I0187712

Thinking the Faith with Passion

The Paul L. Holmer Papers

VOLUME ONE
On Kierkegaard and the Truth

VOLUME TWO
Thinking the Faith with Passion:
Selected Essays

VOLUME THREE
Communicating the Faith Indirectly:
Selected Sermons, Addresses, and Prayers

Thinking the Faith with Passion

Selected Essays

Paul L. Holmer

Edited by David J. Gouwens and Lee C. Barrett III

Foreword by Don E. Saliers

Afterword by David Cain

CASCADE *Books* • Eugene, Oregon

THINKING THE FAITH WITH PASSION
Selected Essays

The Paul L. Holmer Papers 2

Copyright © 2012 David J. Gouwens and Lee C. Barrett III. All rights reserved. Except for brief quotations in critical publications or reviews, no part of this book may be reproduced in any manner without prior written permission from the publisher. Write: Permissions, Wipf and Stock Publishers, 199 W. 8th Ave., Suite 3, Eugene, OR 97401.

Cascade Books
An Imprint of Wipf and Stock Publishers
199 W. 8th Ave., Suite 3
Eugene, OR 97401

Revised Standard Version of the Bible, copyright 1952 [2nd edition, 1971] by the Division of Christian Education of the National Council of the Churches of Christ in the United States of America. Used by permission. All rights reserved. Unless otherwise noted, biblical quotations are from this version.

www.wipfandstock.com

ISBN 13: 9781498212496

Cataloging-in-Publication data

Holmer, Paul L.

   Thinking the faith with passion : selected essays / Paul L. Holmer ; edited by David J. Gouwens and Lee C. Barrett III ; foreword by Don E. Saliers; afterword by David Cain.

   xx + 354 pp. ; cm. — Includes bibliographical references and indexes.

   The Paul L. Holmer Papers 2

   ISBN 13: 9781498212496

   1. Philosophical Theology—Addresses, essays, lectures. I. Gouwens, David Jay. II. Barrett, Lee C., III. III. Saliers, Don E., 1937– . IV. Cain, David, 1940– . V. Title. VI. Series.

BR85 H5745 2012

Manufactured in the U.S.A.

In Memory of
Phyllis J. Schulberg Holmer
1924–2009

Contents

Foreword

WHEN PAUL HOLMER CAME from the University of Minnesota to join the faculty of Yale Divinity School, his impact upon students and colleagues was both immediate and long lasting. He brought a rare combination of Socratic style, a new form of philosophical theology, and a deep brand of Lutheran piety to his teaching and writing. He had been used to pugnacious repartee with philosophers such as May Brodbeck, Herbert Feigl, and Wilfrid Sellars, and with the aftermath of Wittgenstein in so-called "linguistic" or "analytic" philosophy. His concern for conceptual clarity, fused with genuine religious earnestness, was arresting. These qualities are discernible in the pages that follow.

Students came to understand that theology was not a "subject matter" so much as it was a passion, an activity that was required by faith, but an intellectual activity that could also generate and sustain faith. Yet Paul Holmer never mistook theological discourse for God, nor for living faith. Thus we can fasten Anselm's famous dictum *fides quaerens intellectum* as well as Augustine's "I believe in order to understand" over the doorpost of these essays. Holmer did not suffer empty-headed comments and questions gladly. He could spot, as Kierkegaard might say, academic and religious "twaddle." What piqued him was the thoughtless or casual theological remark that led nowhere because it had no process of thought behind it. Clichés were to be avoided. Paul Holmer was unhappy with philosophical and religious pretense. His desire was to get readers and hearers to "think for yourselves."

The reciprocity between Kierkegaard and Wittgenstein in Holmer's essays becomes more palpable the more one reads. Both figures demand a certain austerity of thought—one luring readers into the task of existing and to the possibility of becoming a Christian, the other requiring strenuous, if disconcerting, conceptual labyrinths of inquiry in order to avoid philosophical misunderstandings. Yet both reveal how taking thought requires more than intellectual finesse. Holmer's teaching took students and colleagues into the depths of this reciprocity. I once used I. A. Richards' term "interanimation" for this feature of his work. He grudgingly observed that it was too elegant a term for the hard work involved. Clarity that makes a difference for the life of faith, and for the integrity of speaking, and for the practice of the moral life—that is what Paul Holmer was after.

These essays were often first heard *viva voce* in his lectures, in seminar discussions, and in "common room conversations." It was my good fortune to have jointly taught for several years with him at Yale a now famous course entitled "Emotions, Passions, and Feelings." During those years we heard him working live in the classroom on ideas that appear in several essays, published and unpublished, especially those essays found here in Part Four ("Theology and Emotions," "The Human Heart—The Logic of a Metaphor," and "About Emotions and Passions").

The publication of this collection gives us a sense of how this uncommon teacher has made a lasting impact on students and, indeed, on a distinctive way of thinking theologically.

Don E. Saliers
William R. Cannon Distinguished Professor
of Theology and Worship, Emeritus
Emory University

Editors' Preface

P AUL L. HOLMER (1916–2004) served as Professor of Philosophy, University of Minnesota, from 1946–1960, before becoming Noah Porter Professor of Philosophical Theology, Yale Divinity School, from 1960–1987. Following his death in 2004, the Holmer family gave The Paul L. Holmer Papers, comprising thirty-eight archival boxes, to the Yale University Library, Divinity Library Special Collections.

Having carefully reviewed the Holmer Papers Special Collection at Yale Divinity School, the editors believe that the publication of these volumes of *The Paul L. Holmer Papers* will serve to illuminate three important aspects of Holmer's contributions to theology. In volume 1, we have painstakingly reconstructed Holmer's unpublished, and much-rumored, book-length manuscript on Kierkegaard, presented under the title *On Kierkegaard and the Truth*. In the present volume 2, *Thinking the Faith with Passion*, we have chosen some of the seminal essays that represent the wide scope of Holmer's thought and interests. In volume 3, *Communicating the Faith Indirectly*, we present another aspect of Holmer's thought and work as philosopher and theologian, including both his reflections upon, and his practice of, the sermon or religious address.

In volume 2, we have selected essays that represent four significant areas of Holmer's contributions as a scholar and teacher: his essays on Kierkegaard; Wittgenstein; Theology, Understanding, and Faith; and Emotions, Passions, and Virtues. Holmer was famed as a teacher at Yale Divinity School, with a range of courses that sum up well his extensive interests: "Readings in Kierkegaard," "Wittgenstein and Meaning," his two-semester course in "Philosophical Theology," "Classical Theism and Its Critics," "Emotions, Passions, and Feelings," and "Vices and Virtues."[1]

1. On Holmer as a teacher, see David Cain's afterword, and our Appendix, the articles or book chapters by Stanley Hauerwas, Mark Horst, Robert C. Roberts, and William H. Willimon, as well as Phyllis Holmer's letter responding to Willimon.

In composing this volume of selected essays, we have chosen published and unpublished essays. Many of these essays, whether published and unpublished, circulated at Yale in typescript during Holmer's tenure at the Divinity School. As Holmer's colleague David H. Kelsey shared with us in personal correspondence, Holmer's essays represent "a piece of the recent history of American theology that has been remarkably influential on the current scene through Paul's students, but folk in the field generally have no sense of where it started and its context-of-origin."[2] This volume attempts to fill in that context-of-origin, allowing further appraisal of Holmer's thought, including his strenuous reflections on Kierkegaard and Wittgenstein, as well as his influence on recent interest in emotion concepts and virtue ethics.

The intended audience for this volume is academic, and will include philosophers, theologians, ethicists, and literary scholars. Because Holmer wrote in a classical British essay style that avoids technical jargon, many of the essays will appeal also to a broad educated public.

These essays may also shed some light on the complex range of questions concerning how Holmer's work may relate to the "Yale School" of "postliberalism," especially in George Lindbeck's employment of Wittgenstein in *The Nature of Doctrine*. Early in his book, Lindbeck states, "I am particularly indebted to my colleague Paul Holmer for his understanding of what is theologically important about Wittgenstein. Some sense of the lessons he has tried to convey over the years is provided by his essay 'Wittgenstein and Theology.'"[3] Holmer's essay, originally appearing in Yale Divinity School's *Reflection* in 1968, is reprinted in this volume. While many people are aware that Holmer contributed something to the "Yale School," they are unclear concerning exactly what it was; indeed, Holmer is often mentioned as an important but shadowy figure. We hope that these volumes might fill that lacuna, giving insight both into Holmer's contribution, but also the distinctiveness of his thought.[4]

2. David H. Kelsey, personal email correspondence, August 9, 2005.

3. Lindbeck, *The Nature of Doctrine*, 14n28 (see Appendix).

4. Few have explored the connection between Holmer and Lindbeck. An exception is the recent, sympathetic account in Robert Andrew Cathey, *God in Postliberal Perspective*, 49–82 (see Appendix).

For indeed, Holmer's thought is distinctive. Holmer was careful to eschew labels and resisted being associated with any particular school of thought. As will be clear in these essays, Holmer did not advocate for a school of "Kierkegaardian theology" or "Wittgensteinian theology," or indeed a "theory" at all, this part of Holmer's strongly "anti-metaphysical" and "anti-theoretical" bent. Holmer's concerns were, rather, following Kierkegaard and Wittgenstein, to foster close attention to the particularity, the "depth grammar" or "logic" of the concepts employed in "the language of faith," with a reminder that this language is "foundational" in the sense that the language of faith is "constituted by concepts that are capacities."[5]

Brief comments may be offered on the background of each of these writings. All previously unpublished materials are from Special Collections, Yale Divinity School Library, Paul L. Holmer Papers; the sources of previously published essays are noted below.

Holmer's engagement with Kierkegaard, amply demonstrated in volume 1, is reflected in volume 2 as well. Striking about Holmer's approach to Kierkegaard is how Holmer eschewed popular "textbook" characterizations of Kierkegaard as an "existentialist." In addition to the book-length manuscript that we have constructed in volume 1 of *The Paul L. Holmer Papers,* Holmer wrote a great number of essays on Kierkegaard, and we have selected four essays on Kierkegaard for Part One of this volume that highlight several features of Holmer's understanding of Kierkegaard. We offer first Holmer's essay, "Kierkegaard and Philosophy," presented at the September 1966 University of Notre Dame conference on "Philosophy in an Age of Christian Renewal," and reprinted from Ralph M. McInerny, ed., *New Themes in Christian Philosophy* (1968). In the Holmer Papers collection, Holmer's handwritten note on the top of the first page of a typescript of this paper states: "read at Moral Sciences Club, Cambridge University, Feb. '65." The second essay, "Kierkegaard and Logic," is reprinted from *Kierkegaardiana* 2 (1957). Holmer had extended experience teaching logic at the University of Minnesota, and this significant essay highlights Holmer's own interests in Kierkegaard's deep concerns with logic. We then include "Kierkegaard and Theology," another important essay from 1957, reprinted from *Union Seminary Quarterly*

---

5. Hauerwas, *Wilderness Wanderings,* 145 (see Appendix).

Review, that highlights Holmer's reading of Kierkegaard on meaning in religious discourse, the importance of passions and interests, "the pragmatic significance of the person of Jesus Christ," and "re-reading the human situation." Finally, we include Holmer's remarkable essay on Kierkegaard's *Fear and Trembling*, "About Being a Person," previously published in the volume edited by Robert L. Perkins, *Kierkegaard's* Fear and Trembling: *Critical Appraisals* (1981).

Part Two includes three essays on Ludwig Wittgenstein. The first essay, "Wittgenstein and Kierkegaard: The Subjective Thinker," undated and previously unpublished, links these two thinkers, particularly relating Wittgenstein's "forms of life" with Kierkegaard's "stages on life's way." The second essay, "Wittgenstein and the Self," is reprinted from Richard H. Bell and Ronald E. Hustwit, editors, *Essays on Kierkegaard and Wittgenstein: On Understanding the Self* (1978). The essay presents a close and detailed reading of Wittgenstein's writings, focusing on Wittgenstein's explorations of the concept of selfhood and personal identity. This is followed by "Wittgenstein and Theology," published in Yale Divinity School's *Reflection* in 1968, the essay that Lindbeck cites in *The Nature of Doctrine*, in which Holmer advocates not for a "Wittgensteinian" theology, but "something more modest," in untangling conceptual knots concerning theology, belief, and knowledge of God.

Part Three of this volume turns to "Theology, Understanding, and Faith." It begins with Holmer's polemical essay, "The Academic Game and Its Logic," undated and previously unpublished. This essay on the logic of "understanding" attacks the "logical morphology of scholarly writing and the lecturing style," including "comparing and contrasting, classifying and subsuming," rather than, more humanistically, letting "the imagination and thought of [an] author become our own." In the next essay, "About Linguisticality and Being Able to Talk," undated (but no earlier than 1974) and previously unpublished, Holmer engages the phenomenological tradition concerning "language," in Gerhard Ebeling, Martin Heidegger, and Professor Calvin O. Schrag. The next two essays, "About 'Understanding'" and "About Understanding and Religious Belief" are both previously unpublished, from around 1977, and show Holmer's attempt to explore the particular shape of "understanding" and "not understanding" as complex first-order human capacities (or incapacities), logically distinct from second-order theological reflection. Finally, we include Holmer's "The Nature of Religious Propositions," reprinted from *The Review of Religion* (1955), wherein Holmer teases out the question of the cognitivity of "religious propositions," against both metaphysics and emotivism. This early essay may be fruitfully read in relation to Holmer's later reflections in *The Grammar of Faith* (1978).

In Part Four we conclude with some of Holmer's significant essays on "Emotions, Passions, and Virtues." Holmer was a pioneer in the philosophical and theological exploration of both emotion concepts and virtue ethics. Turning first to emotions, we include "Theology and Emotions" (1973) and "About Emotions and Passions" (ca. 1973), both previously unpublished. This is followed by another unpublished paper from ca. 1973, "The Human Heart—The Logic of a Metaphor." One of Holmer's great concerns in his own reflection and in his teaching centered on the logic of "happiness," and so we include "About Happiness and the Concept, 'Happiness,'" previously unpublished, and written around 1975.[6] In "Something about What Makes It Funny," from *Soundings* (Summer 1974), Holmer explores laughter and humor too as eminently human capabilities. Finally, the last two essays present Holmer's reflections on "vices and virtues." In "The Case for the Virtues," an unpublished typescript from around 1976, Holmer investigates "virtue ethics" as an important corrective over against much ethical theorizing. "About Thankfulness," undated and unpublished, fittingly concludes this theme of emotions, passions, and virtues, as Holmer turns to a careful reflection upon the logic of a particular virtue, that of gratitude, seeing gratitude as an emotion, an attitude, a disposition, and nothing less than a virtue, one that, as the apostle Paul makes clear, can be commanded: "Let there be thanksgiving" (Eph 5:4).

Holmer wrote many of these essays before concerns arose about inclusive language. The editors have not attempted to conform Holmer's writings to current practice, but beg the reader's indulgence, and note that Holmer's own practice on this shifted in later years.

6. An earlier version of this essay appeared as "Theology and Happiness," in *Reflection* (March 1970).

Acknowledgments

THE EDITORS ACKNOWLEDGE THE following contributors to this project. First, we thank Professor Linnea Wren of Gustavus Adolphus College; it was she who suggested that the editors examine The Paul L. Holmer Papers that had recently been donated by the Holmer family to Special Collections, Yale Divinity School Library. At the YDS Library, Martha L. Smalley, Special Collections Librarian, greatly assisted us in surveying the wide extent of Holmer's papers. Joan Duffy, Archives Assistant, ably helped us in procuring photocopies of selections. Robert Osburn, formerly of the MacLaurin Institute, was helpful in early stages of this project, as he was again, along with Ruth Pszwaro, at its conclusion.

Thanks are due also to Don E. Saliers for offering the foreword to this volume. Jack Schwandt and T. Wesley Stewart also provided helpful comments on the project.

Brite Divinity School provided a generous Summer Research Stipend for work on this project. April Bupp of Lancaster Theological Seminary deserves special thanks for preparing the manuscript of volume 1. At Brite Divinity School, Joseph McDonald as graduate assistant provided superb editorial skills, and Karrie Keller, Petite Kirkendoll, and Victoria Robb Powers assisted in typing and proofreading of volumes 2 and 3.

We thank David Cain for writing the afterword and for supplying the photograph of Paul and Phyllis Holmer.

The editors warmly thank their respective spouses for their consistent, gracious support and encouragement as we labored on this project.

We are grateful for the following permissions:

"Kierkegaard and Philosophy." In Ralph M. McInerny, ed., *New Themes in Christian Philosophy*. Notre Dame and London: University of Notre Dame Press, 1968, 13–33. © North America, University of Notre Dame Press; used by permission of University of Notre Dame Press. World rights outside North America: used by permission of Special Collections, Yale Divinity School Library, Paul L. Holmer Papers.

The copyright of the following essay resides in the author's estate, and is used by permission of Special Collections, Yale Divinity School Library, Paul L. Holmer Papers:

"Kierkegaard and Logic," *Kierkegaardiana* 2 (1957) 25–42.

"Kierkegaard and Theology," *Union Seminary Quarterly Review* 12.3 (1957) 23–31. Used by permission of *Union Seminary Quarterly Review*.

"About Being a Person: Kierkegaard's *Fear and Trembling*." In *Kierkegaard's* Fear and Trembling: *Critical Appraisals,* edited by Robert L. Perkins, 81–99. University, AL: University of Alabama Press, 1981. Used by permission of the editor.

"Wittgenstein and the Self." In *Essays on Kierkegaard and Wittgenstein,* edited by Richard H. Bell and Ronald E. Hustwit, 10–31. Wooster, Ohio: College of Wooster, 1978. Used by permission of the editors.

"Wittgenstein and Theology." *Reflection* 65.4 (1968) 2–4. Used by permission of the editor of *Reflections*, Yale Divinity School.

The copyright of the following essay resides in the author's estate, and is used by permission of Special Collections, Yale Divinity School Library, Paul L. Holmer Papers:

"The Nature of Religious Propositions." *Review of Religion* 19.3–4 (1955) 136–49.

"Something about What Makes It Funny." *Soundings: An Interdisciplinary Journal* 57.2 (1974) 157–74. Used by permission of the editor of *Soundings*.

The following previously unpublished essays are used by permission of Special Collections, Yale Divinity School Library, Paul L. Holmer Papers:

"Wittgenstein and Kierkegaard: The Subjective Thinker."

"The Academic Game and Its Logic."

"About Linguisticality and Being Able to Talk."

"About 'Understanding.'"

"About Understanding and Religious Belief."

"Theology and Emotions."

"About Emotions and Passions."

"The Human Heart—The Logic of a Metaphor."

"About Happiness and the Concept, 'Happiness.'"

"The Case for the Virtues."

"About Thankfulness."

Abbreviations

JP   Kierkegaard, Søren. *Søren Kierkegaard's Journals and Papers.* Edited and translated by Howard V. Hong and Edna H. Hong, assisted by Gregor Malantschuk, 7 volumes. Bloomington and London: Indiana University Press, 1967–1978. The abbreviation is *JP*, followed by the volume and entry numbers. For example, *JP* 1, 400.

KJN   Kierkegaard, Søren. *Søren Kierkegaard's Journals and Notebooks.* 5 volumes to date. Edited by Niels Jørgen Cappelørn, Alastair Hannay, David Kangas, Bruce H. Kirmmse, George Pattison, Vanessa Rumble, and K. Brian Söderquist. Published in Cooperation with the Søren Kierkegaard Research Centre, Copenhagen. Princeton and Oxford: Princeton University Press, 2007–. The abbreviation is *KJN*, followed by the volume and entry numbers. For example, *KJN* 3, Not13:41.a.

PART ONE

Essays on Kierkegaard

CHAPTER I

Kierkegaard and Philosophy

KIERKEGAARD IS SO MANY-SIDED an author that it is difficult to make him a member of any philosophic school. And because his pages do so many things, he can be variously assessed. So, he can be read for his biting polemic, as did Georg Brandes, the literary critic: "It is impossible to describe his procedure. One must see him chisel his scorn into linguistic form, hammer the word until it shapes itself into the greatest possible, the bloodiest possible, injury—without for one moment ceasing to be the vehicle of an idea."[1] Or others will find his inventive prose simply interesting and will mark him down as an estimable literary artist. Of course, his religious seriousness cannot be missed, and there has been no end to the number of judgments of his place in the theological community.

But Kierkegaard was also a philosopher. It will be the argument of these pages that he was a radical philosopher, one who was shaking up the conceptual schemes of his day, but more, one who proposed a new way to conceive of some philosophical tasks and a new demeanor for the philosopher. On this point Kierkegaard's attack is more radical than Kant's critical philosophy, and its temper perhaps begs comparisons with Wittgenstein's later reflections. For like Wittgenstein, Kierkegaard is intent upon some relatively circumscribed issues within a wider context, but what he projects, and even concludes, makes a fundamental difference to all kinds of people doing intellectual work. In neither instance is it a new philosophical doctrine that is to be learned as much as it is a number of things by indirection. The attack, the definitions of the issue, the multifarious-

1. Quoted in Swenson, *Something about Kierkegaard*, 24.

3

ness, the way to proceed, questions of what matters most—these are the effects of their writings.

But it will not do to look at Kierkegaard and see what one would expect from authors of the present. He has been examined by neo-Thomists and comes out looking like a halfway scholastic, almost but not quite. The existentialists see him as the instigator of their movement. The distinguished Swedish scholar, Torsten Bohlin, thought Kierkegaard to be the greatest rationalist of all, with a hidden conviction about realities, adequate to logic, mathematics, and all the abstract words of our language. Others have seen his pages, strewn as they are with "despair," "doubt," "dread," and "guilt," to be the rationale for a very subtle existentialist psychoanalysis, deeper than all the rest. It is also tempting to see him as a critical and non-speculative philosopher, maybe even an analytic philosopher, intent upon small issues rather than large, a kind of spy (as he likened himself) or a detective rather than a ruler and a pontiff.

It is very difficult not to be a sophist and sell other people's ideas. Furthermore, it is altogether too easy to betray another thinker's ideas, especially if they are radical and new in form, by using the conventional rubrics and quasi-scholarly devices of the intellectual establishment. Not only is it morally wrong to use others' lives and thoughts for giving honor to oneself, for playing academic games, and for getting to hard-earned results by cheap secondhand means, but it is sometimes plainly deceptive to do a scholarly précis.

In Kierkegaard's instance it is not as though he could not have written the results of his reflection if he had wanted to. Or, with Wittgenstein it seems plausible for the reader of his *Investigations* to say: "The whole point is his philosophy of language; if he had stated that, we could then see how it all fits together. In the absence thereof, I am going to begin there and you will see how his philosophy depends upon it." Apparently this is how many professors consider their tasks. Thereby the job is also botched. So, too, with Kierkegaard. Everyone who satisfies the inclinations to summarize his point of view, to get at the gist, to supply it to others, to tell you what he was "really" doing, is also prone to betraying the aim of such a philosopher. For the philosopher's point is in part to create discomfort with such goings-on, but not by giving you his point.

In what follows I can urge only that one look at Kierkegaard's literature and weigh it a bit more here than there. And there are four such emphases that will probably help the reader to discipline himself, see things a bit more clearly, and, above all, stop collecting philosophical opinions and, instead, think hard. If that happens, Kierkegaard's philosophizing is not in vain. These four are his way of doing philosophy by examples, his theme about "dialectical structure," his original attack upon "concepts" and what they are, and his prevailing program for philosophy.

I

First something about his way of going about reflective matters. Kierkegaard made a great deal out of the concept of "indirect communication." So he said the man who had concluded that no one ought to have disciples is easily misled into formulating a doctrine, namely, "that a man ought to have no disciples." If he then organizes his students, writes a book or two, gives lectures popular and technical, appears on TV, and consequently gets a lot of disciples, something is wrong. But it is hard to say just what. For indeed he seems to have concluded something. He believes it very ardently, with all his heart and almost every day. Furthermore, if someone asks him what it is that he has learned after all the turmoil, he wants to say what it is, namely, "that a man ought to have no disciples."

But to have the students lining up and, for the price of a shave, as Kierkegaard says, even being willing to carry the doctrine further—who knows, perhaps analyze it too—all the while being most ardent disciples, this is at least worth a smile. Suppose someone says philosophizing is an activity, and then the disciples become philosophers of the doctrine that philosophizing is indeed an activity. Is not this the time to laugh out loud? Instead of learning the activity, most people learn the objective teaching, "philosophy is an activity." Once again philosophy becomes a matter of stating, defending, arguing a major point of view. And they are no better off than they were, except now they have one more point of view to entertain. Suppose a teacher says, "Love thy neighbor," and then, "Love thy God with all your heart, soul, mind, and strength." All those who hear agree most heartily and spend exceptional talents upon showing how right it is to love neighbors, how decent and politically sound, how good for the neighbor and the lover, society and the world. Others will with ardor tell us, too, that "love" must not be misunderstood—it is "agapeistic," not "erotic"—and that you ought also, in order to be safe, to know something about your neighbor.

Kierkegaard's point in this is that most of us slip into a way of handling a range of topics—let us call them as he did "ethical and religious"—that seems circumspect, intellectual, in fact, the only way to do it. The intellectual establishment is simply so constituted as to do it this way. All kinds of solemn words are used like "understanding," "knowing something," "being intellectual," "getting clear," "being objective." So it is not only a matter of moral evasion—for example, a refusal to do something, a reluctance to obey—but according to Kierkegaard it is also a philosophical matter. For the net of language, the array of concepts we all use, are betraying us too. Kierkegaard was not one to blame the language as if it failed because it is made up of words, or to blame concepts because they were concepts. Instead it is the very style and, broadly speaking, the form of the reflection that is wrong. Among other issues, it is also the matter of making philosophy into a kind of knowledge.

We began by saying that Kierkegaard chose to do philosophy by examples. And here a word about his literature is necessary. He wrote thirty-five books in less than eight years, from 1842 to 1850, from his twenty-ninth to his thirty-seventh year. Besides, there is a twenty-volume journal spanning a twenty-year period. Primarily the formal literature will concern us here. It is exceedingly odd. It is in two groups; the first is written under pseudonyms, more than a dozen of them, each of which in a firsthand, first-person singular manner, expresses (and I use the term advisedly) a way and a view of life. But many of them criticize, evaluate, and compare one or more ways and views too. So the literature crosses, this way and that, the terrain of aesthetic, ethical, ironic, cynical, ethical-religious convictions. *Either/ Or*, a two-volume work, starts the authorship and canvasses certain enjoyment views, where pleasure is thought to be supreme, where health is what matters most, the conviction that ironic detachment is the best attitude in the long run. The second volume, by a staid judge, shows us a man whose values are communal, who has a sense for duty, who feels obligations, and who is extremely critical of his friend or friends of volume one, to whom he addresses his lengthy epistles.

Something of the same leisurely style permeates the rest of the literature too. So, through another spate of pseudonyms and six more books, *Fear and Trembling*, *Repetition*, *The Concept of Dread*, *Stages on Life's Way*, *Philosophical Fragments*, and the *Concluding Unscientific Postscript*, a large array of attitudes are stated, all kinds of concepts are made explicit, arguments are proposed and countered, and more examples offered. But the interesting fact about this literature, what Kierkegaard called "authorship" or "my literary productivity," is that he thought this was the corrective to the philosophy of his day. Hegel was the prince of the philosophers in Denmark during Kierkegaard's lifetime. But the question was how to attack him. Kierkegaard found a direct attack or a "direct communication," another philosophical doctrine and scheme, a misunderstanding. What philosophers had to do if they were going to handle also the problems of existing, ethics, and religion was to look very closely at existing people. Kierkegaard says philosophers have forgotten what it means to exist. The familiar has escaped them. But it is no good telling the philosophers what it means to exist, for they are, like most people, anxious to have it summarized as a message. Actually they have to be *taught* to remember what they already know.

Philosophy has to be adequate to such a task. Instead of making the ordinary give-and-take of everyday life a "manifestation" or a "symbol" or a "representation" of something profound and deep, Kierkegaard believes that these examples are all there is. They are not trivial or cheap. A philosopher who wants to think about matters of ethics and religion must begin with these, not with abstract concepts. The examples are the thing, and this is why Kierkegaard begins with them.

Kierkegaard's theme is that issues of ethics and religion only count for anything to individuals. William James reports that the Shah of Persia refused to be taken to the Derby Day, and said, "It is already known to me that one horse can run faster than another."[2] The Shah made the question of "Which horse?" trivial. But all questions,

---

2. James, *Principles of Psychology*, 2:675n.

including those of religion and ethics, can be made immaterial by subsuming all their answers under a common head. Imagine what races and games would be if the crews and teams were to forget the absolute distinctiveness of Cambridge from Oxford, Yale from Harvard, and think of the two as one in the higher genus, "university." Philosophy has falsified the ethical and religious issues, made their resolutions seem trivial, by conceiving them so abstractly. The sovereign way to indifference, whether to evil or to good, "this" or "that," lies in converting everything into the thought of a higher genus. Kierkegaard's philosophy tries to teach the reader to take oneself and one's problems with complete seriousness—so, too, the other man's. His examples are not simply illustrations of more abstract points. By being often ordinary, they are intrinsically worthy of reflection just as they are. They do not need to be construed as much as remembered and penetrated.

What is the purpose of the literature, then? In one sense the literature is philosophy as it is, plus being a reminder of where the examples worth philosophizing about are. The literature idealizes and typifies the range of real men and their options, choices, attitudes, passions, and reasoning. That literature tries to frame the world of existing men and to get the literate man to pay it strict attention. Better than that, it might be the means whereby a man learns to take himself very seriously, so that, at least respecting ethical and religious issues, he does not think he has to look at China and Persia first, or find the rhythms of "being *qua* being," or wait for a concept to meet its antithesis before he can decide anything.

The philosophy around him Kierkegaard thought to be quite a joke. It had become a cultural force, for it had informed all kinds of intelligent people. That man who saw the sign in the window saying "Pants pressed here," rushed in, stripped off his trousers, only to discover that the sign was for sale, Kierkegaard likens to those who see "Reality" in the philosopher's window, rush in, and find also that only the sign is for sale. Philosophy proffers itself as the missing knowledge, which to know is also to become good and wise. Kierkegaard could scarcely restrain himself on the pretensions of systematic philosophy—like Plato, who says in one of the dialogues, "Where the promise is so vast a feeling of incredulity creeps in." Kierkegaard's examples show instead a variety of ways of life, all kinds of similarities and differences; but he does not pretend that these differences are being resolved in a new and subtle synthesis; he does not invent a higher or more transparent way of relating these opposing views; he does not suggest that philosophy gives prognoses for the future. No, the wisdom of life is to be gained only when one sees in detail how men exist, how they make up their minds, how bereft they are then of philosophers' help. Wisdom has to be purchased with effort, passion, deep caring; and it cannot be summarized and disseminated at secondhand.

One purpose of Kierkegaard's literature is certainly to make a man see what is already at hand. Those examples, those pseudonyms, have one advantage over real persons—they are exaggerated, even a bit bizarre, so that they make one sit up and take notice. But there is something else too. Each book, perhaps we can say each pseudonym, is seen in a context, a way of life, of evaluating and addressing the world around him. Part of Kierkegaard's philosophical point, made by his literature as a totality ("my literature," "my literary productivity"), is simply that it does justice to the way the existence of men is. If one is going to do philosophy, respecting ethics and religion, the examples have to be multiple, the concepts numerous, the literature a little more casual, insinuating the hard cases, and not being formal and abstract.

Most writers on the philosophy of religion and even ethics have rather slight sympathy for the nuances of spiritual attitudes and their related concepts. Their description of moral and spiritual attitudes is very much like those naïve paintings that depict a landscape in general, to fit everything but finally nothing. Therefore, to describe religious faith as devotion to an ideal, without distinguishing the differences between ideals, or to describe moral life as living under an obligation, without distinguishing the differences between obligations, never bothering with the all-important matter of the "how" involved, is about as illuminating and intellectually satisfying as it would be to describe man as an animal and leave out any further specification. Kierkegaard's examples offer both a more precise intellectual orientation plus an exceedingly rich and concrete psychological delineation of the variety of ethico-religious behavior. His ample field of examples makes it necessary to find a wider range of concepts;

and this is, of course, how his criticism of other philosophies is made good. Once one remembers the range, the simplified schemes, the generalized concepts, are no longer pertinent.

Perhaps, some will say, this is not enough to distinguish Kierkegaard from a first-rate novelist. Indeed Kierkegaard spoke of his literature as being "poetical productivity," but he also said he was a poet-dialectician. So we must then turn to what he called "the dialectical structure."

II

Kierkegaard deemed the Hegelian dialectic an artifice. He did not quite know what to make of "dialectic" in Plato's dialogues either. How then does he refer to himself as a dialectician? And how can he be said to have erected a dialectical structure? In truth, his dialectical structure is not very much. But what there is, he thought, however paltry in quantity, however meager in promise, to be intellectually straightening.

Again a word about his pseudonymous books. While he was writing out that variegated literature, via his poetically conceived authors, he was also unraveling a few topics that are conventionally the prerogatives of philosophers to discuss. For example, his author, Johannes Climacus, writes a kind of meta-account on the earlier literature. The name "Johannes Climacus" is taken from the reputed medieval author of *The Ladder of Divine Ascent to Paradise* (a work as recently translated into English as 1959). This monk is said by Kierkegaard to have attempted to climb into heaven on a ladder made of syllogisms. His modern Johannes is a thirty-year-old student of philosophy, very detached, urbane, witty, a common-room type. He has a problem, but only in that learned off-hand way of most academic people, of discussing what a modern would call the "logic of. . . ." He is concerned with "the objective truth of Christianity," not, of course, because he is a Christian or because he believes Christianity is true, but only because Christianity seems important because it offers so much and he has heard it said that there is something called "the objective truth of Christianity."

My point here is not to abridge his book, so we will let many strands of his discussion go by. Only one theme can be noted. As Johannes Climacus gets to work on this truth-issue, all kinds of things go wrong with the discussion. He tries four different loci in which he can put together "objective truth" and "Christianity," including a very sophisticated philosophical locus, and nothing quite works. There are strains and stresses, and the author is at wit's end just how to diagnose his difficulties, when suddenly a literature begins to appear. They are, of course, Kierkegaard's earlier pseudonymous writings. And they are discussed in the middle of the *Concluding Unscientific Postscript* in an odd appendix called "A Glance at a Contemporary Effort in Danish Literature." This appendix is more than a glance, for as the pages go by, we discover Kierkegaard using that literature not as proofs, not as premises, but as the place to look. Something has gone wrong with "objective truth" not only in relation to Christianity but also in relation to ethics. Gradually, looking at those other examples, this author, philosopher that he is, begins to formulate other concepts that are at work within those contexts. These turn out to be new ones, quite different than those already proffered the young scholar by the philosophic culture that was his in nineteenth-century Denmark. Thus he, indeed, begins to use the word "truth," but he also links it with subjectivity, not only objectivity, and tries to show how this linkage already obtains in the discourse, the behavior, the argumentation going on even now among the less philosophical authors. There it occurs naturally—one might even say spontaneously.

One matter that emerges is that the familiar way of saying that a given teaching—say, either in moral discourse or in Christian teaching—is true, itself gets to be suspicious. So Kierkegaard develops, in some independence of the logical and epistemological traditions of the nineteenth century, deep misgivings about taking sentences out of moral and religious usage and bracketing them. When this is done, the sentences are said to be either true or false. Kierkegaard pours scorn upon that kind of superior philosophizing that he finds early and late, misuses of doctrine, in Hegel's writings and in popular literature, that pretend to know the "truth" of a proposition in contradistinction to other more ordinary uses of the sentence. He denies that there is a superior philosophic concept of truth, a meta-concept; and part of the point of his reflection upon truth and subjectivity is plainly to show that the seriousness and gravity of a passionate religious (or moral) subject makes the meta-concept, this philosophic concept, gratuitous. It is superfluous at best and distracting at worst.

The "dialectical structure" that Kierkegaard was proud of is really another net of concepts, by and large separable from those used in natural science, in historical studies, in logic. Furthermore his "dialectical structure" or "edifice" is not that of the Hegelian philosophy either, which purported to include all the rest. Kierkegaard is very wary of such general conceptual schemes that propose to cover the entire range of thoughts and things. In contrast, he is only prepared to say that a system of existence is not possible, but that a system of logic is possible. For even this "dialectical edifice" is not anything very much in itself—it is only those concepts, not quite a system, that permit one to talk about ethical and Christian matters without falsification.

This way of philosophizing is primarily a matter of clearing away the obstacles in the way of describing and understanding some difficult matters. Laying bare the "structure," "the edifice," "the way to think"—all these metaphorlike words suggest that philosophers are beholden to the repetitive, the reoccurring features of behavior and thinking in a given area. The motto for the *Philosophical Fragments* is from Shakespeare: "Better well hung than ill wed." And here the titles of the books too are pertinent. Philosophy has to be done in bits and pieces, in fragments (though rather large ones sometimes). Philosophy is unscientific, according to the *Concluding Unscientific Postscript*, but not "unscientific" only in the ordinary sense of "science." Rather the aim is to show that here this reflection must be *uvidenskabelig*, nonsystematic, insinuating, and open to the study of pathos and passion, as these also contribute to our own language, our aspirations, our morals, and our religion.

Criticism is accordingly directed against all those philosophic schemes whereby a mediation is proposed between the various spheres of discourse, for example, between ethics, historical science, and Christianity. The point again is made by showing by a kind of *reductio ad absurdum* and citing of cases that this vaunted "mediation" is absurd. According to Hegel, concepts themselves were rich, inclusive of oppositions, actually syntheses as they were, and hence capable of what Kierkegaard calls a "flip-flop." Kierkegaard's intent is to show instead that concepts are specific, but, when grouped, constitute a sphere or stage, a universe of discourse. Transition from one, going to another, is by what he calls a leap. So, all the knowledge in the world about Jesus of Nazareth that historians are able to assemble will never convert into or "mediate into" statements like "He is God." And this is so because the meaning of "God" in Christian circles, he contends, is not a compound of historical assertions. There is, thus, a kind of logic of terms that is the proper discernment of philosophers.

But is this to say there is no place where these different "universes of discourse" (the expression is used advisedly because Kierkegaard does so) impinge upon one another? Kierkegaard's point is that there is something he calls "the simultaneity of the individual factors of subjectivity in the existing subject." To be a man means that one is a loose and uneasy synthesis of passions, of dispositions, of emotions— these are also a part of us. And he chooses to call the philosopher reader's attention to the fact that much of what is treated in "an objective fashion" when aesthetic and moral judgments, religious creeds and plaintive pious words are stripped away from that context of feeling, purposing, wishing, and the rest of the subject life, are thereby truncated, even falsified. It is not that all aesthetic, moral, and religious language is simply expressive either. Instead, he shows us how the concepts therein involved are only possible when the passions are powerful and genuinely operative. The point is a simple one, namely, that the meaning of these kinds of discourse can only be encompassed when the passion and the subjective life are included.

Kierkegaard has no easy answers. He seems to think that the creation of a logico-epistemological tradition in Western philosophy, by which all the concepts and order were assumed to be epistemic, is an oversight. He offers his array of authors and their literature to show that "emotions" and "passions," those factors that have been scorned as subjective and mad, wanton and ruleless, can be and are ruled and are ingredients in aesthetic, moral, and religious concepts.

Therefore, the dialectical structure, loose with many overlapping edges, is the name for a range of concepts, from aesthetic to ethical concepts, those relevant to an ironic detachment, to religious-ethical living, and Christian faith. Besides there are, of course, those of a strict kind, of a formal logical scheme, and those of the sciences, historical, and natural. Kierkegaard's criticism is that the rational philosophers had made these all parts of a single system. Kierkegaard does not, in turn, write out a pluralistic scheme, but he does show us, via his literature, how absurd a single "system" is when all the cases are considered.

To make this case by his "stages" theory, Kierkegaard used both algebraic formulations plus imaginative and even emotional expression. Not since Plato has the history of philosophy seen so intimate a fusion of the poetic and dialectic. Kierkegaard's philosophizing repudiates the popular notion, but also Plato's, that reason and passion are almost mutually destructive of one another. Instead he has supplied a kind of map, a logical one, of the emotional cosmos.

III

But there is also a third pressure exerted by his literature that makes it distinctively philosophical. For what we have noted thus far has to do really with the sweep of the literature. As an extended piece of literature, almost like a long book with many chapters, there is an argument going on against the panlogistic thought. After due editing and a running commentary upon the literature and its several aspects, some abstract concepts begin to loom up: the use of "faith" in religious contexts, he shows, is not really like "belief" or "faith" (in the ordinary sense) when used in other contexts; then there is "truth" used in a religious context. Jesus saying, "I am the truth . . ." quite clearly does not use the same concept "truth" as in "I speak the truth; I assure you I am not lying." Right or wrong, Kierkegaard believed that his authors, and hence he himself, had sufficiently isolated "the dialectical structure" in ethico-religious discourse and reflection to show that such reflection and discourse could not be assimilated to the "dialectical structure" or concepts teased out of history or of other sciences.

In all this there are criticisms of great detail going on too. These can be seen in each book as one moves along. Furthermore, the detailed analyses are corroborated and made richer by the journal, in which all kinds of topics are examined and mulled over, returned to, taken up in ever-new ways. Kierkegaard began his philosophical career where his contemporaries were. He thus treated concepts as if they were some kind of supramundane things. He uses "essence" rather freely as if there were an "essence" of anything you please. Hegel's philosophy plus his reading of Plato's works created his climate of doctrine. Early in his career he is much inclined to think that Socrates made a very good try at finding the meanings of words but that Plato really succeeded, thus to round out the inquiry.

This much one notes in the sundry tendentious philosophical quarrels he has with himself, and we have them at length in the journals. Of course, they are mixed up with all kinds of other things too, as the discussion of the Wandering Jew motif in Western literature, the Don Juan legend, the various stories of Faust. So, we see his "poetizing" going on, elaborating and exploring all the potentialities of these stories, the moods involved, and so on; on the other side is the ostensibly serious dialectical discussion, quarrelling with Plato and other ancients, a few lines from Tertullian or Aristotle, then Descartes (and a short book-length entry on *De omnibus dubitandum est*). Gradually it looks as though he brings these two strands together, and his literature is the token thereof. Concurrently and gradually the interest in those abstract entities, those forms, those transcendent ideas, fades away. He starts as a conceptual realist; he ends with no precise position but with the performances that are his literature.

But this does not mean that the concepts are not firm, even though their foundation is different.

In subsequent works one can note how exactingly he labors. In every one of his books very small conceptual issues continually arise. A relevant example is the *Philosophical Fragments*. That book pictures Socrates as a teacher. But Socrates does not want disciples because he says, ironically, that he does not have the truth or anything else to provide. In fact, he is only a midwife, most ignorant and barely able to ask questions. Kierkegaard lets his account be told rather leisurely so that soon the reader can see for himself how the expression "teacher" applies to Socrates, also how "truth" works between the teacher and the learner, why Socrates cannot justly claim a disciple and is only an "occasion" for the student's learning. In contrast, there is another man, apparently Jesus of Nazareth, who is a teacher too. But in this context, "teacher," "disciple," "learner," "belief," and all kinds of other expressions get launched for us in an entirely different context. Again the aim is clearly to have us see that the same word, "teacher," has an altogether different meaning in these two contexts, so that finally Kierkegaard himself talks about concepts of teacher in one context as over against another concept of teacher in the other.

A fascinating side to all of this is that Kierkegaard's interest in essences and Platonic entities, and "being *qua* being," simply fades away. It did not happen at once, and it did not altogether free his writing of all kinds of these components. In fact, there seem to have been projects with which he became dissatisfied just because he could not quite keep himself as oriented to the particulars as he thought necessary. He found his capacity for abstract reflection, for making distinctions, akin to his poetic talent. Gradually he had to bring this capacity under strict control. Surely, however, there are lapses. But on one occasion he outlined a book called simply *Logical Problem* by Johannes Climacus, his philosophical author. Its first section was going to be entitled just that; its second section was, oddly enough, going to be "Something about the Form of the Religious Addresses, with Special Regard to Aristotle's *Rhetoric*." In the notes concerning this project one can see how easily he projected a general abstract title like *Logical Problem* but also how quickly the execution of it became a matter of placing the issues in specific contexts, with regard to sermonic discourse and Aristotle's *Rhetoric*, especially those passages bearing upon morals and politics. With restraining reflections like these, always bringing him back to specific contexts, he finally decided upon the *Postscript*, itself more in the tenor of the latter rather than the former.

And this is the story of the whole authorship. Also every one of his books in a fashion provides an analysis of a specific concept, invariably by reference to the life histories, moods, and passions of people. Whenever there are practices, habits, established ways, there he finds a concept to spring forth. These detailed analyses, of differences between moral "guilt" and "sin," "doubt" concerning truth-claims, and "doubt" concerning oneself, and many more, make each book useful in itself, quite apart from the purposes it might play in the literature as a totality.

Kierkegaard's smaller books, like *Fear and Trembling, Sickness Unto Death, The Concept of Dread, The Concept of Irony,* and *Repetition,* have seemed to some scholars of the past generation to be a comparative philosophy of values. But he called them plainly "psychological studies." His psychology, however, had little in common with contemporary behavioristic psychology. Kierkegaard is a descriptive psychologist, but always in terms of meaning and significance. He does not even envision problems of causal explanations of human behavior or the isolation of mechanical and dynamical structures of psychological happenings. To the extent that Kierkegaard is a psychologist he is indeed more literary than experimental or scientific. But he is more properly described as doing philosophical psychology, for he is everywhere detecting, isolating, then describing with those concepts, to show us that feelings have inherent order, structure, even systems, that valuations fall into groups and types and are not random, that emotions are not a meaningless mush like the "skin and squash" of Kingsley's caterpillar. This piecemeal kind of analysis goes on volume after volume, page after page. His exploration of emotions and passions, via his examples, allows him to confute the popular conviction that all the relevant concepts are indefinite and vague.

IV

But Kierkegaard also retains something of that high calling of philosophers too. This we shall note in conclusion. There are several guiding ideas going through the maze of his works. One is his purpose of explaining and solving "the riddles of the life of reason and freedom." But Kierkegaard did not want to do this in such a way as merely to increase the store of human knowledge. He had diagnosed one evil of his day, present to the intellectual set, not least the philosophers, as a confusion of knowledge with the problems of daily life, and he did not intend to contribute to this confusion, he noted, by adding a few more paragraphs to help make a systematic result. Philosophy was a discipline upon intellectual promiscuity, which forced thinking men again to the awareness of what it means to live; and to this end he placed the variety of personalities who think and speak for themselves. Thus, he thought, there would be clarified for the reader various stages, or moments, or representative attitudes toward life. His writings state these distinctively, in exaggerated fashion, because actual life rarely allows us to see them separately and clearly. He is brave enough to think that clear, even boldly conceptual, strokes can be morally helpful.

Thus we have an aesthetic attitude, an attitude governed by categories of the pleasant and the unpleasant, the interesting and the dull. The life of morality is seen governed by categories of duty and self-realization. The first is endowed with all the seductive gifts of intellectuality and culture and is expressed in a series of brilliant aesthetic essays upon a great variety of topics: "Mozart's *Don Giovanni*," "Psychological Sketches of Literary Heroines," and "The Diary of a Seducer," a wonderfully beautiful but terrible picture of a diabolically clever but thoroughly unmoral personality, an analogy to Don Juan, clothed in the garb of a lofty intellectual sophistication. The moral man, in contrast, is a man of dignity and poise, who writes letters of warning and ethical admonition to the author of the first part, in which he discusses marriage and other personal issues with a firm touch, but not with showy brilliance. Kierkegaard's philosophizing here is twofold. All kinds of concepts become clear, knots are untied, confusions are dispelled, mostly by the resolute clarifying and ordering of concepts—ideas, notions, arguments—to their correct location. In fact this is preparation to coming to understand them all. But, Kierkegaard also considered it important for a philosopher to "show" these alternatives, *A* and *B* (later the Christian, too), without inventing a foundation, a ground, a common court of appeal, an objective standard, and so on. He leaves it to the reader to decide. He shows that being free here means a genuine choice.

The subsequent volumes, as we have noted, use the same method, albeit by throwing light upon the religious life. So, *Fear and Trembling* and *Repetition* also deal with psychological matters that might dispose one toward religion; *Stages* recapitulates but adds to *Either/Or* all kinds of psychological situations that are transitional to the religious life. Finally Christianity is brought to the fore, but once more the aim of philosophy, as well as the literature penned, seems not to ground these in something more fundamental or to provide some foundations for these choices. There is no substructure, nothing to reduce them to. The philosophical literature that he pens then has little in common with antitheses like realism or idealism, empiricism or rationalism, voluntarism, pragmatism, or ontology. For there is a powerful, luminous reflective energy surging through his literature that makes all such classifications and points of view very inadequate means to lay hold of what he has said. Like Plato in the *Gorgias*, Kierkegaard also presents contrasting views of life; but unlike Plato, who uses Socrates as the ethical representative to conquer each of his antagonists by superior argumentative skill, Kierkegaard refuses to allow a philosophical victory for even the view of life he espouses. Philosophy remains *descriptive* and *neutral*.

In the *Gorgias* one view of life conquers because it is fortunate enough to have the abler protagonist; not so in Kierkegaard's literature. Kierkegaard does not believe that dialectical skill and the management of concepts, if these are what make a philosopher, are finally the means of ascertaining the best life. Instead, as his literature unrolls, it becomes clear that one representative differs from the other often in the quality of pathos. Therefore, moral and religious living depend, not upon intellectual giftedness, however ingredient these may become, but upon intensity, passion, deep needs that are immediate to a man.

Philosophy, in this respect, has something to do with forms of life, but it is not a form of life itself. But we return to an earlier category, namely, "indirect communication." For as Kierkegaard sees it, philosophy has mostly been trickery. It has proposed to communicate directly, as if there were a truth to be had by which such issues could be settled. Kierkegaard believes philosophizing might indeed help his serious reader, but only because the questions at issue might be clarified for him. But he is not coddled, tricked, or allured; and the responsibility for a view of life can never be anyone's but each man's himself, there being no authority, no indisputable facts, no ontological ground, to influence his decision by the intrusion of an alien prestige. This matter of indirect communication is given a multiform interpretation in Kierkegaard's literature. In the last analysis he so understands it to be appropriate to the very heart of Christianity, for here is God helpless in the hands of enemies, even on a cross, while the mob "barters" for his clothes. Again, his own earlier literature, plus the Bible and the homely ways that men always must make up their minds on faith and morals, supply the occasion for his chastened view of philosophy.

A few subsidiary elements can be just noted with brief comment. Some of these I do not profess to understand nor have I put them to the concentrated tests of long preoccupation. In the *Phaedrus* Plato has Socrates say that as a lover of knowledge he must admit that he is an almost complete stranger to the surroundings of the country, since he can learn, not from the trees or the country, but only from men who dwell in the cities. Diogenes Laërtius reports that Socrates came to the conclusion that the study of physics was not man's proper business and began to moralize in the workshop and the marketplace. Kierkegaard reports something like this too. Early in life, with the help of a relative who was a distinguished scientist, he saw the attractiveness of being an industrious collector of facts, and he was tempted by his organizing talent to look for a synoptic view of the whole. For a variety of reasons he gives this up. And I believe it is a mistake to say that this predisposition is merely a preference for the study of ethics and psychology as over against other objective disciplines. Something else is at stake here. His conception of philosophy is being slowly forged. And I believe it fair to say that he increasingly knew where to look.

In considering modern philosophies it can scarcely be denied that the best talents and keenest dialecticians have been spent upon very impersonal problems. But Kierkegaard considered logic and metaphysics but an introduction to the business of real philosophizing. He, therefore, chooses to look very hard indeed at the comparatively uncharted realm of the personality. Of course, we have had spates of interest and systematic discussion upon "values," but invariably in a wrongheaded metaphysical way. Kierkegaard, over one hundred years ago, refused such value-talk; instead, almost like a modern, he placed such concerns in the actual situations and began his philosophical work there. Its distinctions are clear-cut: it has been elaborated with an extraordinary wealth of poetic talent and pulsates throughout with the most exalted passions.

For the fundamental purposes of such philosophizing, Kierkegaard turned to the familiar language, the ways of daily life, and literature already hallowed by long use. The concepts and methods of natural science he declared were quite irrelevant, and most scientific research a mere distraction. And the attempts to apply the results of natural sciences to the problems of every human life were only prolific breeders of confusions of thought. In his day it was the exaggerated emphasis upon a philosophical contemplation of history that was a specifically demoralizing practice of the learned. He predicted that in the next generation it would be the study of the natural sciences and the misuse thereof by the philosophers that would bring a corresponding demoralization in its train. He enjoyed in a sardonic way the theory, attributed to some Mormons, that God is not precisely omnipresent but moves with extraordinary velocity from star to star, and he hails this discovery as the symptom of the improvement which theology may look forward to attaining when at last the discoveries of the nineteenth century, the mechanical inventions, and all the curiosities of the natural order are made fully available for the philosophical theologians to spiritualize further the conception of God.

Already in the nineteenth century there was a predilection for the ideas and methods of natural science in philosophy to be held to argue the possession of a sense for the concrete and the real, while conversely, a lack of sympathy for this kind of philosophizing was believed to convict one of remoteness from the actual. But Kierkegaard was brave enough to insist that another kind of philosophizing was realistic and possible. Dialectic became in his hands an instrument of clarification, a tenacious way of sweeping away the cobwebs of illusion—philosophic, scientific, or otherwise—to make room for human ideals and purposes. Therefore, it was, too, a means of self-discipline and, incidentally, also a discipline of others. Kierkegaard thought this was the way Socrates philosophized too. But the temptation to do as Plato is always close to us; for, he says, Plato transformed dialectic, more or less clearly and consciously, into an end in itself, and the abstractions developed by this dialectic, this philosophizing, became the supreme realities. In short, Kierkegaard admits to being an existential thinker, while others become speculative metaphysicians.

Kierkegaard has only a "way," plus a few concepts, and no objective results.

Descartes had to seek a radical reconstruction of the basic concepts of science in order to relieve a sense of intellectual bankruptcy. With respect to issues of life and conduct he tells us he was anything but radical. He will observe the laws of the land, accept the tenets of the religion in which he was nurtured, and model his conduct upon that of his most respected but moderate contemporaries. And he will leave theology to others, in not presuming to bring its problems to the test of personal reflection.

Kierkegaard reverses this Cartesian distribution of emphasis. He examines where Descartes accepts, and accepts where Descartes reflects. The upshot is that his philosophy becomes also an "existential dialectic," a work that includes philosophical psychology, an unmasking of the concepts, but also pushes them to the purpose of the clarification of the issues of daily existence. It seeks to offer whatever clarification it can to the incessant striving that makes up our daily life. To this extent only is Kierkegaard an existential philosopher. Here is philosophy being practiced to accentuate those issues of existence. Even the fundamental and persistent traits of our striving can become concepts to the philosopher. But just as a drunken driver who lets the horses take him home is also a driver, so also all men are human. But being human is also a task, which may be evaded or shabbily executed. Certainly we all have status—we are all human; but we also have a task. So being existing persons, we have status and task. Kierkegaard tries to make philosophy relevant not only to the status but also to the task.

With biting irony Kierkegaard has traced three stages in the evolution of Christendom. In the first stage the martyr was the representative Christian; in the second stage it was the monk; then came the modern age, the flowering of science, culture, and philosophy, when the representative Christian has become the learned professor. There is, he says, in every professor, every professor of philosophy most particularly, an obstinate and almost inextinguishable persistence in apprehending everything as "Knowledge," just as a certain type of Englishman years ago was reputed to look at everything as a subject for a wager. This professor in us, this philosopher in us, says

Kierkegaard, is longer than the longest tapeworm; only God can extirpate him so as to make a man.

Let me close with a typical Kierkegaardian anecdote, used by him in his *Journals* to illustrate this point: a raw recruit is being instructed by a corporal in the bearing and behavior of a soldier. "You must hold yourself erect in the ranks," says the corporal. "Aye, aye, I understand that," says the recruit. The corporal continues: "And then you must not talk while under arms," he says. "Oh, is that so," says the recruit, "very well, I am glad you have told me, so that now I know about it." "What the devil," says the corporal, "didn't I tell you to keep your mouth shut?" "Aye, aye," says the recruit, "don't be angry with me; now that you've told me, I'll be sure to remember it."[3]

---

3. Quoted in Swenson, *Something about Kierkegaard*, 93–94; cf. *Papirer* VIII 2 B, 81:14 (*JP* 1, 649:14).

CHAPTER 2

Kierkegaard and Logic

KIERKEGAARD IS CERTAINLY ONE of the most prolific thinkers of the nineteenth century. And he bids fair to becoming also one of the most influential. Though there are numerous testimonies to his persuasive powers, especially among religiously sympathetic readers but also among many of his intimate critics, there are to date relatively few studies of his dialectical powers and the implementation of these in his writings. This statement is not made simply to draw attention to the lack of critical philosophical studies—there is such a lack despite the plentitude of secondary works—but also to highlight those factors in Kierkegaard's authorship that gave validity and intellectual form, this independently of one's persuasion or proclivity, religious or otherwise. Kierkegaard was also a philosopher and, furthermore, was so acute intellectually and more particularly logically, that he articulated his writings with their enormous persuasive content with an apparatus, simple and chaste, for which any contemporary analytical and anti-metaphysical philosopher would be justly proud. This is not to say that he was an analytical thinker in the contemporary Anglo-Saxon and Scandinavian senses of the term—he was too many-sided to be a member of any school—but by the canons of even today's rigorous philosophical movements he was certainly a philosopher. He may have had too many strings in his bow for modern readers but it hardly seems plausible to accuse him for a richness of personality that most of the rest of us are but the poorer without.

Without the support of the environment and by efforts that intellectually considered must have been prodigious, Kierkegaard defined his position against the most formidable philosophical positions of the day. Not only did this demand courage, but in his case there was more involved. He had to forge the weapons for his attack in virtue of his own understanding. That he did this in two different directions is sometimes forgotten. On the one side, he opposed the Church of Denmark, though his polemic is aimed, of course, at features of organized Christianity everywhere, with an extremely well articulated view concerning the meaning of Christian belief and practice; on the other side, he opposed the metaphysical philosophies, and especially Hegel's, with humor and wit, precision and exactness, all of these held together by severe views concerning the limits and validity of human speech. The neglect by his readers of this latter feature is perhaps to be explained by the fact that the religious interest is both so obvious and so attractive that little else is expected. But Kierkegaard's writings are here deceptive. What is apparent on the surface, the give and take of the literary creation, is analogous to the parts of the iceberg above the water level. Seven-eighths are below the surface and make possible the portion that is apparent. So too with Kierkegaard's literature. The logical and epistemological views that make his writings so effective as argument, that make his issues conceivable, are usually hidden but are not, for this reason, either irrelevant or unimportant.

An attack upon another's philosophy is not in itself unusual. But it is the mode of Kierkegaard's attack that marks him as a philosopher and thinker of first rank. He does not quarrel with particular factual claims within a philosopher's writings nor does he do as rival metaphysicians frequently have done, namely, show that all of the facts can be accounted for by another metaphysical hypothesis. He chooses instead to level his attack at the possibility, the logicality, of the metaphysical factual claims. The possible is his philosophical domain. He leaves the factually real to the scientists and scholars. The sallies addressed to the metaphysicians are directed to the logic of their discourse as well as the ethical and religious inadequacies inherent in taking such extravagant claims seriously. Detailed considerations of the limits of validity, of coherence, of non-contradiction, of system and sundry other logical values, are replete in his papers and incidental remarks. That all of this impinges upon religious and ethical considerations that admittedly were of paramount concern to Kierkegaard goes without saying; but it is likewise true that if any of his remarks on the most abstract issues have validity, they have validity independently of Kierkegaard's literature too.

In what follows I am intentionally trying to sketch the features of that seven-eighths which is hidden to view. I am admittedly dependent here upon the casual remarks, the jottings and notes of the *Papirer*, the footnotes within the literature proper. But still I admit to constructing logical views, systematic structures, where they do not obviously obtain. The references given in the notes at the end are intended to give only an approximate clue to the important materials, enough, however to indicate why I believe the views herein articulated are congruent with the Kierkegaard literature.

I shall here address myself to three questions whereby Kierkegaard's philosophical and logical positions can be illumined: What is logic? Is Kierkegaard a logician or logical? What are his specific insights?

I

Logic is for Kierkegaard the disciplined inquiry into the meaning structure and principles of knowledge. Unlike modern logicians who might say as much, Kierkegaard does not exercise himself greatly on questions concerning the methods of knowledge, partly, one suspects, because the climate of opinion was not very rich on this topic in his Denmark. Logic is, by him, not conceived to be immediately methodological nor a biological weapon. Throughout his literature he seems to make clear, too, that logic is a spectator's science; it is broadly descriptive. But the question is—of what? It is surely not ontological description; for this is the almost constant criticism made in the *Postscript*, and every other occasion permitting in the literature, of the Hegelian philosophy.

Kierkegaard is a singular *via media* thinker. Denying that logic is ontological, or a science about being, does not entail the affirmation that logic is an arbitrary invention, or simply conventional, or only rules like those governing a parlor game. He seems to be insisting that logic is a descriptive science, but descriptive principally of the structures implicit in the meaningful use of language. Logic describes the idealities, rules and norms, principles and criteria, in virtue of which meanings are communicable.

It is interesting to note that Kierkegaard always roots the prescriptive functions of language in the subjectivity of the user and hearer of the language. Unlike many post-Hegelian philosophers who disparaged both human subjectivity as the locus of anything important and the tendency to make all language descriptive, Kierkegaard did not posit two realms, one of fact and another of value. He did not suggest that logic, aesthetics, and ethics were prescriptive because their objective correlates were values; instead he explored the character of subjectivity and came to the conclusion that it was not completely arbitrary, nor was it formless and to be discounted. His authorship therefore vindicates subjectivity, ethically by the contention that it ought to be each man's concern, and intellectually by insisting that it had formal and regular features and was subject to categorization.

Thus, on logical matters he can admit that there is a facticity to the meaning structure of language that acquires its prescriptive power, its oughtness, in the general interest (a subjective factor to be sure) that we all have in making language meaningful. Without the wish on the part of would-be knowers, logic is only a descriptive science. Just so, too, can Kierkegaard's views on ethics be described. From one standpoint, everything he says about ethics can be couched also in a disinterested form appropriate to ethical theory. But, admitting a personal responsibility for stirring the reader to new ethical enthusiasms, Kierkegaard used every literary device available to keep the reader from reading him dispassionately. However, he was under no illusion, for he continually asserts that the ethical exists as an ought only in virtue of a movement within the man. So too, we might say on matters of logic. It is a tool to everyone with the wish and interest to be meaningful and therewith logic has immediately—as immediately as the wish is present—a prescriptive character.

For Kierkegaard, then, it is meaning that is the vehicle of knowledge. Obviously enough, meaning is a possible vehicle of other functions too. That structures of various kinds are involved in meanings seems to be a major burden of the long history of logic. Thus, concepts, judgments, propositions, inference, categories, etc., are all names for parts of the structure of meaning. But how these structures could possibly refer to a real world and things outside of discourse has been a tempting question that has continually strained philosophers' intellectual modesty. That the relation between meanings and the world was also a meaning structure, that it was itself logical, has been a kind of secular piety overarching vast difficulties not otherwise amenable to intelligent discourse. It is relatively recently that criticisms of such brave pieties have become fashionable. Kierkegaard's criticisms of Hegel are directed to this very issue. He denies that the relation between discourse and the world discoursed about is itself a logical relation. Meanings are logically interrelated, but not meanings and the world. Likewise, and here he may seem to be out of step with modernity, the position that says that there are no meanings in knowledge is inadmissible, not least because it denies the genuinely descriptive character of logic.

Logicians formulate principles that become, in virtue of their usage, laws. This is what is meant by saying that certain ideal values are implied in different kinds of meaning. Order, truth, consistency, system, simplicity, definability, etc., are seemingly the conditions of meaningfulness. To describe these is a major responsibility of anyone who studies the meaning structure of knowledge. Such "values" are different than methods, either special or general, relevant to the sciences. Knowledge, Kierkegaard insists, is a synthesis of logical and a-logical factors. Human experiencing is individuated and cannot be communicated in its original forms. But knowledge that is a synthesis of experience and logical factors is communicable. The meaning structure of a language is the vehicle of the communicable. Thus, logic is the science of what, in a language, makes it communicable and cognitive. To say that logic makes knowledge meaningful or even language meaningful is again to invert the order of discovery and to play Zeus all over again to the order of reflection. Logic is the description of what is involved in knowledge. Logic does not then invent or impose. It becomes normative only if the meaningfulness thus described is desired.

This, in brief, is what Kierkegaard's views on logic add up to. That persons are logical without knowing the subject matter of the logicians is a fact. But this is only to report via persons what one would expect if a meaning structure were implicit in knowledge. Persons do know about the world and themselves without first recognizing logical forms. They have knowledge without possessing knowledge about that knowledge. But the reason for stating this position here is principally to draw the reader's attention to a facet of Kierkegaard's thought and writings that is almost completely neglected. For the position here described is the position from which Kierkegaard attacks the pretensions of idealistic logic. Some of the reasons for saying this will be noted in the ensuing sections. If the above account is correctly to be attributed to Kierkegaard, then we can say that he is one with contemporaries in denying that logic is a description of ontological structures, but that against both the ontological logicians and the contemporaries he asserts that *logic is descriptive* of knowledge and hence is neither metaphysical nor purely formal (except when considered in abstraction from knowledge).

II

There is certainly a difference between a logician and being logical. The logician, I take it, is one who makes his subject of inquiry what for the other man are the tools of reflection. The logical man may also be a logician, but properly, we mean by a logical man one who uses the tools of reflection correctly, so that the meaning of his language is apparent. He may or may not reflect upon logic but certainly he uses it. The question is therefore appropriate: Was Kierkegaard a logician or was he logical?

In respect to the first question it seems clear enough that Kierkegaard was not a logician in any of the usual senses. He did not, for example, write a treatise on logic nor did he suggest at length any new logical theory. The appearances seem to be against him in this respect. But, on the other hand, if we ask whether he was logical, the answer is certainly in the affirmative. He is not irrational or illogical in any wide sense of either term. With almost maddening regularity Kierkegaard too escapes all neat summary remarks. His logicality is not simply inadvertent nor is it as fortuitous as one might assume from the literature by and about him. For, despite the lack of what one might call strictly technical and detached works such as might qualify for the label, "works on logic," Kierkegaard did provide a whole series of judgments about his own writings. He did what in the modern idiom is called, providing a language about his own language. More strictly, he provided a literature about his pseudonymous literature.

In an older philosophical language, probably a little more appropriately expressive for Kierkegaard's accomplishments, Kierkegaard wrote with a high degree of self-consciousness. Hence his logicality is not accidental or haphazard. When you read him at any length you acquire the strange feeling that this man has just about exhausted in his own person the possible vantage points from which his works could be viewed and judged. And a logical and detached standpoint from which the norm and validity of specific works as well as the entire authorship can be understood is never very far from the reader's grasp as he reads Kierkegaard's books, principally because this standpoint is so frequently invoked, though not expounded, by the author himself in his running commentary which his footnotes, his accounts of the books, his journals and papers, yes, and even his letters, give in such abundance.

Kierkegaard's books are many in number and are ostensibly possessed of two kinds of meaning; one kind of meaning is intrinsic to each work, the other extrinsic to each work and provided by the role of each book in the entire authorship. Kierkegaard's sweep was a very broad one and his literature taxed his own ingenuity as well as his readers. Just what all of the pseudonymous works were aiming to do and how they hung together with all of the religious works was not immediately clear. Whether one must assume that Kierkegaard's literature was too complex to let his plan stand clearly forth is a moot point for the literary critics, but what Kierkegaard did do is obvious enough, he supplied a written explanation. Whether his *Point of View for My Work as an Author* is correct in its factual judgments about the earlier works is again an issue for the critics but that this book provides another standpoint outside of the kind given in the earlier works is the interesting point to note for any philosophical reader. For here one does have in fact discourse about his earlier writing. True, it is a language that provides a kind of *telos* for other books; but even this admission does not negate the significance of there being also a standpoint from which the author could comment upon aesthetic, ethical, and religious standpoints. The latter tripartite division is said to be an exhaustive classification of ways of living one's life (i.e., if one admits the Christian to be a variant on the religious). If there is another point of view from which all of them can be described and written about, what is this point of view? Certainly it is not another way of living one's life. But it would seem that such a disinterested standpoint is exactly what Kierkegaard would have called a logical standpoint.

This standpoint is compatible also with the standpoint that permits Kierkegaard's critiques of other logicians in the *Fragments* and *Postscript*. Also, it seems to be identical with that which permits the incidental remarks, sometimes in footnote form (notably in *The Concept of Dread*), that are frequently and specifically on questions of logic and even logical theory. And if one adds to these still somewhat casual appearing sources all of the remarks on logic and epistemology to be found in the *Papirer*, then one has an imposing array of testimony for the existence of another standpoint, a logical and disinterested standpoint, from which Kierkegaard could write and could construe (albeit only logically!) the life views within his literature as well as all else that were his as a most richly talented poet-dialectician.

It behooves Kierkegaard's reader to distinguish carefully therefore between his anti-intellectualism and what might seem to be an anti-logicality. Because the metaphysicians of the idealistic variety invariably use logic to define the real and because they claim that the categories of the real are the categories of logic, Kierkegaard's criticisms of this position are easily construed as criticisms of all logical reasoning. They in fact are not this at all. He is protesting against those philosophical rationalisms that purport to find that intellectual categories, or more particularly logical categories, are descriptive of something more than the meaning structure of knowledge. For Kierkegaard the objectivity, and in a limited sense, the real, to which logic stands related, is knowledge. His crossfire is directed to those who wish to make categories descriptive of the world, of history, of God, or of anything else, metaphysical or empirical. That there may be knowledge about any or all of these, he grants. But logic and rationality in Kierkegaard's sense (somewhat analogous to Kant's) has as its subject for analysis meaningful discourse and not the world. An intellectualism that seeks to mitigate the differences between categorization and facticity, between the non-logical and the logical, is a confusion for Kierkegaard. Kierkegaard finds no logical or epistemological ground for identifying logical categories and those of reality.

He does admit however plenty of extra-logical grounds. The admission of the latter, however, is fatal for the intellectualist's claim, for this is to admit that non-intellectualistic interests or non-logical motives are essential for intellectualistic systems.

None of this is to say however that Kierkegaard is anti-logical. He is not "anti" system, order, or precision. For if the categories of logic are not the intimate definers of reality, they may still be the intimate definers of knowledge. And knowledge may in turn be about almost anything you please, even fictional entities and/or God, and still be logical. The extramental reference of knowledge is another issue altogether that logic cannot construe nor explain. Readers of Kierkegaard's literature well know the importance of "the leap" in this regard. While remembering that Kierkegaard did not write *in extenso* about logical matters, it is not difficult to construct something of his logical theory from his many criticisms of the kind of intellectualism represented by Hegel and the Hegelians of his own day. For purposes of brevity I enumerate a few of his criticisms:

A. He protests first and always against giving logical categories immediate empirical and factual content. He denies that they are historical, theological, metaphysical, etc. But he does not deny that there is historical knowledge, knowledge of nature, and with serious reservations that demand special attention, a kind of religious knowledge called theology.

B. He rejects any understanding of an implicative relation or a logical conclusion that imputes ethical or religious significance to the logical consequent. The neutrality of logic is as relevant to the premises and the conclusion as it is to the inferential transition and nowhere within logical discourse is it possible to slip from the neutral and the logical to the non-neutral and the ethical or the religious.

C. He deprecates also the identification of validity and truth. Though he distinguishes sharply between the truth of sentences and religious and ethical truth, he distinguishes equally sharply between both of these and the kind of claim usually described by the word "validity" that a logical conclusion possesses.

D. He strikes out too against the extension of other logical values, most clearly perhaps "system," to non-cognitive issues. What he has to say about the passions in respect to aesthetics and religion bear immediately upon this problem. Here he wishes to free the passions from the artificial and restricting formality that an inappropriate logical categorization imposes. That there may be knowledge about aesthetics and about religion again may be the case but then logic would describe properly the meaning structure of aesthetic and religious discourse. It would not, should not, predispose aesthetic creativity or appreciation nor a religious decision.

E. He protests too against the extension of the truth that is the logician's to analyze, viz., truth as a quality of a sentence or "propositional truth," to all other enterprises and especially ethics and religion. Kierkegaard denies categorically that any kind of propositional truth is of direct and immediate religious and ethical importance. The assent to cognitive truth is not a religious act. This is the point made indirectly by the insistence that religious and ethical truth is a matter of subjectivity.

F. All of this can perhaps be summarized under Kierkegaard's general repudiation of an identity between the logical and the real. But to say the latter within the appropriate context is Kierkegaard's merit. For he does not deny the possibility of knowledge of the real—he is not like Bergson, supposing that conceptualizing is *ipso facto* a deception—but he does again deny only that logic and reality are co-extensive.

When drawing distinctions between "logician" and "logicality," between "anti-intellectualism" and "anti-logicality," and especially in reference to Kierkegaard, it is well to remember that he was throughout his career of author a polemicist. He was delightfully argumentative. One of the ways to most clearly describe his ideas is to determine what he was against. In contemporary theological language he was a "dialectical" thinker. Again in contradistinction to the idealistic tradition, Kierkegaard decried the panlogical efforts to include even ethics and religion within logical sequences. He proposed that there was an existential dialectic, a qualitative dialectic, separate in kind from a logical dialectic. The first was non-logical and had to do with the life of passion and interest—it was dialectical only in the sense of being descriptive of the opposition, the give and take, of the inner life; the logical dialectic is that which gives anything about which we can have knowledge its argumentative and structural form. As dialectician, Kierkegaard is logical about non-logical matters and this is what makes his polemic so biting and gives irony to his entire endeavor. But he is not inconsistent. In order to draw the distinction between an existential and a logical dialectic and in order to make this distinction stick against opposition who deny the distinction, he uses a logical form in which to state his case for the passions. He uses poetic and passional forms too—he does in truth have many strings in his bow—but to the extent that he would have created only interesting poetical works, to that very extent he would not have been the polemicist and dialectician that he was. He was at once poetically creative and a logical thinker who used his own creativity for reasons that his intelligence commanded. This is why we can argue that his logical dialectic includes the expressions of the existential dialectic and the poetic content within its own scope. But if what he has said about the life of passions is true, then it is also relevant to note that the existential dialectic, the life of passions and the conflict of passions, is itself not the logical dialectic. The oppositions within logic are contrariety and contradictoriness and these are essential to the understanding of the relations between anything conceived. That the confrontations within the life of the passions are something quite different than logical oppositions, this is, of course, the burden of much of the Danish Socrates' literature.

As will be subsequently noted, Kierkegaard was acutely aware of the fact that his own literature was both a poetic achievement and yet an argument. As an argument it was informed by principles of logical reasoning. This can also be said about the bitter fight against the Church and the surprisingly bombastic literature produced during 1854–1855. If Kierkegaard is correct on the delineation of what logic is, then it is appropriate to draw the distinction already noted between validity and truth, and I believe it becomes possible to draw a distinction between the validity and the truth of Kierkegaard's attack upon the Church. His argument is valid if his premises are correct. His premises are discussed and discussed again in the earlier literature. To say this is not to say that they are true. However, this is to draw attention to the fact that it is invidious and logically fallacious to accuse him of logical faults when one ought to criticize the truth of his premises. But the latter is not easy. It is altogether too simple for most readers to read the earlier writings, even to praise them, and then to explain away the later attack upon the Church as if it were not integral to the earlier. This from the logical standpoint is a major fault. Kierkegaard's systematic acuity was not wasted—his literature whatever else one might say and feel about it is an expression of a masterful polemicist who kept his argument always to the point. If he has faults they are not logical in kind.

III

But with all of this it behooves us to turn to the consideration of Kierkegaard's specific logical achievements. One must note always that his literature is logically unified. It is internally consistent; it focuses diverse materials upon the same issues; it provides a description of the life of subjectivity but does it also in the spirit of objectivity and detachment. The literature is about the problems of existing but is ordered and articulated by a logicality that remains almost hidden but that helps to press all of the books to purposes that are Christian in intention and "edifying" in Kierkegaard's special use of this term. Because it is meaningful and because the literature is discourse containing an argument, logic is a necessary instrumentality for both writing and understanding its structure and purposiveness. The complete account of Kierkegaard's intellectual prowess could not be written without a very detailed examination of the internal consistency and logicality of the literature adjudged as a unit.

But again an indirection must be noted. The literature includes discussions about many topics, many of them of great interest to philosophers. Logic is not treated at the same length as some of the rest of these. For example, music, language, the Bible, duty, passion, system, truth, sin, faith, speculation, etc., are all discussed and in surprising detail. Supposing for the moment that Kierkegaard occupied a kind of vantage point while writing about all of these other topics, then it should be possible to discern this vantage point or at least to approximate to its description in virtue of (a) identical (and self-identical) characteristics in all of his judgments about different things, which characteristics are formal properties not identical with any described by the literature, and (b) the fact that his descriptions of other topics give us the outlines when pieced together of logic itself. One of Kierkegaard's pseudonymous authors gives us precedence for this latter use of the literature when he tells us that by going to the "utmost boundaries" of the "kingdom" best known to him, namely language, he can then discover also the boundaries of the neighboring kingdom, music. By describing with precision so many other spheres of intellectual interest, it is almost as if Kierkegaard has circumscribed the sphere of logic without ever quite entering it.

And we are not without his direct comment on these issues either. Repeatedly Kierkegaard defines his logical ground (albeit briefly most of the time, *in extenso* only once, and then in a polemical situation where other issues are of paramount concern). Nonetheless, putting all of these sources together, we can state a number of theses that seem in fact to state Kierkegaard's logical position. These are sufficient in number and rich enough in quality to occasion a revision in judgment about his status as a thinker. Granted that he is not a logician in the ordinary senses, still he shows the diagnostic and analytical powers of the greatest of them. He seems actually to have anticipated privately what are some of today's public logical modernities. Therefore, despite what has been said, he begins to loom as a logician and a very good one.

In what follows I shall list some of the theses that seem to me to give a clue to Kierkegaard's logical theory. These are not in any order of importance. These are, in most instances, constructed and constituted in their present form, from contexts in which other issues are discussed. But I point each thesis toward a logical consideration, and this intentionally. I shall in each instance state first a thesis and then add only sufficient comment to relate each thesis to others.

1. The logical standpoint is one of disinterestedness. Disinterestedness and logicality cannot perhaps be completely identified. The Stoics talked about "apathy" and gave this psychological state of personality ethical and even religious significance. Kierkegaard's aesthetic pseudonyms do the same. Kierkegaard believes that the state of disinterestedness is the *sine qua non* of logicality, but to make such

disinterestedness a life-view was to impute more significance than it could ever contain.

2. Ethical and religious standpoints are instances of interestedness. There are qualities and kinds of interest and therefore there are kinds of ethical and religious positions and ways of life. These are described in Kierkegaard's own literature. There is, however, only one logical standpoint, if pure disinterestedness is attained. Logic is centripetal.

3. Logicality is the necessary condition for all knowing, including the knowing about ethics and religion. Logic does not describe the necessary conditions for being ethical or being religious. Logic therefore describes the conditions permitting intelligible discourse even about passional matters. Disinterestedness is the necessary condition for "discussing" and "knowing" about interestedness.

4. Interestedness is the necessary condition for being human. To substitute a state of logical disinterestedness for a form of interestedness is to confuse a noetic condition with a moral condition. The logical standpoint is neutral and properly amoral; to impute moral qualities to it is to negate its neutrality.

5. Identity describes the condition under which knowledge can be remembered (i.e., known by the same person in different moments of time and in different psychological complexes or states of mind) and communicated (i.e., known by different persons). Logical connections and the acts of inference are between identities in different complexes of things, of thoughts, of meanings. The law of identity in *logic*, therefore, describes a minimal condition for knowledge and communication.

6. Tautology is the highest logical principle. The identity between premise and conclusion is the guarantee of validity. That there is nothing new in the conclusion describes the paucity of logical discourse but from the point of view of disinterestedness this paucity is the token of certainty and validity.

7. There is no proof for logical laws or principles. Insofar as logic describes the meaning structure of knowledge it is "descriptively" either true or false. But insofar as logical laws are true and therefore

"ought" to be obeyed, it becomes ridiculous to assert their truth. They describe only the conditions for valid inference; they do not provide logical grounds for being logical. Logic is not its own proof.

8. There is a necessity described by logic that is implicative necessity. There is a necessity that is "for" logic that is not described by logic. The first is logical necessity; the second is a pragmatic and psycho-logical necessity. There is no logic mediating between persons and logic or being logical. The only proof for logic—or better, the ground for being logical—is the demonstration of the pragmatic need or the absurdity of being illogical.

9. Logic and non-logical (existence, e.g.) are not logically related. But reflection secures a homogeneity between all things by first convert-ing them into possibles. Logic provides a homogeneity in possibility, in knowledge, only by disregarding through abstraction the actuality. Existing things as conceived are logically amenable. That the world is an "existing (not as conceived) logical homogeneity," Kierkegaard finds to be a gratuitous and unwarranted assumption. To assert that this is true *sub specie aeternitatis* is to pretend to a standpoint that is not the logical standpoint.

10. The heterogeneousness of "existence" is an expression for the dif-ferences between passions and thought and also for the difference be-tween the thought of a thing and the existence of the thing. Reflection translates actuals into possibles and thus secures homogeneity within possibility, which homogeneity logic then describes. A contrary and non-logical effort is to convert possibles into actuals, out of homoge-neity and out of possibility into the heterogeneity of existence.

11. All necessity is implicative, not causal. It is a metaphysical leap to impute to natural events and history the necessity characteristic of natural and historical knowledge. The necessity describing logical relations and any and all possibles does not describe nonlogical rela-tions. Logic describes the necessity within the meaning structures of knowledge, not truths of knowledge, not the world.

12. Logical movement, from premises to conclusions, is a necessary movement. It is sharply differentiated from *kinesis* or change in na-

ture and from qualitative changes within human subjects. Logical movement is between possibles; *kinesis* or motion is (from the logical standpoint) the transition from a possibility to actuality; ethical and religious change, conversion, repentance, a new life, etc., is to deny one kind of actuality in favor of another, which is at present only a possible. It is to *become* a possible.

13. Knowledge is a synthesis of the real and the ideal. Logic describes the duality but does not explain it. Metaphysical logic purports to describe and/or explain nature and history as a duality. A non-metaphysical and non-ontological logic describes only knowledge. It does not nor can it explain or construe the duality that the world and knowledge is.

14. That ethical-religious truth is "subjectivity" is from a logical point of view a sentence purporting to be true about an objective state of affairs. Kierkegaard's logical theory permits the objective and logical and disinterested understanding of this assertion without mitigation of the religious and ethical standpoint on the one hand or the logical on the other.

15. That "ethical-religious truth is subjectivity" is itself of logical and empirical significance:

a) As a sentence it stands within a systematically related group of sentences that detail the limits and validity of cognitive meaning structures. This sentence has therefore validity within Kierkegaard's delineations of the logic of meaningful sentences.

b) The sentence purports to be true about matters of ethical and religious fact. Whether it is or not, is another question. In principle, the assertion can be treated as an empirical hypothesis.

16. Logic permits of a high degree of certainty. The certainty about knowledge that is what logic provides is of a different order than the certainties within or of knowledge. The certainties of knowledge about knowledge are greatest where only the ideal meaning structure is described; knowledge about knowledge becomes hypothetical also to the extent that the duality that knowledge is must be described. Logic is most certain because it seeks to describe that which is self-

identical (not as some contemporaries say because it is all a matter of staying consistent with one's original definitions).

From all these, and there could be listed many more, it becomes clear that Kierkegaard's logical reflections describe a *via media* position in logical theory. He was a formalist in logic but with significant differences from most contemporaries. He did not believe that logic or reflection stood logically or reflectively related to any content. He believed the meaning structures commanded by reflection were in truth empty of content and by themselves without existential and metaphysical significance. His case against the ontological logicians makes this quite clear. But, on the other hand, he does not make the logical forms simply inventions either. He believes them to be discovered within the knowledge enterprise that again did not wait for logicians or the logical forms before beginning. Once discovered and isolated it is clear enough that a reference to a non-logical content is not itself a logical matter. The content of the logical forms (which is what knowledge is) is gained only by extra-logical and intentional acts. But again to speak of logical forms as if they were pre-existent is a mistake. They are abstracted from knowledge and have separate existence only to the thought that abstracts them.

Kierkegaard refuses all of the extreme resolutions of the problem that can be raised respecting the relation of the logical and the real. He refuses to translate the homogeneity of essences to the realm of existence as do all the intellectualists of human history. This is his case against Hegel finally and, most particularly, against the Eleatic philosophers of the ancient world. But, against the other extreme he is equally opposed. He refuses to translate the heterogeneity of existence and the inner life to logic and the realm of essences. This is his point in denying so candidly the Hegelian effort to introduce movement (*kinesis*) into logic. His position keeps him a kind of dualist. All of the unities are logical; the differences and the clefts between people, between people and thoughts, between thoughts and things, he accepts to be what they are. Philosophy, and certainly not logic, is no legerdemain by which to discover their underlying unity. No metaphysics heals the breaches; no ontology gives any understanding of the duality. Kierkegaard has no philosophical instrument to make the world different than it appears.

Kierkegaard's understanding of logic secures his intellectual modesty. To retrace his thought on metaphysics is a refreshing and novel mode of seeing how his understanding of the province of validity tempered his hopes and his conjectures about what may or may not be the truth about nature and history.[1]

---

1. Paul L. Holmer's note (with updates by the editors: *JP* refers to *Søren Kierkegaard's Journals and Papers*; *KJN* refers to *Søren Kierkegaard's Journals and Notebooks*):

A Note Concerning Sources

I should like to suggest that the principal sources for the remarks here offered are Kierkegaard's *The Concept of Dread*, *Fragments*, *Postscript*, and volume II of *Either/Or*. Numerous places in the *Papirer* are important too, of which I list only a few: I A, 317 (*JP* 2, 1567); II A (entire section) (*KJN* 1 and 2); II C, 20 (*KJN* 3, Not4:9, Not4:9.a); III B, 177; IV A, 68 (*JP* 5, 5624; *KJN* 2, JJ:79); IV B, 118 (IV B, 118:1 = *JP* 2, 1246); IV C, 62 (*JP* 2, 1245; *KJN* 3, Not13:40); IV C, 63 (*JP* 2, 1595; *KJN* 3, Not13:41); IV C, 66 (*JP* 2, 1598; *KJN* 3, Not13:41, Not13:41.a); IV C, 79 (*JP* 2, 1602; *KJN* 3, Not13:50); V B, 5–8 (V B, 5:8 = *JP* 2, 1340; V B, 5:10 = *JP* 3, 3081); V B, 49 (V B, 49:1 = *JP* 3, 3653; V B, 49:14 = *JP* 3, 2343); VI A, 335; VI B, 88; X 2 A, 195 (*JP* 6, 6532); X 2 A, 328 (*JP* 1, 1057); X 2 A, 439 (*JP* 1, 1059). Also, the incomplete "De Omnibus Dubitandum est" (in Kierkegaard, *Philosophical Fragments, Johannes Climacus*, 113–72) is appropriate as are the lengthy ruminations about logical problems, indirect communication, etc., that were parts of projected books included in the *Papirer*.

Victor Kuhr's *Modsigelsens Grundsaetning* is an able work on these matters and David F. Swenson's essay, "The Anti-Intellectualism of Søren Kierkegaard," *Something about Kierkegaard*, 95–118, is a penetrating endeavor by a student of modern logic to show what Kierkegaard's criticisms of intellectualism actually meant. To both of these, and a host of others, I am, of course, greatly indebted.

CHAPTER 3

Kierkegaard and Theology

K IERKEGAARD IS ONE OF those rare men of reflection—he is too many-sided ever to be a founder of a school of thought. He is not quite properly Lutheran, certainly not scholastic enough; nor is he only an existentialist or even pre-Barthian or anti-metaphysical or an irrationalist. He illustrates the motto that prefaces *Philosophical Fragments*, "Better well hung than ill wed."[1] Though many of his readers have tried to assimilate him to commodious categories, he does not quite fit. For surely no author with such a regard for logicality can be justly described simply as an irrationalist; neither can a devotee of intellectual tradition and a person of catholic tastes and sympathies be seen adequately only as a man of revolt, existentialist or otherwise; and though there is an "either/or" bringing distinctiveness to human discourse and choice, yet it must be remembered that Kierkegaard believed in the powers of personality to synthesize otherwise discrepant factors. Though tragedy and suffering were not alien to him, still he was convinced that Christianity was a happiness view and that faith is the victory that overcomes the world.

To describe Kierkegaard's significance for theology has been made difficult rather than easy by the scholarship about him, for often he has been claimed to be Lutheran or on the road to Rome, anti-intellectual or too intellectual, anti-church or pro-Augustine, too psychological or too theological or even both. Actually Kierkegaard is much better as a theologian than his theological critics and adherents make him out to be. He is a radical thinker. He is more concerned with the substructures than with the super-structures and, on almost

1. Kierkegaard, *Fragments*, 2.

every page, his interest is directed toward that kind of issue which is elemental and from which perhaps several intellectual elaborations can be made. Simply because he talks about matters common to so many positions taken by schoolish thinkers, it becomes almost an adventure to find him a therapeutic but Christian positivist, or a neo-orthodox theologian, or the father of existentialism. Besides being mistaken most of such claims are trivial and an indictment of the scholar who makes them.

A most general point about Kierkegaard perhaps deserves to be remembered. Kierkegaard was, intellectually considered, a diacritical thinker. He was able to make and to sustain distinctions. He excelled in the use of diagnostic abilities and was able throughout his career (brief as it was—he began writing in 1841–1842 and was done about nine years later) to ferret out the skein of possibilities with the utmost of logical rigor. This is the aristocratic and technical side of the man and his authorship. Here he sought to be rigorous, exacting, precise, in fact everything that any scrupulous man of intelligence discovers necessary for intellectual transparency. But the other side, and equally important, was his abiding interest in the synthesis proposed by Christianity for human personality. At once Kierkegaard commanded those dialectic and pathetic (i.e., capacities for pathos) talents that enabled him to indulge and yet to study those pervading emotions and commandeering interests that make existing distinctively human. The point then is that Kierkegaard combined an analytic intelligence with an ethico-religious and synthesizing passion. His authorship endeavors to dignify as well as to express the nobility of the simultaneity of factors within the personality, and especially as this is constituted by faith in Jesus Christ.

All of this should caution the reader against too quickly summarizing Kierkegaard's thought. Reflection moves by distinctions and exclusions and bifurcations but existence is, like the mock turtle soup of which one of his pseudonyms speaks, full of everything. Knowing that the exclusions in thought might not entail exclusions in being, Kierkegaard is very wary indeed in circumscribing what is real. Thus he does not deny metaphysics all meaning simply because he denies that thought and reality are one. Nor does he deny the objectivity of Jesus, of actual existence, of canons of thought, simply because he

notes the importance of subjectivity and the difficulties of the ontological logic of his day. And he is not quite a sectarian and a vol-
untarist on distinctively Christian matters simply because he notes
intellectual and ethical discrepancies on matters like the Church and
the sacraments. But neither is he meekly traditional here either.

Surely Kierkegaard was a wise man. He knew that intellectual
extremes were daring and even exciting but here common sense was
his guide. His intellectual affirmations were tentative and subject to
recall. But ethically and religiously he sought decisiveness and maximal risk-taking. The leap of faith was an act whereby the personality
constituted itself, whereby character was formed. To keep oneself
ethically decisive while admitting intellectual uncertainty was part
of Kierkegaard's admonition towards the good life. The fact that an
erstwhile Christian culture had blurred this difference and the fact
that philosophers had proposed ontological understanding, the understanding of being itself, as the bridging of the gap, led Kierkegaard
to his task of reintroducing Christianity into Christendom and making numerous viable intellectual distinctions all over again.

Four issues will be here adumbrated. Though these might indicate Kierkegaard's relevance to contemporary theology, still more
it is hoped that they may incite that kind of enthusiastic attention
deserving a man of pervading Christian compassion who was simultaneously an aristocrat among the *cognoscenti*.

I. The Meaning of Religious Discourse

First it ought to be noted that Kierkegaard addressed himself to the
problem of the meaning of religious discourse. It is a commonplace
among students of eighteenth- and nineteenth-century theological
literature to note the difference between saving theology by convert-
ing its statements into metaphysical claims on the one hand and historical claims on the other. The Gnostics had even tried, much earlier,
to vindicate theological claims by showing that no historical claims
were essential. And today, once again, there are fervent endeavors
among the theologically inclined to show that theology can be de-
mythologized and, further, that commitment to Jesus Christ does
not entail a commitment to a metaphysical schematism. All of this

is part of the large and vexing inquiry into the meaning of religious discourse.

It is perhaps a dubious distinction to impose upon an author, namely, that he wrote on a topic relevant to men of a century later. Besides, Kierkegaard wrote on this topic only indirectly and in consequence of a concern with the question of the locus of religiousness. Though Kierkegaard knew too that the Christian religion had permeated our customs, our literature, and our language with glory and hope, he was not content to let the contemplation of these objectivities be the primary religious act. He contended against Hegel, not so much because his empirical descriptions were either wrong or absurd, but, rather, because Hegel denied in his grandiose interpretation the religiousness of human subjectivity. It is Kierkegaard's merit to have stressed the fact that theological language, whether this be the language of the Bible or the more formal discourse of the theologian, corresponds also to human subjectivity.

Unlike other thinkers who make a point by excluding too much, Kierkegaard does not deny the possibility of objective reference to theological language. However, his point is a pregnant one, and fraught with all kinds of as yet unexplored implications, namely, that religious discourse is not religious because it conveys results. The point of religious language is not to communicate results as much as it is to stimulate the process of experience and thought that will reconstitute human personality. Ethico-religious truth is, in other words, not a quality of the language itself but is rather the process, the striving of the human subject to be a definitive individual.

Though this kind of point is frequently made, and usually clumsily, it is to Kierkegaard's credit that he makes it with both an aristocratic intellectual intent of clarifying the muddle that the learned create on these matters, and an earnest religious endeavor of showing that the simple man as well as the learned share the condition in their subjectivity for the realization of the highest truth that Jesus Christ is. Kierkegaard had no sympathy with Spinoza's religion in which God is actually the sum total of the logical predicates available to an aristocratic mind. Likewise, the translation of the language of Christianity into that of the logic of historical existence, which Hegel tried to effect, Kierkegaard protests on both intellectual and moral grounds.

But, as yet, Kierkegaard is relatively untried on these matters. However, one hundred years ago he admitted the objective uncertainty of theological pronouncements and hence was not disturbed by biblical criticism of his day nor would he be chagrined by the confessions of intellectual incertitude in ours; but, withal, he noted that the primary question was the quality of one's own life, his own subjectivity, and that no theological sentence was religious in meaning until the appropriation process was stimulated and human passion aroused.

I am bold enough to suggest that recent theology is positively amateurish on these matters. Kierkegaard's epistemological and technical acumen holds a great promise for future formal inquiries upon which so much theology depends. But even more than this, Kierkegaard was a master at etching out the devotional requisites of Christian religiousness and not least of his disinterestedness is expended on the task of reflecting himself out of the aesthetic, the philosophic, and the aristocratic, and back again into the devotional and the simple.

II. The Importance of Passions and Interests

A second consideration marking Kierkegaard's theological relevance is his disclosure of the importance of passions and interests. Few authors have been so marvelously equipped for this kind of task as that Dane. He wrote effortlessly and gives the impression of writing with the immediacy that the bird sings and the flower spreads its fragrance. It is no wonder that he thought of himself as a poet. Once his literary goal became clear, his authorship comes forth almost completely free of those niggardly and finite calculations marring so many artistic and literary productivities. He wrote out of his own inwardness that was rich indeed and in a style not calculated to please his public but one adequate to his own insight. But, for this very reason, he succeeds in writing out of his own pathos and writing his way into the pathos of another individual, his reader. If nothing else, the Kierkegaardian literature is so rich in pathos, so replete with those dimensions of human subjectivity that are truly universal, so expressive of refined passions and concerns, that here alone it will bridge long spans of time and continue to challenge moral turpitude and laxity.

Such honesty, sincerity, and flaming concern, expended as it is in an authorship that defines religious truth not as sentences to be learned but as dynamic becoming of the self, are theologically important by themselves. But Kierkegaard did more. He described the casual and efficacious role of interests and passions in the greatest detail. He brings together what are otherwise so often separated in Christian tradition. For him, the emphasis upon the objectivity of Jesus' existence, of the Atonement, and other divine acts, does not deny the existence or the significance of subjectivity. In fact, it is his intent not to correct Protestant theology here as much as it is to supplement its account by showing that subjectivity too can be orderly, that it can and indeed must predispose the person. Instead of distrusting subjectivity as Lutheran dogmatics and Church practice suggest, Kierkegaard delineates carefully the role of despair, of dread, of guilt, this to make clear that no one is a sinner deductively and only because the dogma says that all men are sinners. A subjective state does correspond and Kierkegaard is apt at pointing it out, all the while skillfully noting the differences as various objectivities, laws, mores, God, Christ, are engaged.

But more than this, Kierkegaard notes too that the content of Christian religiousness is finally passional and interestful, not conceptual. Not only are modes of subjectivity the cause of religious striving but the appropriation of religious teaching, and of anything else religious that is objective and social, leads to another mode of subjectivity. Even love, the *agape* of the New Testament, must be a passion. Kierkegaard felt a responsibility as author to lead his reader out of subjectivity and into the contemplation of objectivities only for the sake of the new subjectivity that Christian faith, hope, and love are. Surely this is of a distinctive note in theological and philosophical writing and worthy of very careful attention. Few authors have been as successful in saying this in a congruent manner as was Kierkegaard. For he destroys as he moves along his own authority and calculates the effect of his writing in such a way as to augment the passional response within the reader.

Kierkegaard, as also noted in the previous section, is here proposing a new basis for the discussion of theological issues. In centuries past, when theologians were able to talk with impunity about the final and efficient causes of nature (this because the physicists already did so), when men of religious learning could espouse easily the fortunes of God in the progress of men, then there seemed little reason to believe that human subjectivity was naught else than a mirror, confused and distorting indeed, of the passing scene. But Kierkegaard is suggesting that the inner life is not a mirror of the outer existence. It is not a chaos, not a random or caused array. Kierkegaard's literature is the disclosure of the life of subjectivity as a cosmos, capable of being mapped and described, in some respects independent and in ethico-religious senses most important of all. By saying that an interest in and a passion for existing is the reality that men can actually practice and own, Kierkegaard proposes a kind of metaphysics, not only compatible with Christianity and the New Testament, but also a new point of departure for theological discussion.

III. The Pragmatic Significance of the Person of Jesus Christ

It may seem amiss to say it but Kierkegaard seems also to have rediscovered the pragmatic significance of the person of Jesus Christ. All kinds of books can be written about Jesus Christ just as they can about Plato, each book taking account of the history of the teachings, of institutions, of the criticisms of either, and all of this being a documentation of the significance of the man. Each book thus written is in turn an item in history to be understood again as a part of the growing significance of the man. But it is Kierkegaard's point that as true as the respective historical accounts of Plato's and Christ's significances might be, still this is not the proper way to describe the bearing upon human interests of the person of Jesus Christ. As important as scholarship might be, Kierkegaard brings a correction to the view that grows up where religious studies are pursued and taught, namely, that by increasing the scope and broadening the grasp, the personal and intense religious response will follow as a matter of course.

Certainly it is true that Christianity has its own tradition and that this is both extensive and refined; likewise there is an institutionalizing of the idea which has resulted in the Church becoming a formidable power in the affairs of men; and not least, rightly or wrongly, there are external authorities, men and books, that are reputed to keep the keys to the treasures of life eternal. Kierkegaard neither denies nor affirms with enthusiasm the above views. But what he is concerned to point out is the fact that no one of these is, nor all of them together are, in such connection with the individual that the Christian's response is ever passionless, habitual, or trivial. Instead there is the person of Christ and He is the paradox. This latter word, "paradox," is intended by Kierkegaard to safeguard the uniqueness of the Christian's object of interest. Paradoxicality describes that kind of relation and object that Christianity and Christ are.

On the object side, Christ is the paradox because no premises offered to reflection can make loyalty and faith to Him a necessary and inevitable consequent. He is neither obviously God, nor inductively speaking, even the greatest man who ever lived. Even if He were the latter, still an absolute commitment would be incommensurate with the approximative and necessarily hypothetical conclusion. But on the subject's side, there is paradoxicality because He is the object of interest, offense or faith, scorn or worship, without that kind of justification that decisiveness seems to ask. The interest that He asks in His own existence and person is an interest not congruent with self-interest nor is it congruent with that reason that we all invoke quite concretely as the reflectively organized common sense of mankind. The contrariety of interests on the subject's side is many-sided of course. Disinterested analysis and reflection suggest a suspension of decision while the guilt and concern going with it counsel the need for a resolute decision; it does not quite seem to be in one's own interest to deny oneself and his interests in order to save oneself. Jesus Christ seems to be asking that men live by dying, that they win by losing, that they get by giving.

Kierkegaard's theological fecundity is again rich on two sides. On the abstract and formal side, he has produced and argued with exactitude the doctrine of paradoxicality and several related doctrines that constitute in part, surely, the prolegomenon to future Christological discussion—even if like other prolegomena this one too may help to circumscribe the inventiveness and exuberance of speculative thinkers. But, on the ethical and practical side, Kierkegaard is even richer. There is an almost lavish outpouring of literature from his pen on the consequences in human existing of an active relation to and interest in the existence of Jesus Christ. This again does not lack exactness and form but rather vindicates the view that Christian subjectivity has its aesthetic features, its suppleness, its variants, and even its sophistication. Where most authors are pedestrian and flat-footed and at best can repeat biblical rubrics with only slight elaboration, Kierkegaard can both illustrate in his own person and sketch for his reader the dramaturgical feature of Christian inwardness.

Not least of the relevance of the figure of Jesus to the person is the fact that a response to Him is not exclusively intellectual, or emotional, or dutiful. It is to Kierkegaard's credit again to have corrected the intellectualism of Protestantism and brought ethicality and empirical behavior back into consideration. Kierkegaard insists that religiosity too is a living synthesis of the personality in thinking, feeling, and willing. The aesthetic factors are not extirpated, the ethical is not abnegated; instead Kierkegaard delineates the richness of the faith relation by showing that even many sets of categories cannot quite exhaust it. All of this is testimony to the personality values that Kierkegaard discovers to be a consequent of the contemporaneity of Jesus Christ.

The thesis that contemporaneity with Jesus is actually possible involves Kierkegaard as it has everyone who thinks about it in numerous problems, epistemological and theological. Kierkegaard repudiates the use, though not necessarily the truth, of the substance doctrines and other gambits of the past. Instead he suggests that Jesus Christ exists as the contemporary only when one's own interest and passion is Christ-like. His suggestion is that the historical Jesus when viewed detachedly and disinterestedly is not the eternal contemporary. But when one forgives trespasses, as the prayer of our Lord suggests, then we are forgiven; when one loves an enemy, one is loved. But one is not loved because of one's own love, one is loved contemporaneously. Kierkegaard too is concerned to say that one's deeds do not merit God's attention. The presence of Christ is not a disinterestedly guaranteed and objectively warranted phenomenon. Again I can only urge that Kierkegaard's reflections here are most suggestive and seem to bear out the New Testament as well as augur well for further consideration.

IV. Re-reading the Human Situation

Last, and briefly, Kierkegaard has read exceedingly well the features of human existence. Many of the listeners in the pew have noted that things in the world are not quite the way the preacher has described them. When one hears the pulpit fulminations about the horrors of sin, and these horrors get no amplification other than that provided by either gross sensuality or misuse of public trust, then it certainly becomes difficult to fit the theological categories to every man. Kierkegaard corrected the interpretations, not by reforming the dogmas but by examining again the way it is we actually behave. Thus he sees us as sinners when we are sensual but also when we are most spiritual and moral. Nowhere does he suggest that sensuous delight in the things of the world is *ipso facto* sinful.

But all of this is part of his long essay in re-reading the human situation. Every issue he touches, the faith and reason controversy, the question of original sin, the significance of music, gets a new and creative treatment. If one analyzes all of this, it is surely the case that Kierkegaard makes his reader see that one's own personality, not history and not nature, is the locus for the presence of God. The larger orders may have their teleologies, God is undoubtedly present in all things occasioning their working together for good, but it is still men who must love God. Again, Kierkegaard does not deny in order to affirm—his domain is personality and he dares to believe that Christ died for every man and that the paramount concern must be to become a Christian. Once the inner teleology is taken care of, then the natural and historical scene may be read for what it is worth.

Hence it is that Christian faith is not alien to personality as Kierkegaard understands it. The otherness of God, the distinction between God and man, are not treated in anything but human terms. This must be remembered about Kierkegaard for he is only mistakenly associated with these traditions that emphasize God's transcendence in non-human categories.

Perhaps few writers have said so much about the glory of our common humanity as Kierkegaard did. Not a little of that glory is evident in the very fact that so much can be known and said about being human and being Christian. For Kierkegaard too, being Christian was a human perfection, not to be gainsaid because it is human nor slighted because it is finally a matter of grace.

In a day when human nature is in such bad repute, when the very fountainhead of sin-talk seems to be Kierkegaard, it might be well to discover how careful he was, how anxious to do justice to the sensory capacities, the aesthetic refinement, the genial admixture of pluses and minuses that we all are. The diatribes in his literature are reserved for those who have leveled all the valleys, who have straightened all the paths, who have taken the heights and depths of personal expression away from their fellows. All of those who, impressed by the engines of society and anxious to secure conformity to God, country, and duty, and who have slandered man by taking the adventure away—these are Kierkegaard's foes. That they include the clerics too, he was quick to note. His enthusiasms were, instead, for the restoration of passion, of expressiveness, of the individual's caring mightily. His literature is an attempt to restore the individual and his idiosyncrasies to a place of honor. For it is by rubbing that Aladdin's lamp, one's own personality and subjectivity, that one discovers God in Christ reconciling the world and oneself unto Himself.

CHAPTER 4

About Being a Person
Kierkegaard's Fear and Trembling

I

KIERKEGAARD WAS SO TALENTED and so witty that even as a young man, when barely thirty and his authorship just beginning (1843), his personal reputation already assured the sale of much that he wrote. So an acquaintance came to him one day complaining that in good faith he had purchased *Two Edifying Discourses*, assuming their author's cleverness and diverting propensities. Kierkegaard could only promise him his money back, if he so wished, for that book was surely not the expected idle elegance.

In a strange but commanding way, however, Kierkegaard's life and authorship never suffered comparison. It was not as if Kierkegaard wrote so much better than he lived or that he indulged designs of human life that he was reluctant to perform. Kierkegaard of all people knew very well that his wit and his talent, even though they were the means to his writing better than others, were not an indulgence granting him the right to act worse than others. His powers were so easy and his endowments so profligate that flights of fancy, sallies of wit, and spates of pleasantries could frame his rigors of argument and lighten his severe dialectical distinctions. As a reader, therefore, one can never willfully choose Kierkegaard's poetic delights and omit his intellectual thrust and still say that one had understood his books. Likewise, to thrill with Kierkegaard's argument and to neglect his passional appeal is surely to miss his point, whatever the book.

This is to remark, then, upon two features of Kierkegaard's relationship to his own books. First, his life does not tell us much of what his writings portend. And this is not because his life is so much less than his writings or vice versa. His writings are not a personal expression, and he practices a craft that is not subjective, not self-disclosing, and surely never emotive or directly passional. He does not illustrate, clearly enough, the popular conception of what an existentialist writer should be like. Second, though he wrote a great deal about his books (in the *Postscript*, in *The Point of View for My Work as an Author*, and at length in his *Papirer*), he never quite gratified that easy deceit that an author is "in a purely legal sense the best interpreter of his own words." Neither did he assume that because he, the author, had intended this or that, that the reader would be helped by a confession to that effect. Nor does he allow one to assume that because something is promised in a preface that it is, therefore, realized in the text.[1]

Both of these points are negative, and they could be used to suggest that Kierkegaard was a rank subjectivist, illustrating the notion that there are no objectivities and no criteria for the arch existentialist that he is supposed to be. But this, too, would be wrong, for Kierkegaard was neither a subjectivist nor an existentialist in any of the popular senses. He is not even "schoolish" or an advocate of a philosophic position or cause. Even if the historical objectivities of his life and the clarity of his intentions were available—as I think they can be with little effort—Kierkegaard scoffs at the notion that these give the meaning of his books. So, the broken engagement with Regina, serious as it is in being a moral breach, is not a clue to the meaning of *Fear and Trembling*. Some critics have insisted that the earnestness in showing that there is a teleological suspension of a moral duty must reflect a deep psychological need to justify breaking a promise and restoring a little continuity to his life. But surely even this must be a mistaken interpretative notion.

But these denials do not require that a book's meaning is whatever the reader declares it to be. There are not as many meanings as there are resourceful readers. Kierkegaard suggests over and over again a large number of limitations upon such wanton interpretation.

1. Remarks to this effect can be read in the "Appendix: A Glance at a Contemporary Effort in Danish Literature," *Postscript*, 225–66; for the quotation, see 225.

Also, the things he says about his entire literature, when he considers it as a totality, and what he says about particular books seem to provide a *confinium*, a limited arena, in which restraints are not only being asserted but in which a certain range of logical considerations are brought to bear by the author. There are logical curbs upon the person who suggests that meaning is private or social, or that there are multiple meanings, or that meaning, in any case, is only subjective.

This is an exceedingly important consideration for an author like Kierkegaard. For there is a way in which he, too, writes an entire literature whose spirit is outside the main strands of Western theological and philosophical thought. Something like Wittgenstein who said this kind of thing about his pages on mathematical and logical problems, Kierkegaard did not write in easy congruence with the pedagogical style of his day nor with the popular theology and philosophy. Wittgenstein said very tellingly about an early work that it did not build "ever larger and more complicated structures," that it did not add "one construction to another, moving on and up, as it were, from one stage to the next." On the contrary, it stayed where it was, seeking clarity and perspicuity right there, and "what it tries to grasp is always the same."[2] Kierkegaard wrote no new metaphysics, contrived no new doctrines, and spun no theories about fundamental matters. In this respect, he was not an originating thinker, for he was not carrying further the thought of the age and he was not suggesting an unheard-of mutation. Therefore, his works spoke to the age and yet were not what the age required. Kierkegaard himself said both of these things.

If one had thought there was nothing different in either Kierkegaard or Wittgenstein because they did not realize an expectation one might entertain from the thought of their day, then it looks again as if another standard way to assess their meaning is being disparaged. And so it is. But this again does not imply that there is no right or wrong understanding or that the literature means what one chooses it to mean. The bugaboo for so many academic people is always subjectivity; for subjectivity suggests that carefully acquired learning, deep acquaintanceship with a period of culture, and scrupulous detail about the problems of reflection to which an author

2. Wittgenstein, *Philosophical Remarks*, "Foreword," 7.

addresses himself are irrelevant to ascertaining what that author is about. But often what is forgotten in this context, bracketed by the cryptic notion that either one must be objective or otherwise subjectivity runs riot, is that such dichotomous reasoning is misleading on a whole range of issues. Just what issues and why—that will be part of the point of subsequent remarks.

For in what follows, I want to allude to another set of conditions that bear upon understanding the sort of religious and even deep matters of the human spirit (we could call them ethico-philosophical) that Kierkegaard writes about. Our considerations will bear upon the meanings that constitute his books, not least *Fear and Trembling*. It might be tempting to say as a very singular critic of our time has done, "the meaning of a book is the series or system of emotions, reflections, and attitudes produced by reading it. . . . The ideally true or right 'meaning' would be that shared (in some measure) by the largest number of the best readers after repeated and careful readings over several generations, different periods, nationalities, moods, degrees of alertness, private preoccupations, states of health. . . ."[3] But here the question of "meaning" and the related issue of "understanding" are described as though the reader's capacities required either an anterior consensus or the assistance of the literary critic. Kierkegaard thinks that there are times when the critics can help; but he is more concerned about a kind of understanding that does not come because of an intermediary and, in fact, cannot come about in that way. Instead, there is an understanding and meaning that only the reader can engender but one that is not, for that cause, subjective, private, or idiosyncratic. Other conditions can be transmitted, but not the meaning. It is the logic of such meaning and such understanding that obtains between the story of Abraham and its reader, between the New Testament and its authors, between oneself and a page of moral advice. There is a logic not only between propositions but also between spoken sentences and their speakers or readers. This is then to anticipate our remarks.

3. Lewis, "On Criticism," 56–57.

II

Johannes de Silentio asks about Abraham: "Who is capable of understanding him?"[4] And right away we sense a great difference between Kierkegaard and most religious authors, including learned commentators. For one thing, he always shows us that religious matters are discontinuous and heterogeneous with our ordinary *patois* and about the world and our common life. The fact is that if we think we have understood Jesus' crucifixion, his dying for our sins, and Abraham's tough and ready faith, then Kierkegaard is certain that all our descriptions and talk about them are much like language on a holiday, that is, not meshing at all with our lives. But the issue is starker than that. Who is in the position (*istand til*), who has the capacity (*duelighed, egenskab*) to understand? Understanding requires more than knowledge and especially knowledge given you by a third party, say a learned critic. And "capacity" here does suggest that one must have some room in his life (perhaps like the expression *rummelighed* suggests), but that can be deceptive too.

No, the capacity is not merely a matter of capaciousness, nor is it simply a skill. So, most students in a modern university can be taught to read Hebrew and some will read a great deal. Some will read so widely in ancient lore that they will have access to the history hidden from the rest of us. But if Kierkegaard is right, these skills and all the attendant advantages they bring will not add up to the capacity to understand Abraham. The difficulty here is not to be met with more information or even with an historical empathy.

The difficulty to which Kierkegaard alludes here is a breach of consciousness itself, something far deeper than a different culture, a nomadic people, another ethos, etc., could suggest. And it is not a breach like that between the cultivated and the bumpkins, the drooling idiot and the person of taste and discrimination, or the scientists versus the persons of letters. Neither is it like that between the good and the evil, drastic and thorough though this breach might be.

The breach of consciousness of which Kierkegaard speaks has to be differently conceived. But first we must sketch a bit what we mean

4. Kierkegaard, *Fear and Trembling*, 29. Other references hereafter are to this Lowrie translation unless otherwise noted. The occasional Danish references are to the convenient 1962–64 edition of the *Samlede Vaerker*. *Frygt og Baeven* is 5:7–112.

by a person being conscious. The familiar feature that stands out in being conscious is simply that people typically learn to see, hear, think in an "about" mood. That is, their attention becomes focused and their psychological activities become transitive. They see the world, hear sounds, and some go on to talk about the world around them. The most familiar way we have of summarizing all this is to say that people begin to learn "about" something. They acquire knowledge. Of course, this supposes a variety of strengths and capacities, skills and crafts. The result is that knowing the world is done in social ways, in language that must be public and for purposes that are recognizable and by and large stateable. But the principal feature is, again, the transitivity, the intentional and referential thrust that is given everything psychological, so that it becomes a medium for "aboutness."

There is nothing in Kierkegaard's pages to suggest that knowing the world does not have all kinds of advantages. Kierkegaard is not an anti-intellectualist if by that one means that he suggests any other way to understand current events, or the past, or even the physical world around him. He never says (like Bergson) that a concept must deceive because the concept is static while reality is in flux and that, therefore, knowledge is only like the movie, an illusion of motion created cinematographically. Neither does he say (like John Locke) that we know only our ideas and not the world itself. There is no pervasive skepticism putting knowledge or the reflective consciousness into jeopardy. On the contrary, Kierkegaard trusts ideas and concepts because general skepticism is only a bit of nonsense. So, we can say that becoming a reflective person, acquiring a reflective consciousness, is like moving from a *terminus a quo*, which in this case is ignorance, to the *terminus ad quem*, which is knowledgeability.

The point is that human beings are host to a certain kind of consciousness. We become conscious "of," become attentive "to," more and more in extent, if we so choose, or contrariwise, we become competent in respect to ever greater detail, if we so choose. Either way, humans begin to distinguish themselves from animals by acquiring all that allows them to intend the world in its very rich and ever-changing manifold. In brief, we could say that man shows spiritual potential by this kind of development. And, of course, we can extend ourselves to new instances, to things heretofore unknown and even to those deemed unknowable. I believe Kierkegaard thought that this kind of cognitive personality growth was *uno tenore*, almost without a breach and in a single breath, and mostly without serious crisis and confounding personal disarray. Here there need be no paradoxes, except local ones to be resolved by better conceptual tools and a refinement of judgment.[5] The limits of thought keep getting moved by better observations and better hypotheses.

So, there need be no paradox in technical scholarship about Abraham. Instead, a refined knower finds more generous rubrics and a host of ways of subsuming him, all of them congruent with the concepts of the learned fields. But more, if one chooses to see Abraham as an anomaly, then one can be quite content to let him be still unexplained, if knowledge does not quite cover his case. One can trust to future scholarship when more evidence will be on hand; and this does not make for a paradox, only the acknowledgment and minor discomfort that some things are not yet quite done. But, the point then emanating from this consideration is that becoming responsible intellectually is an achievement that Kierkegaard does not disparage. There is an *ad quem* and it is feasible.

The difficulty that makes for a deep paradox lies not in the knowledge, but in another form in the consciousness of the human, for there is a diseased and sickened consciousness that begins to grow in all of us, even alongside the growth of knowledge. Unless this "growth" is confronted and directly attacked, Kierkegaard finds that all can well be lost, for there is an almost naïve and simple passional notion that gets added to the normal intellective abilities. It is that the human personality itself, the spirit of man, will take care of itself in the growth of knowledge and correlative skills. Because knowledge is accumulated gradually and incrementally, almost as the expansion and fulfillment of native immediacy, so it is assumed that the personality and spirit of a person is achieved by the same lineal and intel-

---

5. Kierkegaard would have enjoyed Wittgenstein's discussion of paradoxicality in the *Remarks on the Foundations of Mathematics*, in which part of his aim is to show that the paradoxes alluded to by certain theorists of mathematics can be taken care of by harder thought and by confining the discussion to narrower limits. "Something surprising, a paradox, is a paradox only in a particular, as it were defective, surrounding. One needs to complete this surrounding in such a way that what looked like a paradox no longer seems one." Wittgenstein, *Remarks on the Foundations of Mathematics*, part V, no. 36, p. 186.

lective development. The person being normally educated does not typically confront a paradox, and his understanding may be balked but usually by a difficulty for which he is presently unprepared or an ignorance not yet requited. If Abraham had had only more to learn, his frustration could have been temporary, and all of us can understand that kind of dismay. Again, though, the point is that the growth of knowledgeability is defined to be enough for the development of the personality, for then there would be no paradox and no persistent crises in understanding. At least, this is how it appears to most of us. Everything spiritual gets subsumed under a general single-level learning theory.

However, we often find our wants and wishes to be at odds, and the pursuit of knowledge often augments that kind of self-cognizance. But if this quixotic character of oneself is made manifest as we learn this or that, then the paradoxicality (if that is what we wish to call it) is only in the subject, not in anything objective. It is made out to be a temporary emotional aberration—something that one will get over in time. And that, again, is not quite what makes Abraham difficult to understand. For we all can empathize with psychological conflicts and we all can say things that are consoling, if not profound, about this kind of difficulty.

III

Now to return to the consideration of consciousness again. It is Kierkegaard's contention that consciousness is not fully developed when an individual learns to intend in cognitive ways the world around him. Or the development of the capacities to see, to hear, and to know the world around one, even if one should become a virtuoso of science and scholarship, is not to become all that a human being should be and can be. Here another kind and quality of consciousness is supposed. Kierkegaard at this juncture surely is not advancing a theory or proposing a novelty. Instead he is putting what is probably a very common, almost commonsensical, awareness into more conceptual and formal terms.[6]

6. "I have no wish to discover novelties, but rather it is my joy and my darling occupation to think upon things which seem perfectly simple." Kierkegaard, *Concept of Dread*, 76.

Consciousness becomes something quite different when a person learns to make himself an object of attention, concern, and even knowledge. This is to intend and to purpose oneself, and this kind of transitivity is for Kierkegaard the hallmark of spirituality. This is why he says in *The Sickness Unto Death* that Christian heroism consists principally in venturing to be oneself, not being "humbugged by the pure idea of humanity or to play the game of marvelling at world-history."[7] The diametric opposite is to be spiritless and that is like never being conscious of and, hence, never learning to be responsible for, what one has made of oneself. Perhaps this is like the state of those the Apostle Paul describes (Eph 4) whose minds are futile, whose understandings are darkened, who are alienated from God, who are callous and cannot grieve anymore. Here one has hardness of heart. But to be a self, granted what human beings are, requires that interest and enthusiasm, concern and passions, be developed for the quality of one's own life. Here one cares and manifests a kind of pathos. Thus a self relates and constitutes itself. This has to be an intentional activity and supposes that one takes into consideration what one already is. Here the *a quo* and *ad quem* are different. Hence, too, being a self requires understanding, not of just anything and everything, but of oneself.

This is where Kierkegaard again thought that science and scholarship, and philosophy too, could easily mislead one. Unfortunately, some kinds of knowledge and philosophical reconstructions of that knowledge lead one to the notion that one must surely have to understand the totality first, and that only then will the parts, including the self, be seen in the right perspective. If the whole of history can be made at all sensible, it could seem plausible to think that such an understanding would give one access both to the past and to oneself, as a matter of course. But so, too, with "being," with "reality," with "Nature": for a man seems to be but a part of all these. In this fashion, then, understanding oneself becomes an episode within a broader compass. And this kind of learned and sophisticated mistake is a deeply ingrained one, and it is not quite corrigible by a casual reminder.

7. Kierkegaard, *Sickness Unto Death*, 142.

In fact, Kierkegaard seems to think this mistake is both logical in form and ethical (or moral) in motivation. For we want to avoid self-concern and all the attendant components of self-consciousness. This is the moral side, for none of us finds that getting clear about ourselves is very pleasant. We begin to feel guilt, we grieve a bit, and we suffer all the wounds—remorse, remembrance of broken promises, slights, jealousies, contriteness—that have given self-consciousness its bad name for so many centuries. The trouble with you, we say to others and perhaps to ourselves, is that you are too self-conscious. "Forget yourself" seems like the open sesame, a command that opened the robbers' den in the *Arabian Nights* and will unfailingly open the self to better health, too.

The logical side is that we subsume the self as a part is to a whole, as a component is to a totality, as an atom is to the molecule, or even as Hegel, as an episode in the temporal unfolding of the System. But the self is not an object like that mode of thought suggests. Nonetheless, the mode of reflection is still suggestive and easy, besides being eminently plausible, and it allows us to think that selves are nothing unless they are like compost, which gradually becomes solid ground—but only after it first ferments, then becomes peat, and then a usable soil. The community or society looks like the reality toward which selves are contributory.

Kierkegaard says, in contrast, that a self is not a substratum, not a hidden essence at all; instead, it is a kind of relating activity, a relation, which by developing a consciousness of itself actually constitutes itself.[8] For this reason being a person involves activities, a willing of a goal for oneself, an emotionally rich concern over what one can be, a thoughtful assessment of what one already is. All of this is a matter of making emotions, pathos, wish, want, hope, understanding, thoughts, not bare essences, hanging in a kind of limbo, but instruments that are directed "to" and are "about" the self. This is the energy of life of which Kierkegaard spoke so often. He could not understand a man of learning developing such a consuming passion for his learning that he would ever give up the endlessly taxing and consuming thought about himself that would make him a responsible human spirit. "Not understanding oneself," then, would be the penalty for being totally

8. Ibid., 146.

objective. Kierkegaard thinks it would be the most frightful way to live: "to fascinate and surprise the world by one's discoveries and one's brilliance, and yet not to understand oneself."[9] This would not be another way to be a self, a genuine alternative; rather it would be a default so serious that there would be no self at all.

For being a self is a matter of wanting, wishing, not just anything, but a certain quality of life and subjectivity. However, only by being a subject can one be a subject, and that is not a transition; it is an energent, a "leap" as Kierkegaard calls it. One must become a subject by making oneself, not others or the external world, one's object. But not disinterestedly, for that could only be in virtue of not seeing what is there. For Kierkegaard thought that there was a logical, not a fortuitous and accidental, connection between seeing what one was and a kind of concern. To know oneself was, immediately, and without qualification, to become concerned. It would be impossible in the strongest logical sense of *impossible* to know clearly and acutely what one was and not, therewith, to be passionately involved. That is why self-consciousness is a different kind of transitivity. It is not simply knowledge turned inward. We can be students of other people and neither love them or hate them, without, in fact, caring about them in any way. Here the "about" character of our thought, the reference and predication, is logically independent of any kind of "ought." But with oneself it cannot be so, for to know oneself is not like knowing a substratum stuff or an object at all. It is a little like knowing God, who is never an object, but is always a pure subject. So, too, other people may be objects initially to one's glance, but the more pure they are as subjects, the less can they be viewed as objects. But with oneself, there is only the activity or the lack thereof, the relation or the lack thereof, and there is nothing to see but only something to be. There is nothing much else there.[10]

The self is that transitivity that gets its substance by being a "how," by not being a what, a thing, but by making itself a subject. To be a subject at all is to be conscious, to be intending the world in a rich variety of ways. But this one does by no single means, neither by

9. Kierkegaard, *Papirer* VII 1 A, 200 (*JP* 3, 2820; *KJN* 4, NB:87). The translation here is my own.

10. Here the argument of the *Postscript* is presupposed. But Kierkegaard also said these things in numerous places in his *Journals*.

thought, emotion, or will, but by all these and more—by emotions, wish, desire, and love. But to making oneself one's own enterprise and field, this marks out the beginning of a spiritual life. Then guilt, fear of failure, and anxiety get their root in the person.

We are speaking, however, about Abraham, whom Johannes de Silentio cannot understand. Think, therefore, about a kind of self-consciousness that is natural and easy enough. For early in a lifetime, we discover that some things distress us and others please. It is not long before we begin to tune ourselves almost like an instrument in order to gain gratification, enjoyment, and the agreeable in contrast to their opposites. Soon we become conscious of capabilities and powers that we have or do not have by which to find greater pleasure and reduce the pain. All this Kierkegaard has described already in his writings on the aesthetic stage. In a variety of ways, a move can be made to another qualitatively distinct style and manner of intending the self. This is the ethical; and here Kierkegaard is indeed fulsome and detailed. Once more, his point is that an ethical quality can be realized in independence of one's cognitive grasp of the rest of the world. For there are two dialectical streams that meet in the individual, and they never become one. On the one side, there is the skein of concepts within which and by which we construe the world and others as objects. Herewith we know the world and acquire a kind of consciousness that is "about," "to," and "of" that world and all that it contains. This is one conceptual scheme, as moderns would say, or a set of them; but Kierkegaard speaks mostly about a kind of dialectic, a skein of concepts. Nonetheless, the ethical stage also brings into birth another stream of concepts; but they are first (in a logical sense) and foremost developed in virtue of a person's apprehension and consciousness of himself or herself. These are the concepts in which we articulate our understanding of ourselves. They get their content not so much from learned schemes about ourselves as from the informal but necessary kinds of self-judgments by which we must live.

These two kinds of dialectic, one existential, the other cognitive, are not internally related; persons can be religious, aesthetic, or ethical and still have the same science or scholarship. But an individual must often entertain two conceptual schemes, one of the former group, while also being informed by general cognition. The individual is the point of synthesis or is the synthesis itself. Kierkegaard would have us remember that all human beings are in this strait, if they develop any consciousness of themselves at all. To have the latter supposes the development of subjectivity and passion, concern and interest, but these in turn are also qualified and determinate in at least one of three ways, aesthetic, moral, and religious.

Something could be said about the generic features of this synthesis, but I refrain because it does not bear directly upon the question of understanding Abraham. Something else and another kind of crisis of consciousness is shown us there. And that is to approach the telling point. Abraham's life shows us something in and of itself; and that feature cannot be adumbrated or lifted up into a higher synthesis. There is no higher conceptual unity or synthesis. A life itself is the synthesis or the crisis, as the case may be, and this is the price to be paid for a highly developed human spirit.

How then was it developed? Kierkegaard supposes Abraham to have been living under ethical categories and, hence, to have evinced an ethical kind of subjectivity, understanding, and consciousness. This means that he cared, and that he strove to construe his life and behavior in accord with laws and precepts. These were not, nor could they be, merely inclinations and hunches, wish-fulfillments or chancy proposals. Rather the ethical must be defensible and public, and in terms that are congruent with something available to all. Laws, rules, and obligations are like that. Here is the arena in which "rightness," "good," and "ought" get their standardization and force. And the point is that a consciousness, a proneness to intend oneself, is thereby given form and morphology. Kierkegaard thought there was something incumbent in human nature itself that would typically lead mankind from the aesthetic to the ethical and not the other way around. But with the ethical comes also a host of new concepts and these, in turn, become a good part of ethical behavior itself, and not just its cause or its symptom. The thought pattern that is produced is both a pattern for the deeds as well as a part of ethical behavior.

Abraham was like good men everywhere, a man subject to ethical judgments and also a subject who could make his judgments and live thereby. But this community of moral understanding can only obtain when and if the proper conditions are met. The rules and laws are not subjective, private, whimsical, or arbitrary. They are public, universal, stateable, and binding on all. But so is an ethical life. The only exceptions that can be envisioned are among those who have chosen not to play the game, who are drop-outs. There are, clearly, nonteleological suspensions, when a will falters, a thought does not obtain, there is a failure of consciousness itself. In effect, there is a suspension of the rule when we circumvent it and no longer admit it to be binding. But then there is usually a lapse in consciousness itself.

Abraham, again, was not guilty of a moral lapse. If so, we could understand him in the loose sense that we all know about moral lapses and suffer them often enough. Abraham was not victimized by a preference, by a wayward disposition, in contraposition to his settled moral conviction. If so, again we all know about such instances and hence he would not be baffling. Kierkegaard's point is that Abraham still has a determinate and ethical quality of consciousness even while he sets out on his trip to Mount Moriah. He suffers no lapse of that consciousness, but he does suffer a breach of that consciousness in this peculiar way. While willing the law and maintaining a continuity with his fellows and his son in a consciousness that is shared, in concepts that are in common, he now finds a duty from God that he cannot speak about, that is not for everybody, that proposes a way of intending the world and Isaac that seems idiosyncratic, odd, and indefensible. How can we understand that? It is as if the tools of understanding were inadequate.

IV

Here, then, we have a very deep paradox that will not be remedied by information, not by more discursive knowledge, not by enlarging the cognitive conceptual scheme. Nor is it a matter quite of changing God into one more ethical agent, as if he too is and must be part of that game. Must the moral laws obtain for God as philosophers have said about the laws of logic? If so, why? Is it really the case that the paradox is due—as Wittgenstein suggested—to a defective surrounding? If so, it might help to get the surrounding enlarged and bring God in. Let us suppose, for example, that God, indeed, must share the moral consciousness, or more plainly, let us suppose that God is good in the manner that people are. Then the context would not allow for a paradox. God would know everything and his ethicality would be more subtle. The environment would not now be defective—God's command would be thought of as being something like the tragic hero's behavior, which looks paradoxical but is not if you know what the hero knows. This kind of hero is tragic, for he cannot get rid of the tragedy; but the terrible oddness of the paradox and the divided consciousness that ensues is overcome. So, too, if one believed that moral concepts and precepts held for both God and men, then one could in principle understand God by understanding the moral laws. God would be plausible in the longest possible run.

This, too, is the secret of the great philosophical "isms." For they propose bringing everything under a single conceptual scheme, by reference to which the defective surroundings are rectified. Most such large-scale views tend to place all dichotomies within an underlying synthesis and all disunities within a deep and invisible unity. So, too, with Hegel's philosophy, which envisioned all the conflicts of human consciousness as resolvable once one saw each component as if it were but a phase in the unfolding of an all-inclusive cosmic consciousness. In that view, there are no fundamental paradoxes and no crises of understanding that have an irremediable finality about them. They need not be suffered. For again, Hegel is quick to invoke a picture of rationality, a kind of equivalent of the mind of God, in which diametric opposites, even contradictories, are never quite that; they are always in the process of being resolved. To recall Wittgenstein's remark again, Hegel is prone to think that paradoxicality lies in the environment's being defective, but only by its never being the totality. When the totality is considered, all paradoxes and contrarieties vanish.

Søren Kierkegaard thought, on the contrary, that Abraham's confrontation with God led to a paradox that was *not* going to disappear even as one began to understand the metaphysics of God and/or reality. For to know God better was precisely to suffer a divided and wounded consciousness. God was not like a totality; instead he was and is a subject, like the individual. The individual becomes a subject by ethical cultivation, and the law itself feeds a consciousness in which obligation rules. Kierkegaard was convinced, as serious students have been for centuries, that obligation roots easily and appropriately in people. One can take obligation out of theories and the social scene, but one can scarcely remove it from people. So deep is the need for an obliged outlook and a life justified by fulfilling an obligation that this way of construing the world and oneself invariably seems like personal maturation and the pinnacle of self-development. So with Kant and Kierkegaard; and so, too, does Kierkegaard think it must have been with Abraham. A consciousness that feels a debt and owes a life of service is not imposed merely from the outside. Instead it is incumbent, and it is a realization of a capacity and not a triviality created by externalities.

So Abraham has a consciousness that is formed and ruled in the direction of being universalized. It is articulated by a rule and by a duty that brings passions and impulses, deeds and proposals, under its sovereignty. This is how it must be with mature and responsible persons. Furthermore, the very logic and morphology of such a consciousness is that it is understandable to the subject, for everything transitive and outward-directed within its competency is ostensibly covered by the rule. What is not so covered is, again, construable by the rule by virtue of its being an exception to the rule, a lapse. Besides, the rule is not a rule if it obtains only for oneself. The logic of a rule is that it must obtain between other ethical agents. It is a guarantor of understanding, but not only for successive moments of time and hence for promoting a kind of self-identity; it proposes a community of persons within whom moral sense can be promoted. It rules between and among all other subjects.

However, the point that gives the poignancy to Abraham is the fact that his consciousness of himself is identified by an ethicality that envelops God, Isaac, the future, Abraham's people, and the promise by which Abraham lives. God also has been seemingly a party to this truly solemn and glorious conception of Abraham's life and destiny. But that would be a small thing if it stayed only a story. Rather, the story proposed a kind of publicly defensible mode of life for Abraham, within which moral factors were operative. Abraham's consciousness of himself, his subtle ways of evaluating his tasks, his self-justification, were all herein bracketed. He was not the tragic hero who had a small but important fund of secret knowledge by which anything odd could be further explained. Everything was explicable by recourse to a plan, his life, the promise, and the future.

Therefore, God's new command meant a terrible breach in Abraham's consciousness, for it was not as if Abraham had failed God. Being a part of a fellowship of the lapsed, most of us are prepared for defection. But here was a more fundamental and terrifying kind of bifurcation. Abraham suffers a call that is urgent and authoritative, a call from God himself, which is unsupported by the context of the promise and not vindicated by the picture of the future. It has no tissue of reliability, no supporting texture, no arena of reasons backing its force. Worse still, Abraham has to reconstitute and realign the most precious achievement of a lifetime, his own consciousness and evaluation of himself and his tasks. He had had years in which to achieve a self-composure and to make himself recognizable to himself. He had gained self-understanding in the only way that any of us can, by becoming a self.

And that is, finally, where the issue lies. To be a self is to have made the self. Most of us do not understand ourselves because there is nothing much to understand. We get a self and something to understand only by constituting ourselves. We have to wish, to hope, to want, to love, to promise—and more. By doing all this we acquire a self. For the self is not a thing but a relation that relates itself to itself. By wanting steadily and long, a kind of definition of the person ensues. We are knowable by the fact that we have always wanted this or that. We become clear even to ourselves, as to who and what we are, by the intensity and constancy of our wants, wishes, and loves. And if we have never wanted or desired with steadiness and intensity, it is also the case that our lives have scarcely any definition at all. We never arrive at the goal of being a true self. This is Kierkegaard's point through his entire authorship and surely also has to be said on behalf of Abraham.[11]

The issue is not abstract. Every person achieves all this only when the wants and hopes, etc., are themselves transitive. That is why consciousness itself comes to define being a self. After a while, Abraham was conscious of himself, but only because by living a promise and by being obligated by a commanded destiny he had acquired thereby his selfhood. Consciousness involves transitivity in two senses. One

---

11. This is the thrust of *Either/Or*, especially vol. 2. But, again, it is the theme of the entire "stages" notion. The "stages" are like the "grammar" for the task of becoming a self.

becomes an identity, first, by wanting, by being obligated, and by wishing with all one's heart. This makes possible the second kind of transitivity, that of being allowed a thought of who and what one is. Abraham had both. There is more, though, for this is the way in which Abraham became a subject rather than an object. To be a subject requires that the transitivity of which one is capable be turned to the task of making something of oneself. This is a capacity; its realization means that one becomes a true self and a human subject.

However, Abraham had a history with a God who was also a person and a subject. God was not a "force" or a blind power or an "id." God was a pure subject. Abraham's life had been put together by a trust in that God whose will and promise encompassed all things. That God had dominion. Because God was a subject, he could not be conceived apart from loving Isaac, fulfilling a promise, realizing the teleology that had been painfully apprehended by Abraham. The seal on all this was an abiding and deep confidence that Abraham had gained concerning God and the people. Abraham's certainty was too deep for a hypothesis and more encompassing than any theory. Abraham's whole life, as well as God and the fate of a people, all hinged on the reliability, predictability, and communicability of that certainty. From that certainty, everything else flowed. And it was Abraham's consciousness that had been the instrumentality for God's promise and for the establishment of the people of God. Had Abraham failed here, then all could have been lost. But he had not failed. He had kept the faith, nurtured the promise, admonished the people, and projected the future with unswerving loyalty.

And then came God's new command! How could this be understood? I think it right to say that Abraham's capacity could not be stretched that far. For a moral kind of understanding is a kind of capacity. It comes like other capacities only when certain conditions are met. When one's reasoning abilities have been nurtured in a moral manner, then they are also limited in that same manner. It is as if a way of forming one's life, by formalized and rule-ordered wants and duties, also provides and forms one's reasons. For the business of reasoning also belongs to people and it, too, reflects what people make of themselves. More than this, it is that the rules of reasoning are the criteria; but the rules of reasoning are finally a part of the very grammar of how we are living, behaving, wanting, and judging. The criteria become manifest in the way we live. And Abraham had so conformed his subjective life that it had become moral; but moral means that it was in accord with a grammar and a kind of rule-consciousness that a way of living, itself, made manifest. To violate the moral consciousness was to trespass upon the very logic within which lives made moral sense. But "sense" and "meaning," "order" and "rational," are all parasitic upon a grammar that our lives lay down.

Abraham had laid down a very rich and sonorous career. Its morphology allowed his consciousness to judge what was sensible, right, and in accord with God's will. He could not doubt that, for doubt would make no sense unless it was within that orbit. Then he meets God again. And what makes God so unfeasible and so difficult now is not that the moral concepts are being stretched a bit to cover new circumstances; instead, these concepts are being abrogated altogether. "Sense" itself is at stake. It makes rubbish of a promise to make it and then destroy the means of effecting it. So, the crisis for Abraham is not something one can get over by a little patience or by rehearsing the fundamentals all over again. Matters are more serious. Another kind of faith, another quality of consciousness in Abraham, is being asked for.

And that is the very point of the paradox. Faith of the Abrahamic sort is a new move for the consciousness itself. It asks that a subject project himself, make sense of his life, not only by congruences that are established in a calculus of right and wrong, but also to be prepared, on occasion, to establish a kind of criterion, to make a certainty, by a community with God himself. Then, between oneself and God a new grammar will develop, a new rule-consciousness will emerge, and a new confidence will be manifested. This kind of living will have to be intentional and willed; it will be teleological, not a lapse. For a moral lapse is like a failure to intend the rule, and it goes on in the absence of a telos. For Abraham, the business of following God looked nonteleological, but, oddly enough, it was not. Only Abraham and God could know that. Toward the rest there had to be silence.

V

Kant says: "A *conflict of duties* (*collisio officiorum s. obligationum*) would be a relation of duties in which one of them would annul the other. . . . But a *conflict of duties* and obligations is inconceivable (*obligationes non colliduntur*). . . . two conflicting rules cannot both be necessary at the same time."[12] If Kierkegaard is right, Abraham's life and faith have led him to entertain two diametrically different kinds of duty. Thus his consciousness of himself is at stake. How can he go on? Unlike Kant, however, Kierkegaard does not think that there is a single logic or a single set of criteria to which one can have recourse, according to which one duty will appear derivative or lesser. For the criteria, along with the logic and/or the grammar (which provide the criteria), are precisely what either morals or religion themselves establish. They are the source of the criteria. Therefore, the crisis cannot be resolved by recourse to a standard outside the morals, nor do the standards of morals become standard outside the limited moral context. For Kierkegaard would have it that a remark that says ethics is universal does not (because it cannot) make sense unless one thinks of its rules applying only in a context or in a stage of life.

Abraham is also unprepared for a God who is not measurable by the criteria that seem most fundamental and even necessary. For Abraham, like the rest of us, must have thought that the ruled use of "good," "right," "in accord with the promise," and other such working-concepts simply had to obtain for all others and for God. But suddenly he is up against a God who calls for a breach with all that. The break hurts so much because the pathos of Abraham's life and the very quality of his subjectivity are at stake. This is not a matter of rules being abrogated—it is more like a violation of his integrity and a sufferance of an incapacity. His way of coping, his capacity to think the future, all that is in abeyance. And for Kierkegaard, unlike Kant, there is no more fundamental arena of rationality in which such issues can be entertained and perhaps resolved. Making moral sense is part of the enterprise of making sense of our lives. Logic and rationality are not fundamental to all that except in the jejune sense that logic might articulate the common conceptual necessities of our language uses, be they cognitive, moral, aesthetic, or religious. These formal criteria

12. Kant, "Introduction to The Metaphysic of Morals," in *Doctrine of Virtue*, 23.

show us that, indeed, we live and think our way into conflicts, but the criteria surely do not get us out of them.

Kierkegaard shows us Abraham, whose life has been defined by a practiced pattern of expectation, promises, and behavior. Surely what it means to say that this is to bring one's particular life under a universal is to note that Abraham's conduct was subject to criteria that were recognizable by both God and other persons—the people living under the covenant. The important point is that what is a universal and recognizable duty is so only because there is a context that has made it possible. That context is neither mankind nor all the world nor everybody; there we would have an instance of an "illegitimate totality." Any totality of which we speak in a responsible way has to be "all of a limited class" or we soon lose our moorings and sense itself. There is nothing being said if we make the totality all of mankind.[13]

Abraham's duties to Isaac and others were duties to particular people, family, friends, and Jews bound by a tradition. There was nothing more fundamental or more dutiful lying behind Abraham's covenanted life. He, too, had had to decide and the duty was the consequence, not the cause. Here, indeed, then, was Abraham's connection with an ordered ethicality. But Kant and most of us would have it that there must be a "categorical imperative" or a necessary duty that embraces and orders all other duties. Or others would conclude that there is some kind of "rational unity of mankind," within which our *ad hoc* reasons get vindicated, or by reference to which every decision can be explained and made manifest.[14] However, the story of Abraham shows us something else. We do *not* owe our daily reasons or the thrust of our daily speech to intercourse with "all" men. Furthermore, there is no general morality, no standards for all, and there surely is nothing called a duty for all. After receiving God's new command, Abraham suddenly could not speak to Sarah and Isaac,

13. My debt to the theory of logical types is plain. And convenient references here could include several of Bertrand Russell's logical writings. Note Whitehead and Russell, *Principia Mathematica*, vol. 1, especially the Introduction and Chapter II, 1–3, 37–65. Also Quine, *From a Logical Point of View*, 90–94, where Russell's idea of types is stressed as a solution to paradoxes arising in logical theory. My use of the idea is only suggested by the components of the argument. Russell does something quite different.

14. This kind of point is made by Karl Popper in *The Open Society and Its Enemies*, 2:212ff.

with whom and for whom his life had heretofore been lived. And understanding him, accordingly, became impossible.

But this is to say that the "rational unity" is not all-inclusive. On the contrary, Abraham shows us that there are real conflicts. But these conflicts are not just on paper or of a sort that a general logician might celebrate in a pair of contradictory propositions. Here the conflict is suffered. Abraham has no resolution at hand and no higher wisdom to consult. There is no impartial court and no set of hidden reasons to be precipitated out of the confrontation.

This brings us again, therefore, to the issue of what it means to be a self. The self is not an object. (That remark is, of course, a grammatical remark, as Wittgenstein would have said.) There is no truth waiting to be discovered that tells us what we ought to do; neither is there a duty beckoning our resolution and the surcease of the difficulty. Instead, to be a self is to have a capacity for self-clarification only via the "bloody" and long way. There are rival ways of carrying on our lives. If there were not, our selfhood would be a joke and living a lifetime would be like a waste of time. But existing is momentous partly because so much depends upon "how" we do it, not simply "that" we do it.

Kierkegaard uses the story of Abraham to show us that being ethical and being religious are not the same. The temptation is to elide them, and that is what Kant did in his *Religion Within the Limits of Reason Alone*. But there is no vantage point, no logical point of view, outside morality or outside religion that tells us which one we should be. Abraham shows us in particularly sharp relief that the point of intersection between the two is very deep. But depth means here not an intellectual complexity. Instead, Abraham's self-consciousness, how he thinks of himself and gives his life a justification, the very criteria that his life has laid down, these are confronted by another set of criteria, another way to be; and there is no friendly assimilation of the one by the other. Instead, there is conflict and momentous consequences.

Abraham can only clear up the conflict in his consciousness by changing that consciousness. This, however, is a resolution. This means that he has to decide; but by so doing he also clarifies his own life. He had no outside recourse, no data to consult, no evidence to assess. This is how deep the difficulties then become. For reasoning and thinking and speaking and understanding all have limits; we can do them only where there are connections, continuities, and a certain kind of rule of good sense. Our reasoning and understanding get noted in the language we speak and in the ways of life we live. So, too, with Abraham. But the link with all this is our decision to share the way of life and to be, hence, a part of the rationality and a subject in the reign of moral order.

The oddness of faith does not lie only in what is believed. Abraham is said to be the father of faith. Now we might be able to see why. For here we can begin to see what is required. A life like Abraham's shows us something that words cannot say. But now it is not merely biographical information that does that job, but the very manner of life and the way Abraham went on. He decided something momentous, and he did it alone and without the guarantee of companionable talk and the support of the environment. His life and his way give us a clue to what faith is. These block out, in a kind of schematic way, the room that faith requires in a life. We begin to see how fear and trembling are a component and appropriate accompaniment. The anxiety is not a symptom of ill-health and temperamental lapses. The fear belongs to Abraham because the question, "What ought I to do?" gets no answer. There can be no answer. There is no way to decide that faith is right or that ethics is better. Here no scale is available to be consulted. Abraham answers with his life—and even then the question is not answered; it simply falls away. Everything "finite," as Kierkegaard says, is suddenly restored. But think how momentous the decision was!

It is almost as if what Abraham's religion requires of all of us is the admission that nothing matters so much as how we live and decide. The force of any society is obviously felt by almost every individual in it. Most of us probably say something about that. We are indebted to our language, for we do not make it as we speak. We are indebted to our common life in a myriad of ways. But being a self is not only to be a byproduct. And all that socialization might have lured us from the romance and terror and sheer fun of being a person. For there is a voluntary thrust we all must make if we are going to be faithful to God that is not just the same as trustfulness and loyalty and fidelity within the institutionalized contexts. For Abraham's faith shows us that there are limits on all that rationality and on the moralizing effect of our common life. As selves, we stand outside that tissue. There is no embracing morality and no single standard. God is outside all that, too. But being outside does not mean one must stay outside. To be a moral self is also to join up. But one can fall out, too.

There is, clearly, the nonteleological move, when one does not will at all. Kierkegaard thought this meant an aesthetic mode of life, which, while it was a style of life, was not ethical just because of that fact. Then there was a teleological suspension, too. Abraham could not show us the reason for it, but his life shows us—again, it does not say—what is involved.

Is there such a thing as understanding Abraham? Perhaps two reminders are now in order. Kierkegaard's *Fear and Trembling* gives us a kind of understanding that is general and schematic. It shows us via the category of the stages that there is a kind of morphology to one's life and that it is not utterly random and fortuitous. Here Wittgenstein's notion of a "grammar" is useful and begins to move us a little more surely into the details. We begin to get the hang of some human endeavors, not least Abraham's, by knowing where the differences between morals and belief in God, even faith itself, begin to swing off. So much for one kind of understanding, it is slight and perhaps a surface recognition, it is not without its illumination. For we begin to see this via the grammatical remark and see it for ourselves.

The other reminder is of a deeper kind of understanding that is projected for us by this same book. But it is projected and cannot be delivered to us. For it requires a deep kind of activity. If one becomes faithful, then one's consciousness of oneself is moved by the wanting, wishing, and caring that made Abraham faithful and the father of faith. By so doing, one surely would also know God. Within that decisiveness, a new rule, a new life, and a new understanding would ensue. Maybe, then, everything finite would come back again. All of life, the past and the future, would make sense. So it was for Abraham.

Kierkegaard thought that what happened to Abraham on Mount Moriah could also happen on a heath in Denmark. Perhaps it could happen anywhere. The logic that makes it even conceivable is the rational accompaniment to the emotions that were Abraham's—the peculiar fear and trembling that were a sign that his life was being judged and formed.

PART TWO

Essays on Wittgenstein

CHAPTER 5

Wittgenstein and Kierkegaard
The Subjective Thinker

I

WITTGENSTEIN SAYS: "WHAT HAS to be accepted, the given—it might be said—are facts of living."[1] This remark seems to have been changed by the time the second part of the *Philosophical Investigations* was written to read: "What has to be accepted, the given, is—so one can say—*forms of life*."[2] The difference between "facts of living" and "forms of life" is interesting, though it must be that what Wittgenstein enumerates as "facts of living" ("give orders," "render accounts," "take an interest in others' feelings," "establish the state of affairs thus and so"—there are many others) do make up and form lives. But the point I wish to stress here is that these facts of living, these forms of life, are given.

It is important to note, also, that the concept of the "given" is being remarked upon by Wittgenstein with a peculiar force. For a kind of philosophical convention had apparently taken over that word, "given." It has been easy to say that what was "given" to us in our most elemental and plainest state, when we were unlettered, infantile, and utterly unsophisticated, was some kind of experience, maybe a "blooming, buzzing confusion" (in William James' words), something raw, blind, and undifferentiated.[3]

---

1. Wittgenstein, *Remarks on the Philosophy of Psychology*, part I, no. 630, p. 116.

2. Wittgenstein, *Philosophical Investigations*, part II, p. 226.

3. James, *Principles of Psychology*, 1:462.

Again it has seemed, almost beyond argument, that knowledge has a foundation and a starting point in something being given to us. So what one comes to when one analyzes knowledge is that there is a kind of given "raw material" upon which the mind works. This material is just there, not produced; it is given. But the life of the mind is so interesting because concepts, reflection, and activities of the intellect constitute that given stuff into ideas, thoughts, and something recognizable. Wittgenstein's interest is clearly not in summarizing the history of this familiar notion, but he does invoke the word to an altogether different effect.

Thus he tells us that instead of the "unanalyzable, specific, indefinable," being the character of what we have to accept, the "givens" are definable and describable. They are discernible and analyzable. For they turn out to be facts of living, "that we act in such-and-such ways," and these are forms and modes of behaving and living.[4] They are not dumb nor inchoate, nondescript nor ineffable. So what is given does not wait upon the active intellect before it can be known, nor does it have to be constituted into something before it begins even to have character.

Wittgenstein has effected a change in the use of the word "given." For agreement between different persons and understanding something that was said, perhaps some time ago, does call for there being something in common between us. And it has been typical to say that experience, sense data, or the "undifferentiated perceptual field," was our common starting point, as if that were what was given. But Wittgenstein will have us think differently about what permits agreement and understanding. The ordinary way of thinking about noetic experience or about "knowing" is being side-stepped. Because he is trying to *describe* the way we actually do come to understand one another and not to idealize or to reconstruct knowing, he says that the agreement point is neither something like a raw datum nor is it an opinion, but it is in the form of life, those describable ways of acting that form our lives.[5]

They are discernible, though not always easily so. The difficulties of determining when a life is formed and what forms it are not

---

4. Wittgenstein, *Remarks on the Philosophy of Psychology*, part I, no. 630, p. 116.

5. Wittgenstein, *Philosophical Investigations*, part I, no. 241.

Wittgenstein's problem here. Instead he stresses that the facts of living, the kinds of activity, are the crucial factors. Here is where the agreement roots and where language itself gets its vitalities and communicability. Agreeing in language—in understanding, opinion, and what is true or false—is dependent not upon a common pool of experience, as though it were the given, but upon the facts of living. Once we share those, experience, language, and opinion begin to make sense.

II

If the forms of life have to be accepted because they are given, as Wittgenstein said, then we have to ask—"To whom are they given?" The answer is plain enough. They are given to a third party, not to the first party. In Wittgenstein's pages the concern is not directed to understanding oneself or trying to fathom one's own speech. Rather, when I even try to imagine another language I cannot do that without imagining a form of life. And if my own talking and writing is responsible and intentional, it is that because it is already a part of activities that have and are forming my life. The point is, in trying to understand others I am sometimes helped when I see that our failure to understand is in consequence of our not sharing some ways of acting, those ways of living. And if these ways are deeply established, then I am up against something formidable and truly deep. They are deep, not because they are intrinsically obscure, obtuse, or beyond speech altogether, but because they account for so much. So much can be attributed to them, perhaps how you hope, whether you hope, how you love, how you judge, indeed even your language and the games you play.

Maybe we have trespassed. Those facts of living, those forms of life are different to me than they are to other people, surely as different as my relation to my words is from other people's.[6] We are tempted to think that a form of life is a kind of pattern into which we fall, maybe a social inheritance, maybe an established cultural practice, which we do in fact manifest. But it is not quite this if we try to describe ourselves and do nothing more. A form of life is complicated, because after a while the phenomenon of hope gets a place in it. But hope

6. Ibid., part II, p. 192.

could not be there if language were not there already to propose and to project the hope. So a child or an animal does not hope until some facts of living get laid down. But the language is already part of the form of life, not just an expression of it. So, too, with promising. If one is a person who keeps promises and exacts them, too, then promising both forges a life and yet depends upon a language that grants that possibility.

The point here is after a while people become people and human when facts of living count for something with them. And people are so very important, so formidable, because their lives are formative. They would not be humans at all if this were not so. Wittgenstein found that even language, which can be abstracted from people so easily, which can be talked about as though "it" develops, changes, lives, dies, means, fails, etc., must be put back into people's activities, games, even their forms of life, before it will say anything and make sense. Yet "it" does not do that, for it is people who say things and people who mean this or that. Yet people are not stones or things. They are not finished; they are always acting, hoping, grieving, and talking in such-and-such ways.

This is also what makes people and their form of life something I have to think from, not to. When I am up against a formed life, I am presented with something. Here we do not have an argument, a theory, or an opinion. Wittgenstein's point seems, again, to be that here is what is given. But it is not obsidian or traitless, beyond reason or discourse, not like a blind percept or a featureless psychical blur. It is recognizable as hopes, loves, griefs, taking interests, and acting in certain ways, in turn, are. So arguments, opinions, and theories might well take place within these ways of living and seeing, rather than the forms of life taking place within the former.

Other people present themselves to me. Not always, but often enough, I am baffled by what I hear. If the talk is serious, then I cannot revert to a nameless experience which is the given. In fact, what that leads to can never elucidate very much, for the task of moving from that given, call it experience, to the welter of disagreeing theses can barely move at all, especially when the given itself is never articulated in and by itself. Wittgenstein's point is, instead, that I can recognize some differences for what they are, namely, disagreements in forms of life. But this is because they are given in actual persons.

III

But a form of life is "given" like this. Your form of life is given to me, and I cannot do much with what is given. My form of life is not given to me in quite the same way. In fact, my form of life is vulnerable, in part at least, to the way I think, act, take up the world, intend, purpose, and plainly live. So it becomes a little odd to say in a general way, without very specific qualifications: "What has to be accepted, the given, is—so one can say—*forms of life*." An odd move would make that seem plausible, from the context in which the concern with the grammar of language and knowledge is paramount to the context in which morals and religion is paramount.

In the former I discover that the description of language in use requires me to know something more than the words. Not everything meant by the language is said by the language—I do have to grasp what the language is being used for and the range of activities that are bound up with its efficacy. I cannot get any deeper into what is involved than seeing that the very grammar and logic of the discourse depends upon something that is not in flux, that is established, that is given.

Typically, however, I do not talk to myself. I do not inform myself by my own discourse. I do not often have to surmise my meanings. In those instances when I do talk to myself or when I write for myself in a journal, I do not come up against something formidable, namely, my form of life. On the contrary, talking to myself or writing for my eyes only is not a matter, usually, if ever, of ascertaining what my form of life is so that my discourse will now make sense, but simply trying to make sense. One thinks out all kinds of things and the pen or the word becomes the very instrument of the thinking.

The form of life here is not given to me. My thinking and talking is, for me as for you (in the first person), the very means of achieving and establishing, projecting and describing, those facts of life. In the first person, we discover that we have to lay down those conditions. We have to hope, to promise, to tell the truth, to use words responsibly. Hence we become responsible in good part for forming our lives. And the form of life is not given to me; instead, it is an ethical requirement.

Obviously I do not start clear nor continue clear on these matters. Sometimes I am befuddled by ignorance and sometimes by odd
incapacities. So it is easy to say that one believes in God's providence
and that God has the whole world in His hand. Suddenly I find that
a local frustration is building into something very big. I feel miffed,
overlooked, and wretched. I start to talk about the uncertain future
of the world, the breakdown of culture, and tragedies in the making.
There is no quality left in the land and hell looms up. But this need
not start with something small and a spate of disgruntlement. It could
be World War I, and one could say with an established English statesman: "The lights are going out all over Europe." He said it, however,
with such pathos that it was as though God had died and everybody
was dependent upon his or her own devices. Such thoughts are not
far from us much of the time. Our thinking becomes vulnerable,
depressed, and utterly dependent. Meanwhile, we have also said we
believe in God and His providence, even perhaps the thought that He
has the whole world in His hand.

I am supposing that such a batch of talk and conjecture makes
for a muddle. What one cannot assume is that a form of life was given
here. It may well be that I put all this down and then say to myself that
with the God of the Bible, who has the world in His hand, that there
can be no ultimate tragedy, that not all the lights ever go out, that my
vulnerability to the passing scene, is because nothing is established
in me. But I may be unclear about the whole business. Maybe I want
to stop talking about God's providence altogether; maybe I want to
snatch hope where I can and be like everyone else—maybe be hopeful
only when political fortunes warrant it.

If so, then one is discovering what it is to have a form of life.
And one can change that by hoping differently, believing differently,
evaluating oneself and one's prospects in certain ways. Thus, again,
the facts of life are not given to me in the same way that the facts of
my life might be given to you!

IV

What Wittgenstein said on these matters looks elemental and truly
plain. I, at least, cannot argue with most of it, mostly because it is

made up of logical remarks coming out of very close descriptions of how our language does in fact work. If there were debatable theories mixed in or dubious opinions spicing up the account, I think I could spot them. But I do not find them. Nonetheless, I do find that his way of getting to forms of life is only one way of thinking. I do not quarrel with it. Maybe it could be characterized in another mode. In his formal writings, Wittgenstein lets all matters of the soul, all questions about the health of the spirit, all concerns about a form of life, be conspicuous by being left out altogether or being kept tacit. But in his letters to Russell, to Engelmann, and in the pages of *Culture and Value*, he speaks more directly.

It is almost as though doing hard thinking, doing philosophy for Wittgenstein (and many other professionals too) has to leave the forms of life, those facts of living, to someone else. He says that he cannot utter the word "Lord" with meaning (i.e., about Jesus of Nazareth); but he does say that it "could say something to me, only if I lived *completely* differently." And he notes that believing in the Resurrection of Jesus is not a matter of overcoming doubts about the evidence on the historical plausibility of the narratives. Instead he says, "It is *love* that believes the Resurrection. We might say: Redeeming love believes even in the Resurrection. . . . what combats doubt is, as it were, *redemption*."[7]

I am citing these instances (and earlier considerations in this paper too) to show that Wittgenstein did concern himself repeatedly with the condition and nature of the human subject, but not in his typically philosophical works, mostly by the way and in letters, conversations with friends, and in his notebooks (which now are the *Culture and Value* volume). This seems to me to be not an oversight, for the intensity of his writing and the quality of his thought takes care of itself very well indeed. And there are all kinds of things left for others to do also.

Thus, it seems to me that the thought of Kierkegaard that each of us can and must also be "subjective thinkers" is relevant. And I believe that that very concept "subjective thinker" has a grammatical force too. It is a piece of genuine philosophy, and it tells us something about what we are as people that we are prone to forget. In fact, it

7. Wittgenstein, *Culture and Value*, 33.

brings into reflection life, into our consciousness what Wittgenstein has illustrated and given so many instances of, from the *Tractatus* to all of his later pages, and yet which he does nothing much by way of pulling together. Kierkegaard uses "stages on life's way" in manners somewhat like Wittgenstein's "forms of life." The logical force of these two sets of words is similar in many instances.

But a difference is very large. For Kierkegaard says that every one of us can also by thinking become an agent in actually forming our lives and constituting those facts of life. As I have noted, however, Wittgenstein says that too. But he addresses such matters furtively and almost as though "thinking" has to be objective and about only the language and the relation between thought, language, and the world. There is a reluctance to pull "thinking" into matters of subjectivity, into the context and game of producing and sustaining a form of living.

But for Kierkegaard there is such a thing as "a subjective thinker." And he is at pains to show how becoming a subjective thinker is the only way to approximate and enlist ethico-religious matters. It is the medium, the language-game, for such matters. This kind of thinking and thinker is not rhapsodic, random, nor merely expressive. It is not subjective, meaning idiosyncratic, private, or arbitrary; but it is subjective, meaning about one's mode of living, the quality of one's life, and, as Wittgenstein says, "what is needed by my *heart*, my *soul*, not my speculative intelligence."[8]

It looks to me as though a happy alliance could be struck between Wittgenstein's reflections on what we might call objective matters and Kierkegaard's on the character of subjectivity and subjective thinking. It seems to me that Wittgenstein recognized that when he read Kierkegaard. I am sure that Kierkegaard would have endorsed Wittgenstein's reassessment of logic and doctrines, philosophical and theological, if he could only have read him.

8. Ibid.

CHAPTER 6

Wittgenstein and the Self

I

WITTGENSTEIN WAS QUITE SURE he was going to be misunder-stood. Whatever else his authorship was, it was not one more permutation in kind upon the long history of philosophical reflection. Of course, there are some subtle continuities between his pages and other logicians, between his interests and certain metaphysicians, between his topics and those of Frege, Russell, and even Plato. And with considerable strain one can construe him in relation to Vienna, to analytic philosophy, to empiricism, to classical philosophy, even to Kant and Schopenhauer. But none of this helps very much.

One can, indeed, tease out of his pages new views on what philosophy is, novelties about truth-tables, striking themes linking the use of language with meaning, startlingly original suggestions about the worth of the *Principia Mathematica*, and a veritable panoply of aphoristic remarks that look like theories in embryo. However, this does not help very much either. For one will not understand him better by spelling out theories on his behalf, as if his pages are theory-laden without his quite knowing it. Furthermore, it would be a shocking betrayal of everything he said were it to be restated in forms of writing and ways of talking, in concepts and schemes, that themselves distort his thought and make him plausible but conventional, pedagogically useful but intellectually a misrepresentation.

There is striking force to his suggestion that philosophy is an activity and not a body of doctrines and that it does "not" issue in more propositions and theses.[1] Certainly from the beginning to the end of a lifetime of writing and conversation, Wittgenstein was not one to allow easy assimilation. "I should not like my writing," he says, "to spare other people the trouble of thinking."[2] But this is not an idiosyncrasy of manner or a peculiar quirk of personality. Early and late, there are reasons issuing from both what he was thinking about and also from the very processes, the mode of the thinking and the style of the writing, that gave him the case for saying that he could not communicate results. Instead his pages have to stimulate the reader to having thoughts on his own—not borrowing them nor allowing anything vicarious.

No wonder, then, that he was likely to be misunderstood. His thoughts are difficult; but finally, the difficulty does not reside in the fact that they are utterly confounding, nor too abstruse, nor fantastically technical. Certainly there are prerequisites for getting at much of what he writes about, and these are more than good will and general culture. One must have some near-professional competencies to understand some of what he is about. However, there are other causes for most of the misunderstandings, for their persistence, and for their occurring among sophisticated and academically qualified readers. For one thing, Wittgenstein eschews the conventional pedagogical apparatus, the accepted patterns of writing, and most of the pieces of the logical frame within which ordinary scholars and purveyors work. What is deemed to be the minimal sign of rationality, the necessary logical scheme, the obvious ploys—point-of-view, hypothesis, presupposition, argument, doctrine—these, and more, are simply not traded on at all. For in very subtle ways, to rethink Wittgenstein in such terms, in such concepts, is to illustrate how nonsense is made and remade. That is his point; and he does not want to spread more nonsense. This is why, too, his thinking cuts so deep; it forces a new kind of writing upon the author himself and also a new kind of receptivity upon the reader. If it does not do the latter, then one misunderstands, and one's misunderstanding, like some philosophical

---

1. Wittgenstein, *Tractatus*, 4.112.
2. Wittgenstein, *Philosophical Investigations*, x.

problems, even gets a depth about it. The misunderstanding involves one's attitudes and even an outlook.

But another kind of difficulty is likely when we confront the Wittgenstein pieces. One cannot, I believe, conclude that Wittgenstein was exaggerating late in 1919, when he told Ludwig von Ficker, a publisher and an editor of a general cultural periodical, that his manuscript (subsequently the *Tractatus*) would not be easily understood; for its subject matter would seem alien to Ficker. But the fact is, Wittgenstein says that the book is not alien at all ". . . because the book's point is an ethical one." He goes on to say how it is ethical, namely, his pages draw limits to the ethical from the inside; hence there are two parts: ". . . the one presented here plus all that I have *not* written. And it is precisely this second part that is the important one."[3] There is, in brief, an intertwining of factors here and almost an "indirect communication," as Kierkegaard noted on his own behalf. For what is said directly is but one part, may be indeed "unassailable and definitive"; nonetheless, it is a little thing that such problems be even solved.[4] But readers of Bertrand Russell's "Introduction" to the *Tractatus* will know how profound yet plain, how almost expository, Wittgenstein's distinguished teacher and older colleague made the whole book. That "second part," Russell tends to omit altogether. That intertwining and that indirectness are simply not part of our ordinary academic experience. Wittgenstein had even said to Russell in an earlier letter that the "main contention" had been missed. He notes:

> The main point is the theory of what can be expressed (*gesagt*) by prop[osition]s—i.e., by language—(and, which comes to the same, what can be *thought*) and what can not be expressed by prop[osition]s, but only shown (*gezeigt*); which, I believe, is the cardinal problem of philosophy.[5]

3. Wittgenstein, *Briefe an Ludwig von Ficker*, 35–36. Wittgenstein's words are: ". . . denn der Sinn des Buches ist ein Ethischer." The translation above is by Brian McGuinness and is found in Wittgenstein, *Prototractatus*, 15–16.

4. Wittgenstein, *Tractatus*, Author's Preface, 5.

5. Wittgenstein, *Letters to Russell, Keynes, and Moore*, no. 37, p. 71. This particular letter to Russell, written in English, comes from Cassino, Italy, and is dated August 19, 1919. The distinction between saying and showing is central, of course, to the *Tractatus* too, as well as the later writings.

So already we have the ethical and the logical as, respectively, unstated and stated factors here, but, more, we have some things stated and other things shown. Our point again is that the difficulty Wittgenstein creates for his reader is chiefly here. He expects capacities of understanding in the reader that are token of a rich and variegated life, almost levels of human vitality, of passion and feeling, also insight. It is as if he flatters the reader with the thought that one's life is so finely textured and so thick with content, so subjectively developed, that the ethical will, of course, be immediately adjacent even if the text does not provide it, and that one will see with practiced glance the issues even when they are not overtly expressed. It is probably not a mistake to assume that Wittgenstein believed that the *Tractatus* and surely the *Philosophical Investigations* would even be a means of capacitating the reader in these directions; but he was not sanguine.[6]

Russell's *Introduction to Mathematical Philosophy* was sent to Wittgenstein in a prisoner-of-war camp in Italy. He read it and then responded: "I should never have believed that the stuff I dictated to Moore in Norway six years ago would have passed over you so completely without trace."[7] And with almost heart-rending pathos Wittgenstein tells about Frege's failure to understand the *Tractatus*, at least its themes, and then says: ". . . it is *very* hard not to be understood by a single soul!"[8] With such masters of logical theory already failing to grasp his point, and Wittgenstein being in a prison camp with all kinds of uncertainties before him, it is a wonder that he could keep his confidence about his manuscript. He can even dare—a very young man—to say to Russell, the established and Nestorian figure in the

6. "It is not impossible that it should fall to the lot of this work, in its poverty and in the darkness of this time, to bring light into one brain or another—but, of course, it is not likely." Wittgenstein, *Philosophical Investigations*, x.

7. Wittgenstein, *Letters to Russell, Keynes, and Moore*, no. 36, p. 70; a letter of June 12, 1919.

8. Again from the letter of August 19, 1919, Wittgenstein, *Letters to Russell, Keynes, and Moore*, no. 37, p. 71. Correspondence with Frege must have been going on for some years, so this was not just another case of misunderstanding because of slight exposure. Note here the "Historical Introduction, The origin of Wittgenstein's *Tractatus*," by Georg Henrik von Wright, in Wittgenstein, *Prototractatus*, 1–34, especially 13–14.

new logic: "*. . . don't think that everything that you won't understand is a piece of stupidity.*"[9]

The *Tractatus* sets all kinds of limits. More properly, perhaps, it is not the author who does it as much as it is the sheer logic of language that does it via Wittgenstein's book. What lies on the other side of the limit is nonsense, by the logical standards which apply to propositions; and for most of us who read these things, that, in effect, puts ethics, transcendental matters generally, the foundations of logic, the meaning of life, the issues of the self, and much else of first importance, into a kind of limbo. Suddenly, all of that—granted its importance—is beyond our grasp and almost inaccessible. But Wittgenstein's books, and the *Investigations* can be included here, do set limits, if not to the thinking, to the expression of thinking; and the poverty of our own lives is such that if we cannot have these things in propositions we cannot have them seemingly at all. Thus it is easy to conclude that all such matters are nonsensical. Wittgenstein does not say that. He is supposing that we have a first-hand access to such matters, not via propositions, and that what setting limits does is to force that recognition. It is the person who has to have the richness otherwise, the transcendental stuff; and it is no surprise, then, that after so many centuries of learned talk, Wittgenstein should see that his work is outside the streams of thought of American and European civilization.[10] For the learned have put what he wants to show into sayings, the ethical into propositions, and the meaning of life into schemes of argument. In another context, Wittgenstein says that it is almost "unbelievable" the way in which an issue becomes ". . . completely barricaded in by the misleading expressions which generation upon generation throw up for miles around it, so that it becomes virtually impossible to get at it."[11]

Wittgenstein thought there were grave mistakes in his *Tractatus* and that the new thoughts in the *Investigations* could best be understood only in contrast with and against the background of his earlier way of thinking. But this suggestion about how to understand does not touch the difficulties noted above. For the later pages require as

9. Wittgenstein, *Letters to Russell, Keynes, and Moore*, no. 36, p. 70.

10. Note Wittgenstein's "Foreword," November 1930, to *Philosophical Remarks*, 7, a book edited from Wittgenstein's posthumous writings.

11. Wittgenstein, *Philosophical Grammar*, part II, no. 40, p. 466.

much of the reader, if not more, as do the earlier. Many things are different, but still the *Investigations* puts great stress upon the games the individual chooses to play, the way he or she plays them, and even how a life has been formed. These, too, lie outside the language and cannot be quite said. So, the limits upon understanding, the restraints upon grasping even Wittgenstein's later work, may, in part, be due to a kind of mislocation of the issues—in a very profound sense; deepened by the reconsideration of what the logic of certain kinds of issues entails, this might be called a logical matter.

But it is time to turn to the issue of these pages, the problem of the self. For the quality of oneself matters greatly to Wittgenstein, as we have already noted. In what follows, I wish to discuss the self in several contexts. First I will note something of Wittgenstein's comments about himself, mostly in his letters. I am painfully aware of the inappropriateness of concern with a thinker's life in most instances, and I shall try to avoid any irrelevant conjecture or psychological interpretation. My case will be a logical one anyway. Next, we will look at the concept "self" as formulated in the *Tractatus*. Thirdly, some discussion of the concept in the *Investigations*, where William James' reflections are considered and the issue rethought so carefully. Then, in conclusion, a reconsideration of the concept "self" around the notion that concepts themselves have been understood in a new and lively way. How this relates to certainty, doubt, and being a person will amount to another conception of philosophy and of thinking.

II

There are silly things said about Wittgenstein's thought; and one of the silliest is that it is only about words. But say that and it is a small step to concluding that Wittgenstein must have been a shriveled and half-developed personality. On the contrary, he was a richly endowed and many-sided personality. One cannot fathom his negative remarks about the limits of philosophy until you know how tempted he must have been by edifying philosophy, spiritual talk, cultural syntheses, generalized metaphysics, and serve-all concepts.[12] There was a great

---

12. All of this does not suggest for a moment anything negative about his interests in Kierkegaard, Augustine, Tolstoy, Dostoevsky, Samuel Johnson, and others.

deal in him to which all of these could appeal. And the power and authority of his logical strictures can only be appreciated by someone who knows how much there was to inhibit. He was rich in proclivities, but his logical scruples were exceedingly exacting too.

The early Wittgenstein gives us two sets of reflections on the self and they do not quite seem to match up. Or do they? He says, for example, a number of things about himself in his letters that do not seem to get any illumination or any analysis in the *Tractatus*. For the moment, we can leave the question whether they should or not. His philosophy is one thing, his personal life another. So in 1912, he says to Russell:

> Whenever I have time I now read James' *Varieties of religious exp[erience]*. This book does me a *lot* of good. I don't mean to say that I will be a saint soon, but I am not sure that it does not improve me a little in a way in which I would like to improve *very much*: namely I think that it helps me to get rid of the *Sorge* (in the sense in which Goethe used the word in the 2nd part of Faust). Logic is still in the melting pot. . . .[13]

Logic was looming very large for Wittgenstein, and he could tell Russell later that: "It's extraordinary, isn't it, what a huge and infinitely strange science logic is? Neither you nor I knew that, I think, a year and a half ago." Amid the most strenuous efforts to get logic straight and in the same letters discussing these efforts he can say: "Inside me, everything is in a state of ferment." "Every day I was tormented by a frightful *Angst*. . . ."; "My life has been one nasty mess so far. . . ."[14] But nothing is quite so poignant as a judgment about himself which he notes in a letter of mid-1914:

> But deep inside me there's a perpetual seething, like the bottom of a geyser, and I keep on hoping that things will come to an eruption once and for all, so that I can turn into a different person. I can't write you anything about logic today. Perhaps you regard this thinking about myself as a waste of time—but

---

But, here again he read these authors from within his distinctions earlier alluded to, and not as philosophers who "gassed"—i.e., tried to bridge these distinctions.

13. Wittgenstein, *Letters to Russell, Keynes, and Moore*, no. 2, p. 10. This one dates from June 22, 1912.

14. Ibid., respectively the four are from letter no. 24, p. 45; no. 23, p. 43; no. 25, p. 47; no. 27, p. 54.

how can I be a logician before I'm a human being! *Far* the most important thing is to settle accounts with myself![15]

The point here is not to stress facts that are unpleasant or that explain Wittgenstein's writings. But it is, rather, to note that Wittgenstein was concerned with himself, apparently with what he was as a moral person, and that he had all kinds of words at his behest to describe himself. It surely would be a mistake to think that such remarks as these were about particularized matters in his life, his sexual life, his temper, or a failure to get his work done. For he was acute enough, and surely candid enough, to name particulars. Instead the words here show a concept of the self that is in command. And there is a rule-governed character to his language about himself that indicates how deeply it had permeated his life. For it is not only to Russell that he writes this way, but also to Engelmann. In early 1917, he says: "I am working reasonably hard and wish I were a better man and had a better mind. These two things are really one and the same."[16]

The strange but familiar business of judging oneself was not at all alien to Wittgenstein. All of this has an analogue in St. Augustine who tells us in *The Confessions* that one day the pretenses were stripped from him and ". . . the time had now come when I stood naked before my own eyes, while my conscience upbraided me."[17] The concept of self stood obviously right in the middle of Wittgenstein's life—and for a long time, not just episodically, and often because he was so very concerned about himself. All kinds of words are used: "accounts with myself," "better human being," "better man," "inner struggle," etc. It would be a mistake to lump these too easily, but also a mistake to assume that a different concept is being deployed with each differing word.[18] For he was castigating, judging, and correcting himself in ways here that are usually thought to be moral, and the concept "self"

---

15. Ibid., no. 29, pp. 57–58.

16. Engelmann, *Letters from Ludwig Wittgenstein*, 5.

17. Augustine, *Confessions*, bk. 8, ch. 7, 169.

18. Wittgenstein thinks it wrong to insist on the use of certain words and phrases, as if there is a one-to-one correspondence between a word and a concept. Rather, he says: "What I actually want to say is that here too it is not a matter of the *words* one uses or of what one is thinking when using them, but rather of the difference they make at various points in life." Wittgenstein, *Remarks on Colour*, part III, no. 317, p. 59.

comes forth quite naturally. It has its place in that range of concerns and judgments. The very plainness of all this forced Wittgenstein to the same kind of recognition that he articulates in the *Tractatus*. He tells Engelmann:

> But what am I to do? *I am clear about one thing*: I am far too bad to be able to theorize about myself; in fact I shall either remain a swine or else I shall improve, and that's that! Only let's cut out the transcendental twaddle when the whole thing is as plain as a sock on the jaw.[19]

The practices here are unmistakable and well established. They go on much later too. Wittgenstein suffers when he is not clear about some intellectual issues and when he cannot work. But these, too, cannot be altogether divorced from the other questions about the kind of person he is.[20] Once more, that strenuous concern, that worry about the quality of life, was also what made the concept "myself" and "self" very substantial. For it was "his" life that was the concern, not life in general.

There is no doubt that Wittgenstein's letters bear out very well a theme he was striking in his early notebooks. "The I, the I is what is deeply mysterious!" he says in 1916. And he is not talking only about the concept "I." That I "is the bearer of ethics," and "If the will did not exist, neither would there be that centre of the world, which we call the I, and which is the bearer of ethics. What is good and evil is essentially the I, not the world."[21]

The themes of the *Tractatus* on the self are anticipated in the *Notebooks*. "The I is not an object," we are told, and, therefore, though we objectively confront every object, we do not confront the I. But ethics is inexpressible and is not a part of a propositional scheme, and the bearer of ethics, the I, is outside all of that too. For good and evil come about through the subject, the I, but that I is not a part of the world and of propositions.[22] And, herewith the rift between what

19. Engelmann, *Letters from Ludwig Wittgenstein*, 11.

20. For example, when staying with Keynes in August 1925 (noted in Engelmann, 55), and in a letter to Moore in 1937. There he says: "My work hasn't been going well since I came back here. Partly because I've been troubled about myself a lot." Wittgenstein, *Letters to Russell, Keynes, and Moore*, no. 34, p. 173.

21. Wittgenstein, *Notebooks*, 80.

22. Ibid., 76, 79, 80.

is shown and what is said, between what is not expressed and what is expressed, acquires histrionic thrust. Wittgenstein is not dismissing ethics and moral concern, as if it were a nothing; for his letters show us how powerful these cares were for him. That concept of the self, exercised in his letters, has an enormously tangled and replete context. It is rich, variegated, and important. But the difficult matter to understand is the very status of the concept "I." For as we turn to the *Tractatus*, we will see that the logic of language will not give it the substance that his everyday concerns actually have already done.

III

Wittgenstein tells us that a book entitled "The World as I Found It," ostensibly complete, would include a report on the author's body, accounts of what were subject to his will and what were not, but nothing about the subject. From the point of view of such an account, there is no subject ". . . for it alone could *not* be mentioned in that book."[23] One can assume that the subject here is the bearer of ethics, the self, the I, that he admits to being troubled about, who is there, amid plants, animals and stones.[24] In a peculiar manner, then, we can say that the ordinary working concept, "I," has no logical status—at least it does not belong to the *Tractatus*. And this is as much as to say that this ethically rich and essential notion has no philosophical status. That remark, "no philosophical status," is not a bit of whimsy. It is as much as to say that the ethical "self" or "I" does not lend itself to sense. If it does enter into language like the *Tractatus* describes, it will be bogus talk.

But, Wittgenstein knew that there was a way in which another concept of the self—and it is another concept expressed by the same word "self"—did become philosophically appropriate. "What brings the self into philosophy is the fact that 'the world is my world.'"[25] The

---

23. Wittgenstein, *Tractatus*, 5.631.

24. Wittgenstein, *Notebooks*, 82. "A stone, the body of a beast, the body of a man, my body, all stand on the same level. That is why what happens, whether it comes from a stone or from my body is neither good nor bad" (84; October 12, 1916).

25. Wittgenstein, *Tractatus*, 5.641. In the *Notebooks*, July 1916, 74, Wittgenstein also says: "The world is *given* me, i.e. my will enters into the world completely from outside as into something that is already there."

self is not a part of the world but a presupposition of its existence. But this concept of the self is a philosophical one, and it is not surrogate for the human being, the body, the soul, or even whatever psychology describes. It is a kind of metaphysical "I," a limit to the world, not a part of it.[26] Seemingly, a concept of self then arises, like Phoenix coming out of the ashes, not because a person is the bearer of good and evil, but rather from the analysis of what it is simply to have language and to have a world. Both "world" and "language" are limited—they are not indefinite and without qualification. Both are "mine."[27] But the "I" there, the "self," is a logical concept; it plays a role in the logic of language and of world. It is needed logically. And the limits of language mean the limits of the world, but more, the limits of "my" language mean the limits of "my" world. Adding difficulties perhaps, we can say that logic pervades the world, and logic sets limits to both language and the world. We cannot have a world or a language without it being mine.[28] Thus this concept of the self is needed to round out the complexities and logic of language and world. It is there necessarily, not in virtue of observation.

But this metaphysical subject is not to be found in the world.[29] So there is no state of affairs that is being pictured. This must be one more instance of Wittgenstein's "fundamental principle," namely, "that whenever a question can be decided by logic at all it must be possible to decide it without more ado." And related to that is a kind of corollary, that when we have to look at the world for an answer to such a problem, that itself shows that we are on a completely wrong track.[30] In the *Philosophical Grammar*, Wittgenstein insists that the way one goes about, e.g., a proof already determines the sense of what is being said and proved. "Tell me *how* you seek and I will tell you *what* you are seeking."[31] These two concepts of "self" are different. Our point will be served only to say that the concept sought out in the

26. Wittgenstein, *Tractatus*, 5.641. "The world is *my* world . . ." Ibid., 5.62.

27. Ibid., 5.62.

28. Ibid., 5.6; 5.61. Cf. "The I makes its appearance in philosophy through the world's being *my* world." *Notebooks*, 80.

29. Ibid., 5.633.

30. Ibid., 5.551.

31. Wittgenstein, *Philosophical Grammar*, part II, no. 24, p. 370.

Tractatus does a very limited job indeed; if it were used elsewhere as a foundation for talk in daily life, only nonsense would ensue.

It must be the case that nothing in the world pictured by propositions or, for that matter, nothing in the propositions themselves, reveals an existing self. It is almost as if Wittgenstein knows that too well. There is another way of concluding what he did. For it is the whole of thought, the whole of language, the world and not a state of affairs within it, that requires the self, or at least, the concept, "self." For, Wittgenstein thought it absurd to have language without the self, so, too, for a world and language. Ideas and words have to belong to somebodies; otherwise there is no sense to them. Yet in saying this, we cannot admit that Wittgenstein is putting very much into that self. His later writings require not a bare logical subject, but a person, a mouth, situations, and living contexts. That is the normal accompaniment of being a self, and all of that does not get in here. Here he is doing a kind of metaphysics, not description. Thoughts, words, world have to be owned, almost as William James had insisted too. And it is interesting that Wittgenstein does not ask the question he thought was so crucial in his later reflections: "Is the word [self] ever actually used in this way in the language-game which is its original home?"[32]

So, then, we have two concepts of the self. The informal concept that is used in his letters is not very precise, but it is still very powerful; and it is hard to miss what he says using it. In fact, this use of the concept is an instance of an everyday usage. But the formal concept in the *Tractatus* does not suggest anything like the *Investigations*, where he says: "What *we* do is to bring words back from their metaphysical to their everyday use."[33] That has to wait further development.

Obviously, neither is the concept "I" in everyday life identical with the concept of the "I" or "self" as one might have it in any one particular and erstwhile descriptive discipline. We do talk about the "psychological" concept of a person, perhaps contrasting it with "sociological," "physiological," "anthropological" and, maybe, even an "historical" or "literary" concept too. Somehow our own command of "I" is not given us by the sciences of the self. Where then do we get it? The *Tractatus* tells us it is frankly metaphysical, being required by

32. Wittgenstein, *Philosophical Investigations*, part I, no. 116.
33. Ibid.

"world," "language," and even "thought." There is something in all of this that is right. For the concept "I" is not representative, the I is not an object. "One of the most misleading representational techniques in our language is the use of the word 'I,'" says Wittgenstein a decade or so after the *Tractatus*, "particularly when it is used in representing immediate experience, as in 'I can see a red patch.'"[34] And to say it does not belong to any one discipline, is in part a recognition of its transcendental character—it does transcend all kinds of contexts. The "I" is, however, also made clear for us by the grammar and the variety of uses. But that lies in the domain of the *Investigations*, where the grammar, not a particular context and not an artificial metaphysical use, does give one the essence.

IV

Wittgenstein says:

> You have a new conception and interpret it as seeing a new object. You interpret a grammatical movement made by yourself as a quasi-physical phenomenon which you are observing.[35]

Perhaps we have with the self a picture that has obtruded itself upon us and it is of little use. That deployment of the word "I" gets caught up in the picture of a subtle identity, the true "me," and "I" starts to mislead us by being representational. But we are not sure of just what. We do seem sure that the fact that I say: "I see the room's odd shape" is to admit that the visual experience of the room cannot just hang there. It has to be somebody's experience. So, we are prone to make a philosophical point out of this kind of familiar bit of language. The "I" begins to look like a name of something. "'I' is not the name of a person, nor 'here' of a place, and 'this' is not a name. But they are connected with names."[36]

Ownership of images, moods, emotions, pains, thoughts looks like a necessary acknowledgment. And it is true that we must talk about the person who has such experiences. But the "I" looks like a

34. Wittgenstein, *Philosophical Remarks*, part VI, no. 57, p. 88.
35. Wittgenstein, *Philosophical Investigations*, part I, no. 401.
36. Ibid., part I, no. 410.

more particularized identity, which has to be there even for others, before their proper name and even my own can be used. We are still prone to get that concept "I" caught up in a theory or a definition, or even a search for the plain facts. We want the true doctrine about the "I." Instead of learning contentment with the many responsible uses of "I," we want to infer to something more fundamental. That "I" looks like it is being used referringly, like a name, but not to my body, but to something without a body, the real and immaterial ego, within the body.

Perhaps without stretching the point, we can say again that Wittgenstein could not have written so well and so ardently about these matters if he, too, did not feel attracted. William James' common sense and plain talking must have greatly appealed to him. So, we read James saying that:

> All men must single out from the rest of what they call themselves some central principle. . . . *Now*, let us try to settle for ourselves as definitely as we can, just how this central nucleus of the Self may *feel*. . . . For this central part of the Self is *felt*. . . . it is at any rate no *mere ens rationis*, cognized only in an intellectual way, and no *mere* summation of memories or *mere* sound of a word in our ears. . . . *it is difficult for me to detect in the activity any purely spiritual element at all. Whenever my introspective glance succeeds in turning round quickly enough, . . . all it can ever feel distinctly is some bodily process, for the most part taking place within the head. . . .* In a sense, then, it may be truly said that, in one person at least, *the "Self of selves," when carefully examined, is found to consist mainly of the collection of these peculiar motions in the head or between the head and throat. . . . our entire feeling of spiritual activity, or what commonly passes by that name, is really a feeling of bodily activities whose exact nature is by most men overlooked.*[37]

Here the ego becomes an activity of a physical sort. And Wittgenstein finds that trying to lay hold of something directly here is a little like saying: "At any rate only I have got *this*." There is something appealing about James here but also something wrong-headed. One insists upon getting at the *this*—the uniqueness, and James, at least, had

37. James, *Principles of Psychology*, 1:298–302.

moved from the silly business of positing an immaterial ego. But, Wittgenstein notes:

> James' introspection shewed, not the meaning of the word "self" (so far as it means something like "person," "human being," "he himself," "I myself"), nor any analysis of such a thing, but the state of a philosopher's attention when he says the word "self" to himself and tries to analyze its meaning.[38]

By 1930 or so, Wittgenstein was insisting on something different: "I want to say the place of a word in grammar is its meaning." And years later: "A meaning of a word is a kind of employment of it."[39] James and the early Wittgenstein had made mistakes about the "I." But the mistakes were plausible because:

> The idea that the real I lives in my body is connected with the peculiar grammar of the word "I," and the misunderstandings this grammar is liable to give rise to. There are two different cases in the use of the word "I" (or "my") which I might call "the use as object" and "the use as subject."[40]

Thus, he goes to show that when we are saying "my broken arm" and "I have grown six inches," we are identifying a person; and that the importance of this "I" and "my" use, here, is in consequence of the fact that we might be recognizing the wrong person or associating all sorts of things with the wrong individual. At this juncture, there is a kind of logic of information governing the use of "I" and "my." The point is then a kind of grammar governs the "I" and gives us the capacity to use the word in a certain way. More broadly, there are situations and "games" we are involved in that occasion our using "I" in an informational way.[41] But the "I" as subject puts the stress

38. Wittgenstein, *Philosophical Investigations*, part I, no. 398; no. 413.

39. Wittgenstein, *Philosophical Grammar*, part I, no. 23, p. 59, and Wittgenstein, *On Certainty*, no. 61, p. 10.

40. Wittgenstein, *Blue and Brown Books*, 66.

41. The expression, "the logic of information," occurs in *Remarks on Colour*, part III, no. 335, p. 62, but his point is that no one, not even the psychologist, tells you what "seeing" is. Therefore, he, too, uses "seeing" without his learning constituting it. But something like this has to be said about "I" too; for no one teaches us the term in an overt way. And what the "I" is, when you say "I have a bump on my forehead," supposes the use of "I" before the bump. Cf. *Remarks on Colour*, part III, nos. 327ff., pp. 61–62.

elsewhere. There we get sentences like, "I see the rings around the moon," "I feel the temperature rising," "I hear the echo," and "I have the pain." There the logic is different, for the question cannot occur: "Are you sure that it's you . . . ?" The point is such that the language does not secure your recognition nor give reasons for doubting it— the "I" does not identify you nor point you out. But here I believe we need a sharper distinction than "object" and "subject." For in these latter cases, the language is "of" the seeing, hearing, feeling, etc., not "about" them. The "I" assumes its role without a case being made for it. In the *Tractatus*, Wittgenstein had said that an ethical way of life would not be important because the facts of the world would be changed; instead, the limit of the world, that metaphysical self would be changed.[42] Language, too, could not change, for its grammar was co-extensive with the logic of the world. But in the later writings, language itself does not belong to the world, it belongs to people. But it belongs to them by being a part of pain-behavior, of loving, of caring, of wishing, etc. Then the "I" falls into place in all of that. Language does not choose the mouth which says it, as the *Blue Book* notes, for the person has to say it.[43] The rules of the game simply are that a person cries, contorts his face, also says some things. But the "I" is not always a demonstrative pronoun—its logic is not standard. The "I" assumes a role in a game that already goes on.

So we have another concept of "I," giving us a very elemental and almost primitive certainty. Once more, we must remember that early Wittgenstein thought that being a self was being the bearer of ethics. The world was a limited whole; and there are surely times when we all want to say that sort of thing. But to say it, is to recognize that one speaks not from inside the world, but from the outside. The "self" is a limit, is on the outside, and if the person is happy or unhappy, the world as a whole waxes and wanes.[44] But the admission that the world is subject to such vast predication, that it can be this or that, is obviously a piece of metaphysics; and again, to say it, is to talk nonsense (according to the *Tractatus*). The self has to be almost speechless in the *Tractatus*; and that is why his letters from the early period are so

42. Wittgenstein, *Tractatus*, 6.42–6.43.

43. Wittgenstein, *Blue and Brown Books*, 68.

44. Wittgenstein, *Notebooks*, 78–79, and *Tractatus*, 6.43.

touching, almost plaintive. For the letters and the early book do not support each other.

But if we follow the *Investigations*, we have our attention drawn to some of the same facts. Indeed the world is this and that, happiness makes us see the world differently. But now the place of language is shifted, and expressly in the direction of fitting it to that subject, that person. That "fitting" does not happen because of a philosophical doctrine; rather, it takes place when games are being played and lives are being formed. Then the "I" is an emergent in a life-history. It is not only the ethical subject, however, that is brought to our attention. Rather it is that language, all language, belongs to people, to subjects. And these subjects do a variety of things, they are involved in "games," and one cannot know the significance of what is being said until one knows how a life is formed, how a deed is done, how the language works. Then the ethical subject, who had no language save at the expense of galimatias (in the *Tractatus*), now is the veritable necessity in meaningful speaking.[45] There is, apparently, something plain about this matter. It must be something like this, that if one knows the "seeing" language, the "pain" language, not just "about" it (for that will not help), but knows it because you also "see" and "have pains" and talk accordingly, then that "seeing," "feeling," and experiencing pain already puts the "I" within your command. And this "I" is not an inference from an experience to the owner of the experience (as the footnote from Frege's essay suggests), nor is it a logical necessity like the "limit," but it is a capacity, a power (a subject) made by one's living and its context. The subject is there as a certainty—it cannot be doubted. The subject is laid down; and our very ability to speak at all supposes that we are subjects just as the speaking exercises and is a

45. "If everything is idea," says Frege, "then there is no owner of ideas. . . . If there is no owner of ideas then there are also no ideas. . . . I am not my own idea; and when I assert something about myself. . . . then my judgement concerns something which is not a content of my consciousness, is not my idea, namely myself. . . . Therefore the thesis that only what belongs to the content of my consciousness can be the object of my awareness, of my thought, is false." In "Thoughts," included in Frege, *Logical Investigations*, 21–22. It is reflections like these of Frege that are the point of departure for so much of Wittgenstein's work. But the issues stayed with him. Years later he tells Moore: "In one sense 'I' and 'conscious' are equivalent, but not in another." Moore, "Wittgenstein's Lectures in 1930–33," 309–11; the quotation is from 310. And the issues noted above from the *Blue Book* are discussed here, too.

part of our pains, feelings, hearing, wishing. Language becomes what it is because of what we make of ourselves. Hence the variety and rich manifold of the grammar of "I."

But is this a case of calling something the "I"? Do we have two things, the I and the "I"? Do we know the first introspectively and then use the "I" accordingly? The reader of Wittgenstein's pages may think that once more the force of this kind of reflection is to give up the transempirical and transcendental self altogether and probably settle only for a use of words, even a linguistic fiction. However, one factor stays alive from the *Notebooks*, through the *Tractatus*, and into the *Investigations* and the later writings, *On Certainty* and the *Remarks on Colour*, namely, that the most important matters of all are not susceptible of philosophical formulation and exposition. So, there still is no philosophical doctrine about the self. Frege, James and his early writings notwithstanding, the self is firmly in place and not in virtue of philosophy or anything introspective or very special.

But it is time to sum this up in another way and in virtue of issues that Wittgenstein's literature has put within our reach. For Wittgenstein has not given us a new philosophy, if we mean by that new resolutions to old issues, in this case the problem of the "self"; instead his influence is of a more subtle sort. He has pushed certain obstacles aside and caused us to see what we ordinarily overlook. Once that happens, we are enabled ourselves to think something, even be something (and these two do blend), that our reflection previously had estopped. To these we now turn.

V

Surely the metaphysical self drops out of the *Investigations* too. There is nothing to say philosophically about the self. On the other hand, a long look at everyday usage will show us that "I" is not the name of anything, Cartesian, mental, spiritual or inner. It does not, finally, designate an owner, but it does not stand obliterated either. For something else besides philosophy brings it into everyday use.

We are at a point once more where a certain kind of reflection tends to force something upon us. And a passage in the *Investigations* can here be used as our point of departure. There he worries about pain-behavior accompanied by pain and pain-behavior without it. He goes on to say:

> We have only rejected the grammar which tries to force itself on us here. . . . The paradox disappears only if we make a radical break with the idea that language always functions in one way, always serves the same purpose: to convey thoughts—which may be about houses, pains, good and evil, or anything else you please.[46]

Language is not only "about"; it is also "of," and this in a rich variety of ways. More particularly, we can say the difficulty cuts even deeper. We all share an assumption with philosophers like Descartes, Locke, perhaps Plato, that a concept is also about something. It is likened to a copy or an image in the mind, as if then using "I" meant that one ought to have a copy of the I in mind as one spoke. Once more, the concept is supposed to be about or otherwise it is unclear. Wittgenstein's point is that mastery of the concept "I" does not require a picture of the I at all. Instead, being able to discuss oneself as happy, joyful, even in pain, requires nothing like a copy. Other competencies are effected by the language, so that being able to tell about pain, joy, and dismay, these and more, are also done in language and with the help of "I" or "my," etc. The role, therein, is what we mean by the concept. We do something—we do not necessarily convey images, thoughts, or copies.

A kind of skepticism tends to overcome us if we do as James and Frege, even Wittgenstein, had done. The "self" looks like a fiction, an owner, immaterial, even a "motion" between head and throat.[47] But the skepticism arises also because we cannot resolve the issues in the terms that such discourse provides. So, we slip from one to the other, we take positions; we decide one time this way, another this way; or we might even become eclectic and try to be fair to all thinkers and admit that the self is mysterious. It is so mysterious and deep, so inexpressible, that almost like God, all notational schemes are thought inadequate. We might then want a new system of concepts, more refined and better able to lay hold of the essence of selfhood. In any case, this leaves the self quite uncharted and our best thought cannot

---

46. Wittgenstein, *Philosophical Investigations*, part I, no. 304.
47. Ibid., part I, no. 413; also *The Blue Book*, 69ff.

deliver. And the unfortunate consequence is that we are left uncertain and without confidence. What looks like the foundation, the self, is what is least certain; and our thought life, if not our ethical endeavors, seems to be vitiated. There is no hinge on which the door of life can swing. A kind of reflection then keeps us looking for an answer without there being a method for finding the solution.[48]

But Wittgenstein also knew that such skepticism was deeply wrong. More than that, the lack of certainty about the self must be in consequence of the wrong orientation. The quest does not make sense. Those two senses of "I" come back again. "I" in "I am overjoyed" is different than "I" in "I have twelve toes." If the grammar is different, then the understanding of one is of a kind different than the other. Is Wittgenstein right? In the second instance, we can say in response: "I had never noticed"; "I wouldn't have thought it of you—the way you run and walk is no different"; "Can it be? You have never told me before." In the first instance, the way of understanding the language does not require that you know the person better, that you make certain of a fact; instead, the words here require that you too be a subject, that you know what it is to get in on joy or pain. The language fits kinds of subjectivity, it expresses a kind of realized capacity and achievement in the person; but it is not like a sigh or a grunt. Language also is part of the capacity and the ability, not just an expression of it. Wittgenstein's point is that most language actually gets its logic and rule, its morphology and recognizable intelligibility, from standard practices and activities. After a while the "I" comes forth naturally and holds everything in place. All that a philosophical interest can do is to describe that emergence, it cannot justify and does not need to. And, above all, we cannot treat the language as if it needed further elucidation and explanation, if it is already doing a recognizable task. The role needs no justification.

In that first instance, to understand what is being said vitiates the question: "You mean yourself?" That question is nonsensical and is completely pseudo. For saying "I am overjoyed" is part of being joyful, just as "I have a pain" is part of being pained. Therefore that real "I" that Wittgenstein had to indulge non-philosophically in his early letters, that he could not get into the *Tractatus* except illegitimately,

---

48. Wittgenstein, *Philosophical Remarks*, part XIII, no. 149, p. 172.

that working "I" is seen to have a legitimate birth, non-philosophical to be sure. It is there and has to be reasoned "from," not "to." The more there are small achievements, the joys, griefs, hopes, thoughts, wants, the more there is to be linguistically exercised. Thus, one's language will be as rich and many-sided as the achievements of joy, grief, seeing, hearing, etc., will give occasion. More than this, the concept "I" only begins to take shape for us when there are these small achievements. That is the grammar of "I." The "I" is ingredient in all of these achievements.

Put in another way, the criteria for self-knowledge are not laid down philosophically or in some meta-language. They are instead laid down by the kind of activities that make up our life. There is no self *per se* to know. For the self is, indeed, not an object. But it is not a "nothing" either. There is no characteristic self-activity; certainly neither consciousness nor thought are truly singular marks of personality.[49] But there are all kinds of other activities. And self (and "I") when studied conceptually turn our attention to how "I" is tied up with living, with responses, with actions, beliefs, and feelings. Therefore, if it said that Wittgenstein is a linguistic philosopher and worries about words, then there is a point. But philosophy is a conceptual study, and it issues in a grammar—a rule or rules—that tie us up with a kind of natural and human history. To get clear on "I" is, instead, like becoming aware of the forms of human life in which "I" is at home, and, more, it makes us aware of the kind of person we are.

But there is a kind of certainty that we all need. Skepticism is a kind of fault. That "I" which is brought into philosophy as a limit was not actually the "I" used by Wittgenstein when he spoke in a moral way about himself. But the *Investigations* have changed that. The two strands are brought together. Philosophy has no special concept of the self. The only concept or concepts of the "I" are those born because the "I" is the bearer of ethics, but also knowledge, pathos, and art. That use of "I" to which we have been alluding is natural and unquestionable, but only if a kind of capital accumulates. There has to be valuation, judgment, and responsible pathos. Once there are all

---

49. Note here Wittgenstein, *Philosophical Investigations*, part I, nos. 412ff., and *The Blue Book* again.

these, the "I" shows itself. It then has a substance, and its identity is not in question.

This is how Wittgenstein's later reflection shows us that philosophy does not have to produce concepts at all. Instead it can study them, but only if other capacities have already produced them. And this is the point. A human life is also a growth in capacities and powers. One of the most impressive of all concepts (also a power and a capacity, not just a general word) is the "I." But we have to study what it does or rather what people do with it. Language is not only about capacities, but language (not least general words) is also a way to exercise the capacities, to effect the power, to be something. Language becomes the medium in which the concept grows; and to see its role is all that is required in understanding it. After a while, the "I" is used for a genuine achievement, the self, the I. For that is how a life is. It is also being made, and the word "I" or "self," "me" and "my," only become appropriate when some things have been done. To be uncertain about who you are, about one's identity, then is no longer a philosophical problem at all. Rather it is a moral problem. For if one is a subject, or subject to thoughts, virtues, judgments, the concept will be there.

The bane of the philosophical schemes, perhaps the psychological, maybe the theological also, is that here only skepticism can reign. The effect of their way of posing the issues is a series of pictures in which all criteria for certainty were and are removed. (Hence Wittgenstein's worry about the pictures that our learning produced!) But if Wittgenstein will be followed on these matters, then we begin to see that there is a wisdom of life available after all. Philosophy might lead to real wisdom despite its linguistic bent. No, precisely because of it! One sees that the certainty about who you are cannot be borrowed from a philosophical doctrine. But it can be achieved by a quality of deed, feeling, talking, and thought. This is what Wittgenstein tells us finally about these familiar psychological verbs. For example, we all can look if we have eyes, but we all do not see. We have ears and are able to respond to sounds, but we do not hear what is probably available. The difference is that looking is an activity, but seeing is a capacity. One can describe "looking" in non-personal terms, just as "feeling" can be captured in S-R graphs that mark intensity. But "feeling grief," like "seeing the detail," bespeaks a growth in the person.

The locus is not a place, it is a person. Language is not only an expression of the self, it is also a powerful means of being one.

Such a conversion of activities into capacities is what being a person entails. The more dependent we become upon our capacities, rather than our activities, the more use we have for an "I." Finally the problem of personal identity has no single resolution, for there is no single criterion.[50] There are a host of them. But the problem takes care of itself, not by being answered by a philosophical doctrine, but by disappearing altogether. Almost, if we live right, the self is there at hand—we are persons. This is a long road, and a bloody one to a fundamental certainty. But, at least, there is no cheating on the way.

---

50. "What am I getting at? At the fact that there is a great variety of criteria for personal '*identity*.'" Wittgenstein, *Philosophical Investigations*, part I, no. 404.

CHAPTER 7

Wittgenstein and Theology

I

LUDWIG WITTGENSTEIN'S THOUGHT IS not easily summarized. I shall not attempt it. But its thrust can be exploited without it being summed up. Consider, for example, the following lovely passage from his pen:

> Why is philosophy so complicated? It ought to be altogether simple. Philosophy unties those knots in our thinking that we have unwittingly put there; however, this requires movements as complicated as the knots. Though philosophy's result is simple, its method, if it is to arrive at that result, cannot be. The complexity of philosophy is not in its subject matter but rather in our knotted understanding.[1]

Wittgenstein wrote that passage when he was a relatively young man. He had already published a very complicated book with a very complicated title, *Tractatus Logico-Philosophicus* (1921). Ten years thereafter he was still doing philosophy and still in a difficult way, but he was aiming not so much at the big topics, reality, truth, and being, as at the knots in his understanding. As he went on, teaching and writing for the next twenty years (he died in Cambridge, England, in 1951), he increasingly strove to untie the knots or, to use another metaphor, to dissolve the problems. Philosophical problems

---

1. Wittgenstein, *Philosophische Bemerkungen*, 52. Translation my own. This passage was penned between January 1929 and September 1930.

can be considered in a variety of ways. Despite Wittgenstein's negative demeanor, he gave great dignity both to the problems and to philosophical activity by showing how deep they were, how complicated the knots, and how strenuous and technical one had to be to get rid of them. His criticisms were not cheap strictures or easy dismissals.

Right here was one of Wittgenstein's biggest points, namely, that philosophical problems were like knots, also like "bewitchments" of our intelligence. Most of them were like "deep disquietudes; their roots are as deep in us as the forms of our language and their significance is as great as the importance of our language."[2] Instead of crediting the problems with a kind of face value and then seeking still another answer to them, Wittgenstein tried to describe how we got into such confounding problems. He did not seek any new information nor advance any kind of theory; but he looked very concertedly at the workings of our language—concepts, names, forms, rules, grammar, beliefs enshrined in familiar expressions (meaning, sensation, thought, intend, feel, know, etc.)—in order to see how knots in our understanding developed. Most of Wittgenstein's literature bears him out: "The problems are solved, not by giving new information, but by arranging what we have always known."[3] And, in part, philosophy becomes also a treatment, sometimes even a therapy, often a technique, not for resolving the problems as much as setting the man straight.[4]

Philosophical problems always seem to be foundational, ultimate, and inescapable. They are invariably talked about as if their subject matter were extremely subtle phenomena, terribly hard to get hold of. Or, like theologians talking about God, it seems that, of course, there is a God, but our experience is too gross, or our language is too crude, or we are finite and He is infinite, or something of this kind.[5]

Then the problems of philosophy—and theology—seem to root in this fantastic incommensurability, where we get only a myriad of answers and somehow have to content ourselves therewith. We are tempted to think that philosophers and theologians have to be more

2. Wittgenstein, *Philosophical Investigations*, part I, no. 111.

3. Ibid., part I, no. 109. Also, no. 119, no. 126 and no. 127: "The work of the philosopher consists in assembling reminders for a particular purpose."

4. Ibid., part I, nos. 254–55; also note *The Blue Book*, 58–59.

5. Wittgenstein, *Philosophical Investigations*, part I, no. 436.

subtle and refined in thought because there is also a more subtle knowledge of the fact still awaiting our discovery.[6]

II

But our concern here is with theology. There are many ways to relate philosophies and philosophers to theology. We have all read about "idealistic," "Platonistic," "Aristotelian," and other kinds of theology, made into "kinds" by philosophies. We can suppose, too, that there might be "Wittgensteinian" theology some day. But I neither wish that nor need it, and I can only urge something more modest. But even that modest attempt would be a failure if it only gets theology up to date or if we think the latest is sure to be best. If there is any point to reading Wittgenstein with the hope that he might help in one's theological difficulties, it might be because one could paraphrase him like this:

> Why is theology so complicated? It ought to be completely simple. Theology also unties those knots in our thinking that we have so unwisely put there; but its ways in untying must be as complicated as the knots are in tying. . . . The complexity of theology is not in its subject matter but rather in our knotted understanding and personality.

If anyone has tried to understand Christianity in our day he finds himself led down a very difficult path indeed. For as soon as he starts to think hard, he is led to theology. Kierkegaard told about the man who saw the sign, "Pants Pressed Here," in a window. He rushed in, stripping off his trousers, only to be told that the sign was for sale. Kierkegaard thought it was like that with the philosophers and reality. Sick of sham and make-believe, a man hears about philosophers and reality; but all that there is, is one more system for sale, highly recommended to be sure. And about God, is there any knowledge about Him anywhere to be had?

Of course, there are all kinds of theologians, and they are quite smart fellows. They do all kinds of respectable things, like lay bare

---

6. In Wittgenstein, *The Blue Book*, 58, he says: "There is no common sense answer to a philosophical problem." But he argues that one can be cured of the temptation to attack common sense.

presuppositions, relay the last word from here and there, explore implications, make inferences, historicize, synthesize, and analyze. And one seems churlish, boggling over such endeavors. Besides, theologians have good reasons for arguing that their subject is difficult. It has a long history, there are built-in complications—myths, history, "truth," spiritual stuff in flesh, necessity, contingency, finite and infinite. In addition, it has all been kneaded into a tough dough that can be fashioned into a thousand loaves! Besides, considering that God's ways are not man's, there is an even deeper reason for the uncertain shape of the loaf. The point I want to make is that often theology, like philosophy, is most disappointing when it is most obviously prosperous—when there is not only one theology but dozens of them. All one seems to get is points of view and not knowledge of God. Everything seems well until one tries to make up his mind between Christologies, theologies, and theological anthropologies. In virtue of what does one decide?

Instead of knowing about God, via the theology, one gets a new kind of problem, namely, trying to understand theology and theologies. One began trying to understand God and hoping that theology could help; one ends up trying to understand the theologies. If it were clear that the difficulties were only due to the simple ignorance of the learner, that would be, however uncomfortable, at least tolerable. But it is not quite that, either. For precisely in those respects where philosophy and theology blend and pool resources, there too Wittgenstein's animadversions about philosophy seem to fit also theology.

Therefore, the thought that Wittgenstein brings to all of this is not the possibility of a more subtle theology—one that will hold the field for a generation or two. Neither does he say such stupid and sweeping things as "all theology is nonsense" or "thinking does not pay." He gives no consolation to the thoughtless or to the impatient. He is not against thinking, but he also thought about the problems and how we got ourselves into such morasses, where disagreements proliferate and confusions multiply. Instead of yielding to an easy skepticism, it seems to me that Wittgenstein's work urges more concern with details and closer scrutiny of the source of the theologian's puzzlement.

One way to put this is simply that most of us are dissatisfied with the way the Bible and hymnody and catechetical teachings—let us call this a kind of notation—talks about Jesus, God, and the world. For the moment, let us admit that this notation is rather pervasive and common. It may hold us in its grasp. Yet we are inclined to think that certain facts are not taken into account, that some of our experience is omitted, that this system of notation is old-fashioned and inadequate. We want a new notation, a new scheme, a new set of concepts, and a new language by which to say everything that was said in the old notation, plus taking cognizance of the differences. So, theology begins to lure us. And it is no answer to anyone to say that "the Bible says . . . ," or "my church teaches . . . ," or "in the words of an ancient hymn. . . ." The old notation is precisely what is inadequate (so we think), and we cannot satisfy the quest by clever restatements.

So, theologians, like philosophers, begin to write out notational systems, some of them plain, some of them subtle. All of them seem dependent upon the earlier, but most of them are not simple restatements. Of course, some of them are that, but these often seem no better than the originals. Theologies that are existentialist, phenomenological, neo-metaphysical, idealistic, etc., often look as if they are getting at more subtle matters. Furthermore, they seem to be giving one the *minima*, the foundational fact or concept, upon which the rest depends. But the difficulty is that there is no agreement. Nowhere is skepticism so learned and disagreement so profound. Yet we all are inclined to think that there must be something there to be discovered, that the *minima* have not yet been properly described.

Wittgenstein thought that the source of such conviction lay very deep indeed. I have no doubt that some Christian factors feed this source in additional ways. For one thing, Christians are inclined to put God among the invisibles, the intangibles, the really "real" behind appearances, etc. And God must be a fact, ultimate and final. So, whatever the sources that Wittgenstein thought drove intelligent people to disparage their working speech in favor of a more subtle and refined one (I am not talking here about the scientists' preference for a language alien to the man on the street), these seem to be compounded by impulses throbbing among the religious!

I have no cure-all. But Wittgenstein said in a letter to a friend (1917): "I am working reasonably hard and wish I were a better man and had a better mind. These two things are really one and the same—God help me!"[7] Maybe only some things in theology are a public craft. Theology, too, has become a business, and its integrity is often vouchsafed for it by public criteria. Wittgenstein had to break with obvious public criteria in order to philosophize about "knots in understanding." Perhaps it is appropriate to say that "knots in understanding" also pervade theology. If so, this will make theology harder work rather than easier. It will ask for more passion rather than less. Such work will not make it a "game" in an invidious sense, but it will demand greater congruence between our thoughts and our form of life.

III

We are strongly inclined to think that: "God's truth is independent of whether men believe it or not." So, we might also want to say: "God is in Christ" and "Christians believe that God is in Christ." If one says the former, then we say something that is theological. The second, about what Christians believe, is more like saying that a certain group of people have come to a theological view.

Those two statements have quite different uses. If one asks about the truth of the second, we do quite distinctive things to ascertain what is what. Our measures and rules are different when we discuss whether or not there is "believing" than when we discuss whether God is in Christ. If someone said: "I'm going to find out whether Christians believe that," his statement, on the face of it, at least, would not be absurd. But if he were going to find out whether God was in Christ, we might think him a little odd. Can one do research on that? Can one examine documents to find out? Has some testimony been overlooked? Does testimony count?

Still, people have said: "God is in Christ." Maybe one wants to say that such a saying is only one man's point of view, or that the original speaker was trying to say something else, or that the being of God is somehow being addressed with those words, or that the words are

7. Engelmann, *Letters from Wittgenstein*, 5.

only an expression! If we say any of the latter things, it might well be that we have a theory that all we ever have on such matters is a point of view, or that what is before a speaker's mind is always imperfect when made public, or that "being" (or "God") is always supposed by any descriptive language, or even that words are also like a cry or a grin or a smirk—speaking inadvertent volumes!

But I note these because all of us are prone to accept a strong view like: "God's truth is independent of whether men believe it or not," as if that surely must obtain. However, when we mention a particular case, "God is in Christ," we begin to see that there is no expert judgment to which we can repair. It is not testimony that proves it, for proof is not quite what we can have. If I said: "two times two is four," then I say something mathematical. Again there is no expert on "twos" and "fours" who assuages doubts and establishes the case. Instead this business called mathematics is both an activity, such that men have made it, and a branch of learning, and hence not arbitrary. Most things false in mathematics are like abrogations and exceptions. And about these particular issues Wittgenstein has said a great deal.[8] However, if one said, "Mathematical truth is independent of whether men believe it or not," the view is quite without a context. Does it make any kind of sense to say it? Always? What are the measures for its truth? We do not know whether the view makes any sense at all.

If everybody believed that God was not in Christ, would God still be in Christ? Now we may be inclined to say "yes." What is wrong with that? Well, for one thing, we have probably coasted on some analogies. Two and two make four whether Johnny believes it or not, but that does not say that mathematics is independent of all belief whatsoever. No, mathematics was constituted by the activity of mathematicians—it is now a game with rules. Is theology only a game? Not quite like mathematics: "The mathematician is an inventor, not a discoverer."[9] The Apostles were not inventors of the Gospel the way mathematicians invented numerals and the rest of mathematics. Or, were they? Is theology a kind of knowledge of God that can be stated independently of being believed?

8. Wittgenstein, *Remarks on the Foundations of Mathematics*, part I, nos. 163ff., pp. 47ff.

9. Ibid., part I, no. 167, p. 47.

I suspect that Christian beliefs seem dismaying to most persons—at least in hymns, Bible, and simple teaching forms—also because so much seems to depend upon "believing." We feel thwarted and confined by having to believe. In mathematics, "believing" seems rather trivial (except when we consider that without mathematicians doing it, there would not be any). In a Christian context, whether one believes or not is a religious test *par excellence*. And there are peculiarities. God is like a judge or even a teacher, whose examination is not meant to inform others about the subject matter but about the person examined (whether he believes or does not). Right here, we seem, nonetheless, constrained to say that our theological interests are higher and more refined. We want to know whether God is in Christ or not. To say, "I believe that God is in Christ, but it is not so," is a blatant contradiction. Why, in heaven's name, and on simple logical counts, too, does it not make sense to ask: "Isn't it so?"

Theology, in one of its forms, gives expression to the conviction that there ought to be knowledge of God, independent of belief. Most "belief" looks like a transition into knowing, a temporary mind-state, vanquished by knowledge. We have a kind of standard forced upon us by the notion of being rational, namely, that we first find out whether it is so, then we, too, will believe. And our theologies tend in the direction of feeding this conception of rationality. However, this may well be the biggest knot in our understanding, the cramp in our thought, that produces some of the theologies and our misgivings about them when we get them. For they do not satisfy us, nor do they untie the knot. Nothing quite fills the bill.

But just why there might be a difference in "belief" in respect to Christian teachings as over against other kinds of "beliefs" (e.g., Goldbach's theorem, or "that the chair will hold me") is lost to us by a very learned way of speaking.[10] We say that we believe in propositions and that propositions have to be true, etc. The words "belief," "proposition," "true," already have put our considerations into a mold. It seems to make no difference what we deal with so long as propositions are involved. "Belief is belief," we are inclined to say, "all that matters is 'what' you believe." With such elegant simplicities the web of thought is spun around us. To break out takes an enormous effort

10. Wittgenstein, *Philosophical Investigations*, part I, nos. 574ff.

indeed. Breaking out means that one looks at the teachings again, at the very homely details.

There is something about Christian believing that makes it a constant struggle. One has to hold fast, almost in spite of the way the world is. One is tempted to say, in spite of the way that theology is, too. But surely something is wrong. It must be that part of the theological task is to free us from misleading analogies and the making of ideologies in Jesus' name. Maybe theologians also have to describe, not invent, and get clear the limits of language for us once more.

Wittgenstein was once mildly chided by a friend for his lack of faith. Typical of him, he did not blame it on to the age or the rise of science or modern culture. With a perspicuity that was almost alarmingly honest, he clearly saw that the lack of faith and belief was not a fault of life and society as they are. And this is what is so moving about the man, this is what makes him a teacher who gets one into the Christian arena despite his professed lack of faith. He never blamed the world. He saw that the issue here was himself, and he never let go of that, as far as I can tell from his pages. But in response to that friend's inquiry, Wittgenstein said:

> I am clear about one thing: I am far too bad to be able to theorize about myself; in fact, I shall either remain a swine or else I shall improve, and that's that! Only let's cut out the transcendental twaddle when the whole thing is as plain as a sock on the jaw.[11]

There seems to me to be something moving and right about that remark. Furthermore, it puts us in the right frame of mind for thinking about Christianity. It might even help us to keep our theology directed against everything that clouds the simplicities and destroys both our confidence in thinking and our faith in God.

But Wittgenstein's work is also safeguarded by his fine irony. Kierkegaard said that some readers of his literature would complain that it was too scientific to be edifying and too edifying to be scientific. About Wittgenstein's works we can say confidently that its technicalities are aimed at making us think right, but to think right requires that we live right. Few thinkers have been so technical and so disinterested as he was, but few thinkers have forced us to such hon-

11. Engelmann, *Letters from Wittgenstein*, 11.

esty and such scrupulous self-understanding. It just might be that one can be edified in such a context too. Maybe these are the requisites of theology as well as philosophy.

PART THREE

Theology, Understanding, and Faith

CHAPTER 8

The Academic Game and Its Logic

W HEN I FIRST READ Plato, I was struck by what seemed to be
his first article, namely, that the corruption of morals would
begin with the banishment of truth. When one is new to academic
pursuits and when the thought of being a teacher still seems exciting,
this case for the truth has a delicious prospect that makes being a
self-conscious intellectual not an indulgence but a necessity. But now
after decades of teaching and rather arduous professional life, I am
not quite sure just what being a professor and university teacher and
researcher has to do with maintaining or even ascertaining the truth.

However, I am not here going to indulge in the canards of our
craft. For example, and despite the title of these remarks, I do not
think that the interests of university administrators are frequently or
always contrary to those of teachers and professors; nor do I condone
the popular idea that more money and more positions is what the
schools need in order to do their jobs; and surely it is not true that
research always freshens the intelligence and teaching dulls it. So, notions of self-governance, of more subsidies, and of less teaching, seem
to bespeak shallow diagnoses.

Because I have lived with a wife who is a very active teacher
in the public schools, I have seen the role of clichés and of simple
resolutions in public education, too. So in wider circles of education
the administrators pacify themselves and the public with a TV set
for every room (which soon is never used), with "new math" (which
is quietly pushed aside after countless books have been purchased),
with "individualized instruction" (which puts cherished teaching
patterns into abeyance for another season), then a good dose of sex

education (when that is the vogue), and lately, with computers (which are modern and obviously the answer).

It is a large and egregious mistake for educators to claim great advantages over the rest of the world when their diagnoses are as time-bound and their proposals as fashion-dictated as any that sellers and buyers might indulge. Much of the flailing about with methods, with curricula, with learning centers instead of libraries, with endlessly adding courses of study and being modern, is something that we do because we can do it. These seldom represent deep thinking of the issues and clear-headed analyses of the prospects.

Administrators and teachers alike do also have misgivings and thoughts about pupils and themselves that are on target, but then they profess that they can do nothing about such issues because of unions, of the law, of parents, of the "system," and, one hopes, of their own self-reluctance. Instead, we talk about research, about lengthening the school year, about computers—again, because we can manage all of these. Furthermore, by taking on open classrooms, new grading systems, and dozens of other large-scale policies, we can invoke another odd and covering concept, that of "experiment." So the jargon for a half-century or more has been that all these new proposals are part of "experimentation." But one looks in vain for the controlled inquiry, for the criteria, for the disinterested evaluation that would make the concept "experiment" meaningful. Most of this is bosh; and as educators we are on general issues like the professors of English, Bible, and philosophy, who instead of teaching the actual literature, religious thought, or philosophy in themselves, do what they can, namely, talk about the biographies, the circumstances, and anything else that conceivably might be relevant. So, we go around the educational issues and the proprieties of learning and teaching and talk about what we can—budgets, tools, policies and endless "experimentation." Much of educational talk, for the schools and the universities, is trivial and shallow—and expensive.

However, we also must sometime address the issues where they are. And this is not so much a question of talent as it is fortitude and patience. If we do have a stake in the truth, we must, on occasion, look for something besides a consensus and we must seek also a kind of personal readiness. Furthermore, despite the huge outpourings of money and talent, the educational tasks are not necessarily thereby aided. Instead there is another set of factors that vitiates education. These factors envelop both administrators and teachers, and they will not be addressed by a new method or longer days or endless hours of discussion. These are issues of attitude and also modes of thinking that have us in their grip. These sometimes put truth in a secondary role and give priority to pedagogy, to teachability of ideas rather than their intrinsic worth. Admittedly such matters seem abstract, but actually they are not. They have to do with personal proclivities and specific habits of thought and procedure. So they are within reach of all of us. But they seem to have happened to us inadvertently and almost by the way, so mostly we are not aware of them at all. They are so commonplace that they seem the only way to think and behave. Besides, they have administrative power and money behind them, so they seem irresistible.

Instead of now placing the blame on the administrators and other power-brokers in the world of education, it might well serve us to look first at a feature of all of us, administrators and teachers alike, to see if something, probably unwitting, has not happened to us that keeps integrity and even the truth at bay. So, in what follows, I will sketch briefly a set of attitudes and practices that seem to me to be corrigible, however uncomfortable their admission may be.

I

First it is important to recognize what happens when ideas are treated by analogy with objects, even mental objects. This is a subtle matter, but we do not need to be experts in epistemology or logic to see what is entailed. Instead, it is a function of the way learning, in most fields, is promulgated. Hence, the defect is widely pervasive, and it is inherited with the learning as well as looking almost like a product of it.

What I refer to is the plain fact that the learned now treat the history of any kind of ideas, and they do it in art, literature, philosophy, philology, theology, political theory, etc. Most professors and teachers are products of such training and are most compliant products too. There are few, indeed, who have even begun to question the validity of such teaching. After all, why should they? The lecturer and teacher is in a magnificent position of advantage—he or she now has an administrative role respecting an idea. One can now talk "about" the idea. One can now tender it, manage it, conduct it, execute it, even bring it into operation within the controlled context that pedagogy provides. So, the idea becomes something like a thing, an object, or an event, occurring under such and such circumstances. This is simply the way the academic game is perpetrated, the way it is played.

It is simply not the case that the issues with which we are here concerned can be met by saying that the fundamental task is to encounter the idea or concept in the language in which it was originally promulgated. Most ideas are translatable into any number of natural languages. Except for exceedingly rare instances, what is said in one natural language can be said in another. What we are addressing, instead, is the more subtle issue created by an artificial language-game, that created by scholars, teachers, pedagogues, and the entire industry of which they are a part. This is a kind of trans-language, trans-national enterprise, and it goes on within any natural language. Scholars and teachers are like a craft or a guild; and they recognize each other across otherwise immense barriers of time, cultural differences, and convictional loyalties. For those very reasons, they easily identify themselves as cosmopolitan, non-partying, and free of provincialisms and localisms. No wonder, then, that this scholarly world has the very air of genuine intellectuality and radical rationality.

Again, our question is whether literature, political realities, religious concerns, philosophy, and countless other human solicitudes, can be translated into the media of the scholarly language-game. Obviously, the scholars want to say "yes" and get on with the business. Furthermore, they want to insist that their artificial medium, the more logically defined and intentionally designed language of scholarship, has advantages over the original modes of discourse in being the medium in which the truth or falsity of ideas can be determined and more properly communicated. This game is even identified as a pursuit of truth, almost as if the making of literature, the task of philosophizing, the relentless struggle of religious living and thinking, are but antecedent conditions for the infinitely nobler business of manipulating those ideas in the scholastic modes. Obviously, these are several. There is criticism (higher, lower, stylistic, historical, linguistic); there is a variety of comparative study (cultural, typological, anthropological, etc.), and most obviously, historical study, which now is genitive about art, novels, poems, religious convictions, philosophical views, in addition to human institutions and social life. It is as though the educational ventures themselves, now deemed so useful and even necessary, have spawned these ways of handling the momentous and more primitive human materials. Perhaps no mode of understanding (and that is an appropriate way of describing almost exactly what is involved) is so ubiquitous and so easy to do as the historical game itself. This is what most scholars in what we might call broadly the literary and humanities fields do.

One relates one set of convictions, achievements, even ideas, to others in a series of contrived conceptual schemes, periodizing as one goes along. Once more, the historical scholar can now place, contrast, and delineate in a manner that will construe the original material in arresting ways. I am not denying that all of this, in turn, has a way of looming up as the achievement of recent centuries, as if the human spirit took a magnum leap upward. What is astounding is that the supposedly critical community, the scholars and teachers, should have so easily capitulated to it all, almost without demurring, and with full enthusiasm of the thought that this is the high road to understanding, if not the truth itself.

The result is that ideas, again of any variety, are placed in a context created by the pedagogy. An idea now has a context but an artificial one. For example, the history of philosophy is such an artifice. Soon Aristotle on "form" is contrasted with Plato on "form" and with thinkers early and late who had a stake in "form" or "idea." Questions here are not resolved by research in the original language, even though that is what the technical scholars want to say. So the pedagogues now augment it with work in Greek, Latin, and the European languages. All this supposes the validity of the pedagogical and scholarly ploy and the administrative posture created by the history of ideas, or the history of philosophy, or comparative studies, etc. What is wrong is the pedagogical demeanor itself.

But it would be a mistake to think that one is carping only at a certain kind of historical study. Again the matter is not one to be resolved by cleaning up that particular mode of study and its projection of subject matter. Rather it is that for the sake of getting command, one "administers" the idea, the poem, the play; one displays them in a scheme—a kind of conceptual system that is not that of the original author at all. The idea becomes something different than it was to the author, for it now fits a role in romanticism, rationalism, or medieval thought—the rubrics, systematic and historical, are endless.

There is something very deep about these matters. Most of us as academics, as pedagogues, critics, or historians, cannot quite afford the negative thought. Most of us have gotten used to Kierkegaard criticizing the docents and his saying that he fears falling into their hands. We can acknowledge Wittgenstein's misgivings about the university company and his fear about what pedagogical types would do to his thought. Schopenhauer, Marx, Keats, Samuel Johnson, Eliot, among others, were leery of critics and professors who would serve up the gist or distill the essence of their work. All of them were also critics and wrote about writing. Luther's dismay for his commentators is barely concealed in his pages.

Certainly we are up against something more than mere idiosyncrasies of individuals or a scorn for commonplace abilities. Nor is it useful to invoke, as academics have so frequently, the notion that some are geniuses and pontiffs, and that the rest of us are but journeymen with our tasks to do. There is more in all this than a difference in roles. What seems to be at stake is a serious question about whether ideas, for example (one could speak about "meanings," "understanding," also about the "play," the "poetry," the "art work," etc.) are really like physical objects or coins, and whether they remain the same in whatever hands they may be placed. When one changes the game, does one not change the very stuff itself? Can ideas, plays, works of the human spirit, be administered for the outside like this?

Think of the clergy, too, and the professors of religion. In reading an epistle of Paul one comes away with an overwhelming conception of his struggle to resolve fundamental issues of his life. But a second-hand academic account turns his tortured reflection into something called a Christology, about which one can now say that it was or was not clear in such and such details. Now one can entertain Paul's thoughts without any of the chaos he suffered and still supposedly know what he was about. We now can treat those thoughts detachedly, securing for our readers and hearers an accuracy and a logical precision that were lacking in the more primitive use.

Sometimes persons of genuine achievement do not help us very much when they insist that their work is simply the fruit of much application and a ready will. This is what Kierkegaard said about his thirty-five books written in eight years and Bach about his enormous musical outpourings. What we forget is that such single-minded attention to the tasks bespeaks enormous humility and a capacity to say "no" to a thousand impulses. Here there is what most of us could only describe as a kind of suffering. But to be educated in and by poetry, music, great thoughts, and religious living, without having to reduplicate such conditions, is now the promise of general education. It is as though higher education of the human spirit is now available at cutrates. We now have invented an administrative-pedagogical posture, which can be acquired rather easily, from which everything noble can be approached disinterestedly and objectively. But it is a real question whether the subject matter is really the same. Do concepts and poems, thoughts and passions, keep their identity just because we use the same words?

II

However, the answer to such a question or a train of such questions is not easy to give until we see for ourselves what is involved in the conceptual scheme that most scholarship and teaching entails. For it is, in the academic scheme, as if Aristotle, Bach, Keats, and Wittgenstein had to have a theory, a view, a point of view, or at least a proposal to believe. This all-embracing scheme tends to intervene and place what others have said and done in another kind of very plausible intellectual embrace. This artifice is thought to be topic-neutral, almost the way in which we think that a natural language itself is topic-neutral, permitting all kinds of values, itself requiring none. So, the academic scheme requires that every thinker have a theory or a point of view or a doctrine. So in the history of metaphysics it is assumed that everybody has one just as in the business of teaching ethical themes even Heraclitus has to have a distinctive ethical view. Because Aristotle uses the word "form," he must have a doctrine about "forms." But in such cases, the original thinker's use of the word, perhaps as a concept with a variety of uses, is now put to a use the original thinker knows little or nothing about. This theory-talk, for example, puts a use of the word into a different relation to the thinker than he, in fact, originally exemplified. He is made to speak in a manner that he, in fact, never did.

The original thinker probably used a word with power and authority for a specific range of things. But now if he has a theory, that very supposition requires that his theory be an alternative to other possible themes, that his use of the word is consequent to evaluations and conscious decisions, that he argued to something (for this is required of theories), that he deemed his theory justifiable for relevant reasons. Or, think about this peculiar style-consciousness that a certain kind of literary criticism imposes on kinds of literature. Soon we get a picture of a host of styles, an author exemplifying one, a picture of the author's responsibility to a style, and all of this chiefly because the relation to the style is posited by the survey mode of the meta-discourse. Again the logic of theories and of styles, the very grammar and shaping of them in the learned discourse, is not the grammar of them, neither of their surroundings nor their use, in the first instance.

The teleology governing much of this pedagogical lore is very simple and very seductive. We are being asked to give our allegiance to a scheme of ideas—be it Marxist, or a more neutral historical scheme, or a development of doctrine outlook; or the evolution of styles, of ideas, of the novel. Initially we read authors because they seem to have understood and articulated something, the Gospel, the social scene, some poetic imagery, the physical world. Most teachers apparently cannot do that easily. But neither did the primary authors do it easily. But, teachers do what comes easily and which they can learn from each other, namely, understand this abstract scheme of ideas. Besides, students and readers can get into this train of ideas far more readily, too. Now our access to understanding the authors is via the understanding of the scheme of ideas. There is only one difficulty. The topic has subtly changed, for the topic does not stay the same simply because the second scheme is proposed as a culturally enriched mode of the first.

By force of the very teaching devices, literary figures now stand in a different relation to their literature in the history of literature than they did originally. Of course, someone might say, that is precisely what the history of literature is supposed to do. True enough, but this is to admit that the history of literature and its truths, if such there be, are not the aim of the literature itself. But the access that pedagogy supposedly supplies to the student is an access to the primary material itself, not chiefly to hypotheses of a comparative or an historical variety. Furthermore, the issue is not whether the criticism or the history or the developmental scheme is not literature in its own right, created by the scholars. Surely there are critical and historical hypotheses that are also consequent of the genuine endeavor to find something out. The interesting fact is that the scholarly industry wants it both ways: first, that scholarly endeavor be productive of a literature with intrinsic validity and scope; and, secondly, that such scholarship, such precise and careful reading, be also the sesame to the original texts. Whether these matters are ever clearly articulated, the latter is the way that teaching goes on. And this latter view is what is being criticized.

The end of all this can be very harmful. It produces a kind of learned sophistry, a mode of plausible appreciation of all kinds of material that falsifies most of it thereby. For modern modes of lecturing, the contemporary textbook literature, the suave covering of the field that is supposedly one's ingress to the issues—all of that conspires to be objective and detached, ultimately reasonable and fair, and impartial and universal in appeal. Yet it betrays the original literature. No one knows this quite so poignantly as the originating authors themselves.[1]

But as scholars we ought also, on occasion, to brood a bit upon the very logical morphology of scholarly writing and the lecturing style. Not only are we sometimes painfully pedantic and sometimes

1. Immanuel Kant worried about the lack of popular appeal of his work, especially the *Critique of Pure Reason*, but concluded that a popularization cannot be attempted in studies demanding such concentration. But he is invariably concerned with the task of writing an exposition about his work. So, in discussing Eberhard, who had done a kind of scholarly précis, he shows his correspondent, Carl Leonhard Reinhold, why the secondary language about his work cannot do what his book itself already did. See Kant's letters to Reinhold, May 12 and 19, 1789, in Kant, *Philosophical Correspondence, 1759–99*, 136–50. Also note his comments to Christian Garve, 98–105.

disguised ideologists—these are plainer to see—but we also malform the material we are seemingly so intent upon presenting fairly and objectively. This happens in another subtle way when we dramatize an author by placing him in the extremely heady context that historical perspectives and surveys permit. Soon we have Kant juxtaposed against British empiricists, Horace Bushnell against Schleiermacher, Aquinas against Luther, and Samuel Johnson as a precursor of the romantics. Pedagogy and convenience soon give us generic titles by which to subsume styles, doctrines, and points of view. The authors themselves begin to look like embodiments of period characteristics, and they are construed as typifications and responses to historical antecedents and conditions, about which they were frequently innocent. But that makes little difference. The scheme gets to be the teaching material; and if it is ample enough, everybody fits.

To the extent that this way of administering scholarly material works, it is invariably a snare. But it does make stubborn and hard materials, highly individuated, amenable to a secondary treatment. Almost by definition, just about anything can be put into an historical embrace and also into a survey of the field. And the teachers and their *patois* about the original materials is now the medium of the understanding—and of the misunderstanding. This, indeed, is a kind of game. It is complex and many-sided, but obviously, it can be learned, promulgated, and popularized; for it simply is.

The falsifying side of all this does not become manifest, though, until one looks at the logical features that are normative in such scholarship and teaching. For this range of ideas (and styles, poems, etc.) are, in relation to one another, now treated in a supposedly objective medium. The medium of treatment is logically different than the linguistic medium in which each author writes. Then they appear to be true and/or compelling only as if that were a peculiarity of the author or his age. In the survey, they have a kind of non-ideological and non-persuasive detachment; they are, again, like physical objects, just there. So, the attitude soon is fomented among readers of and listeners to academic materials—not the sciences so much as the humanities—that the academic survey gives you the truest and most objective standpoint. Then a kind of skepticism becomes the normative posture towards the material. The skepticism bespeaks an air of superiority, as if Kant were prejudiced towards categories because he believed them to be necessary, or Pope bewitched heroic couplets, whereas we, who know a little about everything, are now skeptical about everything, too. The logic turns out to be that those who know history or have an academic vantage point by which to survey a field are cognitively qualified in a manner that the participants and practitioners are not. This seems to be something almost dangerous to teach. It purports to offer the truth, but it is a truth which is not the truth of any of the bodies of discourse being administered, nor is it quite a genuine historical hypothesis either. Instead it is a kind of pseudo-skepticism, produced not by evidence carefully marshaled, engendered rather by the artifices of the pedagogues' games.

This skepticism is actually produced by the artificial situation in which literary pieces or arguments or points of view have become something like options. But such options probably did not obtain for any original thinkers. Instead, they are made into options by being presented as such in an academic milieu. Therefore, the skepticism is appropriate enough; for granted what the scholars' account will permit, there are few compelling reasons for accepting one style or one view as over against the other. The logic of academic talking makes the reasons originally adduced for a point of view only a part of the passing scenery. To choose a view requires that one choose the reasons, but the age alone makes the reasons. Thus, the skepticism gets exceedingly encompassing.

But this is not all. For the demeanor that we have instead is also congruent with the way in which institutions of learning are also professionally administered. There is a coincidence of aim between the administration of the institution and this current way of administering ideas and subject matter. To this we now turn.

III

Thus far we have tried to show that the logic of forcing the various kinds of literature into the academic ways of thinking and talking makes the literary material into something quite different than it originally was. It speaks now to a different range of concerns. And skepticism is now given a different kind of status. Through the ages doubt and skepticism have looked like the pathology of thinking; but this kind of scholarly and popular teaching now indulged in colleges and universities makes it look like the health of the intellect. It appears that one has to go to the university to become deeply uncertain on fundamentally important human matters. Knowledge is now the sesame to a kind of convictionless life. The fullest possible account—a survey of the domain and/or a history of the literary piece and its issues—now tends to justify a deep disquietude about the validity and authenticity of primary literary expressions. Everybody earlier in time looks like a bigot, interesting but not quite objective.

This is made even less tolerable by another disturbing feature of modern academic life, namely, the existence of the office of the administration. There is no intent here to name persons or to indict individuals, as if special culprits were the target. Nor is the intent simply to add flames to the controversies between dean and faculties, as if their interests must invariably clash. Again the issue is a logical one. It has to do with that outside vantage point, be it the dean's or president's or whoever's, who feels it necessary to look at scholarly domains and interests and adjudicate their demands and assess their claims respecting one another. The issue here is the high degree of overlap that develops between this powerful advantageous perspective and that of the editing and overseeing of ideas by modern scholarship. For what often makes the administering of ideas so feasible for modern scholars is simply that this is what deans and presidents also do, and they have also the money and power to keep the enterprises going. Along with the foundations and their leadership, the university authorities tend to reward all this new kind of non-partisanship. It fits our democracy, our lack of conviction, our multitudes, and the non-ceasing plea to be fair and disinterested.

The need for a disinterested place, from which one can adjudicate competing desires and claims, is obvious enough. Thus, administrative offices are a necessity. But the teacher who finds it easier and more plausible to address a variety of students and colleagues and to do that by treating ideas and styles as physical objects, will also find that so doing will create a disposition in him- or herself as well as in the students. Unfortunately, the professional administration that universities need also makes that same disposition almost a necessity. Teachers have learned to mix up ardor and variety and, subsequently, to serve up and dazzle young people. But a variety of ideas can become a habit, and entertaining a variety is not to get into any one idea at all. A certain kind of eccentricity develops, along with a deadening of persons to the deep issues involved—maybe both. Ideas are entertained. Just as the teacher yields to one idea after another, just to create interest besides doing up the field and the history, so the student does the same, without ever being possessed or transformed by any one of them.

For the administrator who cannot know much of the detail of any of these fields, the attitude has to be that of the benevolent outsider. Anything that purports to be a field and has a faculty population has to be given a kind of status. By and large, administrators are not stupid, neither much better nor much worse than the faculties. Except that the administration mode of looking at the domains fits into the peculiar mode of thinking that pedagogy also produces. However, the administrators have power and authority to subsidize. Hence their attitude becomes one that can never be examined or seriously questioned. Toleration towards opposites rather than sharp polemics and argumentation now becomes a social necessity. Almost everything is tolerated. The administrative is absolutely generous towards the chaos in beliefs. Nothing looks foundational and everything proffered by the learned is on par. This must be why we now have such a proliferation of beliefs offered to students and an almost total lack of criticism anywhere. For now to understand almost anything means putting it in the spectrum, or in the array of the curricular offerings. If there is any merit, it belongs only to the popular domains that are elected, for all other kinds of genuine intellectual reasons for or against become inaudible and invisible. The big word here is pluralism. This is almost the guarantee of intellectual sagacity.

Furthermore, this modern intellectual excitement is the specialty of the contemporary statesmen of learning. They see and comment on the panoply. They like to comment on the growth of knowledge and the multiplication of fields, for that is what the office of administrator permits and offers. Seeing all these issues from the outside is to see pluralism—now in everything: religion, politics, philosophy, literary enthusiasm, and argumentative preferences. This is sociology of knowledge with a vengeance. All of this creates the hoax that the modern world is so different from previous ages that even Heraclitus would be unable to cope. Now the administrative task is to keep the spectrum evenly populated, for the word gets around that the presence of these alternatives marks superiority. To have the plurality is to be just to the way things and people are. The new norm for departments and groups is to be representative, never partisan, dogmatic or one-sided, and never convinced. Pluralism is not just part of an indicative remark—it is part of a normative requirement. Furthermore, it is as if the administrative vantage point is the truly superior intellectual count. It is here that the ultimate and ruling judgments that establish the merits of learning are, in fact, being made. Again, the foundation officers, the impresario faculty who see their specialties in the larger spectrum, and the deans and presidents now coalesce.

This is how we get something like the modern "establishment" in academic contexts. Differences of view that once incited argument and polemics and that are part of the problem in the endeavor to establish the truth are now in themselves made highly acceptable. A new kind of wisdom, beginning simply as a concession to disagreements one does not even try to settle, now get backing. If one talks long enough about all of this one can soon convince oneself that this miscellaneous plurality is a grand invitation to human potential and a realization of humanity, garnered after the centuries. Actually this is also to make a virtue out of chaos and intellectual incoherence. This does not make for a higher truth at all, only for a ploy convenient to half-hearted intellectuals and teachers and a policy for administrators that gives very crude credence to the mad disarray of modern university life. It is not true that pluralism marks off the contemporary age from ages of superstition, of religious credulity, or of dictatorial conformities. Obviously enough, there have been profoundly different and fundamental views of life, differing ways of governing, and a plethora of faiths and hopes, since time began. But that kind of pluralism has been long acknowledged and enshrined in terms like "autocracy," "democracy," "Christian," "Jewish," "unjust," "just," "hedonist," "altruist," etc.

The contemporary pluralism no longer bespeaks a genuine dilemma or a shocking paradox out of which the real intellectual life begins. It makes the intellectual life one of absorption and appreciation of the plurality, not a demand for a momentous choice. This kind of pluralism creates an artificial mood, one made by the academic manner of projecting otherwise very demanding alternatives. Again, this is all a part of the aesthetic and disinterested perception that university policy now makes the typical cognitive-like access to momentous matters. This becomes part of public relations and is the politic way of both addressing divisive topics for the human spirit yet rendering them innocuous. One can then assure the clientele of seriousness, on the one side, yet a seriousness that will never be invidious or non-democratic, on the other. Here we have the new case for fairness, for equity, where all the major options still get their erstwhile expression.

By this time it must be clear that I think this state of affairs reprehensible. It makes modern institutions of learning one more shallow purveyor, a kind of education indeed, but one that settles for an exceedingly cheap kind of sophistication. This is why contemporary television and radio, let alone a popular press, is a real rival to the educational scene. For nowadays, argument, dialectics, and saying yes or no, is bad form and seems not to be affirming others, not quite liking people. Instead, where education is supposedly higher, we get a wider variety and the antecedents are multiplied. Perhaps it is all a part, too, of the truly faulty notion that education can and must be made easy for all those who are un-benighted. By creating vast inclusive institutions with laudable social aims, we have also stimulated the laziness of both faculty and students. Surely an idea of Leibniz's is no easier to put to use today than it was in the first instance. But it is now as if ideas are going to be costless, almost to be gotten by reading and listening, usually without any turmoil, personal change, or really giving up anything else. Faculty and administrators together have helped create a new kind of university learning and teaching. But it is surely about time that we also question its implicit logic.

IV

David Hume once remarked that it is infinitely easier to defend the negative; and the poverty of positive remarks herein may well serve his theme. Is there nothing, then, to be done? Surely much can be said about these matters that will be helpful and even remedial. At this juncture, though, it looks as though any criticism here is a superb vanity, almost like arguing with a custom. But that is a good part of the difficulty. For the humanities particularly are subject to the effects of these academic transactions. These precisely are the subject matter fields, where, to absorb the material—theology, literature, philosophy, art, music—is also ostensibly to become more humane, civilized, and urbane. Here the content is personal and vulnerable, albeit not directly and immediately. But our point is that the academic devices, even though one reads primary materials in preference to secondary, are usually such as to create a kind of neutral skepticism and the framing of the materials creates an objectivity that looks like the superior intellectual posture.

It may be difficult to distinguish between direct propagandizing and indirect communication of these fundamental human possibilities, between dogmatizing and taking with utmost seriousness the need for decision on issues of aesthetics, morals, and a form of life. But part of the shallowness of which we have complained is that in order to avert the former, we (both administrators and faculty) have also averted even the opportunity for the second. We have made pluralism, relativism, superficial appreciation of opposites, tolerance of all beliefs, and all lifestyles, the educated posture. And all of this also because we have created a kind of unreal and artificial objectivity—a mode in the collegiate game—the norm on such crucial human concerns.

Surely it is about time that academics rethink all of this lest they be hoisted on their own petard. To avoid an invidious subjectivity, we espouse a kind of objectivity that makes the forming of the subject life—what thoughts, pleasures, imagination, art, faith, are supposed to do—almost suspicious. In addition, it is as if we explain everybody's subjectivity, everybody's inner life, their convictions, loves, hopes, and thoughts, by methods which make our own accidental and an embarrassment if reflected upon. But this state of affairs can be thought about by intellectuals and can be remedied from within. Otherwise, we invite a kind of sullen anti-intellectualism that thrives on the poverty and convictionless character of modern intellectualism.

Almost endlessly there is this odd strife between the humanities and the sciences. And we have an array of proposals about the humanities and Western culture, constantly titillating the faculties, most of them only compounding the difficulties. For few of us dare to attack the fundamental questions. We always think this must belong to somebody else's specialty. We are inclined to think it is a professional matter for epistemologists or maybe a curriculum specialist. Or we look for generalists who are otherwise the pariahs of the collegiate scene. But such matters belong to anyone who is willing to think with and about the grammar of our common life. That is within reach of all of us. However, it costs something to make that clear. One has to be willing to face profound objective uncertainties, to see what one actually needs and wants. In fact, one has to be educated by great literature and art, not educated about it, in order to begin such an inquiry.

But surely there is something short of this available to the teachers and scholars too. After all, we can begin to teach intensively if we want and if we dare to do so. We can stop comparing and contrasting, classifying and subsuming, and let the imagination and thought of the author become our own. Anyone who thinks he can do that for a dozen philosophers, or all the romantic poets, is a plain fool. Then we can make our teaching both the very organ of and the occasion for human genuineness. Instead of treating ideas as physical objects to be discoursed about in the about mood, we will show by our teaching that they are ways of being significantly human.

CHAPTER 9

About Linguisticality and Being Able to Talk

I

W E CAN READ A great deal about "the problem of language" in major theologians and philosophers of our time. It is hard to say exactly what is involved in that "problem," except that one of the theologians says that in it "all the questions about the world and man and history are increasingly concentrated." And that is about right, for the problem of language masks a dozen other issues. Our theologian can say the above because he also believes that: "when God speaks, the whole of reality as it concerns us enters language anew."[1]

But there is also another kind of concern that some philosophers have manifested. Martin Heidegger finds that language is not constituted or made up solely by thought and thinkers. Language is not quite a system of conventional signs—it has another depth. It is as if language sometimes comes out of an "encounter," and language thereafter, has to be assessed as a whole, even thought "about," and not only "with." "Being," as he would have it, presses itself into language, from which, the thinker then can determine more precisely what reality is. Language speaks, Heidegger says, and this in addition to the fact that people speak with and by it.[2]

1. Ebeling, *Nature of Faith*, 182 and 190 respectively.

2. It is almost as if language memorializes and articulates more than a speaker knows and says—hence the mystery of a living language. Note Heidegger's *Holzwege* (1950, 1957), especially "Wozo Dichter?," 248–95; see the English translation, "What Are Poets For?" in *Poetry, Language, and Thought*, 89–142.

For language cannot be understood solely as the articulation by a person of a discovered intelligibility and order in the world or even in being. Instead, language is more—it is the veritable dwelling place of "being," where reality articulates itself and is progressively made manifest. Something happens in language that is pre-conscious. No wonder then that "linguisticality" becomes something of a feature, which has to be assessed to get at metaphysical issues. And out of that kind of context, we can get a little glimmer as to why Heidegger wants to take the pages of Hölderlin and other poets almost as a datum for getting at fundamental reality issues.[3] Language in this account is something of an event; it has to be understood not only by what it says but also by what it is.

The issues here are radically different than Russell and Whitehead describe a sentence to be. For example, in the *Principia Mathematica*, they note that a proposition can be a fact when you consider it simply as an item occupying space on a page or on a blackboard. Then it is a geographical fact. When it is heard, it is an acoustical fact; when articulated, a psychological happening and fact. But Russell and Whitehead make the point that they are concerned as logicians not with these kinds of facticity, but with the logical properties of truth and falsity.[4] Whitehead and Russell insist that logic concerns itself with language chiefly because it proposes truth and/or falsity. So, their concern is with the truth-function, but not with the truths. As a matter of course, they, too, are concerned with more than what is being said by any one speaker. But their interest is with general rules and functions that a language in use evinces and by which speakers can ostensibly make sense. Heidegger is, I believe, fumbling after something general and transcendent to any one speaker's contrivance, but he invariably castigates the logical interest. Along with Professor Calvin Schrag, whose work will be noted later, Heidegger seems to think logic overstandardizes and formalizes everything about a living language to the point of falsification. So he dismisses formal and logical matters very quickly.

3. Note Heidegger's *Aus der Erfahrung des Denkens* (published in 1954, but written right after World War II). See also the English translation, "The Thinker as Poet," in *Poetry, Language, and Thought*, 1–14.

4. Whitehead and Russell, *Principia Mathematica*. See especially Appendix C to the 2nd edition, 1:659–66.

Again, then, Heidegger and many phenomenologists continually allude to the fact that a piece of language is a fact, but in such a way that the event-like character of the language demands an interpretation. But more, it is as if language, and to a certain extent thinking too, are fate-laden; for "being" is unveiled and shown not just in what language says but also in what the language, in fact, is. This general feature of language is what philosophy, not logic, gets at. But this feature is not just dangled in something called the philosophy of language. Rather Heidegger himself purports that there is also a subtle framing and predisposing of thinking and talking that roots in this peculiar pre-conscious and pre-psychological meeting of "being" and man.[5] By a slight transposition upward this whole story is easily told also on behalf of theology and God. And a host of exegetes, theological and literary, have been doing this kind of sophisticated hermeneutics on texts for the past twenty years or so.

Heinrich Ott and other theologians have rather quickly exploited the analogues between Christian theology and phenomenological thought, especially Heidegger's; and all sorts of longstanding preoccupations with language have again become freshly appropriate. We have it asserted that "In human language God's own language makes itself heard"; we have another version of "saying" and "showing" introduced, quite different than Wittgenstein's, around the notion of "being" "unveiling itself"; and a major case for hermeneutics is, therewith, declared, because language itself, not just what is said with it, has to be interpreted and understood.[6] The search for understanding becomes evanescent and extremely difficult, for there is nothing quite simple to understand. It is not as if a person can comprehend, again, only what is being said; for the compounded difficulties of "linguisticality" are that a piece of poetry, or for that matter almost any piece of language, has a double sense, first, that which is made by it being said, and secondly, by any language being what it is. And the

5. Heidegger, *Unterwegs zur Sprache*. But see especially the brief excerpt, "Language," from this volume, in *Poetry, Language, and Thought*, 187–210.

6. See Robinson and Cobb, ed., *The Later Heidegger and Theology*. Note especially the essay by Heinrich Ott, "What Is Systematic Theology?" 77–111, and remarks of Robinson in "The German Discussion of the Later Heidegger," 3–76. The discussion of Wittgenstein's that is relevant is in the *Tractatus*, 4.121: "Propositions *show* the logical form of reality."

factual character and the logical form that the *Principia Mathematica* pointed out are then not quite analogous.

This sounds like the language showing the user its form or something of that sort, and the language not being able to say that of itself. But matters are not that simple, nor are the issues logically delineated. Perhaps it suffices to promise that language unveils deep metaphysical and even divine matters. I find that all kinds of considerations of how God can be the word and the "logos" and how the word of God can be contained in the words of human writers, now easily obtrude upon our attention. It looks as though this ostensible phenomenological interest in language, in bracketing it in these ways, has shown us more than we ever suspected. Even if the vicissitudes of hermeneutics do not burden every reader, they certainly have a large number. For now we have hermeneutical philosophy in depth upon some issues that were obscure as they stood. One result is another curious kind of theologizing that is dependent in detail upon what look like egregious philosophical mistakes.

In what follows, then, I want to consider anew some issues that have arisen in the philosophical discussions. My interest is twofold. I would like to rid myself and the reader of the thought that language needs a general philosophical accounting in order to be understood. But, also, it seems important to rescue phenomenological concerns from such grandiose philosophical and speculative accretions. It would be well to restore a truly "bracketing" and "descriptive" kind of interest to phenomenology, freeing it from these other imputed depth-factors. Secondly, I want, also, to head off theology from the onerous burden of making the case for God via such extraordinary and finally irrelevant moves.

II

Consider instead how lovely it is to be able to talk! There are situations when we discover a simple pleasure in being able to say something. After surgery to correct a malignancy in his throat, I heard a colleague say: "Thank God, I still can talk!" Obviously, just to be able to make noises, with tongue, larynx, and all the rest of the natural equipment, is something very moving indeed if one has been threatened with premature silence. But there are other cases. For example, that one takes pleasure in talking is shown us in how people talk and is seldom said directly by the talking. We learn about the talker's pleasure as we hear him say this or that. We do not need and indeed would distrust someone's telling us that he gets pleasure out of talking if other factors did not show it already.

Sometimes we are with people who overpower us. Their assurance, their aplomb and authority, silence us completely. Later we recover our poise and our wish, and words seem to come again. As a young student in the presence of Bertrand Russell, I simply could not talk to him. His magisterial bearing and reputation inhibited every word. But then he said something that seemed very absurd—that all study of philosophy must begin with George Berkeley's theme, *esse est percipi*. The stress upon "all," even amid such charm and intellectual prowess, was like a trigger for a rejoinder, and the talk began to flow again.

But there are other cases, too. Sometimes we do not know what to say, and hence we cannot talk. When we learn a little and get at home in the novelties, we find a quiet joy in verbalizing. Or, maybe we have said to another: "What's the matter? Did the cat get your tongue?" All of us have lost our enthusiasm to speak in some situation. Maybe a sorrow has overwhelmed us, perhaps we are too depressed for words, or we have reasons for murmuring that at the moment, at least, "silence is golden."

My point is only to draw attention to the circumstances under which it is gratifying to be able to speak. If I have to say to someone, "I couldn't talk to you before—there were too many things standing in the way," it would be hard to imagine not being very grateful at speaking again. So, successful surgery, knowing our way around, assuaged sorrow, getting rid of the hard feelings—these and more make us appreciate our ability to talk.

But these common matters are overshadowed by the kind of consideration that Heidegger and other phenomenologists have advanced. To get at their range of issues, then, let me turn to a particularly cryptic and brief essay by a leading American thinker who has assimilated and even modified the strong views I have noted. His pages have a depth about them that cannot be denied; but I want to speak to a set of theses that seem to me to be central not only to the author but to a whole catena of thinkers who seem to me to have gone astray. Professor Calvin O. Schrag's essay is "The Phenomenon of Embodied Speech."[7] His thrust is not quite what I have noted as characteristic of Ott and some pages of Heidegger. Mr. Schrag stresses, indeed, the *Dasein*, the particular human being and how he is unveiled, if not revealed, by the very character of speech, not only by what is said in speaking. Already I have noted that "how" a person speaks does show us more than a person does and can say. But this is not enough for Schrag's trained glance.

Instead, the author begins his remarks with the strong assertion: "The ability to speak is a unique and idiosyncratic feature of man." Posing it that way, it seems very plausible for him to take language with great seriousness. Man is an *animal loquens*, not only *animal rationale*. And it is clearly not the author's aim to do what I think might be worth doing. For when a man says, "By Jove, isn't it great to talk again!" and if you did not know that he was saying it after surgery, or after a big fright, or after recovering his tongue, the saying might strike one as odd. We would want to know why something so common as talking could be so valuable. We might want to ask: What do I do with my talking? What is being taken away in enforcing silence upon me? If one were to get a picture of how one's poise, one's confidence, one's projection, how one was going to do and even be something by talking, then one might be getting something substantial to go with *animal loquens*. Of course, it might frighten one a bit, too, to think that so much depends upon so little.

Consider another and different case. A person might realize how few people he offended when he was silent in the hospital bed. No longer was he sarcastic and biting, and he could not even up any account when he lay there in the enforced stillness. Maybe he would reflect like an ancient writer: "Even so the tongue is a little member, and boasteth great things. Behold, how great a matter a little fire kindleth! . . . But the tongue can no man tame; it is an unruly evil, full of

7. Schrag, "The Phenomenon of Embodied Speech," 1–27. All the following references are taken seriatim from that essay. The essay following Schrag's in *The Philosophy Forum* ("About Our Capacity to Talk," 29–42) by the author, Paul L. Holmer, was a counterthesis and includes some of the material in the present essay.

deadly poison. . . ."[8] With such sober thoughts, he might be strangely glad for a respite from his world of talk, where out of the same mouth has come praise and blame, almost like a fountain sending forth at the same place sweet water and bitter. Seemingly, his troubles are less when he has to keep his mouth shut.

Now perhaps we begin to get a little more material to go with that strange expression *animal loquens*. And this picturing might be worthwhile in particular circumstances. If people have become jaded with ordinary life, tired of the humdrum course of events, yearning for big events, which never transpire, it might be helpful for a moralist to restore joy to someone. He could remind another how dismal it would be if he could not speak. Of course, this is not high-minded philosophy; but still, his remarks might be reminders of some familiar things, enough to show him that he has no right being so despairing. Contrariwise, there are those who talk a good line, who are wantonly loquacious, who deceive themselves and others, who do not bridle their tongues. These might need some reminders of how talking is also weighted with responsibilities, that idle speech is a vice, not an unmitigated gain at all. Once again the force of the above kind of reflection is only to reinforce what is often patent but forgotten, that if you are an *animal loquens*, you had better mind your words and manners.

Let us be very clear that not all of this is philosophically interesting. For some of these matters are too important to be left to philosophers or any other special group of experts. Nonetheless, such matters are worthy of a kind of reflection. One can be serious, one can think about such things, and one can learn what to say and what not to say about talking by considering the circumstances, the effects, the purposes, etc., being served. Even if they are not typical of philosophers when they do philosophy, they belong to philosophers as well as the rest of us. But my aim is not to make a case for philosophy, new or old. It is rather to get at what I think is wrong with almost any philosophy of language. I gave some instances of reflecting about our talking which are worthwhile in special circumstances. But reflection about talking, however useful and ancient, does not have to issue in

---

8. Jas 3:5, 8 (King James Version).

something so elaborate and so artificial as most phenomenologists and as Professor Schrag proposes.

Nothing I have said forbids a kind of reflection about what the philosophers have called *Dasein*. For as wrong as the logic of a lot of this is, I find the concern with the speaker via the language not to be a mistake in principle. There is something of a depth sort in the notion of moralists and lately of the existentialist thinkers that a person simply must care for the quality of his or her own being (though I would prefer to say, "his or her life"). After all, people are not brute facts, and they are not quite precipitated into whatever it is that they are. So, something can indeed be said about learning to exist as a person that is not to be said about everything else. But the question of what using language has to do with all of this remains.

Not everything meant by the language is said by the language.[9] For the person also gives a kind of body and substance to his words by whatever he is and the specific things he is doing. So language by itself does not tell us everything. We understand what is being said when we know the situation, the purposes that embrace the words and the relevant activities, even the kind of person who is speaking. Much of what the philosophers and theologians who are cogitating about language in recent years are alluding to seems to have an elemental rightness about it. But some general and abstract "referents" tend to intervene. And their referents and the large-scale abstract nouns make everything immediately speculative and mysterious. I would like to urge that the more common issues be brought to the fore and then, hopefully, the large and metaphysical concepts, *Dasein* and *Sein*, "embodied existence," even "linguisticality" and more, will disappear. But this is something that one will have to see about in what follows.

Therefore, I propose to take up five additional theses that I found in Professor Schrag's pages but that, I believe, are common to Heidegger and many others too.[10] By dispelling these, I hope to

9. This kind of remark and what follows is, of course, in consequence of Wittgenstein's and Kierkegaard's reflections. Not everything done in a language is done by the speaker either. This is why logic is so important, for it describes those formal and rule-like features of language itself.

10. Readers of Rahner's *Theological Investigations*, vols. 1–13, will easily recognize some of these issues in his pages too, for instance, "The Experiment with Man," 9:205–24, and "Philosophy and Philosophising in Theology," 9:46–63.

show that we no more need a "critique of language," than we have here been offered one. We are left with people and their talking again. Furthermore, we are left with the kind of reflection with which I began—a plainer set of considerations about ourselves.

III

We are told that in speaking, "human existence in its manifold concreteness comes to expression." (This is to return to the *Dasein* again.) The reasons for this are fairly elaborate. We are urged to think about words, apparently as they are on the one hand in a vocabulary list or a spelling book or a language text. Here they seem to be standard, orderly and relatively precise. On the other hand, we are urged to think of words as spoken, when we say something with them.[11] Of course, there is a difference between them. They are the same words, yet how different! Mr. Schrag becomes very philosophical even in his description. For he tells us that: "The word as spoken is an *originative* act of speaking."

The interesting thing here is that the author does not explore any examples at all. All the examples I think of do not seem to require the notion of "originative acts" at all. But what distresses me is that no examples are cited. I suspect that he does not believe he needs to do so. For reflection that is supposed to be philosophical is usually very lofty indeed. In the first pages of his essay, the author tells us that we do not need only a "critique of pure reason" but also a "critique of language." I wonder if a lot of expectations are not bound up in that word "critique." Of course, this is a word made standard by Kant's big books, in which he purported to show us how there were principles, transcendental principles too, that were not the subject matter of reasonable activities as much as they were the criteria and authorizing conditions for all kinds of activities. Philosophy was the knowledge of these perennial transcendentals, not the knowledge of the transcendent. In Mr. Schrag's pages, it is surely the case that he is telling us that there must be something always the case, something that has to

11. Hofstadter's "Introduction," ix–xii in Heidegger, *Poetry, Language, and Thought*, shows that Heidegger, too, has castigated the pictures of standard words, uses, etc. Note, too, Heidegger's "The Origin of the Work of Art" in this same volume, 15–87.

be true, something philosophical about talking. But the talking itself gets overlooked.

I submit that he is being misled by a notion that there must always be something philosophical, something necessary and universal, undergirding the familiar range of things around us. So, he latches on to our talking. He makes some distinctions and asserts a few things but nothing that requires the philosophical case he makes. For example, there is indeed a difference between the words cited in a thesaurus or a vocabulary list and the way they are when we use them to say something. But this difference is a function of what we are doing in the two instances. The difference is introduced by something outside of the words. Words in a list are not in their natural habitat and that is the advantage in listing them. Using words to say something is quite the normal role for words.

Doesn't this tell us what we are doing? Is that not enough? It is not the case that words are "standard" in the one case and "original" in the other, say, when we make a speech using them. That way of marking the differences between a list and a speech puts the difference into such a genre that a philosophical distinction seems to flow forth. But something has been forgotten. In one case, we can say we have a standard because that is what we write out at certain stages of pedagogy. It is chiefly the pedagogy and the interest we have in standardizing that creates the list of accepted words, meanings, grammatical rules, and the rest.

Of course, there are differences between listing words and speaking with them, but such differences are neither so binding nor so profound that they demand anything as big as transcendentals to describe them. Our vocabulary is often learned in a different way than our sentences are. We teach words to one another in such a way that words are the simplest units, something like the pieces out of which are fashioned sentences. But this is only the way it appears, for all of us also know that sentences are not just strings of words, except to someone who is only counting the words.[12] All of us compose sen-

---

12. Leibniz in his *Grammatical Thoughts* was bold enough to say that the formal requirements of grammar, declensions, and conjugations did not correlate with what he calls "philosophical grammar" (apparently the "sense" of what is being said). So he says: "Yet a man who speaks a language and neglects these differences [gender, declensions, and conjugations], as I heard a Dominican from Persia do in Paris, is understood none the less." See Leibniz, *Logical Papers*, 13.

tences most of the time, using words, for that is all there is. A sentence is not quite the sum of its parts, if one means that words are parts. So, too, one learns the notes in music first and then sings or plays thereafter. But, what Schrag and Heidegger call the originality of speaking, as over against the dull sameness of the words, is only to remark upon a common feature of sentences and, maybe, of speakers. All of us make up sentences every day of our lives, and if that bespeaks originality then it is too widespread to be so dignified.

Certainly it is true that the role of a word in a sentence can not be computed only from its meaning in a list. Sentences are not functions of individual words. We are prone to make that mysterious. We have to be involved in tasks, in duties, in organized endeavors; and then what Wittgenstein calls "games" begin to give the words their thrust. Besides we decline, conjugate and do a variety of other things with words all of the time, and all of these capacities make up the forces of the sentences.

Perhaps the mystery comes from taking the word in the list to be somehow the standard, as if there its meaning were really captured. Something odd has crept in. There are persons who study words, make up lists and hence standardize them somewhat for the rest of us. However, this is done for specific purposes that ought not to be transposed into anything big and philosophical. We need word lists, standard usages collated, dictionaries written, and synonyms and antonyms drawn up, but all of this is principally useful for kinds of teaching and writing. Collating all of that can be a kind of natural history of words, with all of the privileges and limitations accruing thereunto. Words can be treated also as facts. My point is not to deny that the familiar business of talking is not worthwhile; on the other hand, it is worthwhile because talking and people are what they are. Speaking is not taking dead meanings and dead words, and doing such original things with them that a philosophical exegesis and hermeneutic are demanded. Speaking is, of course, a matter of using words; but to know about speaking (and writing, for that matter) is also to learn that words are actually abstracted out of sentences and that meanings of words are not "simples" out of which meaningful sentences are compounded. So, what Professor Schrag finds so interesting philosophically I propose are obvious and overlooked facts about sentences and our capacities to talk.

However, there is also a danger in saying what I have suggested that simply flattens all the issues. One can conclude that there is nothing to think about and one can become so Philistine and so banal that no problems will be seen. This kind of killing of reflective initiative surely can happen by always involving commonalities and everyday circumstances. So, it might be well to rethink the matters involved. A list of words is different than a sentence, but how? For one thing a list is a form, too, but it is a form for a very definite set of purposes. The forms of a sentence, both grammatically and logically described, are necessary for a wide number of purposes. Logicians and grammarians find sentences more interesting than lists and for obvious reasons. The logical forms go a long ways in telling us what the possibilities and limits of sentences and words in them are. However, they do not tell us everything. People also have to be considered. Once we bring in people, the speakers, then we get a little closer to that *Dasein*, that highly particularized kind of being, that we are. But, it seems to me that the kind of person, his loves and cares; the issues he resolves and those he omits; the odd qualities of character he has managed; the manners and ways he lives—these and more, give the causes and reasons for words becoming so flavorsome and so interesting.

Philosophers have long since commented upon the formal necessities within which words have been given some of their powers. To note these, again, is to revive a subtle kind of reflection too. One can be glad, even more, to have phenomenologists and existentialists tell us about *Dasein*, for that reminds us that particular persons are exceedingly relevant. But the point gets lost when only general words are used. That "originative" factor is only noticeable at all because there are formal matters that obtain throughout. Clearly, the rules do not account for all that is said or meant. Actually, the originality can be accounted for not by something that is purely general and formal, but by the wonderful richness of the human tribe and the variety of activities they find necessary. It just may be that this kind of appreciation is not quite what philosophers can write about any better than anyone else; but it might engender wonder in which all of us can take a little solace. Besides, it might be a source of a homely kind of wisdom again.

Of course, many people are saying things that are not worth saying. The sayings still might be original. Words are still not just noises. A noise makes the sound or is the sound; but words are the sounds by which we say something and/or do something besides make noises. We can say new things with old words. Not every new thought demands an increase in vocabulary. Words are like that, and nothing in their nature is being violated or strained by that accomplishment. After all, that is what having a good command of language means, namely, that one uses words very well indeed. Thus, there is no reason at all for linking an "originative act" with words when all that the concept, "an originative act," refers to is what people do with words in their natural habitat, an ordinary sentence in relevant contexts. Using the words is a skill; but it is more than a trick too. The point is simply that the everyday contexts for ordinary people are quite enough to explain the novelty of most sentences.

Nothing extraordinarily philosophical or transcendental is required here at all. We need no special categories, no principles, no specialized critique, for logic and the speakers are, indeed, quite transcendental as they are. Mostly we need to remember only the large range of examples of word-usages and things people are doing while they talk. All sorts of factors might help, everything from word lists, the act of repeating words and learning words from a list, the difficulties of learning the new sound for a word, spelling a word, even making up a sentence. When we know a word well the sound becomes as irrelevant as the click of a man's teeth as he speaks something important. At one extreme, we have to learn to spell the sound and thus learn the word; at another extreme, we enunciate the word only to say something with it. The better we talk, the more we say. That is a matter of skill, not philosophy. The project is everyman's; and it is too many-sided and too common to be subsumed under any philosophic rubric. Talking is so ingredient in our common life that it has no singular presupposition or distinctive antecedent condition. It is engendered by everything and anything, too much for a generalization or a transcendental critique. The greater a speaker's skill and the richer his life, the more originality. The greater one's general capacities the more one has to say. To conclude thus is to make suspicious those abstract transcendentals by which to establish a critique of language in general. For there are not a few things but many that get us in on what people mean when they talk.

Nonetheless, we might want to admit that there is something transcendental about logic of itself. For the rules of language usage are not given by a single instance of meaningful talk. This is why the form of a sentence is not just "my form" or "your form," and thus the form transcends both my speaking and yours. It has to belong, perhaps, to English, or to a scientist's way of arguing, or to the syntax of questioning or the shape of asserting something. This is no small matter, but it is a far plainer kind of transcendental feature than Schrag or Heidegger suggests. But, then, so is the "I," who speaks, "transcendental," in respect to what he says. He does not say himself—he is outside the discourse the way the physical eye is outside the visual field. Once more, we can say that language only works at all when there is a subject who is speaking it, who is outside that language. This is a case of every person being transcendental in and of himself. But, putting these two cases together seems to make quite enough of a case for transcendentals. However, this is also a very commonsensical kind of reminder.[13]

IV

Mr. Schrag makes something of the following: "Even verbalized speech expresses as much by what is between the words as by the words themselves." All kinds of considerations are knit together here, such as: a concept of "language," around which we can link notions of being controlled, objective, subject to a science of linguistics, "institutionalized speech," etc. In addition, there is a correlative concept, that of "speech," around which are woven notions of "vital relation," uncontrolled and "non-institutionalized" language, language subject to a person, etc. Climaxing the delineation, a distinction is drawn between a phenomenology of speech, on the one side, and a logic of language, on the other. There is an intrinsic claim of each point that could be remarked upon in turn; but I choose to take them as a group,

---

13. These remarks are drawn from Wittgenstein's *Tractatus*, especially 5.632ff. and 6.13ff.

and I hope to show how they lose their force when the above quotation, around which they cluster, is examined in detail.

There is a time to say, simply, "Words are just words." But the time to say that is guarded by circumstances. For example, I might want to say it when I expected someone to do something to help another, but all that he did was talk. Then to remind the other person of how paltry words are has a real sting. But the need here was for some deeds. Or, if someone has spoken at length, it might be appropriate to say: "Words, words everywhere, and not a thought to think." To say "words are words" is not to make a fundamental point, or a minimal one, upon which other points can be added as if it were somehow foundational. However, if one asked: "What did you mean?" and got, for a reply, only a repetition of words, then one could say with due disgust: "Only words." However, that disgust marks something appropriate to the circumstances; and the circumstances have to be right, otherwise even one's disgust is rubbish.

But Professor Schrag's remark seems to take the "word" very seriously indeed. He makes something unexpected and almost unaccountable out of the fact that what we say is not words.[14] We say something with words and there is no one-to-one identity between words and what we say with them. And, it is not even the infinite number of permutations that we could compute for the finite number of words that in turn would give us the full range of all that could be said. The fact of the matter is that Professor Schrag is having difficulty here because he is trying to account for the richness of what is said as if it were a product of the words. That is not the case, quite clearly. Sometimes we hear or see only the word, a kind of noise or shape on paper, and we miss what is being said or done with the word. The isolation or abstraction of speech-sounds, or words, without any regard

14. Here it might be appropriate to note that phenomenologists generally seem to generate a good part of their problems by juxtaposing "words" versus "what is being said," as if this were a fundamental issue. Instead, it might be only that one is looking at language without looking at the language game. When that happens, absurdities abound. This is Wittgenstein's point against Russell. See Wittgenstein, *Remarks on the Foundations of Mathematics*, part V, no. 8, p. 166. But note also Rahner's notions about "an ontology" of symbolism, which arise again, because once having looked at words without their employment being thought integral, he has to get their connections to reality asserted by a single metaphysical thesis (*Theological Investigations*, "Theology of the Symbol," 4:221–52).

for the meanings involved, is strange. Usually we do this because of special interests or because the language has failed us. In the context in which words are coined and used something else obtains, for there the speaker's situation and the hearer's responses are intimately intertwined. The situations that occasion speech are every object and every event in the world. And language is so flexible and pliable in our command that it conjugates and means in respect to everything in a speaker's world. If we were to try to give a discerning account of meaning for every unit of language, we would need an equally discerning knowledge of everything in the speaker's world, and this we do not have. However, words are not even copies of anything, so knowing a thing exhaustively is no guarantee of knowing the meaning of the word for it.

Why is the author so struck with the way language works? Of course, words in the form of sentences say something, whereas words by themselves do not say anything. More accurately, speakers say something, usually in sentences and with words. But it is "with" words. Certainly speakers do the saying, and words are their means. What is needed before one speaks is having something to say. But that does not make language always an expression, nor does it suggest something mysterious about speaking. It is not between the words that something is imparted, but it is by the sentences, made up of words, that one says something. But people do the saying.

The issue about a phenomenology of language versus a logic of language does address an important issue. We can suppose easily enough that a mistake was made when it was said that logic was the science of meanings. For meaning is not a subject matter and logic is not its unique science. But the difficulty is compounded when it is thought that logical conditions solely describe the limits of how language becomes meaningful or nonsensical. Certainly a kind of logical prowess linked with the notions of older positivisms is partly responsible. Thus, there is a point to the phenomenologists wanting to take a wider look around and to watch the language in action. To call this a "phenomenology of language" does, however, suggest more than it can muster. The orientation is right however.

Whatever the merit of doing phenomenologies of everything, from language, to minds, to religion, it seems clear enough that nothing philosophical and necessary, *a priori* or traditionally transcendental, will come forth from a study of the uses of words. Wittgenstein thought about these matters, too, and while noting the importance of rules, gave up very quickly the notion of the sovereignty of logic as arbiter in respect to the meaning of language. When he said that one ought to remember that the meaning was the use, he was not making a philosophical pronouncement at all. Instead, he was urging that by using the words in particular ways, then they came to mean in an equally particular manner. To look at the uses was not to discover something philosophical, but it was to be able to circumvent the need for a philosophical rubric by attending to the people who spoke. This seems to be right, and a reminder of where a real phenomenology of language should lead. To know the use of a word is to obviate the need for further elucidation.

V

Professor Schrag has something to say also about speech and time. It seems to go like this. Language in the abstract looks timeless, whereas speaking in the concrete seems to put past, present, and future together. Something of great substance is being broached here, I suspect; but I am not quite certain how to phrase it for myself. The author has a title for his reflections, namely, "The Temporal Synthesis of Speech." But this is confusing, for it requires that one think that time has three modes, three ways of being for us. If the concepts, "past," "present," and "future" are taken to be names of kinds of time, again as if time were a something to be divided up, then we have all kinds of peculiarities before us. However, something deeper than that is being gotten at. For the author will have us ponder the way the sense of a question will make us think about, not the present moment (when the question is being uttered), but about the past or the future. Not lacking for an ability to think up nouns, he tells us that speaking, not, again, just the vocabulary or a word, adds that sense of "directionality." So without overt referring expressions or obvious pointers, we look to the past or future.

Again, I do not wish to deny that speaking includes these things. We can talk with words, which from one point of view are intrinsically timeless things, about past, present, and future. Time, indeed, is not in the words; but time is not "in" anything, for time is not that kind of thing. Once more we seem to have the need for a philosophical consideration made manifest for us by the way we have conceived matters. We must, therefore, think a bit about those concepts, "present," "past," and "future." By themselves, they are not names either, not at least the way "Fido" is the name of a dog, for there is no object to go with these time words. Nonetheless, they are concepts and they do have fantastic powers for us. Once we learn to talk with them, we can do remarkable things indeed. We can refer to things that have happened, and that is what becomes the province of the concept, "past"; we can hope for better things, and the concept, "future," gets its competencies thereby; and so, analogously, with the expression, "present."

But, my point is, again, to take the philosophical mysteries out of the notion of "speech" by alluding to the plain fact that language is indeed made up of words, but that some of those words are grammatical expressions for concepts. And concepts are not mysterious, even though many of their powers are used without being remarked upon or even at all described for us. Some of those concepts, like those with which we are here concerned, are so powerful and have so many skills tied to them, like hoping, caring, regretting, repenting, feeling lonesome for one's home of yesterday, etc., that it is quite impossible to do much more than reflect over a few examples. However, the few are enough to show us that what the author calls "temporal synthesis" can be seen more plainly as a capacity of a word. A capacity of a word is what makes words other than names; and these capacities to call up yesterday, hope for tomorrow, enjoy the present, these and more, lie within those powers that make words concepts. That is part of what we call the "meaning" of a word. Obviously these powers belong chiefly to the uses of the words, but they are intimately bound up with the word and its permissible uses.

But more has to be said. For what Heidegger and Schrag are after is, very likely, something different. They are not concerned simply with the fact that we can use individual words and concepts to measure and to mark time, for that is a feature of language that does not seem very mysterious. It is not past, present, and future, when named, that are difficult to explicate, any more than is clock-time or other kinds of measurement. Instead, it is the odd temporal-synthesis that takes place in a sentence without temporal words being therein employed. (We are back at Kant's problem.) So, for example, remarks like: "I forget dates more frequently than I used to"; "Let's hope that she will recover"; "Napoleon was a scamp"; "Rivers usually flow to the sea"; "Glaciers account for our interesting terrain"—these and more, already effect a temporal synthesis. Everything talked about seems to be temporally located for us.

Once more, there are ways in which logicians have noted that disjunction, negation, affirmation, etc., do seem to belong to the very form and structure of propositions. But the temporal feature of facts seems to be, not a matter of the form of propositions at all, but rather in consequence of their content and the way the world is. Oddly enough, it is also true that every fact has a temporal character and that universality and generality obtain here without exception. It is not a large step to say, again, that "time" must be somehow transcendental, perhaps in the manner of Kant, who thought it was never quite empirically perceived but was a reason-contributed form in which everything empirical was perceived. Heidegger and Schrag are sensitive to this issue, but the resolution seems to be unnecessarily complex.

For, again, we get the notion of inert and non-temporal words, on the one side, and living speech, on the other. We have noted here a variety of considerations that seem to make sense of the issue but these considerations are piecemeal. Perhaps they can be gathered together in another way without recourse either to Kant's "forms" or to the mystique of "speech" in contrast to "words." Is it not the case that the temporal character of all facts is expressed by the very grammar of the language?[15] Furthermore, even though one might be tempted to impute all the peculiarities of temporal characterization to "speaking," that notion puts too great a burden on the activity. Actually, every proposition contains time in some way or another, but the question is

15. Note Wittgenstein's *Philosophical Grammar*, especially part I, Appendix, no. 5, pp. 215–18, on "Is Time Essential to Propositions?" Leibniz argued in the 1680s that nouns, pronouns, even adverbs had a temporal sense. He is very rich on these questions and seems to suggest throughout a point similar to Wittgenstein's and the argument of this paper. Note Leibniz, *Logical Papers*.

"how?" It is a mistake to assume that "time" is "contained" by analogy with a box containing many "things," for time is not a "thing" at all.

The point is, rather, that the very logic and grammar of language must be reconceived. We have for too long thought that generalities of certain kinds, like truth-functions, "not," "or" and a host of logical constants, could easily enough be described as part of the very logic of the propositional form. But by thinking about the range of concepts and words earlier noted, it now becomes possible to see that it is not accidental, on the one side, nor graphically mysterious, on the other, that all propositions also provide a temporal order for everything. This is not because nature or the world or reality is temporal and propositions somehow invariant and eternal. The breach between logic and reality does not need to be invoked here. Instead, the grammar of a language in a peculiar and very sharp way shows us the harmony between thought and reality. If there is anything metaphysical to be said it can be said via the grammar of our language. Then the contrasting bifurcation between lifeless words and temporal speech, between eternal logic and the flux of becoming, gets another kind of resolution altogether.

Professors Heidegger and Schrag are very close to such a resolution and are in the right locus. This is one point at which the linguistic turn in a certain kind of phenomenology is a turn in the right direction. Furthermore, it begins to move towards the analytic philosophers too. But there is no precipitous breakthrough. The thought of the living grammar, the living rules, of an active and working speech does provide the clue. What is the large metaphysical surge in phenomenology around the powers of "linguisticality" needs to be controlled and mapped a bit. We can conclude, therefore, with Wittgenstein: "Like everything metaphysical the harmony between thought and reality is to be found in the grammar of language."[16]

Certainly Schrag is right to note that much technical language is more dependent upon the pervasive and rich world of everyday speech than is everyday speech upon the precise language of science. But, I do not find this thought very edifying. It seems to me that everyday speech, even in the author's sense of "speech," is rich, but this is so because the concepts, like those time-concepts, are so useful and

16. Wittgenstein, *Zettel*, no. 55.

do so many things for us. But this is what the grammar and logic of these concepts show us. All we have to do is try to talk and think without concepts, noticing the gaps that they leave. We are dependent upon them at every turn. This does not argue for their greater expressiveness or their proximity to time, being, or existence. No, it allows us to say that they are a different kind of concept, authorizing a variety of intellectual and other kinds of accomplishments. So the synthesis is not quite in speech but in the relations between speech, actions, facts, speaker, plus a lot more. Again, this is what the grammar of a working language finally does for us. Nothing very pretentious is happening. Instead, we have very powerful concepts, linking, when used properly, all kinds of activities. This is a remark, then, about words in use, and, of course, about the people who use them.

VI

Mr. Schrag dwells upon the fact that one does not have speech without a body. One does not have the teeth of a comb without the rest of the comb either. More is at stake though. It seems that our bodies also contribute "gestural meaning." Here I can only plead a reading of many descriptive linguists. For I think that they admit the point readily enough. Surely speaking is not so simple as putting on a language, as if it were ready-made, only waiting a passive occupant. Such a view is absurd. Language is bound up very minutely with the general refinement and sophistication of the whole person, body included. All the capacities of the person, his feelings, all the intensifications of his responses, all the specializations of actions of which he is capable, physical or otherwise, interact with one's language. Anything adding to the viability of language has indirect and pervasive effects upon our actions; and the reverse seems to be the case too. Language can make us better listeners, cause us to see more, even change the dispositions of the human heart over a very long run. So there can be no denying the intimacy of body and speech.

One needs no special pleading to acknowledge that speech from the clouds is very peculiar. Of course, people speak, and people do have bodies. We cannot think otherwise. Again, how does one make a philosophical point out of all that? Mr. Schrag is apparently not sorely pressed to do so. He has us recall that bodies are in space, that speech is a feature of bodily persons; and there we have it. It seems that speech must, and that "must" is fairly strong, gather some kind of scope that could be called "spatial." He has it that speech infects space "with value and meaning." Maybe that is what it does, but I find the thought rather hapless. Is it not, again, that our language, our words, when used, also require those abilities to speak of "before" and "after," "up" and "down," and other such places? Maybe that is to put it badly. It is not actually our words that require the ability as much as we, ourselves, do. We can then use words, quite ordinary words, to talk about "over yonder," "the other side of the moon," and many more spatial loci. Indeed, this is quite something, at least if you cannot do it for a while, or if you lack the words, for example, in German or another foreign language.

Once more we are at a crucial point. Just as Kant and other thinkers have wondered about how our language and our perceptions place everything in a spatial locus without invoking spatial concepts directly, so, too, do Heidegger and Schrag. Once again, the logic of all this is the issue. Trying to account for the generality of the spatial locating of everything we perceive tempts us to think that there must be something *a priori*, if not radically metaphysical, about "space" itself. But here Schrag's thought turns to the fact that all language is embodied, and we get some extraordinary reflections about the peculiarity of our having a language that is abstract now brought into vitality by being put into the flux of speech by a body. Once more, it strikes me that the notion of "embodied" language is rather redundant and superfluous. We need to know something else or, at least, have our attention drawn to other factors we have overlooked.

Once more, I find that Mr. Schrag has hit upon something. But it does not lead us the way he thinks it does. Nothing philosophical or existential is required to fill out the account. Instead we need only a painstaking examination of our language. Certainly we can look at words, but that does not get us very far. We have to look at the words when they are spoken, just as Professor Schrag suggests, for here words are used as names, as concepts, to make theories, and all kinds of other things. These do not occur without speakers. They do not even occur on paper, for a language written always has its genesis in speech. A language is spoken. That is where and how it gets used. One needs to look no further to elucidate most of Professor Schrag's queries. But the grammatical tissue, the net of ruled uses, is where the synthesis between non-spatial words and spatial reality is effected. The fact of the spatial character of our language is undeniable. The explanation does not lie in our bodies, but it does lie in the grammar of our language.

VII

Even bigger issues are enjoined in the latter two sections of Professor Schrag's long paper. For here we are told two big things that gave me pause. One, that speaking and thinking are both embodied; two, that speaking is an act of communication, the condition for which is the "inescapable situationality of being-with-others." The latter expression is even more profound in German, so I beg leave to consider it as it appears above. Apparently, "existence" is communal, and, therefore, speech can be communal. There is no world-less speaker, or, for that matter, thinker. So, we are told that the worlds of speaking and thinking reinforce and even require one another.

My misgivings lie with the strong expressions like "inescapable" and "require." There is a plainer way to note some things, maybe more modest things. Isn't it enough to give an account of all of this without going beyond describing our power to talk? People talk, and who is illumined by the additional notion that we are embodied? Whatever is said here seems at best to be redundant and even clumsy. And, clearly, talking has to be about something, call it "world" if you must call it something.

It seems to me to be the better part of wisdom to give the simplest possible account. That, I propose, is done when we gather some instances that are perspicuous. They tell us enough—we do not need to go beyond them, beneath them, or behind them. They are enough in themselves. And what are they instances of? Only language in use, or, plain talking. But talking is both *ad hoc* and ruled. The command of the grammar of the language is what permits us to be original. But this, too, happens in everyday circumstances.

CHAPTER 10

About "Understanding"

I

SOMETIMES A PERSON WILL say to another: "I don't understand what you said. Please define your terms!" One seems to be very close to a paradigm case here, something almost obvious and clear, for what could be more appropriate in such cases but a definition? What are definitions for, if not to tell you what a word means?

Furthermore, is it not almost a standard practice among most bright people to assume that misunderstanding a word means either that one does not know its definition or that one has a wrong definition? And a person is almost churlish or a misologist who refuses to give a definition when all you seek is the understanding of the word. For that is how matters seem to stand, namely, one, that a definition states the meaning of a word, and two, to know that definition is to understand the word. So we get a linkage between word, definition, meaning and understanding.

So much for the moment for words, considered one by one. There are other times when we are puzzled not by a word but by a group of words. For example, I read Abraham Cowley's poem "On Hope" and came across the line:

'Tis hope is the most hopelesse thing of all.

And suddenly I do not know what to say or how to respond. I cannot go on. Even Richard Crashaw's response to it ("By Way of Question and Answer") does not help immediately.[1] There is something surprising about saying that hope is hopeless, as if hope, without which men perish, is itself of no avail; as if hope (which Crashaw says, almost with the entire race) is not "our life in death, our day in night." Here I suppose we might conclude that the poet has gone wrong, that he has said something we cannot understand because he is plainly mixed up and mistaken on the matter of hope. In a given case such a judgment might, of course, be right. However, Cowley's line is paradoxical and initially a block to understanding because of another circumstance altogether. The surroundings are rather defective—almost intentionally so, I suspect—and Crashaw's dialogue eventually completes the environment and thus corrects matters. What was said no longer looks bizarre and quite so out of keeping with what we understand hope to be. "Understanding," then, is restored, not so much to the poem as to the reader.

This kind of help in gaining understanding is, I believe, fairly frequent and, also, clearly in contrast with other helps. I note it to show that it is different from the first example where a practice leads us to something written, a definition, which looks to supply what was needed, but more, which is deemed in itself to be the understanding and the meaning of the word. However, a third kind of case is also apropos. It has affinities to both of the above but is still different in some respects. I note it herewith at some length.

II

There are times when we do not understand something that is said, when the individual words are familiar enough and the syntax is recognizable, when there is nothing paradoxical, and the literary continuities seem to be there. So I read in Aristotle's pages that poetry is "more philosophical than history"; and I confess to not knowing what Aristotle means. When I think I have found out, it all keeps slipping away again. Suppose that I know the individual words and am familiar with philosophers and their books. Now the task of helping me becomes quite different again. When I say that I do not understand,

1. This dialogue poem by Cowley and Crashaw is included in Gardner, *Metaphysical Poets*, 169–73.

plainly, it is not definitions that are missing. In any case, definitions would not resolve the difficulties. In fact, I usually lapse in cases like this into saying, "I don't know what the author has in mind." The difficulty does not lie in the darkness of the words; rather it is that the words I recognize do not tell me what the author meant.[2] Thus I cannot understand. Again, it is not the words, but it is the sentences and the argument that do not make sense. The sense seems to be missing, however familiar the words.[3]

But let me take a harder case. The Apostle Peter, early in the life of the Christian Church, is reported to have been called before a distinguished group of religio-political leaders. One could imagine them, resplendent in their Jerusalem culture, urbane but still annoyed, curious, rather self-consciously responsible "rulers and elders"; and they began questioning Peter about the uproar that the teaching about Jesus and the resurrection was calling forth. Among other things Peter said: "And there is salvation in no one else, for there is no other name under heaven given among men by which we must be saved" (Acts 4:12).

Not much is said in Acts about the distinguished listeners confessing to not understanding that harsh and uncompromising saying. But the rulers did charge the Apostles strictly not to teach any longer in this name, and they subsequently harassed and imprisoned Peter and others. One fellow, a reportedly distinguished Pharisee and councilman, also a teacher of law, made a radical proposal, saying that the Apostles ought to be left alone; for if the teaching were of God, they could not be overthrown, and if it were not of God, it would wither away and the crowds would dissipate quickly enough. One is tempted to think that he had acquired somehow the sense of the situation—and hence understood a great deal—rather quickly.

However, that expression "there is salvation in no one else" has been a very difficult one for many people since. Peter said it in

2. Of course, that circumlocution about "what an author has in mind" can mislead us into a silly business of trying to penetrate his mind. For various reasons, I will later argue that that must be wrong.

3. R. G. Collingwood tells us something comparable in his *An Autobiography* about discovering Kant's *Theory of Ethics* as a young boy and being frustrated. "Disgraceful to confess, here was a book whose words were English and whose sentences were grammatical, but whose meaning baffled me." Collingwood, *An Autobiography*, 3–4.

a context where there were Jewish leaders around. So it was as if the remark had a sharp thrust—this name was the one whereby repentance and forgiveness of sins were to be given to Israel (Acts 5:27–32). One surely could sympathize with those Jews, who, well-trafficked in religious teachings, were suspicious of such a scandalous repudiation of the old and a radical and new departure. Not least, too, when the leaders could see plainly enough that Peter and John were common and uneducated men! It is as if the Apostles were using the old terms, "God," "repentance," "salvation," and more, but then rather spontaneously putting them into a new and different scheme of things. A new religious game was being played—the teachings were mostly the old ones but a new identity and location has been given all of them, by the incorporation of a new name.[4]

A difficulty for the Jew might be phrased: "Why this name?" One could easily imagine another man, a ruler charged with keeping peace in Jerusalem, a man who might have put Roman rule before Jewish law, saying: "I don't understand these fellows. Can't they see that they are disturbing the peace?" A modern reader of the twentieth century, imbued with popular ideas of everybody having a culture, that within any culture one finds a religion, might say: "I don't understand the intolerance here. Imagine him saying 'in no other name'!" A superficial and hasty hearer, one who is impatient with making up his mind at a cost, might comment: "What's it all about? Everybody arguing. Why do they do it? I don't understand!" From the above it should be clear that one could grade "misunderstandings." There are, indeed, kinds of misunderstanding, and no standard case. There is no one thing that is misunderstood and, hence, no one way to address the difficulties, for they are several.

Right here, then, we begin to see that a definition will not help all kinds of misunderstandings, for that supposes a standard difficulty. So, too, another sentence, ostensibly a statement, will not do it either because, again, that supposes a singular locus for the misapprehension. In anticipation of later comments, we note here that "understanding" might actually be so radically different that all such efforts

---

4. Some remarks suggesting this kind of thing—not about religion and Peter, but about Bertrand Russell and mathematical logic—can be read in Wittgenstein's *Remarks on the Foundations of Mathematics*, part III, no. 26, pp. 119–22. The logical morphology is similar.

are bound, almost logically, to fail. What if "understanding" is like having "taste" in choosing clothes? Then obviously one cannot provide "taste" only by giving people your judgments, unless you were also able, thereby, to engender the qualities of life and thought that "being tasteful," "having taste," etc., requires. But this is to anticipate.

We return to a consideration of the Apostle's remark. Misunderstandings would be easy to come by here, and failures to understand much of anything said by Peter could be imagined. But also, there would be a kind of odd understanding that opponents would evince if they said: "The teaching being what it is, send our best teachers after them. That failing, the police. If that doesn't work, to the gallows." However strenuous that seems, there is a kind of understanding here. For the opponent who saw that the teaching was disruptive, required careful consideration and even suppression, is certainly getting a grip on what is involved. One can suppose that the early Christians saw this kind of response as far superior to the indifference of the majority, though more painful. This illustration, then, adds to the variety of understandings.

However, my concern now is still a different kind of proposal. I want to think about the person who hears a remark like Peter's and says: "I wonder what his thought really was?" This remark is a very polite and sophisticated modern way to meet strong and baffling statements. It is much more ingenious and tolerant, too, than threatening the original speaker. It looks better. The *force* of the remark is usually to *suggest* that the reason for the bafflement is that the meaning and the thought are missing. If a way can be found to state that meaning, then understanding will obtain. This becomes a kind of paradigm way to address a whole range of misunderstandings. I want to argue that it is wrong.

For it looks as if the principal role of certain kinds of reflections, often philosophical and theological, is to provide meaning and to restate thoughts so that people can understand. I recognize the motive as being helpful and edifying and part of the noblesse oblige that goes with being reflective, learned, and a professor. It is not with the lofty motive I quarrel at all. On this occasion, I wish, too, to make a few exclusions. I mean to omit from consideration those who want to tell the meaning—and hence provide understanding—of current events, of modern art, of iconography, of the twelve-tone scale, of the student unrest, of rebellion, of racial strife, and the shenanigans of the leading politicians. I am certain that there are large numbers of psychologists and social theorists, along with a few philosophers and many theologians, who will gladly do these things for relatively small fees and in brief compass. Besides we even have theologies of culture, of politics, of the university already written up for those who have trouble understanding these inclusive and strange things. When philosophers got weary with doing that—and chastened besides by all kinds of nasty considerations about what "meaning" was and by a notion that they were journeymen and not pontiffs—the psychologists and social commentators, but also the theologians, took over. But one cannot discuss all of that at once. So, I will confine myself to the specific issue of philosophers and particularly philosopher-theologians, who have addressed the issue of understanding something that another has said. It is language that will be my focus, not least, language spoken out of a depth of concern and interest.

My particular issue will be a literary one. When a text or saying is not understood—such as Peter's "there is salvation in no one else" or Paul's "God was in Christ reconciling the world to himself" (2 Cor 5:16–21)—it is tempting to assume that one can write out the understanding of that text. This, then, comes to be called the theology of the text or even the theology of the author. It is as if one is asking for the thought of the author, the thought that authorized or engendered or accompanied the saying.

The circumlocutions, symptomatic of the difficulty, are: "What is your understanding of that text?" or "What does the author mean?" or "What is the philosophy (or the theology) of that text?" This kind of question is usually met by a response that purports to provide "the understanding," "the meaning" and "the theology" or "the philosophy" of the text. This pattern is very general and seems to be almost a rule for people who read and expound books and sayings. I do not include here all literary critics or all students of literature. My focus rather is a kind of popularization of meta-talk, espoused by philosophers, some literary critics, and certainly by most theologians.

Let me cite an example. "Meaning" became the *raison d'être* of philosophizing—so that when I once asked about the meaning of Shakespeare's lines:

> as if we were villains on necessity; fools by heavenly compulsion; knaves, thieves, and treachers, by spherical predominance.[5]

I, a novice and student, was told by the distinguished scholar and seer of Elizabethan drama, E. E. Stoll, to see the philosophers. One of them, in turn, did oblige by telling me something else, ostensibly the philosophy of the text and the Elizabethan world view of Shakespeare. This loomed up as the royal road to understanding. But enough of that for the moment. It was clear that the meaning of the text lay in another set of beliefs, ostensibly those that Shakespeare had to be also entertaining when writing the above lines.

In the present hour, the mantle has fallen rather heavily upon theologians, who illustrate the pattern most tellingly and often in an undignified and borrowed fashion. The examples are legion and look to be of a kind. Some find "holy history" and a certain picture of man and God, proposed by that notion, to be the understanding of the text; and some find a very abstract statement about human existence and its uncertainties and their resolution to be almost implied and meant by every text; others find process and change to be foreshadowed, or ontology, or something phenomenological, etc. I do not aim right here to exploit any one of these examples. It is rather that tendency of mind, that intellectual disposition, behind all of these. For such a tendency seems to grip most of us and cause us to think that when we do not understand a text "an understanding" is, in principle, to be sought and to be stated. This seems a persistent and almost standard practice and most certainly one that leads to mistakes.

This kind of misunderstanding of understanding, sophisticated and technical as it actually is, is, in turn, very difficult to diagnose. It is the kind of move I am worried about. For I am not proposing to provide the correct "theology" or "philosophy" or "understanding"; instead I want to show why there is none at all to be sought or found in this fashion. Why, in short, the orientation is wrong, and why "understanding" is something altogether discrete and different.

---

5. Spoken by Edmund in Shakespeare, *King Lear*, act 1, scene 2.

It is this issue which surfaces so plainly—in religion and particularly Christian religion—that I want to think about. Perhaps it is all the more odd that this should occur, respecting Christian teaching which is so obviously of the sort which says: "Everyone who hears these words of mine and does them will be like a wise man. . . ."; "present your bodies as a living sacrifice, holy and acceptable to God. . . ."; "make love your aim. . . ." (Matt 7:24; Rom 12:1; 1 Cor 14:1, etc.). The whole literature, Old Testament and New, asks something of its reader while it also provides this and that. Above all, the literature is not a catalogue of its writer's conclusions. It does suppose a discovery and a revelation of something, but not as a conclusion of its author's arguments. It is rather as if one's life will now be grounded and completely remade and the obscurity of everyday life also dissipated. Some kinds of pursuit will, hereafter, be dead for the reader and an arduously sought and discovered way of life now completely alive. If this be its achievement when understood, so that now one rejoices, is glad, is deeply relieved, is on a new path, it is all the more odd that an intellectual habit, one having to do with "how" to understand, should take over and blur the point of the literature.

III

Kierkegaard thought it odd and a misplaced intellectualism that everyone who did not understand what "love" and "God" meant should, therewith, insist upon a definition. So he says:

> The man who really loves can hardly find pleasure and satisfaction, not to say increase of love, by busying himself with a definition of what love really is. The man who lives in daily and yet solemn familiarity with the thought that there is a God could hardly wish to spoil this thought for himself or see it spoiled by piecing together a definition of what God is.[6]

Kierkegaard was very clear about himself and said on this issue that his refusal was not in consequence of laziness nor because his thought was too vague to entertain the request. He refuses the charge that he is simply obstinate or that he does not know what he is talking about. What he is denying is that every request for help in understanding

---

6. Kierkegaard, *Concept of Dread*, 131.

supposes a common pattern or a paradigm. It is the morphology of "understanding" that is the issue. What Kierkegaard is asserting is that a definition is not the way to an understanding of certain kinds of concepts—in this instance, "love" and "God."

For nothing is so natural, once one has assimilated a certain amount of philosophy and logic, as to conclude that a concept is a general term. Of course, we could all then say, a general term must be defined in order to be understood. Nor is Kierkegaard rushing to the other extreme and saying that concepts like that are indefinable a fortiori. His point is precisely that the criteria for "understanding" certain expressions like "love," "God" and "seriousness" are quite different than a general theory of definition or a general picture of meaning might lead us to expect. The contexts for the above words are respectively so different that to abstract them from that working context and put them into the artificial one of "definition" would be to misunderstand them altogether. So, we read him again about the concept "seriousness" (which his author Vigilius Haufniensis is urging upon the reader):

> It is so serious a matter that even to give a definition of it is frivolous. . . . So far as my knowledge extends, there exists no definition of what seriousness is. I should be glad of this, if it be true; not because I am fond of the modern fluent way of thinking which has abolished definitions and lets everything coalesce, but . . . because one does not like to construe in the form of a definition what thereby is made out to be something else and different from the thought that must be understood in an altogether different fashion . . . and loved in a completely different way. . . . To my mind, what I say here shows better than any definition of concepts that I know seriously what the question is about.[7]

Thus, Kierkegaard is not denying that "God" is a concept nor that "seriousness" is either.[8] If he had said "God" was a name only, then understanding, again, would be dissimilar; for a name is resolved by learning what or who is named. The resolution here is often

7. Ibid. Here I have re-translated the passage on pages 130–31.

8. This is specifically asserted in the *Philosophical Fragments* and the thought is developed again in the *Concluding Unscientific Postscript*. Note "God is not a name but a concept," *Fragments*, 51. Also note *Concept of Dread* about "seriousness," 14–15.

quite distinct. And generally with names, it is clear that we are having to do with a somewhat more primitive and easier class of words to understand and to explain. Concepts are unlike names. Kierkegaard thought, furthermore, that most moral and religious concepts were not to be explained and to be understood in the same manner as, for example, class concepts in the natural sciences and general terms used in logic and mathematics. That is why the delineation of concepts and their description was so constant with him.[9] But also psychological concepts were different—emotion words, also words like "reason," "understanding," "belief," "dread," "irony," "anxiety," "serious," "mood"—so different that he proposed that the entire attempt to increase our understanding of these by multiplying our objective psychological knowledge of anxiety, seriousness, emotions, etc. was part of a monstrous illusion.

As far as Kierkegaard was concerned, then, the attempt to get hold of the objectivities supposedly correlative to these words, as if they, too, were names for processes and subtle facts still to be unearthed, was entirely mistaken. He denied categorically, that there was anything there to get clearer about. That's why he can joke about the mistaken philosophers in heaven using a microscope to examine heads to see if they can find out what thinking is! Their and our illusion is deep-seated, and vast. It grows up in all of us and is extremely difficult to sort out.

Here Kierkegaard's sketch is like a radical redoing of the familiar picture we all have of mental life, of thinking, of knowing, of being anxious, in despair, being in dread and a host of the related problems of understanding and meaning. There are some strong resemblances to Wittgenstein's remarks. So, he says, "If God had looked into our minds he would not have been able to see there whom we were speaking of."[10] Why? Because when I am thinking of someone, it does not

9. Readers of the Kierkegaard literature will remember that he wrote about the concepts of "irony," of "dread," of "teaching," of "authority," among others, even using the Danish word for concept, *begreb*, as part of his titles. The "concept" theme also pervades his twenty-volume journal.

10. Wittgenstein, *Philosophical Investigations*, part 2, p. 217, and pp. 225–26. Also note the subtle remarks about an omniscient God and whether, supposing that there are people who go on and on calculating madly until the end of the world, He could know the outcome. Wittgenstein's point is that there is nothing "there" or "anywhere" for God to know. God, too, must calculate. Cf. *Remarks on the Foundations of Mathematics*, part V, no. 34, p. 185.

follow that there is always an internal picture of him that is there in my head to be apprehended. In fact, there may be no process, no internal activity, nothing objective and physiological and psychological, accompanying my speaking about a man. There would be nothing there for God to see any more than there is even for me, or certainly for another person. So, too, Kierkegaard says that despair is not an activity any more than sin is a psychological phenomenon or condition, to be discerned disinterestedly as one would a tropism, an instinct, a pain, or an itch.[11] Despair and dread have to do with ways of being conscious especially of oneself; but "consciousness," in turn, is not an internal state or a self-observable kind of mental activity. Instead, Kierkegaard is at pains to show the reader precisely how these concepts work, how complex they are, and how far we are from understanding them rightly if we only describe them with that sort of learning which is "indifferent." By contrast he chooses another form and another set of criteria that provide the appropriate context within which "understanding" can take place. He is not writing out the understanding or providing a written definition that can then serve as the understanding; instead, he is giving the words their employment, even their role in a linguistic context (as well as a non-linguistic context). Then gaining the understanding is something to be done by the reader. The understanding becomes a feature of a person; and it is not a statement, a definition, or a subtle point of view.

The issue is whether understanding is something that can be defined, bound up within a matrix of language. That is like saying—the meaning of "seriousness" is something that can be stated, if not by a single word, then by other words. To get that meaning is to understand the word, the concept "seriousness." But Kierkegaard refuses to define the term; for he insists that understanding here is not a matter of knowing a definition. However, he does not say that "seriousness" is beyond language or that it can only be expressed non-linguistically. Neither does he say that the word "seriousness" is only a "symbol" and that what it symbolizes is altogether different and can only be felt or experienced. It is not an activity or an experience, say like a flash of light or a pain is an experience. What one does with that word is much more complicated than simply naming a state of consciousness

---

11. Note Kierkegaard, *Sickness Unto Death* and *Concept of Dread*, esp. 14–15.

or describing a dispositional pattern. These might be involved, but more likely the role of the word is complicated by the fact that seriousness is not realized until one is deeply concerned about himself, maybe about immortality and/or the quality of his life. Therefore, Kierkegaard does not so much define the term as show why a man temporarily concerned about a governmental crisis, ". . . about the national debt, . . . about the categories . . . about a performance at the theatre," insisting all the while that he is now very serious, is really comic.[12] Here the language is, as Kierkegaard says, "twaddle," or "nonsense," existing "in order to conceal thoughts—that is, to conceal the fact that one has none" or is not really serious.[13]

Even that language in which one talks about and with the concept "seriousness" needs more than talk to be made sensible. That is precisely Kierkegaard's point. And it is not mere words, even a definition, which gives the hearer understanding of what "seriousness" means. As Wittgenstein said, "How words are understood is not told by words alone."[14] And it is characteristic that he added without further modification, the bare word "theology" to the above remark. Kierkegaard, in order to effect a similar point, sketches the mode of life, the generalities of concern and depth of preoccupation, within which seriousness could be evinced. A whole stage of life, or what Wittgenstein might call a "game" or even a form of life, has to be seen in order to understand what seriousness actually means. Then one looks not to the definition as a formula of understanding, but to a spirited and well-articulated person, within whose mouth, a word like "seriousness" has a definitive role.

So Kierkegaard notes:

> To understand/and to understand are therefore two things?
> Certainly they are; and he who has understood this . . . is initiated into all the secret mysteries of irony. . . . No, but that a man stands up and says the right thing . . . and so has understood it, and then when he has to act does the wrong thing . . . and so shows that he has not understood it—yes, that is comic. It is infinitely comic that a man, moved into tears, so much moved that not only tears but sweat trickles from him,

12. Kierkegaard, *Concept of Dread*, 133.

13. Ibid., 96.

14. Wittgenstein, *Zettel*, no. 144.

can sit and read, or hear, representations of self-denial, of the nobility of sacrificing one's life for the truth—and then the next instant—one, two, three, slap-dash, almost with the tears still in his eyes—is in full swing, in the sweat of his brow, with all his might and main, helping falsehood to conquer.[15]

To use again Wittgenstein's language in conjunction with Kierkegaard's thought, it is as if the meaning of some words is so bound up with a complicated mode of life that the meaning cannot be simply "said" to you. Kierkegaard would have it that nothing will show "seriousness" except a well-developed personality. Tricks with words and pedantic things are bound to fail. To understand some words, therefore, requires that one be "shown" something. And what can be shown only, cannot be said.[16] Sometimes it is the "how" that shows forth. Therefore, the same sentence may be the truth in one person's mouth and a falsehood in another—not because of anything like "relativism" or because of a radical subjectivity—but rather because words are never true simply as words. They need mouths, persons, situations and the right context, even the right feelings, emotions and passions to go with them. All of this is part of the non-linguistic that will frequently have to be shown to you, to be seen by you, before the word or words can make sense.[17]

Kierkegaard recognized all sorts of differences here. There are times when a piece of language does not express everything, in and by itself, because the occasion has to be right. The application and time for the expression, when these are right, show the reader what is meant. For this reason Kierkegaard complains about language being, by itself, "abstract" and hence not telling you very much. On the other hand, when one puts the language back into existence (what slipshod popular philosophy calls making it "existential"), then one has the words and the application all bound together again. This, too, is why oratory and rhetoric is so dangerous in all circumstances where the

15. Kierkegaard, *Sickness Unto Death*, 221–22.

16. "What signs fail to express, their application shows." Wittgenstein, *Tractatus*, 3.262. Of course, Wittgenstein thought, too, that the whole language mirrored what no part of it could say—that is a different point than Kierkegaard made. Wittgenstein rethought the latter issue too.

17. Note here Kierkegaard's difficult reflection on this matter in the *Postscript*, 180–83. Also, in the pages about Adler, called in English, *On Authority and Revelation*, he addresses a comparable range of issues.

meaning can only be seen in the application. Again, this has a resemblance to Wittgenstein's notion that what words slur over, their application says clearly and also to the extraordinary concreteness that is required by his insisting that language makes sense only when it is seen in a language-game.[18] But Kierkegaard has another target, too, namely, the notion that concepts and words can be translated into the language of "pure reason." He denies that there is something called "pure reason" in which words work—again his whole thrust is to show that there is nothing purer than ordinary men and their reasoning. And words get their meanings in these concrete applications. "Pure reason" and its language was for Kierkegaard very much like Wittgenstein's language without a game, super-logic and super-language that no one spoke or could speak.[19] It was a chimera and another kind of sophisticated misunderstanding altogether.

But there are again those occasions when language and what it is about also requires not a translation into a purer and more conceptual form, but the appropriate kind of action to go with it. Thus, the man who wants to stop mutiny can speak all he wants, yell at the top of his lungs, and his words may yet be powerless. Kierkegaard's point is that the very meaning of wanting to stop mutiny requires not only strong language against it but the language plus the speaker's absolutely "unconditional obedience." Then, the very meaning of his words is shown by his refusal to waywardness, by his resolute stand.[20]

But, herewith, I wish to turn to sharper formulations of the case, where it is asserted that an understanding of a text or a piece of language or a part, thereby, can really be provided in something called a theology, or a philosophy.

18. Kierkegaard, *Postscript*, 415ff. Note Wittgenstein's remarks—and the selection could be large in number—in *Tractatus* 3.262ff. and *Remarks on the Foundations of Mathematics*, part V, no. 8, p. 166, where a point is made about Russell's not putting the notion of proposition into an actual game—hence the concepts become too general, etc. So, Kierkegaard notes that the saying "God's word endures forever," would be meaningless perhaps until the moment when you were utterly weary of the world, when it could come to life and become clear and mean everything for you.

19. Kierkegaard's *Papirer* X 2 A, 354 (*JP* 1, 7), but see also the *Postscript* where the language of speculation is treated in the same way.

20. Kierkegaard, *Works of Love*, 121–22.

IV

What I am concerned with is complex. It might be seen in the notion that a philosophy of mathematics, say something like Russell and Whitehead's *Principia Mathematica*, purports to give you the understanding of mathematics, something you would not get by learning to do mathematics itself. I am not able to criticize that book and its detailed logical and algebraic construction in a manner anywhere near befitting its magisterial bearing. But Wittgenstein did criticize it in a very responsible way in the pages that have been put together by G. H. von Wright, R. Rhees and G. E. M. Anscombe under the title, *Remarks on the Foundations of Mathematics*. Instead of the *Principia Mathematica* being simply a clearer and better statement, in ostensibly logical notation, of what really is the same in mathematical notation, Wittgenstein insists that *Principia Mathematica* does not give you the understanding, the same understanding, that doing mathematics would provide. Even the notational system, by being different, introduces something new. So he says that reading *Principia Mathematica* is a "game that has to be learnt"—it is not the same game of mathematics, now simply being done in a new set of symbols or different sets of words.[21] Furthermore, Wittgenstein uses mathematical considerations and *Principia Mathematica* to note a drift in a very deep and tendentious kind of reasoning that most of us get caught up in almost continually. This is to assume that there is a kind of logical structure of the world, surely of all of language, "which we perceive through a kind of ultra-experience (with the understanding, e.g.)." This logic, he says, is "a kind of ultra-physics," describing the logical structure, by reference to which we get to the foundational and ultimate, final and rigid, general and abstract kind of reality.[22] And furthermore we are inclined to think that the logical structure of propositions is somewhere in the background, "hidden in the medium of the understanding."[23]

21. Wittgenstein, *Remarks on the Foundations of Mathematics*, part I, no. 18. But note the following sections too. Then again in Part II Wittgenstein argues that logic is not foundational to mathematics and gives subtle reasons: nos. 3–8; 40–45, etc.

22. Wittgenstein, *Remarks on the Foundations of Mathematics*, part I, no. 8; but note also *Philosophical Investigations*, part I, no. 97.

23. Wittgenstein, *Philosophical Investigations*, part I, no. 102. Readers of Anselm's *Cur Deus Homo* might recognize this kind of thing in the way he uses

It strikes me that what Wittgenstein criticizes so deftly and with such detail is one consequence of a kind of mistaken movement of reflection and language that also produces the "pure reason" philosophy that Kierkegaard is polemicizing against. Wittgenstein has Russell, other sophisticated philosophers, and his own *Tractatus* in mind—as cases of conceiving the role of logic and other abstract and formal concepts and relations as the court of appeal when the ordinary language could not be understood. It was as though that highly refined conceptual net was also more meaningful and more understandable than everyday speech. Logic, especially a precise and highly formal logic, was then a less ambiguous and a more carefully contrived medium for genuine understanding. Whatever the criticism might be of all of this, I think it incumbent to say as Sallust, the renowned Roman did, when speaking of his retirement from public life to write histories, that his readers could be assured that he does this "rather from justifiable motives than from indolence." Modern technical philosophy, Russell and other logicians included, has made people think very hard, and for that one can be thankful. But with the Hegelians and certainly many theologians, the creation of a meta-language, a language of meaning, has often been an escape from difficulties.

To return to the kind of thing Kierkegaard was combating, one needs only to read his *Postscript*. For there a kind of speculative philosophy, mostly Hegel's, is the target. Again, it is as if we have a new tissue of language, a new conceptual system, a skein of thought in virtue of which the meaning of art, of politics, of morals as well as religion is finally to be declared. Obviously as Kierkegaard saw all of this, that higher and purer thought, would "say" the meanings that were implicit in all of the rest. There was no room for something unsayable being shown (as Wittgenstein had said about logic and logical form in the *Tractatus*). The point of philosophy of this highly abstract sort was that it would present the understanding, the meaning, of all of the major cultural enterprises of men. It could be declaratory, explicit, and clear. It was as though all other lesser kinds of speech and activity needed this array of philosophical concepts. Everything else, including Bible, science and even forms of literature needed to

---

"understanding"; the mode of argument by which he shows that Jesus Christ "had" to die whereas the Scriptures just tell you He did; the role of "transcendentalia," etc.

be translated into this new medium before understanding could take place. Kierkegaard admired a thinker who could exercise an "omnipresent autopsy," a dialectician skillful enough to carve up the bodies of thought—but only if he then left them as they were. To convert them into something else was the fault of speculative philosophy. What purported to be a restatement, even a matter of making explicit what was already there, actually turned out to be a deception. So he says about a near contemporary, Heiberg, who had written "philosophically" about immortality "that the answer is very easy, owing to the fact that they have already the question, wherefore one cannot deny that they answer the question, but one can indeed affirm that the question is not what it seems."[24]

But more, if everything—art, morals, religion, and politics—is articulated in a language-medium that is highly formal and abstract, Kierkegaard asserts that any understanding taking place therein is actually a misunderstanding. His point is precisely that the language of art is all tied up with moods, with liking, with appreciation, with disliking, with a variety of aesthetic concerns. To strip all of these away to discern a supposed "dialectical structure," ostensibly purely conceptual, is to leave out what makes art what it is. So, too, with the ethical. He says:

> If anyone were to say that this is mere declamation, that all I have at my disposal is a little irony, a little pathos, a little dialectics, my reply would be: "What else should anyone have who proposes to set forth the ethical?" Should he perhaps set it objectively in a framework of paragraphs and get it smoothly by rote, so as to contradict himself by his form?[25]

Readers of Kierkegaard's *Either/Or* and *Stages*, as well as others of his pieces, will remember that his point was to deny that we could have one language-scheme, a philosophical system of concepts in the "about" mood, which would be an objective statement of the meaning of the aesthete's language and behavior, the moralist's, and of what he called Religions A and B. His literature does not argue the issue, except with a most skillful *reductio ad absurdum*. For by showing that

24. Kierkegaard, *Postscript*, 154. Note analogies in Wittgenstein, *Remarks on the Foundations of Mathematics*, Appendix II, 55ff.

25. Kierkegaard, *Postscript*, 137.

there is a language that inheres in what he calls the stages of life (they are several, aesthetic, ethical, ironic, humanistic, religious, etc.), he makes clear how intimately the meaning of what a man says is bound up with all kinds of things, moods, passions, feelings, interests, lack of interests. His rubric is "stages"; and it is not altogether inappropriate to remark that that term covers much of what Wittgenstein alluded to when he spoke of "forms of life."

Kierkegaard lets that kind of meta-language of meaning, that philosophical scheme, simply manifest itself as absurd. His own creation of poetic and pseudonymous authors, whose talk is all bound up with their wants, their activities, their emotions, their behavior, makes it obvious enough that to understand them one must also see "the warp and woof" of their speech and their activities over a period of time. Their language is "of," not "about" alone; and what it is "of" is no simple factor at all. Kierkegaard never once approached an expression theory of language, but he everywhere places the language that is meaningful in a matrix that is human, concrete and as complex as behavior itself. It is always its pragmatic and what he calls its "existential" feature that contributes to its meaning.

Already in Kierkegaard's day, it was becoming an established practice to write out "the" understanding of the Bible in another language medium, that of a kind of philosophical theology. As already noted, this was an instance of a practice given a kind of dignity and style by Hegel's extraordinary philosophy. That philosophy seems to have captured a pattern of behavior that is early and late among the intelligentsia. As I have noted, it has analogies in Russell, the ideal-language philosophers, certain sophisticated logicians, and apparently, the early Wittgenstein. It has vulgar and aristocratic forms. One can, of course, lump too much together here and claim too many likenesses and forget the differences. But I think there is a way to state something diagnostic that might warrant considering these forms of reflection together. I wish to turn to that in conclusion.

V

Think for a moment about all the theologies there are. By and large they seem to speak to the fact that men do not understand the New

Testament, what Christianity is, or what such and such authors (relatively few, by the way) mean. The primitive materials of the Old Testament and the New are fairly circumspect in quantity and, for that matter, in quality. A certain kind of acquaintanceship and familiarity, therefore, is not only possible but quite often achieved. But this is not enough in order to get understanding. So, a learned industry has developed—critics, low and high; historians; stylists, logicians, students of culture, of society, of psychology, of thoughts have been clustering about. One is reminded of the story of the two fat princes who got all their exercise by walking around one another. In this arena of scholarship, too, things are so well developed that the professors can surely get their intellectual muscle in pretty much the same way. I do not wish to say that there is not something that has been learned and that there are not still things to be learned. Each discipline might contribute as it will. I am concerned here principally with the picture of how understanding will come about.

It looks as though theologies, as well as philosophies, have to be very synthetic indeed. There seems to be no telling from where the understanding might come. If the difficulties in understanding are as massive as everyone seems to think, then one might indeed need linguistics, ethno-linguistics, history—and everything else empirical and/or non-empirical—just to squeeze a little understanding out of a text. The difficulties are formidable, for it is almost too much for any one man to do in an ordinary lifetime. If one must formulate a "theology of" (or one could call it a "philosophy of" too) say a New Testament or Old Testament author, book, age, era, party—and if one must formulate it out of the vast empirical learning (or whatever else it might be, conjecture, insight, hypothesis, "heart unto heart calleth," etc.), then I suggest that no theology, no "understanding," will be proffered that will be worth the candle. For that is a game that simply cannot be any longer played. There is too much material for one man. More than that is wrong, however, for the conception of theology as a "statement of the understanding" is also logically wrong.

Another way to see this difficulty is to start with the competing theologies. Supposedly they are the "understandings," the statements of understanding, that have somehow come forth. But now, how can they be understood? There is something deeply and seriously wrong if a proposition of the New Testament or the Old had two or more complete analyses and statements of meaning. One must suspect the analyses or, better yet, one must suspect whether the notion of supplying an analytic account and restatement of the meaning is an altogether mistaken effort. How did we get into that posture? Besides all that, when one has competing theologies, they no longer are the understanding of something else but instead have become something very difficult to understand in themselves. And that is where we are these days. We cannot even decide which one is the understanding.

Right now we suffer from the plethora of theologies. We can no longer understand them. There are strange efforts to try to put them together and get some sense out of them, but such schemes are so vague and so loose that they seem, at best, platitudinous and, at worst, so formal that they are really quite empty. The contention that theologies are cultural expressions would be apt except that theologies are too different in a simple culture and too much alike across cultures to give credence to the view. Theses of historical development again are impressive by their sheer scholarly weight, but they do nothing to bridge the distinction in logical types that keep cropping up. And here the historical transitions do not tell us very much about the differences in kinds of theologies we now suffer. Theologies, like philosophies, are logically opposed and do not look as though they can ever coalesce. And then there is the dreadful notion, a third option, born of sheer fatigue or absolute thoughtlessness, that keeps coming up, to the effect that every so-called understanding is only "mine" or "thine." This view tries to teach us contentment with the differences on the strange ground that there is only a kind of subjectivism, a kind of relativism, a kind of private slant, even on the issue of meaning. Whether my "meaning" of Plato's or Paul's text matches Plato's or Paul's is seemingly fortuitous at best. Worst of all, this attitude takes alternative theologies to be the sign of opulence and prosperity, as if then one has creativity and fecundity—and, of course, meaninglessness and intellectual anarchy.

To say that a theology or a philosophy is only a personal expression is to give up the enterprise altogether. Then the meaning of a text must always be an episode and be without any kind of rule and order. Admittedly—this is the way the scene looks; but then a deeper diagnosis is in order. The view we have been noting is like admitting that everybody is sick, but never really getting at the cause of intellectual ailment.

This state of affairs is symptomatic of a grave difficulty. For not only is theology not being paid any attention because of its wild cacophony, but, worse still, is it that those who pay it attention now have to assimilate first a general theory about the competing theologies. Besides, there are several of these too, and all of them are highly dubious and, unkindest cut of all, religiously useless. Thus, they are a long way from giving the kind of understanding that a theology offered in the first place.

One might be at a loss in all this if someplace a familiar chord were not being struck. Suddenly it sounds again. It resembles the earlier efforts to get sense out of competing philosophical systems. For there, too, people did the history of philosophy in a desperate effort to find a philosophy; they talked about the evolution of thought and emergent factors; they shifted to logic and a more subtle backdrop against which all the popular statements looked like adiaphora; they tried to show that competing systems of thought could be otherwise understood in patterns, in mutual synthesis, in opposition; and some said the whole business was nonsense and ought to be given up altogether. Then, too, there were positivisms and skepticisms that said philosophy was one more excrescence, for which one was better without. Amid all of that, there were still small voices and I wish only to extend the hints that have been dropped to this theological arena.

Might it be that understanding is not at all something that can be written down, like a theology, a philosophy, a super-conceptual scheme, a meta-language? Granted that, one has to ask two things: what is understanding? and, what is theology or philosophy? By responding to each briefly—and supposing the reader's attention on the issues raised in the earlier sections of this paper—perhaps the academic convention will be thwarted and some kind of answers proposed.

First, about understanding. Certainly understanding is not one more activity or process. While we can certainly say with real sense that "understanding" is something that people do (people, not animals, the dead or inanimate objects), still this kind of "doing" is not like "reading," like "talking," like "peering intently," like "writing," etc.

That is why we can say "stop talking" and expect a response in silence; but "stop understanding" makes no sense at all, because there is nothing to stop, to cease doing. Of course, I can stop trying to understand an equation, but that would be to stop doing the calculating—again, another activity. And the endeavor to make "understanding" a very subtle process, so supple and insinuating, so deeply inward, must also fail. Wittgenstein notes:

> We are trying to get hold of the mental process of understanding which seems to be hidden behind these coarser and therefore more readily visible accompaniments. But we do not succeed; or rather, it does not get as far as a real attempt.[26]

The endeavor must fail because understanding is not an esoteric psychological process at all. And that is not to give up anything foundational or empirical; nor does it counsel intellectual despair.

Instead "understanding" is a capacity. But it is, in most instances, a capacity that is taught.[27] There is the activity of looking that supposes the eyes and the right muscles. But "seeing" is not only looking—it involves all kinds of deft powers, abilities and even discriminations that have to exercised by the individual himself. The capacity to understand is not subject to the same limitations as activities are. I stop reading; reading is interrupted, reading is by the minute or hour; I can command it. Understanding is more like a quality of the person—he has it, indeed, but not like an activity. It is an achievement. He does not lose it by sleeping for an hour; but he may lose it by a desperate life or laziness or not caring. It cannot be clocked, but it does characterize some people's mature years. If you lose it, it is not like a process ceasing or something being turned off. The capacity is gone, like sight in old age, or moral feeling in reprobates, or aesthetic taste in the Babbitts.

Because the Christian religion required understanding, because, too, understanding was a capacity, Søren Kierkegaard refused to take Hegel's philosophical-theology and other theologies in its mode with any seriousness at all. There was a sense, of course, in which

26. Wittgenstein, *Philosophical Investigations*, part I, no. 153. Also note the extraordinary passage in *Zettel*, no. 446, beginning: "But don't think of understanding as a 'mental process' at all."

27. Wittgenstein, *Zettel*, no. 421. Note the remarks, too, in *Philosophical Investigations*, part II, where the questions revolve in part around teaching capacities.

Kierkegaard said Christianity could not be understood, but this was so because granted the way men were, they lacked the capacity to assimilate it. The point of his *Fragments* is to show the reader that Jesus Christ brings the capacity and the condition to the believer, so that faith (again, a passion but also a capacity) becomes possible. Kierkegaard refused to write out another philosophy and one more theology, for any endeavor to do that would, if intellectual fashion were followed, be a betrayal. "Understanding" could not be written out for anyone else—results like that were a travesty and an illusion. Most particularly would this be so, if understanding were really a capacity. Then the aim is to get the reader from no capacity to the capacity. It is, indeed, to activate him but to do it by stimulating his self-concern, thereby producing his capacities.

How similar this is to Wittgenstein. He, too, refused to write out a philosophy, for the whole point was that philosophizing was an activity (*Tractatus*), not results. Even the later works are like that, refusing to take psychology to be a new access to "understanding," "emotions," "knowing," etc.—for that would suppose they were activities or processes (philosophical perhaps)—or refusing to do up another philosophical system or even to refine that of the *Tractatus*—for that would suppose "understanding" was an interpretation, a restatement, as if every instance of understanding was like having an interpretation. But he refused to do anything like that.[28] For to understand a language was more like "being able," "being empowered," or as he says, ". . . to be master of a technique."[29] It does not suppose an interpretation—rather a capacity. It supposes that one knows how to follow a rule or, at least, what to do.

Kierkegaard stressed the "capacity" issue, too, and in a variety of contexts. Early and late in a short but intense literary career, he argued that the understanding required in most of the areas covered by "philosophy" and "theology" was a capacity. But that could not be

28. Note the pages in the *Blue Book* on this issue, 31ff. Also R. Rhees, "Preface," vii–xvi. A good example of Wittgenstein's refined reflection on this kind of thing is to be seen in *Philosophical Investigations*, part II, no. 192, where he says: "When you say 'Suppose I believe . . .' you are presupposing the whole grammar of the word 'to believe'" and not a state of affairs that can be asserted, etc.

29. Wittgenstein, *Philosophical Investigations*, part I, no. 199. "And to *think* one is obeying a rule is not to obey a rule" (no. 202). Again, nos. 609, 634.

conveyed as though we had knowledge. So, he drew a distinction. The communication of knowledge is direct, impersonal and in the "about" mood. Here one does write out the "knowing." But where understanding is the aim—as in morals, religion, even the subtle areas of epistemology and logic—here one is trying to communicate something he calls a *Kunnen*, a capability, a capacity. This requires in the writer a certain kind of indirection, where he will use his authority and his own pages, not to write out a theory but rather to engender a capacity in the reader. Albeit a philosophical and theological writer—or what Kierkegaard would call "a reflective writer"—would not, therefore, simply write out a command or an order either. His pages would have, indeed, an indirection about them.[30] The question would then be, perhaps, of what kind could they possibly be if understanding as a capacity was supposed to ensue? His own *Fragments* and *Postscript* are a kind of answer. For they are, as he says, of an "algebraic" and logical sort, with the addition that he subsequently clothes the issues also in "an historical costume."

His pages are not, above all, the understanding of morals and Christianity. They are in the nature of a treatise on logical problems (which his *Journals* indicate was his first title for the *Fragments*), but a logical account of the kinds of concepts and their connections to emotions, to passions, to actions, that one would find in New Testament Christianity, in the Socratic dialogue, in popular aestheticisms, in the working moralities of his day, etc. Here was the logic in a new mode, a laying bare of what he thought of as the conceptual (he called it "dialectical" too) factors connected with the moods, feelings, emotions, passions (he lumped these under the "pathetic")—and all of it in an historical setting. In a way, this is the pattern of all of his work, from first to last. He is doing "grammar." Then, the aim of it was to show the reader that he had to mime, to mimic, to do something, in order to achieve understanding. Again, there is something here that makes his pages a kind of morphology of stages and ways of life. There are linkages between what a person is, his moods and subjectivity, and what and how he speaks.[31]

30. Kierkegaard, *JP* 1, 651 (*Papirer* VIII 2 B, 83). See also, "The Second Lecture," *JP* 1, 657 (*Papirer* VIII 2 B, 89).

31. This is why the *Postscript* is called by Kierkegaard on the title page "A Mimic-Pathetic-Dialectic Composition."

But lastly we can turn again to the question of what this makes of theology and philosophy. It is tempting to say that if theology does not state the understanding of Christianity it is then nothing at all. But here the judgment is too precipitous. For both Kierkegaard and Wittgenstein this is not the end of the reflective life at all. There is plenty still to do and to suggest.

Here, however, I choose to answer the general question by saying that both philosophy and theology do not state the understanding, which one then assimilates as another gloss upon the original text. Instead understanding is a capacity that one achieves with and by the first-order literature. The purposes of theology and philosophy are not to provide meaning but they ought to disclose the rules that will enable one to see how understanding can be achieved. One might note as an example how the grammar of a language works. Save for the rare grammarian, who ruminates about grammar as if it were the subject matter, the normal use is that one learns from it, not what to say but how to say it. One learns typically, not the grammar but how to speak grammatically. So with logic, one does not learn what to think; but one might learn more than logic too—one might learn to reason logically. But to become grammatical and logical are both very easy—for there are those who do both without the application of gross and violent stimulants—and very hard—it seems some people, even those who teach them often do not quite succeed. This is, finally because both are capacities and not simply bodies of discourse. To acquire the latter is easier for many than to acquire the former.

If one asks, then, what theology does, one can say simply that it provided the rules, perhaps in these contexts where the difficulties occur, by which the capacity called understanding will grow. Depending upon the characteristic issues, this will mean that one will discover how to put on and to use with purpose the language of the Scriptures. This rather than inventing a new conceptual scheme by which to state its meanings! To understand it will suppose a capability; and that might involve holiness, self-concern, honesty, guilt, and all the rest that Scripture already discusses. These do not come by assimilating theories; but the right kind of talk could well force one to look in the right place and to consider the surroundings that one's life gives his words. For misunderstanding in morals and religion, as well as those areas having to do with the pursuit of wisdom, might well have to do with incongruities between the quality of one's life and speech rather than incongruities simply between the parts of speech.

Both Wittgenstein and Kierkegaard discovered this and repeatedly drew attention to it. The interest in metaphysical schemes, whereby one can summarize reality in a paragraph or two, seemed to both of them the height of absurdity. But neither rejected metaphysics save as something to be done only on paper. Wittgenstein, who so succinctly had stated the case against philosophical knowledge of transcendentals in the *Tractatus*, just as succinctly brought the transcendentals back again in his later work. However, with an enormous difference. For the meaningfulness of talk about God, about moral matters, about happiness, all now inheres in whether one is really in that game or not, so that one's life will really bear out one's talk. If there is nothing to go with it—the language will be drivel. By the same token, if one does not understand the language, it very probably will be because one does not choose to be so trained and formed that one can ever find out.

Why else did Kierkegaard say that the principal thing with the New Testament was to be trained by it? Most of us do not want that. We indulge our weaknesses by making "understanding" of confounding matters another intellectual matter. Why did Wittgenstein say "theology as grammar," except that the right rules do tell you what is what.[32] And the essence is expressed by the grammar, but in such a way that the essence in matters of faith, the understanding, is to become the truth, and not just talk it. How words are understood is not a matter of words alone.

---

32. Kierkegaard's theme throughout was training. Note his *Training in Christianity* and *JP* 1, 707 (*Papirer* X 1 A, 658). Wittgenstein's remarks are to be found in *Philosophical Investigations*, part I, nos. 371–73. Also *Zettel*, no. 144.

CHAPTER 11

About Understanding and Religious Belief

THERE ARE MANY KINDS of misunderstanding; and there are many ways not to understand. It is very hard to gather up in a single embrace all that is involved. So, too, it is with understanding. Think how many different qualifications would be needed to explain what is involved in saying: "Oh yes, now I understand!" Indeed the concepts, "understand," "misunderstand," and "not understand," each and all, are highly ramified.

But there are some cases that loom up in some situations and become typical. And it is a few of these types that I want to allude to here. The attempt will be made so to state the cases that an inherent perspicuity will come forth respecting particularly the difficult matter of understanding and not understanding the Christian teachings. In what follows, then, I want to sketch a few instances.

I

A rather extraordinary story is told in Holy Writ about an old priest, Zechariah, and his wife, Elizabeth. According to Luke, these two were promised a son, who would make "ready a people prepared for the Lord" (Luke 1:17). These two elderly and devoted people were overwhelmed with the tardy prospect. They fitted this also into a conception of God and His promised land that had nurtured them and their people for a great many years. Therefore, it was not surprising that when the child was born, everybody rejoiced. The old man very dramatically called the boy "John," even though the name was unknown in the families. More than this, he burst into poetic song, within which he again put the old stories together to include his new son. Among other things, he remembered that God had promised to save the people from enemies and all who hate, for that was a good part of God's oath and covenant, well attested heretofore! Moreover, he dared to add something new, namely, that young John should prepare the coming Lord's way and long-expected prospects among the suffering people.

Years went by and perhaps all of us know something of John the Baptist's story. For he himself preached rather widely, once more fitting the very tangible promises of the earlier prophets to the prospect of Christ's coming. But when Jesus came, things seemed to go wrong. John was imprisoned and one can easily imagine his perplexity. His father's poem, his own preaching, plus all the prophet's love, had linked the Messiah with the crooked being made straight, the rough made smooth, with no more hatred and the abolition of triumphant enmity. But in that lonesome cell, after a lifetime of preparation for a Messiah, so manifest that "all flesh shall see the salvation of God" (Luke 3:6), John's understanding began to falter. In desperation he hurries his friends to Jesus to ask: "Are you he who is to come, or shall we look for another?" (Matt 11:3 and Luke 7:20).

Imagine his disappointment, his chagrin, his hurt! The one who came after him, who was so mighty, who would burn the chaff of history with an unquenchable fire, what kind of Messiah was he to a man languishing in a dirty cell?

Jesus answers him to the effect that the blind receive sight, the lame walk, and the poor have good news preached to them. Not a word about release for the captive John or being saved from the hands of those who hated him. Besides, there came the almost shocking conclusion: "And blessed is anyone who takes no offense at me" (Matt 11:6; Luke 7:23). What an answer to a man who was promised much and was suffering more, mostly because of God!

This is one very startling occasion for misunderstanding. Most of us have a very tender regard for our dearly bought expectations. Civilization, culture, learning, and even the poetry of the fathers can easily enough conspire to mold our conception of what we want, what we need, and what would constitute our fulfillment and happiness.

Nothing seems both so obvious and so essential as our own intimate convictions about what would make us truly content. Unlike most men, John even had a pious father, he had shared deeply in an expectant prophetic tradition, and, besides, had a successful career as a prophesying preacher behind him. No wonder, then, that he could not easily—and that is all we have a right to say (for he must have found his joy)—put it all together with suffering all over again because of the Messiah. It all must have seemed a very serious mix-up.

Then, too, there is the altogether new note. For Jesus says in effect that that man is happy, is blessed, apparently whatever the other conditions, who takes no offense in Him. This is to link, granted Jesus' ministry and teaching, human satisfaction and happiness with hearing Jesus' words and doing them, despite enmity, one's own society, and familiar expectations. Think how easy it is to be offended. It looks as if the Messiah does not care enough, as if He does not see where the problems lie, as if He is not morally and politically committed, as if He does not understand man's needs and visions, his deepest moral cry, and most urgent yearnings for happiness. Instead we hear Him cry: "Happy is the one who is not offended in me."

This surely is an occasion for not being able to go on. For if that is the way it is, then Christianity indeed looks out of step with the most advanced thinking as well as concerned social planning. "Blessedness" has never been a joke; on the contrary, it is the great desideratum and goal of most personal striving as well as the expression of the most sensitive and refined social consciousness. Here, however, one must simply pause and ask himself just what is involved in this conception of blessedness. The Christian teachings are not an obstacle to understanding always because they are other-worldly (though this aspect can be difficult), but rather because they confront the rather plain and heavily trafficked view of happiness (via prosperity, no enemies, no war, no suffering) with another this-worldly proposal, that one can find blessedness in being passionately given to Jesus and His suffering way. And strangely enough, that blessedness can begin with John, in prison, or not, as the case might be.

We do not know the rest of John's intellectual history, though his ignominious fate is clearly transcribed. It is almost as if the enemy triumphed even in a ghoulish and spite-ridden way. . . . Perhaps it was that the education of John did not cease until the last moment. For he had a great deal to rearrange—promises, hopes, poems, fatherly regard, the whole picture of life, enemies, friends, possibilities, even the view of what God was.

Perhaps, too, with expectations and promises being what they are, with human potential being projected and thwarted by social and political ideals, we, too, are very inclined to link God with good as we see it and happiness as we know it. The coming of the Kingdom looks like it may be effected by common cause, by liberality, by God and man in educated tandem. Then our pattern of understanding is made firm by the very degree to which we get committed to these overarching cultural idealities. It is not difficult, after a while, to fail completely at comprehending what is apparently incongruous and out of step.

It should, then, be no surprise to balk a bit at Christianity, which is so radical that it proposes a new conception of happiness itself, almost relieving us of the oppressive burden of the other, while not slacking our will or encouraging effeteness. Once that conception begins to change at least one obstacle to understanding Christianity is removed, not so much by learning as by a subtle change of orientation and heart. One might say, in brief, that if one gets trained to this new way of finding happiness and gets it linked up even with suffering and unfulfilled expectations, then a source of misunderstanding is also done away with.

II

There is another kind of failure of understanding when somebody says: "The trouble is that the word 'God,' is a symbol and it doesn't mean anything today." We all know that this is said also about salvation, sin, repentance, redemption, atonement, heaven, and a host more. If we think that these hang together with God, in a kind of conceptual net, then it makes a kind of superficial sense to say that "it," i.e., the whole batch of teachings, just does not make any sense for, of all things, "modern man."

It is not mine to speak for the whole age, so I confess only to reporting the difficulties. And I know there are all kinds of inspired students of these matters who are preparing themselves to supply a new set of meanings to all of these erstwhile lifeless symbols. According to some, flirting with phenomenology and Heidegger is bound to help; others are convinced, though not altogether convincing, that Whitehead's metaphysics will resuscitate the whole scheme; and some are all for radical surgery and will construe everything in the scheme in the light of a neglected feature, like "obedience," or "hope," or some secret feature of linguisticality. For reasons which quite escape me, others seem to think that a kind of meaning can be salvaged if one strips off everything Godly, divine, and otherworldly, leaving something necessary and ruggedly human by which we can get our bearings again.

It all sounds as if the words are in trouble. They have gotten trite, too familiar to matter, or worse, they have plainly worn out. It is one thing to be alert to contemporary scientific and political ideas, but it is exceedingly dangerous to state them in traditional Christian terms. For then an alien content is introduced. It is another matter altogether to say traditional Christian things in terms that are fresh, imaginative, and contemporary. Nothing said here opposes the latter. If this is where the difficulty lies, then it can be supposed that the realm of meanings is in fairly good health. The difficulty is that there is so little light in or on that realm; it is dusky and dark and one is never sure what one is finding. Words are obvious enough, we seem to think, but their meanings are harder to get at. Once the words and the meanings, like husband and wife, had a happy relation, and where you had one, you had the other. From there on, though, the story gets a little burdensome; for I am not sure if new meanings have somehow happened along (maybe they are emergent the way new women are to a restless husband) and are seeking a word—trying to muscle in or maybe slither in, or whether we really need new words, too, to go with the exquisitely refined and deeply cultured meanings that are now ringing the world.

But vagueness about this relation between words and meanings is almost in order; for again, it is like the disorder between two people, when after a while, one does not know where to put the blame. The difficulty, I suspect, is often simple, seen from the outside, but terribly confounding when seen from within. To point it out from the outside is not the same as resolving the difficulties when they are felt within as the loss of meaning and the inability to understand. But here, unfortunately, we can only say a thing or two from the outside. Perhaps the most singular way to frame the issue is that we all think that in every instance of the use of language there "must" be an interpretation of the word in order that the word mean something. And we continue to think that, over and over again, because we forget that being meaning-blind is like being tone-deaf or color-blind. Being color-blind is a matter of not being able to do something, just as being tone-deaf is not a mistaken interpretation, but is, rather, a lack of capacity. One is not able to hear tones and to discriminate tonal qualities. But not "being able" is what counts.

There is a time and a place for interpretation, even with religious words and teachings. But it is not the case that every use of a word needs an interpretation, or some kind of mental act of assigning meaning, before one has a use for the word. This issue will be described in another context in the third section of this paper.

So with understanding and being meaning-blind. It is an inability to do something. This inability does not depend upon, first, a mistaken interpretation, or no interpretation at all; for interpretation is not required at all. It is not as if one interprets the word first, thereby assigning the meaning, and then, secondly, goes on to use the word. Contrariwise, to understand a word is, indeed, to know its meaning, but that is only to be prepared and poised for one of its uses. The meaning of a word, that which we commonly believe a word somehow has, is a pseudo-object—actually no object at all. When one uses a word, in ways that make a difference and that are recognizable, then, and then only, can we say that the word has meaning. But interpretation is not required in most cases; for the employment of a word is a practice, a ruled use. One simply learns that. To be able to use the word is to understand it.

To say, then, that the word "God" has lost its meaning is usually to misconstrue the difficulty. For most of us are then led to believe that the meaning, which we apprehend ostensibly by an act of thought, call it interpretation, or insight, a "knowing," that that meaning is obsolete, or lost, or no longer correct. Therefore, we cannot, supposedly, go on using the word. But if the use of the word is what we are after, not first, an interpretation, then we have to ask: what uses does the word "God" have? An entirely new perspective then opens up.

Take as an example a kind of human trivialization that has a long history, that called Philistinism. When one is a Philistine in taste, one refuses to discriminate and to exercise judgment. In religious affairs, one is a Philistine when one has no spirit, no vision, and no imagination. Philistinism is the all-too-human proclivity to be average in wish, hope, and accomplishment, to be content with being like all the rest. But even in such a denuded human situation, there comes the striking theme that with God all things are possible. Purposely, we have placed that thought in a Philistine-like setting, in which no more possibility is conceivable than a dull average mentality will engender, and that is very little indeed.

If one asks, within that context, what the God-idea means, one could say without qualification that it is all tied up with the notion that all things are possible. But this is not saying very much, unless one knows when, to whom, and why, one says it. Then the range has to be increased, but not just on paper, for what is required is a non-linguistic exercise and use too. The uses are practices indeed, calculated to get a man out of the narrow tract of experience that has closed in upon him, that makes him think that he knows how things must go, what is very likely, and surely those that can never obtain. So his convictional scheme has to be broken up by the new thought of a God for whom all things are possible. This is not all, though, for unless a hope grips him and unless his boredom and tedium, maybe even despair, are vanquished, the use of the thought has not been realized. But this is not to say that the latter, the new emotion, is always dependent upon the former, the new conviction. They may sometimes vary independently or even happen in non-concurrent order. One might be stirred by the hopefulness of a man who starts with hope before he knows such about God, who is the source and object of that hope.

This is to tell us, then, that the word "God" means something. But how? "God" means something mostly because it has a power to effect differences in thought, behavior, emotion, and long-term disposition towards oneself and the world. This theme about God is a theme about possibility, and that is not so much to be interpreted as it is to be imbibed. It is for the human spirit like oxygen is for human breathing. A new lease on life is what the concept of God provides. Motivations and spirit will return and life will no longer be trivial and meaningless.

How tempting it is to say that the idea of God is old-fashioned and that it has lost its meaning. This is where we earlier met the issue. However, if what we have said has described a new setting for the issues, then it is not the idea that is in so much difficulty as it is all of us Philistines. Perhaps science and popular learning have been construed for us so that we believe that it all adds up to a new scientific determination, which means that there is no possibility, so that the past is indeed prologue. Maybe someone, a teacher or writer, has put science in that picture. But now comes another teacher who says that with God all things are possible. That suggests even another employment of science, an unheard of veto on common sense wisdom, a diatribe on dumb submission. With all of that one is released to new hopes, new fears, new possibilities. And these are the "meaning" of God. To know "about" that is to understand, but in a lesser and linguistic sense: to do these things, to find joy and a lasting hope, is to understand in richer and wider senses. To have been enabled, empowered, emboldened, made strong—these are the uses of the concept of God. Then one understands indeed.

The surface grammar of the word is one thing, and it can be read off the language and what the terms include and exclude; the depth grammar is something else altogether. To be a student of despair and hope, of novelty and boredom, enough to see the tie-up between these and the words, is to know in an altogether different way the rules of life and faith. This kind of understanding is not a function of literature alone but is gained only when one has used the literature to forge one's life—and then thought about that!

Of course, this is to change the focus quite a little. No longer are the words in difficulty but rather it is the human Philistinism that is the cause of the difficulty. For it is very hard to see how one could put the words of the New Testament to work in one's life if one stayed trivial and average in all of one's judgments and behavior. It is this sort of thing that makes Wittgenstein's remarks about a form of life so pertinent. For he saw that there are times when the meaning of a word depends upon the sentence and paragraph in which they are being used. But more, when you know that the whole paragraph is a part of physics or religion or making fun, that that is the game that is being played, you can place the word and surmise a lot about it at once. Then there are times when a dismal judgment of despair is understood far better, or even understood at all, when you know that the form of life in which the words made a difference was, e.g., Philistinism rather than, say, a vigorous kind of activism like that of Napoleon or St. Paul. Not everything meant by the word is said by the word; some of that meaning has to be shown us by the quality of life in which the word has a genuine force. Some of that meaning is shown us by the form or stage of life.

This is to say, then, that understanding certain teachings, especially those of Christianity, is all bound up with seeing the kind of strenuous life that produced those words. And if one places those words in one's own mediocre life or in the familiar context of an everyday life where even moral judgments are seldom taken with seriousness, then a subtle kind of misunderstanding begins to develop. It is as if the triviality of everyday culture that we all share plainly gives no role for such magnificence and extravagance of hope, of novelty and powerful motivation, as the New Testament suggests. One can, of course, try to reconstruct the historical situation that was primary for these sayings, but that is an exceedingly long way around. A shorter and surer way is to change one's own life, make it a little more primitive and plain in pathos, so that it becomes a setting for the New Testament extravagance that is faith, hope, and love, *extraordinaire*.

This is not so difficult as it seems. For our lives are often so lived that deep feelings and plain concerns, consuming self-concern and primitive wishes for happiness have only been masked over, smothered by proprieties, and not actually lost. Our conformity to the world and its fashions has often merely blurred pathos and not altogether extirpated it. So it is almost a self-knowledge, a self-acknowledgment that is called for; a grief that is unrequited, a disappointment that we have lost in being like others when we really wanted to be different, a refusal to see our distinctiveness in the desire for peer approval. When these come back in force—when we let them manifest themselves—then it is like an essay in honesty, an effort in being true to oneself. Then the conditions for understanding the New Testament come flooding into one's life again.

III

We are thinking about "understanding" and what it entails. We have noted one kind of obstacle to understanding Christian things that looms up in the New Testament itself, especially when it locates happiness and blessedness in a way that is exceedingly strange and unfamiliar. But secondly, we then turned to the odd consideration that "understanding" itself is over-intellectualized, as if it always is related to word or words as an interpretation is supposed to be. We offered, instead, a case or two that allowed us to see that understanding was, more often, the ability and capacity to do something—follow a rule, recover equanimity, re-do one's posture towards the world. Now, however, we want to take up still a third focus for misunderstanding.

This has to do with a tendency to misuse and to over-evaluate the general ways of talking that make up much of theology. Not for a minute, though, must one denigrate all general concepts or every remark, theological, or otherwise, that has those powers to make us take in a large swath of the world around us. We will note this feature of theology later. But here we are noting a misuse. For misunderstandings are sometimes very specific in origin, so that we are not able to say simply that we have a problem in the discourse or in the conceptual scheme *per se*. It may not be that all misunderstandings are stateable in general terms because some of them are difficulties that are indigenous to a person, not to a concept, a theory, or anything stateable at all. Under these circumstances, it is absurd to believe that a highly general remark, or a piece of specialized terminology, probably theological jargon, will provide a complete explanation of the individual cases.

A certain conception of the power of theology seems to us to be at fault here. In what ensues, then, I propose to look at theology when it is conceived to be, in itself, an understanding of a text or of a teaching. Perhaps this will make clearer a source of difficulty.

Whatever else theology is, it is not "the" understanding of a text. It might be an explanation, by which one can understand, but it is not in itself the understanding. Think of mathematics, for an example, where someone not understanding Pythagoras and his ingenious notion of the square of the hypotenuse of a right triangle equaling the sum of the squares of the other two sides, is asked to compute it algebraically: if that fails, one can do it geometrically and see the squares. But those are calculations and projections; not the understanding but the means to the understanding. However, the understanding is not in the words, the figures, or the numbers. It is rather an achievement in the life of the person. But a person does not typically understand only once, though it happens often rather suddenly; for "understanding" is not like a flash of pain or an episode like a spell of nausea. It does not go away unless one loses his wits, for it is not an experience, a happening, an event in your psyche, a process going on like the flow of blood.

To be understanding is rather to be able, to be empowered, to have a capacity. And all of these remarks are not about words on paper but about people. With understanding, one might finally be able to speak to the point and see the issues, do the right thing, and make no more mistakes. In the Christian context, guarded by the use of the New Testament and some of church practice, the aim is not to provide the understanding only in a piece of theology, for that is an absolutely egregious error. But theology, instead, is like calculating to a mathematician, philology to a linguist, and discipline of the child to the wise parent, the means to the understanding, not the understanding itself.

Understanding has to live as a capacity, as a kind of potency, in a person. Of course, it can be lost; and in Christian literature we are rather fully warned about the duplicity of worldliness, of the unrepentant spirit, of the hardness of heart, wherein understanding can be darkened and capacity thus lost. So the utmost of care is in order to guard one's life, to keep oneself from falling; for here a fall might mean more than a bruise. Instead one might lose everything, even eternity. Of course, one must be reminded that one is not altogether alone here; for there is a rich and very peculiar sense in which one does not understand in and for himself and in which, instead, God Himself supplies the condition and becomes part of the capacity. But even this supposes a willing disposition and a seeking man; and to be so misled by the world and by one's spirit, so as to think that nothing matters, or that one does not need God is, again, to lose even the grace that will make the difference.

But the issue is, again, what theology is. Surely, it is not "the" understanding; but it might be the explanation by which one understands. It might be the logical portrayal that will end an ambiguity or clear up a confusion, or it might be an argument establishing a point one had not thought of. There is a way to catch all of this up by saying that theology is something like grammar, which does not represent an understanding of a language as much as it does the tools by which to use it with understanding, or a set of rules, again, that are reminders of the way subsequently to behave.

We have often heard it said by proponents of new teaching methods that it is not enough that children merely learn to add, multiply, subtract, and divide but that they should also come to understand mathematics. It is a rather complicated matter to discuss, for we are a little hard put to it to state very clearly what counts as understanding mathematics. Part of the issue is, though, that it does not seem enough for a child to know just that two plus two equals four, when he can know "why" four and not seven or ten. A picture of mathematical understanding includes more things than just giving correct answers, having true beliefs, and being proficient. We might say it like this, then, that much of mathematics is learned as though its variables, mostly numbers, were uninterpreted, mostly raw and brutish. But to interpret them is only another way to allude to the fact that they must be given meaning. Unlike words, which are only words at all because they already have meaning and are usually teachable only when they mean something and when something can be said with them, numbers are terribly formal and empty.

Before we can understand something, even numbers, they have to mean something. "Understanding" and "meaning" are interrelated and very closely indeed. Therefore, in mathematics we begin to get a glimmer of understanding when we get a little rationality mixed up with the numbers, when we know about numbers as sets and can give reasons for the true answers in addition to the answers. But there is more, too; we have to do something with the numbers, such as tell time, estimate this or that and apply them to a thousand relevant situations. In addition, it might be that when one understands one has, too, these facilities by which to do more mathematics. This is, in brief, to give some meaning to the numbers. But this is not done by a theoretical stroke; instead, theories and practices, probably together, insinuate their way into a life history, by forming capacities in the individual. The person understands when he can say "why," estimate, describe, and do a host of things, using mathematics.

So it is also in theology, with differences to be sure, but also in a manner something like this. Theology is a kind of interpretation of religious teachings, but only in the manner of keeping a person from repeating the words of Jesus and the rudimentary commands of the Apostles as if they were formulae. Those teachings, simple and plain as they are and fairly standard through the centuries, are analogous to numbers and do need to be assimilated. But repeating the creed can be like doing sums, without the understanding. One would be a fool, indeed, who learned set theory as if it were another formula and was not able to answer "why" four, rather than three. And theology, which is learned like the creed, is equally absurd if repeated by rote as is set theory; for it is not the understanding any more than is "set theory." Both are the means to understanding and understanding is, again, an achievement in the life history of the individual.

Theology is itself misunderstood if it is thought to be "the" interpretation, meaning, or understanding. But there is something devilishly common and almost plausible about that misunderstanding. There is something about the highly general terms, "being," "ontology," "process," "truth," "reality," and a host more, that makes theology, like philosophy, appear to be about another level or another depth (one can choose his metaphors here) that is more fundamental, truer, better in every way. We are led, almost imperceptibly, into the conviction that if we could only get clear here, we could clear up misunderstandings on everything lesser. But if what I have said makes any sense at all, this picture of conceptual levels and the dependence of our working language upon a super-language is altogether wrong.

A misunderstanding of Christian matters can ostensibly be any one of a number of things. One may have a wrong picture of understanding itself. For if we cannot understand the Gospel until an understanding is written out, surely safeguarded and defended by reasons that command acceptance in public debate, then we are mistaken about both what "theology" is as well as what "understanding" is. For, as I should want to argue, theology has to have good reasons and be unequivocal and clear in order to say something; but this makes it usable only to gain understanding and never to be it.

Understanding, on the other hand, may occur because one has used God's grace, because one is pure of heart, because one has done the things he has already heard commanded. Some may understand because a theologian has explained, with technical means perhaps, how the world is when it is referred to God, when seen as His Creation, when happiness and God are re-ordered. But that is to say that a capacity that is hurt by sin, by deception, by weakness, by dishonesty, by half-hearted thinking, is restored by God working even through, of all things, theologians.

CHAPTER 12

The Nature of Religious Propositions

A RE RELIGIOUS PROPOSITIONS COGNITIVE? That the question can be put at all indicates that the vulgar-vernacular language used to describe and explain them no longer seems adequate. Once it would have been quite enough to ask: Of what are they cognitive? For if there is a single and necessary epistemological standpoint, a cognitive ground to which all propositions are referable, then there are conceivably a common sense and common premises for all learning. This is the conviction about cognition that has sustained supernaturalistic philosophies. For any supernaturalism turns out to be a vernacular kind of language and reflection that construes even moral and religious sentences by analogy with those sentences descriptive of nature. And it is because the convictions and beliefs about the possibility of such cognition itself have changed that the vernacular accounts no longer seem relevant. The issue now is to show how religious propositions can be cognitive at all. Any descriptive philosophic account that takes for granted the possibility of cognitive meaning of religious sentences no longer meets the issue. The issue is now stated in the question: Are religious sentences cognitive?

I

Attempts to translate religious sentences into other linguistic-reflective systems are also fraught with difficulties. It has been the claim of some philosophers that there is a unique philosophical standpoint, qualitatively distinct from all other kinds of standpoints. As

Kierkegaard noted about Hegel, there are those who contend that philosophy is reflexive, a kind of awareness about awareness, in which trans-empirical reals are to be apprehended. Conceivably, then, there are at least two levels from which sentences are to be understood: first, as the expression of feelings, sensory intuition, imagination, and issuing in poetry, moral judgments, religious literature, and even empirical science; and, secondly, from the reflexive philosophic and truly cognitive standpoint. In this latter kind of understanding, the achievement is among others the translation of religious sentences into an even more abstract linguistic system, and the extent to which they can be thus translated is the extent to which they are true. This is by now a relatively familiar treatment of religious sentences by the philosophically sophisticated. Again, this kind of translation coincides with the vulgar view that there is a single philosophical standpoint, that there is a hidden "nature" and "truth" to which such a vantage point gives cognitive access. Here, also, there is ample ground for doubt, for if philosophy is not the cognition of trans-empirical "reals" but only of the forms and modes of reflection and expression, then nothing whatever is gained by translating religious sentences into philosophical rubrics.

On the other hand, it has been irresponsible thinking that has led many technical philosophers who have been otherwise known for their care and precision to insist, without careful analysis, that all religious sentences are simply nonsensical. Instead of the patient and exacting analysis of religious sentences with that kind of neutralization that the dialectical and linguistic tools of technical philosophy permits, we have seen, instead, a quick dumping of religious sentences to the heap called the meaningless. This is understandable psychologically, when one remembers that the vulgar-vernacular philosophies had so defined the religious sentence that even an acknowledgment of the likelihood of its truth seemed to come close to being a religious act.

Religious faith (or "belief" as it too is called) and cognitive belief have been defined so as to be almost indistinguishable in kind. And especially is this apparent when religious sentences and all others claiming to be cognitive are articulated within the same system of language and thought. It has been easy for anyone who denies the cognitive quality of a religious sentence to move too quickly, and by trading on the analogy between religious belief and cognitive belief, to insist that, if these sentences were meaningless, then there could be no faith or belief. This position is clear enough if one thinks about "believing" a descriptive sentence that purports to be true but yet is nonsensical. And contrariwise, to admit that there might be cognitive significance to a religious sentence seems almost to admit that one is a religious man. But this is all the more reason why precautions are in order. The long discussion in theological history as well as the constantly shifting focus in philosophy ought to counsel even more care and solicitude than otherwise. And where the passions and enthusiasms of men are so proximate, as they are in religious matters, more care and precision is essential rather than less.

II

An extreme resolution always tempts the student of these matters. There are numerous illustrations, some of them recent, of such extremes. If one argues that religious sentences are cognitive and make truth claims, then the assent to the truth claim is a kind of belief. If the difference between being religious and being non-religious or irreligious can be cognitively described, then, it has often been urged, this difference is statable in terms of the sentences that are denied or asserted. The use to which creeds and other groups of sentences have been put by religious practitioners is a case in point. But, even here, difficulties have been acknowledged. For even the most avid adherents of creeds have known that assent to the truth claim of sentences is not a sufficient personal qualification to make one religious. Furthermore, the differential between persons that makes it easy for some to respond affirmatively to the sentences and others to respond negatively does not seem attributable to the ostensible truth function of the sentence. Therefore, both from the side of a religious interest and from a somewhat more disinterested cognitive side, there have come serious questions. More typically religiously motivated is the question—how do the personal qualities of the religious life stand related to an act of assent to the truth of sentences, whatever their

content? And the cognitive interest is paramount in the question—
how do we know religious sentences are true?

Beginning on the side of cognition, it is easy enough to insist
that religion is not cognitive at all and that being religious is not "believing," at least in any sense analogous to cognitive assent or belief.
This kind of analysis saves cognition from the apparent absurdities
of religious knowing claims and yet demarcates an area, attitudinal
and emotive, for religion. Arguing from the limits of cognition, one
then proceeds to exclude cognitive components from religion, arguing that religious sentences are not propositions and are not cognitive
but, instead, are expressions of convictions and attitudes. And these
latter are not to be confused with the convictions or attitudes present
when we say that something or other is true.

Then from the side of religion there comes a somewhat similar
rejoinder. Sometimes one must admit that the motives for this kind
of rejoinder are engendered by a need to defend religion against its
learned despisers, but often too the case is made in order, ostensibly,
to keep religious faith distinctively religious. Thus it has been often
noted that, if religious faith is only an act of assent to true sentences,
then this act of belief does not include many of the most important
ingredients of religious living. The insistence upon cognitive religious
truth gives maximal significance to the act of its acknowledgment.
In order to combat the danger of a kind of intellectualism that might
attenuate the stress upon other qualities of the religious life, like love,
a sense of sin, etc., religious thinkers also push to the extreme of
denying the cognitive component altogether. They then identify religious faith, not with belief (erstwhile cognitive), but rather with trust
and confidence and loving. In the latter instance, then, one denies
cognition in religious sentences for the sake of faith understood as
a quality of a man. In the former instance, one denies the cognition
in religious sentences for the sake of the intellectual consistency. But,
in both instances, the cognitive status of religious sentences is denied, and the endeavor to describe the subject's religious act of belief
by analogy with cognitive acts is intentionally decried. And to such
extremes have both recent philosophy and also much of recent theology brought the argument. This is the point towards which kinds of
positivists and some radical fideistic Protestants seem to converge.

But I should like to suggest that, despite the apparent agreement between two parties otherwise disparate, this position is not as significant as it might seem. One may concur in the attacks upon the systematic constructs in which religion has been described without thereby agreeing that all religions are simply non-cognitive. For to say the latter is to neglect the fact that religious sentences are cognitive, but in somewhat peculiar ways. To deny that they are cognitive in familiar ways is pertinent, for most theologians have been so intent upon saying that they are cognitive, without distinguishing the peculiar sense in which they are so, that criticism is deserved. Perhaps, too, religiosity is primarily a quality of persons, not of sentences, and perhaps religious faith is not analogous to cognitive belief; but one can concede these points and still recognize a cognitive content in the religious sentences.

All of this is a token of the confusion that has long been manifest in the discussions about cognition and belief, reason and faith. Most philosophers, and certainly theologians, have shared the view that to admit cognitive components in certain kinds of sentences is to admit certain behavioral consequents. But there are no necessary or even probable consequences between the act of admitting the truth of objective cognitive sentences, whatever they concern, and other acts and attitudes of a subject.

Theologians frequently speak as if the admission of cognitive values in an ostensibly religious sentence "necessitates" the religious life, and philosophers seem to be holding in turn that a non-cognitive attitude (if this is what faith is) "necessitates" that religious sentences be non-cognitive. All of this reflects the confusion created by those who, in construing religious sentences as cognitive, also insisted that the cognitive act of believing them was a religious act of faith. This is an ambiguity closely related in kind to that noted in other places between the "is" and the "ought." But in religious theory, principally because the "ought" is so frequently psychologically described, and also because the transformation of the personality is so paramount, the confusion has been between the statement of a truth (the "is") and the consequences that knowing the truth is supposed to effect (the "ought"). Without noting that the nature of the transition from an objective and disinterested apprehension of true sentences to a subjective quality called being religious is not itself an implication nor a *natural* movement to be described as a relation of cause to effect, the distinction intrinsic to the peculiarity of religious sentences is thereby blurred.

It is with the intention of drawing these distinctions that the following is written.

III

Religious sentences are cognitive, but in a manner that begs elucidation. They are cognitive of a possible way of constituting one's life and daily existence. There are truths about actualities and truths about possibilities. As long as men cannot know descriptively and as an actuality the future that does not as yet exist, they only encounter it as a possibility. A future that is conceived or that is conceivable is a possibility. Perhaps it is to the extent that one has fears and anxieties and concern about himself and others that every man also tries to conceive and plan his anticipated existence. The rules for describing and conceiving possibilities are stringent, but do not by themselves limit markedly the range of possibilities. Sentences about a possibility are true or false about it considered as an object to be described. And this is cognitive truth—truth as a quality of a sentence. Such truth presupposes that we agree about the definition of the possibility before describing it. Possibilities have names and are definable. There is a correctness in respect to that which is defined and named, even if one names fictions.

But it must be admitted immediately that such cognitive truth is not peculiarly religious. For to cognize possibilities is a prerogative of all kinds of persons, and it is logically conceivable that the knowledge of a possibility might be entertained irrespective of qualities more personal and idiosyncratic. Furthermore, one can dawdle with possibilities as do the world's dreamers, the insane, and children. Of course, it is one thing to entertain possibilities and another thing to know about them. The latter presupposes that they be systematic and coherent, free of ambiguities, clearly articulated and defined. But granted this restriction, there still does not seem to be anything peculiarly religious about such sentences as might be said to describe conceived future possibilities. And it is another question altogether to decide which possibility will, in fact, be the one I shall seek to realize.

One might state the matter in another form: To assent to the truth of a sentence about a possibility, even if it were one describing a Nirvana-kind of existence or the converted life of a Christian, does not mean anything more in respect to the subject than that he admits that the sentence is true of the way of life thus named. Everyone who agreed to this description could, ostensibly, from the truth of the description decide not to choose such a kind of life among the several possibilities that there are. Therefore, the admission of the cognitive truth about possibilities does not seem to involve necessarily anything that religion has tried to describe with the word faithfulness or righteousness.

Therefore, it would seem that, to the degree that religious sentences are about future possibilities, they can be cognitive and true, but that the knowledge of this truth is not intrinsically religious. But to say this much is to omit something very important from consideration, viz., the fact that many sentences called religious are also cognitive in a factual sense. At least they claim to be cognitive factually. And it is the supposed factual reference that has made religious sentences appear to be crypto-scientific and hence occasioned repeated conflicts between science and religion. It is typical of the religious literature of Christianity, Judaism, and Islam to make many factual assertions. It is not my purpose here to suggest that all of them, or even any of them, are true or false. The question of which are true and which false, which are meaningless, etc., has to be decided by empirical investigation, and certainly it is only philosophical naïveté that has credited the idea that all of any group of sentences about matters of fact must be true together or otherwise false together. Both religious apologists and attackers have shared this genial error in the past, thus exciting glee that was incommensurate with either the proofs or the refutations.

But there is a kind of factual claim that is intrinsic to some religious statements. Some religions, and most notably those mentioned above, contend that the future possibility is to be discovered in human history. The history of Israel, taken both as a series of events experienced by Jews and as a narrative about those events, is claimed to be a disclosure also of a possible way of existing. Likewise, the life of an historical man, Jesus, is claimed to be the possibility of a new life. In the latter instance, extremely interesting and difficult things are said; for there are those who say that the possibility was created by his words and language, and others who say that his existence itself is the possibility, even if he had not sketched a new life linguistically. But this is a controversy for theologians—the issue at point is that some religions make cognitive claims about historical events and relate these to the cognitive claims about the possibilities.

Cognitive claims about historical events, even the claims that a man existed or that tribes existed, are hypothetically certain claims. And it is important to remember that sentences used by religious men to assert the factual existence of anyone or any group are probable assertions and subject to the dialectic of all sentences about matters of fact. There is certainly no a priori reason why some sentences about matters of fact are more certain than others. Attempts of religious thinkers to make all the sentences of religious literature both factual and certain led to such absurdities as inspiration and infallibility, both desperate efforts to make secure what could not in fact be made secure.

Once again it must be indicated that the admission of the truth of sentences about matters of fact does not, of itself, produce religiosity. It is most difficult to see that sentences about anything you please in the past can become religious in virtue simply of their truth claim. The admission of a man's existence (or assertion that he existed, was of such an age, height, race, etc.), just as the admission of a people's existence and history seem to be left simply as a cognitive act, best achieved in a state of neutrality and objectivity. Thus, granting that religious sentences are cognitive of either a possibility or an actual existent does not sufficiently distinguish them from other sentences to make them religious, for it is certainly possible to admit the cognitive truth of ostensibly religious sentences without losing the neutrality of the knowing subject, and without becoming a passionately religious man.

But at this point it is well to remember again what the more speculative and braver philosophies (and theologies) attempted. We have admitted two kinds of cognitive truths that are ostensibly to be found in religious propositions, but metaphysical philosophies have proposed a way to connect these two and thus make these cognitive truths more specifically religious, much less neutral and detached. First, however, the setting must be remembered. There were and are today people who report that there was an ancient people called Jews, who did so and so. With more detail we learn that they believed they were chosen and that this made them heavy with the responsibility of being priests to all nations. Thus far we have two kinds of cognition: reports about an existing people and an account of a possible way of living (perhaps also the remark that some of them lived this way, others did not, etc.). Other persons might say there was a man, and that by him a new way of life was preached. Classical philosophies in the service of these claims tried to resolve the two questions: Why should the possibility be here? and, Why should I choose this possibility among others? Classical supernaturalism attempts to give a kind of present-tense linguistic description in which God can be understood and described as equally related to past, present, and future. In this present-tense language system, the historical events and future possibilities are treated in non-temporal language, and cognitive links are purported to stand forth between otherwise disparate and discontinuous events.

Thus it was and is argued that *because* of God, therefore the possibilities do exist and are to be actualized. Of course, one cannot deny that the kind of cognition which claims to know that sentences about God are true, appears richer and also appears more religious, in virtue of its subject matter, than knowledge of historical events in their historicity and knowledge of possibilities ever can. But this is the question. Attempts to show that one has cognition of God and that sentences about God are meaningful and/or true are vitiated by epistemological considerations. Therefore it seems both more expedient and befittingly modest to let the cognition of religious sentences rest at what it is, viz., claims about historical existence (in some faiths) and claims about possibilities. Therewith, however, it must be admitted that we do not seem to be in the position to show cognitively why any possibility is thus asserted, or that it ought to be asserted, or that it ought to be actualized. We can only begin with the cognitive assertions and test their veracity if we choose, but not include them in any broader cognitive claim that might seem to make cognition itself religious.

But then the question arises as to whether this analysis does justice to the uses given religious sentences. We have admitted that, as cognitive truths (supposing them cognitive and omitting those that cannot be shown to be), there is nothing intrinsically peculiar either about their content or the act of believing them. There is, in other words, nothing religious in either instance. This is to say that the act of belief in a cognitive sentence is not an act of religious faith. Attempts to enlarge cognition to include a trans-empirical object (God) has the superficial merit of introducing a religious content into the sentence and making the act of believing such a sentence a religious appearing act. In another context I argue that this is theological superstition, and, in any case, it is insupportable on cognitive grounds.

But how can religious faith be distinguished? Religions differ at this point, but let us begin with the most complex first—those religions that make historical claims. Religious faith for such religions does suppose that one believes in a proposition that, e.g., a people or a person did exist. Here there are historical grounds for the belief. The belief is cognitive; its meaning is delineated by the evidence the sentence accounts for. Secondly, all religions seemingly described a possibility—a way of living and of personal being that is at least conceivable, however difficult it may be to actualize. Again, one may believe that the description is true—one may further believe that this possibility is presented in historical concreteness (thus the second is combined with the first). However, neither of these acts of belief by itself nor both together are acts of religious faith, but, depending on the religion, they may be necessary in order that the act of religious faith takes place. (This is an issue that again must be discussed by theologians, for it involves the differentia between religions, most notably those of Christianity and Judaism as over against perhaps some of those of the Orient.)

The peculiarity of the religious act of faith, or belief as it too is sometimes called, is that it requires not simply that I hold certain sentences to be true, but rather that I am becoming the possibility thus described. This latter act is non-cognitive, but probably pre-supposes the cognitive acts noted above. To become a possibility is to admit an interest, an enthusiasm, a passion for the possibility heretofore only cognitively described. The cognitive act of belief is qualitatively distinct from religious faith, as disinterested apprehension is from interested pursuit. The peculiar difficulties of discussion at this point have been more typical of those religions that involve both a disinterested knowledge and an interested enthusiasm, less typical of those religions that minimize the significance of an historical locus for the occurrence of the possibility. But it seems clarifying, to me at least, to distinguish the cognitive sentences, admitting their religious neutrality whatever their religious use, and then also to separate the cognitive act of belief from the religious act of belief as objectivity is separated from subjectivity, as contemplation is from enthusiasm.

The confusion in religious discourse may be described this way: insisting upon the importance of the cognition of a (religious) possibility, religious faith becomes confused with cognitive belief; insisting upon the non-cognitive aspect of faith, religious sentences mistakenly are assumed to be non-cognitive. Here, instead, a distinction is drawn. Religious sentences are cognitive but are not religious in virtue of this. As cognitive, since sentences describe the possibility of a religious life and believing these sentences is a neutral cognitive act. But becoming religious is a matter of having a non-cognitive enthusiasm and interest in becoming the possibility that can be cognitively described. To translate the sentences into this non-cognitive and passionate context is to put the sentence to a truly religious use. Thus, both cognition and faith can be delineated in relation to the same sentences, the first being non-religious and dispassionate, the second being religious and passionate. But a possibility that can be objectively known and yet subjectively reduplicated is properly called religious when it is remembered that the stress is upon the latter, the reduplication and becoming, rather than the former, the act of awareness.

IV

All of this is a proposal that cognitive-appearing sentences in religious discourse once again be examined closely. It is being here proposed that a sentence, for example, in which it is asserted that a man is God (and, e.g., all other sentences about an incarnation) be read as, there is or there was (as the case may be) a man who is (or announces) a new possibility, a new way of life. To say this much is to stay within the cognitive. The details about this possibility that contrast it with other possibilities can be added and usually are in more discourse.

This is to assert further, that men do not have knowledge of a divine being who has divine qualities. Religious sentences, including the above, are phrased as if they do. The mode of arguing by analogy, therefore, suggests that the incarnation is a kind of surprise, because it means the juxtaposition of divine qualities and a human being. Whatever justice this may have done to the passions men have felt, this does not do justice when considered from a cognitive standpoint. For *cognitively* men do not encounter a divine being. Men might call certain qualities, with which cognition has to do, divine, and this for various reasons, some of which might be appropriate. But that these qualities are *known* to be of a divine being is another matter. Here the structure of language seems to have invited the confusion, and many other features of reflective and linguistic usage have sustained it. The cognitive meaning of the God idea is given only by the order of ethical and logical possibilities as this is augmented by long experience of the race. The Hebrews and Christians utilized the first of these (ethical possibilities), certain Greeks the second, and most of Western theology has tried to wed the two into one by insisting the God could be *known* as an actuality, an existing being with attributes. What I am here suggesting is, therefore, only that the cognitive content of religious sentences be admitted to be as limited as it is. To say a man is God or that the world is created by God (to choose another salient example) is to say something cognitive, but, when such sentences are analyzed, they say among other things—this man is (or taught) a kind (to be specified . . .) of possibility or the world and things in it are like gifts—they are given—and can be understood so. It is the qualities of the possibility that are the cognitive grounds for the divinity claim.

The analysis of the sentences of Christian literature into *kerygma* and *didache* made by C.H. Dodd and others, roughly corresponds to the distinctions noted here. The didache sentences, which are defined as moral teaching, are there distinguished from the kerygmatic sentences, which are factual and historical. From a standpoint of an epistemological analysis, however, this distinction is only approximate, for it is characteristic of religious sentences that a declaration of possibility be given within a factual and historical assertion. The didache sentences are specifications of the possibility and identify it in contrast to all other possibilities; furthermore, in the New Testament they enjoin and persuade and stimulate and, therefore, are not simply cognitive but much else besides.

This position here argued does not deny the importance of religious cognition. With rather technical reasons that will be considered in a later paper, it can be shown that the extent of cognitive significance of a religious sentence depends upon the peculiarity and specificity of the possibility it names or describes. That many religious sentences describe only in different modes and words the same possibility may be the case; but that all do so becomes doubtful as one begins to read the religious literature. There are some striking differences among religious and moral teachings. And one must remember, too, that there is no a priori way, nor any ultimate metaphysical intuition from which one can leap into this array of possibilities and decide which is true, which are religious, which are only ethical or non-religious, etc. The fact that the possibility that religious sentences describe is peculiar means that its source in history is a problem. Some religions, at least, do not describe a possibility that is in accord with the wishes of the majority, and this draws attention not only to the question of the source of such possibilities but also gives a clue as to why it has seemed plausible to some to claim that anyone who advances such a possibility might be called unique if not divine.

A related issue has to do with the question of the desirability of this possibility. When persons have argued that religious propositions are emotive or, as Freud did, that they are wish fulfillments, they seem to have taken for granted that the religious possibility expressed the wish. Interestingly enough, most religious theories, i.e., sentences about religious sentences, have denied this. The declaration of the possibility can be cognitively encountered when it is specifically declared, and this should indicate that a religious sentence is not so individuated as to lack all intersubjective reference. But granted this reference, it is argued further that the possibility thus declared is not possible to do or to be, by which it is meant, I take it, that it is not desirable to all who recognize it cognitively as a possibility.

The fact that a possibility must be cognized before it is significantly realized is also a requirement of some religions—this insistence reflecting the view that, otherwise, the religious possibility might not actually be met, because one's own wish might then be determinative. Such niceties again belong to another kind of analysis, but suffice it to note that religious sentences are not easy to believe in. If they were only wish-fulfillments, it would be a little difficult to understand the stress that has been put upon the cognitive and identifiable character of the religious possibility. And, likewise, if religious faith were only unrestrained subjectivity, then it is difficult also to understand the large stress that has been given to showing that faith is something unexpected—this because it is thought so widely that the reduplication of the qualities of life that such a possibility describes is so difficult a matter.

V

In conclusion it might be said that this paper urges that the endeavor to interpret religious sentences as cognitive of trans-empirical realities be given up. And this for two reasons: one, that there is no epistemological warrant for such kinds of assertions (even if there is an intuition of such realities, this would be an event, an occurrence, but not a warrant for the truth of sentences!); and secondly, that the attempt to use knowledge of a trans-empirical Deity as the ground for the possibility so occurring in a given instance and also as the reason for my pursuit of it—this was also a mistaken argument. It seems more appropriate, therefore, to urge that religious sentences can be cognitive of historical events and, also, that they are the occasion for the cognition of a possibly new and definitive form of life. But the religious act of faith is not to believe the truth of the description of the possibility nor even the historical claims. Perhaps such an act of belief is a necessary condition for religious faith, but it is not itself religious, for religious faith peculiarly is the passionate and enthusiastic becoming of a possibility. Faith is not belief—cognitive belief—but is instead a non-cognitive translation of a heretofore cognated possibility into the concreteness of one's idiosyncratic character.

This point of view seems to do justice to both the restraints that are induced by ruled reflection and the uses to which religious sentences are in fact put. What this point of view omits is the luxurious claims that there are cognitive truths about God Himself. But in the nature of the case, these are allowable only from God's point of view! And the attempted simulation of a God's cognitive grasp does honor neither to the religious life nor to the proper use of language and reflection.

PART FOUR

Emotions, Passions, and Virtues

CHAPTER 13

Theology and Emotions

I

IT GOES ALMOST WITHOUT saying that the emotions are often in ill repute. We are all witnesses to diagnostic practices that make most mental illnesses emotional in genesis and character. Besides that, we inherit from Western literature an insidious distinction between the passions, on one side, and reason and the intellect, on the other. The force of that disjunction is to relegate feelings, desire, pathos, and emotions to the raw material of the individual and their dominance to the adolescence of the race. Maturity, both individually and socially, has looked like the conquest by reason over one's lower nature and, of course, the emotions.

It is no wonder then that the emotionally charged pages of great literature and the Bible have seemed a little embarrassing to the learned. Theology often is construed as an effort to state in concepts and in the barest, most non-toxic language, what Scripture does in a more rag-tag, informal, anecdotal fashion. And one of the unfortunate consequences of that single-minded view is a kind of corollary, namely, that preaching can be rhetorical, a little stem-winding, hortatory, and perhaps more plainly biblical and emotional, whereas theology has to be rational, non-metaphorical, and, certainly, non-emotional. I am not arguing that there is not room for a distinction between disinterested analysis and passionate advocacy, maybe sometimes described respectively as theology and preaching; but it seems to me that most frequently this kind of distinction is also invoked invidiously and wrongly.

It comes out something like this: that preaching is addressed to common people, who can only be appealed to emotionally anyway, whereas rationality and theology is for more rarefied souls, with finer timbre and more sophisticated requirements. No wonder, then, that the notion develops that emotional religion is for the illiterate, for the frontiers, for missionary fields, and theological religion is for the universities and the culture-saturated. Furthermore, it is as if all the criteria and the meaning are in the province of rationality, which then can construe and reconstruct, even state in another form, the religion that is more emotional and perhaps popular.

To tread on these grounds is to be fairly secure within the limits of theological, and even philosophical, history. This is the way most of it falls out. One has the uncomfortable impression that most of the academic theological traditions, including Schleiermacher (who is often cited as if he were an exception), are nested together rather comfortably within that broad intellectual matrix that puts emotions and intellect, passion and reason, in opposition. And occasional forays of theologians against Greek modes of thought and loudly expressed preferences for Hebraic mentality seem to me to founder again on the details. For it is the case that massive discomfort and quavering inabilities with the emotions is almost endemic to theologians, no matter how Hebraic, and so it is also, to the theologically trained ministers.

Perhaps it is not surprising, then, that the theologians and the ministers who are creased at all by theological and biblical sciences quickly revert to psychology, probably clinical too, if they seek emotional sustenance for themselves and surcease for their parishioners. On the other hand, those who are sensitive to the emotional features of sacred literature will probably discover that, outside of the early Church fathers, most theologians seem to be playing another game altogether. So, in despair, those sensitive to emotional needs turn to poetry and imaginative literature, perhaps Greek tragedians, where pathos and the emotions get in exercise that links to the Bible far more obviously than does so much of academic theology. Unfortunately, this move also tends to alienate a great deal of modern preaching from its more thoughtful sources.

Above all, it is important right here to recognize that theology can be written in the deliberate avoidance of emotion. Its language need not be anything but absolutely disinterested, even detached. Certainly it can share the disinterestedness of truly great literature. For the best of literature is often the least provocative in any immediate affective manner. But precisely because it describes in such detail and with exquisite choice of material, the reader is all the more able to respond with pathos and feeling himself. For like a great novel, say Graham Greene's *The Power and the Glory*, such literature, without its language ever being an ostentatious item in the exercise of an emotion, can start an irresistible array of emotions like pity, love, and anger. And it is this kind of theological and religious writing that is so difficult to effect; and it is scarcely done at all in our day.

In what follows, I wish to specify some misgivings and some egregious mistakes in four different areas of concern. First, something more about the fear of emotions and the fear of being emotional; then, the related anxiety of never allowing any emotional expression; thirdly, a look at recent theological theories of emotions; and lastly, a brief defense of theologically defined emotions.

II

The fear of the emotions is often couched as the fear of subjectivity. To be subjective in contrast to being objective is like having no standards against having at least one. There seems to be a conception, now almost prejudicial because it is assimilated without any thought being put upon it, that emotions are internal episodes and mysterious psychological phenomena, some kind of perturbation and agitation, mostly physiological perhaps. It is also thought that these episodes and/or processes can and do simply occur. What happens, it is popularly assumed, is that they get linked with other happenings, objective, let us say, but in a fortuitous and accidental manner. In any case, "subjectivity" is like a generic name, a denominating expression, marking off the locus for feelings, desires, wishes, emotions, and a host of other psychological happenings.

This inner world, we are led to believe, has no apparent logic or rules. But it does respond to a range of stimuli, which we might term "causes." Therefore, it is supposed to be in an arena studied by psychology. However, being an inner world, it is therefore also damagingly private, so it does not yield easily to study. If my grief is an inward happening, then it is mine and not yours. Then the force of the remark that it is private and subjective is that it simply cannot ever be yours, nor can I tell it to you or about it with any hope of your fathoming it. For if my grief is mine, really mine, so that I feel its overwhelming power, then I alone can know it. That grief will be an experience-factor; it will be my feeling-event and its qualities and intensity will be mine to suffer just as my hope will be mine to enjoy. Clearly, if emotions are like this, internal events, then access to them can only be from within.

Something like this is forced upon us by the conventional pictures of how emotions root in us. This is why it is said in our popular social-political campaigns that only women can know a woman's feelings, only blacks can testify about the black's emotions, and maybe only you can know how much you love her. For in all these cases, the privileged access is part of the picture; and this access can be used as you will to exclude or to include, as the supposed emotional experience is duly acknowledged. There is, obviously, something obscurely appealing about this kind of claim; but it has to be articulated altogether differently and not, certainly, because emotions are private and inaccessible to others. Surely I do not know the frustration of the defeated, not because "frustration" is an internal occurrence, but rather because I have not yet known nor chosen to know a number of things, and I thus have not appraised them in certain defined ways.

To be able to know the appropriate range of things and to be prepared for an appraisal of them—as fearful, as lovely, as vulgar, as frustrating, etc.—is the principal part of an emotion. Admittedly one's personal history and a range of preoccupations over a long period of time will also equip people with the capacities to make an appraisal that is deeply right and hence emotional. One cannot grieve over the fate of his country unless he has learned to love it; so, too, one must have loved deeply to feel the poignancy of betrayal. However, to say all of that is to admit that emotions are conditional but conditional upon all the factors that make for a significant evaluation and description (the two are not distinctive activities; one often is the other) of a state of affairs, of human behavior, or of the way life now is. There is, after all, an "objective correlative," as T. S. Eliot called it, in virtue of which an emotion is occasioned, right, appropriate, and precise, or vague.[1]

Students of psychology know well that early psychologists thought that there would have to be introspective techniques worked out by which to get at these emotional and other mentalistic phenomena. But the difficulties of doing that led many to behaviorism, in which the objective range of human activity was studied, with the contrary thought often proposed that emotions were not internal and were nothing but the behavior. Others used bits of behavior as if they were the symptoms, and that the emotions, if internal, could be informed and mapped by them. Our argument, brief and dogmatic as it is, is that emotions, like thoughts, are not quite either the physiological behavior or internal episodes. For both the popular introspective views (like most expression-theories of poetry, art, music, and emotion) and technical behaviorism suppose some such views. When they are seen for what they are, it does look as if the theoretical constructs, the "introspectivism" and "behaviorism" and their irreconcilable claims, simply lose their glamor. We do not need them or any other so-called science of human nature.[2] We are left with ad hoc commenting, which has its degree of success and its skilled minority too. In such contexts, it is absurd to ask for the causes of emotion, except in the abnormal instance; the norm for the emotions is to be seen

1. This phrase is used by Eliot in his analysis of what he thinks is the artistic failure of *Hamlet*, where the objective correlative to Hamlet's emotions, he insists, is not manifest. Part of that "correlative" could be, of course, a history of moral concern about incest, long-standing fidelity, respect for the dead, as well as the events involving the usurping king and the death of a father. But much of this is what is not there. Note Eliot's essay, "Hamlet and His Problems," in *The Sacred Wood*, 95–103. Another way to say this is that the emotion of Hamlet is "in excess of the facts as they appear."

2. This is, admittedly, a rather stringent and unsympathetic way to dismiss a common conviction about the importance of a science of human nature. My claim is a difficult one to make plausible and has nothing to do with anti-intellectualism and/or a romanticism that decries order and logic. On the contrary, my argument rests on the logical impossibility of such a science (whether psychology, sociology, or of other kinds of human dynamisms) by which human behavior can be generalized by analogy with the behavior of the stars, of electrons, and of a multitude of other things. This issue is to be argued in a forthcoming series of papers—such as "The Human Heart—The Logic of a Metaphor" and "Something about What Makes It Funny."

in everyday and ad hoc instances, when emotions are the motives and reasons for our behavior.

By and large, emotions, then, are not episodes nor internal happenings at all; however, we cannot deny that there are times when we seethe with anger, though our demeanor be calm. We sometimes feel humble but appear to be proud; we are furious but behave sweetly. However, the large and compelling point is that the emotions are not irrational eruptions, not at least if we are at all clear about ourselves and whatever it is we are responding to. We often talk, as T. S. Eliot has reminded us, as if thoughts were precise and emotions were vague. In truth, there is precise emotion and there is vague emotion. To express precise emotion requires as great intellectual and critical power as to express a precise thought.[3]

For this reason, then, we can be glad for literary giants and even, on what we might call almost secular grounds, the skills of the writers of Holy Scripture. In the making of literature of this sort, it is not that special organs of knowing are at work or a particular kind of epistemic insightfulness presupposed. Rather there is a precision, not so much of feeling and emotions, but of description. Besides, there is an uninhibited use of everyday language, in which the emotions are both freely exercised and described. Such literature is also remarkably theory-free and all the better for that.

But there is another fear of the intellectuals, too, and that is related to the first, but manifested differently. It is that the emotions are vulgar and common. Much of this stems from the fact that emotional life, like intellectual life, is subject to modification and greater refinement. One must distinguish between shallow grief and deep grief, superficial and silly fears as over against pervasive and worthy ones; and so on with most emotions! And it takes culture and some general capacities of a reflective sort to grieve appropriately and to hope with aptness and insight. Emotions that are unrelated become moods, and then they are as irrelevant and as damaging as are thoughts that float aimlessly. It is not the case that we have two sets of criteria, one set that is "subjective," for the emotions (perhaps how genuine the feeling,

3. Readers of Eliot will recognize this theme from his essay, "Shakespeare and the Stoicism of Seneca" (1927), in *Selected Essays*, 107–26. But I am also indebted to Errol Bedford's "Emotions," reprinted in Gustafson, *Essays in Philosophical Psychology*, 77–98.

etc.), and another, objective, and perhaps logical for inner thoughts. Whatever governs one, mostly governs the other; and thoughts and emotions flow into one another almost without differentiation. The fear of God is not an optional and quixotic response to a God we otherwise know. Rather it is that to know the God of Abraham, Isaac, and Jacob, and the Lord, Jesus Christ, is to fear Him. Where the knowing is shallow, the fear will be trivial too.

But there is something, of course, to the notion of vulgar religion. It often is correlative to an otherwise vulgar and shapeless way of living and responding. Religion is often emotional in a trivial way. There are people who weep copiously but who do not, thereby, grieve in the same proportion. Crying is a sign of grief, but only in a certain context and only in some circumstances. People learn to modify and to control laughing, weeping, random movement, twitching, cringing, and many other initially undifferentiated kinds of behavior. For better or for worse, cultivated and urbane people are lately known for playing it "cool." Whether we approve of this pattern or not, this demeanor of equanimity can often enough also be relatively superficial. Grief and joy, fear and anxiety, also suppose remembrance, carefulness, motivation, and a host of factors, other than the obvious ones noted. So if one grows in emotional power and depth, one grieves perhaps a lifetime in very substantial ways without spending very much time weeping. Then the test for grief is the extent and quality of behavior that is modified, but not necessarily through crying.

Considering these things, then, we can say that there is a vulgar kind of emotional display in some religious contexts that will undoubtedly simply wither away with greater emotional understanding and general humane culture. Again, though, there are those who are misled into thinking joy is not present unless there is exuberance and grief unless there is overt mourning. In such cases, a kind of instruction in human seriousness, Christian included, cannot but help. The unfortunate feature here is that even Christian instruction, via either the Bible or elementary theology, is often so couched as to augment the prejudicial view that pits emotions against rationality. For both the pedagogues and the pundits have sometimes concluded this, and both are wrong.

There is clearly something to Christian experience, but it is not autonomous; and certainly it is not a stirring of psychic energies and a release of latent potencies within the individual. But there is something to the concept "experience" here that must be salvaged, but only with the help of discernment into both the emotions and the Scriptures. Certainly, it is logically odd and radically incongruous that a man should believe that he is redeemed without his also feeling joy. Here is a case where "joy," the emotion, is part of the understanding of what redemption means. So, too, is remorse and self-abnegation part of the very meaning of the doctrine of sin. One cannot properly be said to understand either matter if the emotion is lacking. Of course, he might also be revolted by the notion of redemption; but that revulsion, too, would be antipathetically appropriate, right within a certain kind of human condition. But the point is that here theology, considered as teaching in which Biblical concepts are interpreted, would not be contrary to emotions, but would rather give them occasion and definition.[4]

Therefore, there is no antithesis at all between theology and emotions; and one does not exclude the other. The specter of an emotional religion, which finds stimuli in biblical texts, but not instruction, of course must be countered; but not by another absurdity. For the other alternative has often been a kind of orthodoxy that has made belief the major activity of the Christian. Then the rest of Scripture—the fear of the Lord that is the beginning of wisdom, the joy, the contentment, the dauntless hope, the love that will move men and mountains— gets no grounding in Christ Jesus but looks, instead, like a vagrant piety, part of the adiaphora, and only psychologically interesting. A non-theological Christianity would be Christianity without concepts and that is absurd; a non-emotional Christianity, which is without distinctive pathos, feeling, and affects, is a contradiction in terms.

Herewith, however, it might be appropriate to turn our consideration to the absurdities that this fear of emotion has produced.

4. The notion of interpretation here is a very low key one indeed. In teaching mathematics, we can get students to learn to count, to calculate, but keep the entire number system uninterpreted. So, too, we can teach formal logical systems that way, where no meaning is attached to the variables at all. But when we interpret, we aim at "understanding," which means that we want numbers to say something. So, too, with Christian teachings.

III

Almost any man one meets has also learned enough about the world and himself to know that some prospects are fearful, some things are dreadful, that anxiety is often justified, that there are things to be glad about, etc. In brief, we might say that the emotions are simply a part of everyday life, and the kind of makeshift intelligence we need to plan and to know where we are going and why. One of the unfortunate features of the popularization of learning among so many people in our day is also the spread of a strange attitude that often goes with learning. This is a kind of *ataraxis*, "learned indifference," "detachment," and a preference for the disinterested and emotion-free appraisal.

All of us know in general that love can blind you to defects, that enthusiasm keeps one from seeing the faults of one's own work, that despair, fear, and anger can be disruptive and keep one from a just and discriminating analysis. But once more, the very valuable tactical injunction, to be wary lest one be deluded, which is essential to a small-scale matter, is often enlarged to become a large-scale strategy for the whole of a life. Then we get the absurdity of popular stoicism, which makes almost any emotion at all inappropriate. Then men became like walking sticks, devoid of feelings and in a sense (that is meant to be invidious), apathetic.

Shakespeare's *Othello* shows us Desdemona and Othello, at first innocently and touchingly infatuated; but their love for each other is so dreamy and so completely defenseless in a world that contains Iago and all kinds of uncertainties, that the whole play is also a kind of document on jealousy and hapless love. In contexts like that, we are all rather accustomed to hear reason extolled, as if our likeness with the brutes were in our passions and our unlikeness with them in our reason. So Iago says: "We have reason to cool our raging motions, our carnal stings, our unbitted lusts."[5]

The result, though, is unfortunate, because this attitude leads us to eschew emotion altogether and to extol a style of living and thinking that makes emotions themselves to be that part of ourselves that we grow out of. This is, obviously enough, quite intolerable also. It is

---

5. Shakespeare, *Othello*, act 1, scene 3. And Iago's notion is not that we have "cause" or good "reason"; but rather that "reason" in men is there in order to repress emotion and desire.

not as though the emotions are bottled up and must out somehow—for emotions are not inward forces or powers, always seeking expression—but rather that we cannot then live in our kind of world and be the kind of people we are, without caring, without fearing, hoping, planning, wishing, being sorrowful and anxious. All of these are ingredient in the normal way of sizing up the world; and to be without them is to miss exercising capacities that are not just optional, but essential.

It is in this circumstance, then, that a new kind of emotional expressiveness is cultivated, and this under several auspices. Because of the long-standing notion that emotions are inward, it is easy to assume that they seek expression. But if one is unable to express them, then a kind of psychotherapy is often invoked wherein one learns to dare to be himself. The picture is, when generalized, of course, all wrong. It is drawn up as if emotions of fear, dread, ecstasy, and erotic love are seething within, and, furthermore, as if these and their intensities are the defining energies making the human heart and the self, in one instance, different from that in another. The real "me" or "self" is supposed to be lurking in these private constellations of latent powers and thwarted emotional drives.

In such a mythological context obviously almost anything and everything can be said and usually is. For the criteria are seldom very stringent when definitions are so broad. The picture suggests that the self struggles for expression against the inhibitions of conscience, superego, society, the fear of others; and the battle is titanic and terribly histrionic. Of course, the scheme is loose enough so it is bound to fit a large number of cases. This loose fit is also taken to be a kind of confirmation of the view.

But there is more. For granted what looks like an inhibition of inwardness, then religion of a certain kind is invented if not exploited to cooperate with the psychological factors noted. Connoisseurs of these matters are continually arising to tell us that true religion must also liberate people from emotional stringency. And all kinds of religiosity are loosed in the world, ostensibly to free up these dams that occlude the flow of emotion and to allow the real self to come forth. It goes without saying that much of this kind of talk is nowadays almost completely free of any restraint coming from theology. Furthermore, a new use of the Bible is engendered, a kind of swooping down for an exegetical morsel that looks particularly pleasing and is psychologically telling.

In such circumstances, where emotions have been so poorly done by, the Christian church is almost helpless before the new irrationalities of psychotherapeutics and of the frightfully powerful and stimulating popular religion of our day. When rhythm, increased decibels, and incantation of biblical formulae get brewed together in the interest of releasing people from captivity and liberating them to be themselves, it looks rather churlish and downright mean, if not irrelevant, to cavil against self-discovery. It happens, however, that Christianity is not in business to produce this kind of self-discovery. Besides, the psychological view is all wrong. The self is not within; there is nothing within but what the physiologists and plumbers and we ourselves find to be there. There are no emotions there to be found or to be inhibited.

Nonetheless, there is a kind of plausibility about the mistake that engenders much of this. It is simply that people cannot long deny the emotions, for to force the denial of emotions is as much as to condemn people to a deep and fundamental kind of dishonesty. This dishonesty does not have its roots finally in the internal character of emotions, but in the veto that is cast upon recognizing the world, oneself, and others to be what they are. Here is where fright, anxiety, love, and envy get their targets and their justification or the lack thereof. The real and proper way to inhibit an emotion is to show someone that whatever is the object of the emotion does not deserve it. Admittedly, some emotions, like some thoughts, are free floating and have no targets. Here is irrationality indeed. Not all emotions are like that, only some; and for this reason we have standards in the way the things and we are, and these cannot be neglected. It is a standard that is being abjured by those who decry the emotions.

Therefore, there is a point to this quest for honesty. The world is frightful, joyous, and awesome; and one is entitled, if not required, to see and feel it so. Our future is uncertain, our morals are patchy, and our character is reprehensible. Simultaneously, it is an outright travesty of both psychology, as a disciplined kind of reflection, and Christian theology, as the social and conceptual context of faith, to be subservient to such undefined and vulgar views of human nature and the emotions in particular as we have noted. Christian theology has a teaching function that is relevant here, but it has little to do with bringing out the emotions that are supposedly within to their fruition in the self. Instead, it proposes that by referring oneself and the world to God, one will lose the vain and defeating emotions and one will be able to live in hope, confidence, and joy until the very end of his life. But everything that might be normal in such a view is pitched a little higher by the additional concept of eternal life, within which embrace, one's orientation and all passions and emotions will be even further redefined.

Therefore, we might note in passing, that what we have here said about the emotions is not quite theology in the very strong sense of the evangelical context and the very language of faith itself. I am supposing that the Bible is like that and that certain teachings of the pulpit and church traditions are that. But these pages are a kind of *praeparatio evangelica*, an attempt to convince the reader of a few things that will help to make his thought congruent with that more strictly evangelical thrust. The odd despair that many people now come to feel with Christian things is often generated by a kind of thought-scheme, not least about the emotions, which looks like high-minded modern theory and makes us too prone to think the emotions are subject only to causes, of which religious worship ought to be one, or that the emotions are childish and ought not to countenanced by sophisticated moderns. But all of that is nonsense.

On the other hand, the fittingness of the deep Christian comfort and rest, peace, and understanding, must also be insisted upon. Men and their thought-life make emotions ingredient in almost everything they do and say.

It is the nobility of these strains that made Christian evangelical theology at once so fulsome and detailed. For it was as if there were a thousand ways to view this new life and unheard-of possibilities. This is why the contemporary scene, again, looks so paltry. I want to note another feature or two of it, which again will have to be cast in a polemical mood.

IV

There have been a couple of attempts to come to grips with emotion in recent theological writing. In both instances, these serious endeavors have led to such extremity of view that they are almost like ideologies. The first of these is the thesis, related to what has been already said, that the emotions (and, of course, the poets, dramatists, and religious writers who limn them) are the clue to an indelible human nature. This is that there is, in all of us, "an unchanging human heart." Religious-poetical romanticism, usually in combination, projects this notion, often by way of antithesis to modern scientific and psychological views. The other thesis is cast up by recent existentialist theologians and philosophers and is writ large also in some recent imaginative literature. In trying to find a rationale for human life, after the loudly proclaimed demise of metaphysics, some thinkers have posited a new ontological clue to man. This clue is roughly a set of transcendental-like emotions that are said to define his nature once and for all. But now to the first of these.

That there is an unchanging human heart is an exceedingly tempting view. For the notion seems almost obvious. If the ruffian in the pit of the Globe Theatre could respond to the ribaldry of John Falstaff, to the scheming of Iago, to the sweet nothings of Portia, then how does one explain the response of sophisticated people centuries later? Despite differences in morality, social convention, knowledge, cultural context, and all the rest, there is an identity between the rabble in Shakespeare's pit, Dr. Johnson, and the myriads in our time who respond to Lear, Hamlet, Othello, Ophelia, Cordelia, and the shrew who still needs taming. So, the doctrine of an unchanging heart looms up as a kind of explanation.

One might label this doctrine as a piece of metaphysics, inadvertent, albeit literary. Despite the aversion that romanticists, theological, poetical, or lay, feel towards over-elaborated argument and over-subtle inference of schoolish transcendentals, the metaphysical will not be denied. No wonder that the proponents of metaphysics insist that they will still be around to bury their undertakers. For to insist that there is an invariant human heart is, on the other hand, an almost classic instance of how the anti-metaphysicians say metaphysics get formed. From the similarities of language, the language of the emotions (fears, hopes, loves, anger, frustration, disappointment), one is led almost imperceptibly into positing a deeper and invisible bond, perhaps by saying, metaphorically, that here is the language of the heart. From that it is only a step to saying that there is, after all, a sameness about human beings, namely, an identity in human heart.

There is a move from the similarity of language and of emotions to a substantive, that enduring heart, by which to explain and to ground the similarities. But suffice it to say here that this unscientific and literary way of articulating the notion that there is a common human nature, namely, in that human heart, is subject to the same criticisms that we earlier noted of positing, via psychology and related sciences, general laws and statistical subsumption that would etch that nature too. For if emotions are what we have noted them to be, part of the evaluative knowing and appraising that we all must do, then they are, in themselves, the explanations we need. We cannot, in turn, explain them all by reference to something else. In this respect, then, and seen as a kind of logical feature, there is an unfortunate likeness in explaining emotions, in going beyond them, whether it be in the direction of general laws they instantiate or of an unchanging human heart they illustrate.

This kind of metaphysical explanation is odd, coming as it does from people who are acquainted with great literature, even the Bible. The resolution on behalf of the heart always seems compatible with other eternal verities, including, of course, the doctrine of original sin. Other metaphysical-like theories of the emotions, however, have this same attractiveness—witness the enthusiasm for Freud among the Christians and the Jews. For here, again, this way of getting behind the emotions and giving them, in turn, an explanation rather than letting them explain (as we do in ordinary life all of the time—"I stopped because I was afraid," "she doesn't go there because she hates him") has a kind of superficial similarity to and seeming compatibility with a certain theological temptation to explain in a very broad and once-for-all manner too.

Enough, then, of this, except to insist that this is not the way in which one ought to use this metaphor about the human heart. There is no intention here to derogate it because it is a metaphor, nor do I suggest that the concept, metaphorical and all, of the "unchanging human heart," has anything less than a highly defensible function. But that is a matter for another disquisition.[6]

There is another acknowledgment of the importance of the emotions by theologians that is far more popular recently and is, to a certain extent, also more difficult to assess. It is, in brief, that certain emotions are ontological and foundational, trans-empirical and necessary. Here a doffing of the hat towards Kierkegaard is almost always in order, for he is reputedly the father of existentialism. Again, it seems to me that caution about Kierkegaard is always in order, for he is the thinker that argued most carefully that the dialectical (the conceptual, the teaching, the statement of what is the case) must go together with the pathetic (emotions, feelings, human subjectivity). And that was the point also of his stages, namely, to show this intimacy in alternative forms of life. In any case and contrariwise, many existentialists have still proposed a kind of anxiety, dread, or fear, as if all men had it because they were men.

This kind of elucidation of the human condition, then, has made it seem as if there is an ontological state of affairs, an emotional and necessary way that a man has to be, to which the great cultural postures, like Epicureanism, Stoicism, Christianity, and others, are like answers. The picture of what this man is varies slightly: but he is alienated, alone, uncertain, dogged by needs, and pushed into either absurdity or sense by these dominating and emotionally motivating energies. Perhaps all of us have felt a little of the intellectual exhilaration and security of grip that this way of talking has given. It provided many intellectuals a kind of rhetorical thrill along with a few dialectical tools, and together made it look very much as if everything were falling into place.

Besides, existentialism gave systematic theology a tremendous and needed boost. Theologians talked again as if they were getting at something very close to bottom—the ultimate and inalienable feature of every man to which the Bible and God were intimately appropriate. Furthermore there were other cash values too. World literature sprang to life, new drama was written, and the emotions got their long inning. None of this do I want to deny. Also, this way of reorder-

6. Note the essay, forthcoming, by the author, called "The Human Heart—The Logic of a Metaphor."

ing Christian teachings seemed like a new apologetic, and of a different kind altogether.

Instead of everlastingly having to argue the truth or falsity of Christianity and instead of having to discuss in a tiresome way the relation of Christian teachings and the sciences—always in cognitive terms—the neo-existentialisms proposed something different. It was as if Christianity were, firstly, a means to resolve depth difficulties of an emotional sort, not of a cognitive sort. There is, obviously enough, something to be said in that direction that is right. With that I do not quarrel, but the morphology of the argument is the issue here. Instead of seeing the efficaciousness in the life of the individual as a consequence of Christianity's truth, this kind of emphasis proposed that the emotional and moral efficaciousness came first, and the issue of truth or falsity, if raised at all, was secondary. One ought not to suppose that this is necessarily cynical or cheap, for it is not. Whatever else is to be said, the theologies that stated things this way had the merit of being immediately more congruent with the Bible and the manner of the early Christians.

No wonder, then, the hold that this pattern of thought has had upon both the technicians of Christian thought and the laity in recent years. For the emotions were once again taken with seriousness and, in effect, spoken to in a Christian manner. And it is fair to say that this kind of theological conceptual scheme has also increased the perceptual acuities of the depth emotions in the Bible as well as in ourselves and our fellow men. A kind of evangelical ring, perhaps a little hollow, was restored to Christian preaching because of this general way of conceiving men and the world. Certain features of orthodoxy were brought to the fire too. For another thing, it pushed many of the irresolvable cognitive uncertainties into the background, and it allowed a measure of autonomy to the preacher, almost as if he had a fundamental domain to which Christianity addressed itself and within which he could speak without constant intimidation from the sciences and scholarly interests.

In addition, this way of doing theology (seeing Christianity as an effort to confront a distressed and an emotion-gripped man) had a way of putting other things into perspective too. For if there were these fundamental and pervasive emotions, rooted in man as man, then all other cultural enterprises were like adaptations to this same nature and same emotions. Then we had loosed upon the world these numerous theologies "of" this or that, wherein a means was exploited of reading back almost anything you please to these same deep and emotional fundamentals. The theologies of culture have abounded in our day. It looks now as though these emotions were rooted in a human condition that gave a unity to everything that was human; so it was not a big step from theology to general culture.

A kind of theory of meaning seemed to be at work in all this, as if, again, the "meaning" of the Christian faith were more clearly discernible if one saw how Christianity resolved the same anxiety that science, politics, art, and philosophy also sought to resolve. It looked as if we were very close to stating the modus vivendi of all things human. Whatever all of these things had in common as a point of departure then, was like an assurance of a minimal common meaning. Criteria were not ostensibly invented; they were discovered and were hand to glove with the way that men were and always had been, in biblical times all the way to the present time.

From all that has been said, it should be obvious that criticism of this kind of theologizing is not easy; for it has done much to organize reflection and to help put fundamental Christian things, not least preaching, to the fore again. Perhaps this was at a cost; for the revelation of God came to look like almost an addendum to this very flexible and cleverly articulated view of man. Be that as it may, revelation, too, God's word, looked as though it had to be meaningful by reference to what man's nature was, rather than the other way around.

Perhaps enough has been said already to make it clear that the only thing wrong with all of this is the main point. Emotions simply are not like that. Rather, emotions are part of the history of men and one ingredient in the continuous adaptation and judgments they have to make. The existentialist theologies and philosophies attempted to give even emotions a metaphysical status. The meaning of saying that is that emotions are so described that they root simply in man, in any context or even without a context at all. It is as if an emotion exists in a man, independently of situation, occasion, and exactly who he is. All of that is contrary to the very meaning of the concept "emotion" itself. Furthermore, there is no way to ascertain the sense of such an exaggerated and airborne notion of emotion. For all of our fearing, anger, dismay, etc., are "of" something or other. They are deeply contextual. And we cannot ever make sense of an emotion like fear without knowing of what a person is afraid. Fear means nothing much unless it be fear "of" this or that. But all such considerations are ruled out by this kind of non-contextual and ontological manner of speaking of emotions.

In conclusion, therefore, we turn to another kind of issue altogether. We proffer a brief view of what emotions are and how they are tied up in a variety of ways with the concepts we also use to describe ourselves and the world. Christianly speaking, this entails that emotions are defined and constituted in detail by theology and other Christian teachings.

V

It perhaps goes without saying that the Christian teachings are also "conceptual" in character. Nothing terribly aristocratic or lofty is being said thereby; nor is this to suggest that theology, also highly conceptual, is a more noble way to understanding than say simple Christian obedience or relatively untutored faith. But it is to say that God is a concept, not just a name, as Kierkegaard so eloquently said.[7] More than this, "faith," "hope," "love," "repentance," "sin," etc., also, are concepts. In brief, these words are used referringly in Christian contexts. But in order to use them one has to acquire the ability, the know-how, the power, and the capacity. One has to be able to use them within limits, for certain purposes and not all, in order to do a variety of things. Thus, to have a concept is not to have only a supple vocabulary or to be able to recognize a word, but also be able to judge,

---

7. This is argued in *Philosophical Fragments*, 51–52. The same point is made by Peter Geach, *God and the Soul*, who argues the issue out of the pages of Thomas Aquinas. To say "God" is a concept is not to deny that He is a person; but it is to say that "God" is more like "President of the United States" than it is like "Dwight Eisenhower," or more like "dog" than "Fido," like "Prime Minister" than "Mr. Atlee," like "Miss Prim and Proper" than "Alice." The meaning of the expression is larger than it would be in the case of a name; thus "God" also tells us about a kind of life and a form and possibility for one's own life. Being "President" suggests more than a name would, unless you already know that the named person also held that or another office.

discriminate, evaluate, distinguish, say a variety of things. What counts for understanding a concept varies with the concept at issue.

William James spoke about his dog that was disturbing the peace of the New England mountains that James was enjoying on a holiday. In disgust, James insisted that the dog go home, but the dog seemed strangely reluctant. After a while the dog did leave for home and many days later showed up in Cambridge, Massachusetts, at the only house he understood to be a home. James' point was that the dog understood "home" to be a name, not a concept. For a man, a concept, indeed, does have generality and hence can be used to refer to a large number of places. But this long-acknowledged characteristic of a concept, namely, its generality, is often one of its lesser features. For a concept is not only a general term. Behind the term is the use of it; and that person (and the uses he commands) is the nexus between the word and its reference and the term and its explication. The powers and capacities of the user, if these are organized and in a recognizable order, are what are properly the thrust and sovereignty of a concept.

Therefore, the learning of a concept is not an assimilation of a definition; rather is it the achievement of a range of capabilities (such as "home," with above example) that would permit recognition, identification, judgment, all kinds of appropriate action, plus, of course, a permissible range of linguistic activities too. One would, by understanding almost any concept, be empowered in a rich variety of ways, and the deeper and more appropriate that understanding, so, too, the extent of and scope of resources and abilities. Now, to say that Christian teachings are conceptual is to note that Christian learning supposes not a rote memorization of teachings or a polite reduplication of ritualistic saying but, rather, a growth in capacities, personality scope, and powers. The "new life" of which early Christians spoke is not, then, an idle euphemism or an empty figure of speech.

Again to say that Christianity is conceptual is not to exclude the emotions. On the contrary, because Christian teaching is so many-sided, involving examples, parables, stories, argument, history, admonition, plus all kinds of activities like praying, bowing the head, attending church, feeding the hungry, etc., its concepts are also assimilated in a variety of ways. The language of faith is properly embedded in the above range of activities and soon becomes not an interpretation of them but part of the activities themselves. To be exposed to that language is also to be exposed to the range of activities that it engenders, articulates, foments, extends, expresses, but, above all, that it helps to conceptualize. But a caveat must be entered, for a concept is not necessarily more perfectly articulated in speech than in other activities. Again, this depends upon the kind of concept with which one is dealing. So long have concepts been simply understood as general terms (or as universals) that it has been forgotten that this linguistic feature is only one of the realized powers of a concept. The concept really lies further back—it is the capacity that generates the general term and not the term itself.

However, our point is not particularly the linguistic one but is rather that among the powers of a concept is also its exercise in emotional ways. To understand most moral, but especially Christian, concepts, like "God," "providence," "love," "hope," "resurrection," "salvation," is ipso facto also to be made capable of deep and encompassing emotions. So to understand "salvation" is properly to be either repulsed or attracted, not just entertained; to understand "sin" is to feel guilt, maybe anguish, or perhaps revulsion at the very concept, but again there is no disinterested understanding available at all; to understand "redemption" through Jesus Christ's death is to feel joy or to be offended, perhaps to be made hopeful, not thrust into despair. This is the manner in which Christian theology is necessarily bound to a host of emotions. And the understanding of Christian teachings entails the emotional life as firmly as two times two equals four.

Theology in our day is simply remiss in not drawing this to the attention of all; but more, it is logically inadequate besides. For theology is nothing if it misses the logic and shape of the teachings; for that meaning is all tied up, in a delicate and many-sided way, with a host of emotions. More than this, there are specific Christian emotions. Hope that springs eternal in the human breast is not the same as Christian hope; for the latter is logically a function of the story of redemption whereas the former has to do with general well-being and the inveterate and altogether obvious disposition to look for the bright side of every difficulty. These are differing capacities.

This is to assert in another context, then, that emotions do have targets and/or are transitive. It is a mistake to assume that they simply exist in people, as if they were autonomous twitchings of the psyche and were only triggered by occasions and circumstances. The fact is they do not so exist. Emotions are part of the appraisal and judgmental activities of human life. Christianity enters the human scene with an account of God and the world that is calculated to make men judge their future, their prospects, themselves in a different way altogether. This is a good part of what theology helps us formulate, namely, all the differences that would thereby ensue.

Clearly, most of us are taught by common-sense judgments, by worldly wisdom, by the complicity of culture to which we are all heirs, to take the world to be fearful, odd, and taxing in a variety of ways. What we think of as natural emotions are usually the most general fears, hopes, affections that are congruent with the commonsensical judgments we all make. Theology confronts all of that with a polemical edge, for that is precisely what makes up worldliness. Even science and the truths of everyday life get tucked into that commodious matrix. And then we get a host of easily understood emotions that belong to all of this too. Here is where despair takes root, envy gets its hold, jealousy thrives, love gets partial, enmity flowers, and men become damned.

The message is that good tidings do not remove everything that produces emotions. But it breaks up the familiar logic of the emotions. Many people cannot live without pain, but the New Testament does not allow us to luxuriate in the notion that pain is bound for all time to desperation and defiance. Amid suffering, even pain, one can also find a deep joy. The missing feature is supplied—God—who is like a middle term whereby another emotion is projected. Almost all of us have to learn to live alone; and it is difficult to avoid loneliness, that dreadful, debilitating emotion. But again the link between being alone and being lonely is broken by a God who is with us always, even unto the end of the age. Men scream with the consequences of injustice and they wallow in indignation and a deep moral anger. Here, too, there is no necessary link between suffering an injustice and being so hurt that one thinks resentment is completely justified. Even resentment can be replaced, if not modified, when God is remembered.

The world is a very mad place anyway. The deepest kind of unhappiness of all is that fulsome moral and emotional disquietude that grips man after man. The social engineers who would have us believe that being prosperous, healthy, justly treated, educated, cultivated, etc., would lead to a happy set of emotions, like peace of mind, contentment, hopefulness, and just enough excitement to keep interest maximal, are usually themselves doomed to disappointment. It is not that emotions are random or casual, but rather that they are appraisals; and appraisals are as variegated as the people who make them, plus the circumstances. It is not the variables alone that bother us; it is rather that there are so few invariants. That is the way it is for people. The targets keep moving, but so do the people change. This is why emotions are so difficult to engineer: in principle it is not even conceivable, let alone possible.

No wonder, then, that men's lives are so desperate and happiness so fleeting. After a while there is no measure and no standard. Everything looks arbitrary and fleeting, mostly because it is. But Christianity puts a stop to the madness and calms the spirit. It tells us about God who casts no shadow by turning, who is the source for all the days of men. And once we get that at all clear, we are on the path to a peace for ourselves amid war, a hope amid frustration, a love amid spite, an imperturbability amid perturbations, even personal quietude amid the chaos.

The conceptual and the emotional, or as Kierkegaard called them, the dialectical and the pathetic, are delightfully intertwined. It is not obvious that the teachings must *always* precede the emotions; for sometimes the emotions can be learned, first; and their very presence gives good reasons why the teachings are subsequently believed. Mostly, however, the teachings do come first and the emotions subsequently. Any deeply religious man is, after a while, accustomed to emotions and feelings that are of a kind utterly remote from those that are thought normal to everyday life. The birth, life, death, and resurrection of Jesus are the matrix for the God, *ego sum alpha et omega*; but they also provide the lineaments for a companionship that demands a whole range of new concepts as well as new emotions. And these connections and these novelties, their logic and their relations, are the burden of theology.

"Come unto me all ye that labor and are heavy laden, and I will give you rest." This is what Jesus says. In whatever tongue that is spoken, there is always some kind of appeal. It would be odd, indeed, to be completely unmoved. Our suffering humanity stretches out for a little of the comfort of these poignant words. What else qualifies a man to respond other than the weariness, dismay, suffering, and deep discouragement that sooner or later grips almost all conscientious persons. No wonder, then, that so many men stretch out for this loving solace that promises so much and yet asks so little.

CHAPTER 14

About Emotions and Passions

Y OU COULD IMAGINE AN old woman, a little sarcastic about a husband who never did very well by her, saying, "He wasn't much to brag about—he was no good in the house and no help with the children. But one thing is sure, he made something of those stamps." If you wondered what kind of man that husband had been, it might surprise you to learn that he had a very big stamp collection. The more you would learn about him, the more your surprise. For let us suppose he was not much otherwise.

But he did go after those stamps! He went to the stamp store every week, rain or shine; he looked them over carefully and made careful purchases. When he got home, he placed them carefully in books. He looked at them very often; he compared his stamps with other collectors. Above all, he clearly liked the stamps and spent his time and money on them. Furthermore, he gave up other things, like bowling and motorcycles, the local tavern and even the care of the kids, so that he could care for those stamps. Perhaps his wife would have liked him to do something else, but, at least, she knew where he was and what he was doing, which is more than could be said for some husbands.

A man like that is in the grip of a passion. One of the signs of a passion is that it persists over a long period of time. This is what the old widow says when she admits that she has no right to complain, for that was the way he was before she married him. But the passion was gripping—it cut a big swath in that man's life. So with stamp collecting when it survives the early enthusiasm; so with patriotism when it continues after the fevers of war are over; so with a love affair when the excitement of the honeymoon is past. All of these are passions only when they are long, when they cut rather deep, when they command and explain a lot else in one's life.

Emotions are a little different. The boy or girl who is excited over the new stamp and its bright colors might have all kinds of emotions—delight, excitement, surprise! But ten minutes later, the call to do something else is just as enthusiastically embraced. When we are young and still not very well grounded, the world plays on us almost like an organist on his keys. And our enthusiasms come and go, we swell up and down with the circumstances, we cry and laugh, love deliciously and hate passionately, have friends and lose them for mere trivialities. Our emotions are frequent and short-lived. Both the way we think of things and how we take them is fairly shallow and almost flippant.

We all remember swearing lifelong allegiance to people whose names we can hardly remember. We loved with vehemence and disliked with vehemence the same things or people within the day or even the hour. Gradually, we learned to love more deeply and care more firmly. So we can then say that the Christian religion does, indeed, involve us in a whole set of emotions. But they are not at all like those we suffered in our ups and downs when we were young, or probably suffer now. The difference is that the emotions, like love, hope, grief, joy, that are urged upon us by the New Testament, are also held fast by a great and enduring passion.

Think about it this way. We have noted that patriotism is a passion. We can't quite imagine a thoughtless or careless person, or one who is very young, being properly patriotic. For patriotism requires that you care for your country, even when you dislike something, that you stick with it even when you disagree. But that requires more than easy emotional responses. The person who dislikes something and then says that he hates his country is shallow and does not quite understand his country. After a while, with a passion being worked out in our life, we also become able to care for our country even when its policies are not agreeable or its leadership looks rather shoddy. When you are patriotic in a deep way, you can also control those judgments a bit and you don't need to zigzag quite as much.

Remember, too, that stamp collector husband. Maybe when he was young, he vacillated between likes and dislikes, was overwhelmed now and then, discouraged when he saw all he didn't own. But later, though he cared more than ever, he did not wax and wane and he probably never lost his head over a stamp anymore. Nonetheless, he kept buying and pasting, examining and comparing, until he died. The passion was there but the emotions were different.

Surely it is the case that being a Christian is also a matter of having emotions. We would be fooling ourselves if we did not think that we were supposed to learn to hate sins. It is not enough just to vote against adultery, to disapprove of murder, to have a distaste for lewdness. We must also hate these things and then love mercy, kindness, justice, God, and neighbor. But does this mean we must zig and zag in pursuit of experience? Must we be immature? Must we look for a religious jag and make church a place where we can be turned on?

It would be that way if emotions were only what we remember them to be when we graduated and we had a lump in our throat. Or when we got married and felt so overwhelmed, or confirmed and felt so awed and undone; or when we heard the war was over, or that she loved you, or that you were going to get better! There is another way, other than by always collecting episodes and having big times.

That business of learning to love God with all your heart is a big part of being faithful. Here is where your faith also becomes a passion. If you let that love of God stick with you, it's like stamps and patriotism, only a lot better. Your life gets a plan to it—the passion organizes your life and helps to straighten one out. It saves one from shallowness and cheapness and even from altogether losing one's life.

The odd thing is that, of course, being a Christian involves emotions, and very deep and lovely ones too. But you do not need to search them out or ask for extravagant stimuli every day. Just like a true patriot does not need a war every year to feel good about his country, so a Christian does not need a religious bombshell to get his emotions started. If one learns to be faithful, he will, indeed, fear God but also love Him; he will have reasons for confidence and even a quiet contentment. More than this, he will see evil and also hate it mightily; he will uncover greed, malice, and jealousy, and grieve over them too. But, there is more, always more. That passion can be so thorough and so broad that it will make one glad to be alive. Then he can rejoice as the Apostle said he must! "Rejoice, again I say, rejoice!"

CHAPTER 15

The Human Heart
The Logic of a Metaphor

I

WITTGENSTEIN THOUGHT THAT ONE of the most dangerous ideas for a philosopher is the altogether familiar one that we think with our heads or in our heads. The notion gives birth to the conviction that thinking is an occult process, a silent and mysterious activity, going on in ways that are occasionally logical, within an enclosed space called the head.[1] Anyone who has read Wittgenstein's pages knows how deftly he attacks the misleading and strange puzzlements into which most of us are led by that very persuasive picture.

But there is another issue, different in many respects but similar in form, that I want to address, namely, the concept of "the human heart." For one thing, I wish to concern myself with the unfortunate fact that philosophers, along with many other learned people (psychologists, theologians, scholars of the world's literature) seem quite unable to use the expression "heart," let alone discern its logic and powers. More particularly, there is a fundamental dearth of discussion and understanding of the emotions, passions, and feelings. These seem to have been relegated to amateurs, to anyone who wants to be edifying, and to the poets. The concepts involved go without study and discipline. When Wittgenstein was brooding about thinking in the head, I find myself wondering about feeling something very deeply in one's heart. Is the latter more metaphysical than the former?

---

1. Wittgenstein, *Zettel*, nos. 605–6. See also *Philosophical Investigations*.

The omission by the learned is worthy of some thought. So is the effort to reduce emotions and feelings to something physiological. Many of us might think it odd to say that the thought of Napoleon's ignominious retreat from Russia is only a physiological event. So when I say it was ignominious, is that even more clearly my physiology because an emotion is involved?

The concept "heart" is both inescapable in everyday speech and yet embarrassing to acknowledge, at least, for the learned. It does not quite belong to any branch of learning—psychology, philosophy, theology, or even literary criticism. There is something absurd, too, about the fact that Rousseau would have us get rid of analysis in favor of "heart," for such a correction seems to have gotten things mixed up too.

But we can perhaps begin by acknowledging some familiar differences. Shakespeare had a fantastic command of language as well as of mood and feeling in order to write the many lines of anguish that flow from the mouth of Lady Macbeth. But he also wrote his lines for an audience; and many of us can testify how moving they are and almost hurtful in their poignancy. He could put language to an effective emotional use, but he did not bother to analyze his competencies or the emotions involved.

One might concur then with the notion that Shakespeare was able to make language a part of the emotional life. Instead of being about it, it was "of" it, and in a variety of ways. It is too simple to say that he allowed language to express "emotion," for "expression" would then have to cover too wide a gamut in any one of his plays. But clearly the prodigious diversity of everyday speech and the fantastic variety of things we all do with words, besides simply describing things, were provinces in which Shakespeare was an absolute master. What most of us do badly, he did in memorable ways, including the assimilation of feelingful and emotional talk. No wonder, then, that he could speak so beautifully, too, of the kinds of human hearts.

Hence, in *The Winter's Tale*, almost at third hand (a "gentleman" tells another about the King and Camillo, and the audience overhears this account), he so describes the extremities of human behavior that joy also breaks out in the theatre audience. Not much is said, but granted the detailed story the audience already knows, it is more than enough. Where the narrator of the story is uncertain, the audience is not for even one moment:

> There was speech in their dumbness, language in their very gesture; they looked as they had heard of a world ransomed, or one destroyed; a notable passion of wonder appeared in them; but the wisest beholder, that knew no more but seeing, could not say if the importance were joy or sorrow; but in the extremity of the one, it must needs be.[2]

Certainly Shakespeare's skill in bringing a thrill of reconciliation to his audience, not by splashing the principals before one, but by an off-hand bit of gossip, marks him off from most plodding authors and certainly most analytic students. He knew, also, how to put language to work so that emotions would be created, again, not by piling up the stimuli or overpowering the audience with lights, armies, and massive activities. He did it, instead, with the clever use of narrative, integrated, of course, to action, but most of that only reported and scarcely ever seen. So this is a skill, quite different from describing an emotion and different, too, from untangling an emotion concept.

Thus, it is plausible to say that Shakespeare's plays address human emotions and appeal to the human heart in a way that one cannot expect an analytical philosopher's pages to do. His game is different. All of us feel a little suspicious, too, with philosophers who try to be at all edifying. We think they are preaching, and/or being literary or rhetorical. Or, we have clumsy notions of someone becoming subjective when he ought to be objective.

Wittgenstein's remarks in the *Tractatus* (and the *Notebooks*) about ethics, God, death, the problems of life, did take on a kind of propositional form. He had articulated the dictum that "all propositions are of equal value," and shown that there are no propositions about any unequal and transcendental matters.[3] Still he produced those remarkable dicta in what seem to be a propositional form. Thus, these very rich pages always seem a little out of place, almost a concession to weakness and a threat to philosophical disinterestedness. Also, they seem a bit odd—almost as if Wittgenstein's heart was showing a bit. Hardly anyone who comments on the *Tractatus* dares to do

2. Shakespeare, *The Winter's Tale*, act 5, scene 2.
3. Wittgenstein, *Tractatus*, 6.4ff.

much with these passages. Almost anything else (tautology, formal objects, "sense," usually highly detached and abstract issues) seems preferable. It is as if such matters as are of the heart are too intimate, too personal in comparison with these more jaded topics. It is not the transcendental and metaphysical business that accounts for the difficulty. The difficulty with so-called transcendental matters is, rather, that the relation to the person of death, God, the good, and so forth, is what matters so much. To know about these things requires that one see both the object but also how it stands in relation to a person. And the emotions then came into play.

The query, again, is just why do the technically trained, the philosophers, the literary critics, and even theologians (perhaps psychologists) stay away from all of this? If it is technical incompetence, I find that slight disqualification; for since when did philosophers shy away from subject matter because they were not expert practitioners therein? Most historians of philosophy cannot do any philosophy that is noticeable; nor can most historians of religious thought ever speak with religious fervor in first person eloquence, let alone render up a doctrine. And are literary critics able to write a poem or other literature for themselves? But if it is an incompetence or emotional and passional matter, then, at least, we can begin to get a grip on the issue.

Wittgenstein obviously struck a note for some philosophically trained people when he insisted that all propositions were of equal value, and that the ones that looked unequal, foundational, metaphysical, and so forth, were really pseudo-propositions and, in sober manner, without sense. Besides being wrong about propositions, this argument is dependent upon so many subtle considerations that it is hard to conceive it serving as a rationale for large numbers of readers. Anyway the reluctance antedates his argument.

In Wittgenstein's later work, when thinking hard about troublesome psychological verbs, he mentions the expression: "In my heart I have determined on it." He has been worrying about "loving," "hoping," "pretending," "expecting," "understanding," and the strong proclivity to conclude that there are inward processes going on inside of you that correspond with all of these. Then he alludes to "determining in your heart" and adds: "And one is even inclined to point to one's breast as one says it. Psychologically this way of speaking should be

taken seriously. Why should it be taken less seriously than the assertion that belief is a state of mind?"[4] For the conviction that "understanding" and "expecting" and "knowing" are correlative to activities
in the mind is a serious matter. It produces, too, all kinds of mistakes
such as the notion that there must be subtle processes, and that they
are knowable, if at all, only by a strange kind of philosophical thinking or inward cognizing. Besides, there is the large-scale difficulty of
pushing reflection to a notion that there is a mind inside the head.
Moreover, all of this blinds us altogether to the differences between
capacities and activities. Neither Wittgenstein nor Ryle[5] is denying a
man the right to discriminate between "a good mind" and a bad one;
nor are they denying the right to use the concept "mind" in a host of
familiar ways. But it is the mistaken added reflection, mostly philosophical, that has created insoluble puzzles and that is being attacked.

The "heart" issue is like this but also a little different. Wittgenstein
thought the concept "heart" was so firmly established, and not the
worse for that, that someone might be taught to understand the meaning of the expression "seriously *meaning* what one says" by use of the
gesture of pointing at one's heart.[6] So much then, for its establishment
as a concept; to have put your heart into something, so that you really
mean it, might be all right. It would be something else to put emotion,
feelings, and sentiments into the heart, the way thought and decisions
have been put into the head. Surely that, too, would be a mistake.

If one thinks that belief is a "state," "of" and "in" the mind, then,
it seems one could as easily think the heart was the receptacle of
motives and emotions and fundamental inwardness. But here some
differences begin to emerge. For "the heart" is and has been treated
as a metaphor for a very long while (almost since the origin of the
concept), but "mind" has not been.[7] The consequence is that "mind"

4. Wittgenstein, *Philosophical Investigations*, part I, no. 589.

5. The reference here is to Gilbert Ryle, *The Concept of Mind*, where the author
quite clearly is cleaning up the accretions that have clustered around the notion of
"mind." He is not saying we have no rights to the expression.

6. Wittgenstein, *Philosophical Investigations*, part I, no. 590.

7. Thomas Hobbes, clearly enough, in *Leviathan*, thought William Harvey's
discovery of the circulation of the blood and his conviction that the heart was a
controlling organ of the body, a kind of scientific confirmation of the thesis that
the heart also controls man's desires and aversions. It was as if Hobbes used the talk
of heart in these descriptive ways to give a biological and physical foundation to a

has almost always been thought to have a "logic" and to be a proper subject of physiological and psychological inquiry, description, and analysis. Furthermore, a kind of conceptual gravity has been given everything of the mind by linking it up with prose, with philosophy, and with a kind of objectivity. But things of the heart are emotive, poetic, expressive, and nothing if not rankly subjective. Metaphor, yes; but this has been as much as to say that there are no criteria, that the sense is limited to the initiates, and that it all amounts to romancing, which may have its cadence and thrill but all of that a part of the "accidence," not the "essence."

This is to say that the logic of the metaphor, "the heart," has been obscured. One would be a fool to promise too much. There is the one word "heart" and a host of uses. So anything said of a general sort can only be schematic. But a few distinctions can be drawn and a kind of loose morphology may emerge. Perhaps in so doing something else will be made clear, namely, some of the reasons for the academic neglect and the conspiracy of silence on this issue. Maybe one could hope, too, for the use of the term "heart" among the scholarly, even a descriptive use once more.

I am supposing that the use of the concept "mind" has not been vitiated by the thought that there is no mind for physiologists to discover in the head, nor a spiritual thing for psychologists to map; yet "mind" is an inescapable and highly compacted "metaphor," useful in both everyday discourse and on any occasion when one is trying to explain a certain range of behavior. That is, if one plays a certain kind of game, the expression has its vitality—and it has not lost it because of the increase of knowledge or the tardy awareness that it is a metaphor. To this extent, something similar can be said about hearts. It is not as if the expression demands another theory, either to explain it or to replace it. It, too, has a continuing vitality.

---

kind of moral view—that men's hearts were moved to fear of precipitous and violent death above all else. The metaphysical "heart" here gets a biological and physical foundation. It becomes with the help of Harvey's hypothesis a piece of scientific metaphysics.

II

First, there is something to the notion that the expression "heart" as used in most common parlance is a metaphor. "He has no heart for the fight"; "She has a broken heart"; "The heart is sorely charged" (the doctor about Lady Macbeth, *Macbeth*, act 5, scene 1); "Out of the heart are the issues of life" (Prov 4:23); "A process in the weather of the heart" (Dylan Thomas); "Man looks on the outward appearance, but the Lord looks on the heart" (1 Sam 16:7); "for man believes with his heart" (Rom 10:10); "Then let them anatomize Regan; see what breeds about her heart" (*King Lear*, act 3, scene 6); "And the lost heart stiffens and rejoices" (T. S. Eliot, "Ash Wednesday," VI, line 11).

It is almost blatant that "heart," as used in the Bible and most literature in which character delineation plays a role (Shakespeare, Dante, Milton, Kierkegaard, Molière, Dickens), is a kind of place or seat of a variety of emotions and faculties. To characterize the heart, therefore, is like touching upon the essence of the man. For the heart is deemed host to intelligence, to imagination, to attention, to purpose, even to wisdom itself. And when men are glad or sad, it can be as easily said, especially when the gladness or sadness is deep rather than shallow, that the heart is glad or sad. Of course, it can also be afraid, angry, troubled, loving, large, hard, pure, but only when people are that way.

It is an interesting fact of literary history that far fewer users of the concept "heart" are prone to look for a non-metaphorical and theory-like case for it than one finds for the users of "mind." On the mind issue, the norm, statistically at least, seems to be almost entirely on getting to things fundamental almost at once. For it has been widely supposed that there are physiological and psychological, if not metaphysical, foundations for the mind. And some of the mind-theories do, clearly enough, also subsume emotions and often purport to usurp the role of the "heart" too.

But this subsumption of the "heart" is always a marginal intellectual effort that never carries conviction very far and seldom seems to reorient the majority of thoughtful writers. A difficulty is that such theories are usually more esoteric than the phenomena they seek to explain. So the concept "heart" goes on and on, almost from the beginnings of literature to our own day. Here and there it looks as though it has been vanquished for good, but it always came back with its explanatory forces still vague, by some standards, but still unimpaired, by others.

It seems that many users of the term have not been troubled by speculation and even the quasi-sciences of behaviorism and psychoanalysis, because they were invariably using the term metaphorically anyway. This is not to say that it was being used ornamentally or only in borrowed fashion either (parasitic upon a supposed literal use). The Bible writers, the Roman poets, certainly Shakespeare, are never even tempted to play another game on "heart" than the one they are already playing. What the intellectual culture developing around the "heart" does is to magnify the detail of human character, the knowledge of motives, purposes, consequences, and so forth, the effect of which is to credit even further the knowledge of the human heart. It takes a violent breach of intellectual history, one completely scornful of so-called arm-chair and literary psychology and one in which scientific psychology is being proposed, to discredit the earlier lore. But even then, the metaphor, though denigrated by the supposedly new factual description, has survived remarkably well.

It looks to a later glance as if this breach with the tradition was not as empirically grounded as it was claimed anyway. And the psychoanalytic and behavioristic accounts were more like promissory notes, quite unsecured by any factual collateral. Besides, neither of these so-called schools of thought provided any detail on the issues adumbrated by the "heart"; and their very neglect of these issues and the details, usually because they were incommensurate with the methodologies, has left the field almost as widely open as it was before.

Most of the Old Testament writers, despite their naiveté about human anatomy, were never even tempted to give pseudo-scientific accounts of the human heart. Supposedly they thought "physically" to the extent that they knew there was a heart in a man's body, and that when it stopped beating, death ensued. But their use of the term to explain behavior did not seem to obligate them to magnify the physical account. Their use had its own vitality. And the physical use of the term did not logically relate to the metaphysical use in any direct way. So quickly enough, we find the metaphorical uses being extended to name the "midst" or the innermost or hidden parts of the sea, of the earth, as well as of man. Mostly the metaphor works to contrast that in a man, his heart, which will differentiate him from his flesh, his garments, hands, eyes, ears, social standing, even his speech. The "heart" is the index to conscience, to what is private about him, to what has moral worth, to whatever there is about him that promises any moral productivity. It is as if anything that happens to him has to enter his heart before it will be of any abiding worth to him.[8] Above all, God sees and judges the heart, whereas men are deceived and taken in by appearances. The pathos of both the Old Testament and the New Testament is concentrated right here. For the quality of that heart is something that is open to a kind of self-knowledge, and, finally, everything depends upon its quality, even God's judgment.

But again, it is important to note two things. The term works always as a metaphor, even when a heart is required to be clean, washed, and pure. Furthermore, the utmost in pathos is required of each man in respect to the heart; for the very logic of heart is such that it is tied to the concepts of God, of judgment, of responsibility, and even to how much a man is worth. This is quite different from the picture given us in the Platonic dialogues where learning and most inquiry are construed as dependent upon a kind of remembering. Then one who is ignorant needs a teacher to remind him of what he already has laid up in his mind. For the ideas have been his, antedating as they do even his birth. Coming into the consciousness of them is pathos-ridden because it looks as if virtue is knowledge; but more than this, the doctrine of recollection also serves as the ground for the proving of the immortality of the soul.[9] In contrast to this, is, of course the Bible and most of Western literature that stresses "character." For here it is the human heart, with its emotions and feelings, with attendant

---

8. Note here Job 27:6; Deut 7:17, 8:17, 9:4; Isa 14:13. See also related uses in the New Testament: Matt 12:34; Rom 2:15. There are a host of other instances in the Bible that would be worth long reflection, for example, "The Lord looks on the heart" (1 Sam 16:7); "the secrets of the heart" (Ps 44:21); "the heart is deceitful, . . . who can understand it?" (Jer 17:9); committing adultery in your heart (Matt 5:27); "slow of heart to believe" (Luke 24:25); "become obedient from the heart" (Rom 6:17); "tablets of human hearts" (2 Cor 3:3); "that thoughts out of many hearts may be revealed" (Luke 2:35); and so forth.

9. Of course, my debt to Søren Kierkegaard's *Philosophical Fragments* is obvious enough.

and consequential vices and virtues, that looms up as the very center of the person.

Clearly the notion of "heart" is linked with the most crucial factors of our common life. But it does not seem to have suggested, therefore, any endeavor to get rid of the metaphor and try to declare these things in a more literal and non-metaphorical fashion. This is why Shakespeare's words in Lear's mouth are so sardonically odd, because their drift is so contrary to the use of the long-standing metaphor: "Then let them anatomize Regan, see what breeds about her heart. Is there any cause in nature that makes these hard hearts?"[10] Anyone who knows the language and persons well enough to use "heart" knows that anatomy and natural causes do not belong in this context at all. That's another game, and only Lear's intellectual and moral frustration and confusion would give the excuse for such a remark.

It is surely the case that much of the language of the Holy Scriptures is simply riddled with metaphors like this one. But this is not simply because it has to do with religion, as if its language must be anything but literal anyway. Rather, the language of the Bible shares this feature with most wisdom literature (the Epicurean, except when they do their philosophical determinism, the Stoics, the aphorists, Nietzsche, Montaigne, Pascal, La Rochefoucauld, and with the literary seers we have mentioned). Tolstoy, Dostoevsky, Shakespeare, T. S. Eliot, and even Lawrence Durrell[11] write both the language of the heart and also help define it. In fact, the task of talking about people in daily life seems to demand this metaphor too. So, to account for action, all of us—and certainly along with the literary sources mentioned—appeal to fears, loves, hopes, wants, desires, intentions, and motives. This is how we make ourselves transparent to others. It also is the way we understand ourselves and others.

The concept "heart" (for it is a concept while also being metaphorical) gets its authority and force from the fact that it does gather

10. Shakespeare, *King Lear*, act 3, scene 6.

11. In a preface to the poems called "The Death of General Uncebunke," Durrell says: "Not satire but an exercise in ironic compassion, celebrating a simplicity of heart which is proof against superiority or the tooth of the dog." This is, in part, an explanation of the style of these strange carols and soliloquies, and their content too. Durrell, "Death of General Uncebunke," 33.

together many of these familiar and altogether homely expressions, with which we explain ourselves and others. For there is no higher and better kind of explanation to be had of human behavior than the one that accords with our long standing patterns of explanations and that also accords with observation in the given case. So, I watch Macbeth secure the death of his friend, Banquo. How do I understand that unless I know Macbeth's envy, his fear of Banquo's "dauntless temper," and the fact that "under him, my genius is rebuked; as," Macbeth notes, "it is said, Mark Antony's was by Caesar."[12]

To say that I understand the working together of ambition, fear, envy, and downright malignancy in Macbeth's case is also to say that I know the heart of the man. It is as if he is responsible for something, principally, what he has made of himself, his heart, foul and malignant as it may be. But without the need for explaining in this ad hoc and non-generalizing way, that is, without involving laws of behavior or general statistical accounts, I would have no use for the concept of "heart" at all.

My point is that we have a metaphor like "heart" (and another like "mind") only where we are concerned about people with wants, loves, passions of all sorts, and the motley of emotions. And the Bible and the kinds of literature we have listed share the task of addressing people who are like that, and this orientation gives the metaphor "heart" its firm and large place. (The metaphor "mind" sometimes overlaps "heart" but only in part; and it also differs in significant respects, but that is another story.) Furthermore, there is a linkage between this kind of interest and the use of "heart" that is deeper than a polite literary convention. Things ought to be put the other way around, namely, that what looks like a literary and religio-moral connection is a concession to the inescapability of metaphorical talk when granted a certain kind of interest in human behavior.

In his poem "A Song," W. B. Yeats' picture of a heart surprisingly growing old—of desires ebbing, of enthusiasms waning, of zest fading, or ardor dissipating—is a very cryptic and precise way of gathering up a whole catena of behavior. It is not as if the metaphor is here decorative and trivial; instead it is a heavily impacted expression, drawing together a host of considerations that have no other way of

12. Shakespeare, *Macbeth*, act 3, scene 1.

being meaningfully centered.[13] In another poem, Yeats adds almost parenthetically: "Hearts are not had as a gift but hearts are earned."[14] The metaphor here does in part draw things together, but not in the interest of a general theory or some kind of statistical regularity. It is a mistake to assume that Yeats is doing something alternative to, and instead of, empirical psychology or by way of sketching a live option to Freudian psychoanalytic theory. It does not compete with them at all. If we did not have literary artists like this, we would have only everyday discourse.

But this is the way so much metaphorical talk has been rationalized. It is made to appear that metaphors have their role almost to appease, on the one side, the reader's interests, and to express, on the other, the writer's richness of pathos. That argument has been logically all wrong—it reads that metaphors are vague because emotional life is illy defined and without specification; and metaphors and literature invoking them are useful in the intellectual economy only because we do not as yet have more definitive and non-emotional explanations. All of this I say is wrong. For it has made the use of metaphors like "soul," "mind," "spirit," and "heart" look as if they never named anything at all and as if their use was only tolerated until a better discursive and general-law kind of account could be successfully perpetrated.

The fact is, instead, that human nature being what it is, there are no general laws and statistical summaries by which to summarize it at all. At this point, psychology and other elaborated general theories with a psychological interest, like Freud's and Jung's and many others, are not a refinement of ordinary human observation, and they are not substitutes in a formal mode for what we already have in informal and ad hoc fashion in our own observation and much of literary history. If one omits the latter, we have usually nothing at all. Literature formalizes everyday discourse, but science invents an entirely new game.

13. Yeats, "A Song," *The Wild Swans at Coole* (1919), in Yeats, *Collected Poems*, 137. [Editors' note: In the typescript of this essay, Holmer quotes in full stanzas 1 and 3 of Yeats' "A Song."]

14. Yeats, "Prayer for My Daughter" (1921), from *Michael Robartes and the Dancer*, in Yeats, *Collected Poems*, 186.

III

But there is more to metaphor than this. For another kind of point can be made from the fact that many factors in human behavior simply cannot be said at all. Instead they are shown us. However, language is so flexible and supple that language, too, becomes a part of the showing rather than simply about it. So, the expression in the Psalms about the fool "saying in his heart" that there is no God is not a poetic way of saying something plain, namely, that he is talking to himself and concluding that he is an atheist.[15] Instead the metaphor "heart" summarizes what a man's deeds and life already show. It is as if what the fool has done is in putting his life together already shows that he does not believe. Then the heart of the man would make meaningless any words to the contrary.

Here it is the case that words get their meanings not only when they conform to the way things are, as if they copy or reduplicate the world, but also when the words are truly congruent with the heart of the man. The concept of sincerity has a little of that ring, though it is a much abused and rather slight expression. The metaphor "heart" makes a wider variety of demands. For when a man has no heart, that is to say that he lacks capacity, not only skills (which "capacity" also covers), but also room in his life. It is like saying that he cannot rise to grief, or is incapable of joy over this or that, or cannot face yet one more round of difficulties. There is no single and sharp way to put all that, for a multitudinous range of things are involved. And one does not need a law or a generalization either. But more details are always useful, though the details, in a variety of cases, often tend to fan out the cases very considerably.

It is here where the concept "heart" becomes a useful abridgement, without thereby becoming a mistaken effort at over-standardization or even a false universal. The heart is also fickle and changeable, of course, mostly because people are notoriously so. But "heart" as an abridgement is not proposed to satisfy a cognitive interest as is a generalization about a biological or botanical range of specimens. People seldom fit such psychological generalizations anyway, at least when we discuss their feelings and emotions. For the

---

15. Note here O. K. Bouwsma's essay, "Anselm's Argument," in Bobik, *Nature of Philosophical Inquiry*, 252–93.

lineaments and features of human nature are not quite fixed, nor are they wildly random either. Surely, they do not permit quite the precision of a universal or the exactness of science. The difficulty is not that the facts are too difficult to master or the variables too many. It is rather that the complexities and diffusion do not reduce any further, and the application of law-like concepts and too great a precision is plainly logically wrong as well as empirically infeasible.

But there is a kind of order nonetheless. The logic of the metaphor "heart" is such that it fits people as they are. One has to think, therefore, of a contrasting case. We all know about color-blindness, either in ourselves or others. It is, nevertheless, a little difficult to say exactly what constitute the criteria for establishing it. The fact is, nonetheless, that there is widespread agreement, and hence there are criteria in that agreement about the judgments of colors. These judgments are made by those who are not color-blind. From all of this we learn what a given color concept is, and also what is involved in establishing and judging colors, correctly and incorrectly.[16] Admittedly it is from within the circle of those who have the capacity for color discrimination, that the very concepts of color get their determinate characterization. So, with the ability comes the concept, and the agreement follows suit.

The important issue here is that we do have agreement, even though capacities (which from some vantage points look subjective), which are shared, but not universally, are antecedent and requisite. But with feelings and emotions there is, by no means, the same kind of agreement. In respect to colors, we must admit capacities; so, too, with emotions and feelings. But a life of contrition is read by one man as very subtle feigning, another as genuine self-abnegation. Here, too, we admit that a kind of capacity is required for the judgment, but that admission does not issue in agreement. So, we are inclined to push the matter to an extreme and say either that the science of psychology is not yet developed, that there are facts there not yet observed or carefully enough articulated, or, that with us human beings, subjectivity is altogether random, that here there is no order, that the passions stand opposed to reason as the raw material does to the ordering principle.

16. Wittgenstein, *Philosophical Investigations*, part II, p. 227.

For in not being able to produce agreement, we are inclined to say that there can be no science. And to that extent, the argument is right, for there is no science of human behavior by analogy with the science of heavenly bodies. Furthermore, there is no way to project what such a science would look like, when the very facts which we wish to generalize about are not open to that disinterested and non-contextual study we propose. On the contrary, like the judgment of color depending upon those who are normal to make the judgment (who are the makers of the game, whereby the rules are set up), so the judgment of who is contrite, glad, angry, and dishonest involve, also, criteria that are only available to those who know in virtue of capacities. It takes wise men to do these things, we say. But the literary traditions and common life also leave room for the man who has "heart" for these things. The metaphor "heart," as a name for personality qualification, covers a lot of interlocking capacities.

Is this to say that each "heart" writes its own law and declares its own criteria? The romanticists of history would assert the rights of the heart like that. Then the "heart" becomes a metaphor for radical individualism and symptomatic of no standards at all. The more difficult task, almost thankless, is to admit that there is no way to get the kind of agreement we might want (if our expectations are formed elsewhere) about the judgments of the heart, not because they are so random and subjective, but because they are so momentous. Here we have no science and no indelible features that cry out for a scientific generalization. Instead, we have human beings, who are recognizable as persons and not animals, because their behavior is dependent upon so many factors; but more than that, because their behavior is also dependent upon the capacities they are willing and able to realize. Here is the massive *petitio*, the circle from which there is no escape, the limit beyond which we cannot think about these very important matters.

Therefore, to say that a human being has become hard-hearted is like recognizing that what he has done with himself has now made him incapable of all sorts of feelings and concerns. Surely there is a range of indefiniteness here; but the recognition can also be remarkably perspicuous and firm. But it involves not the ordinary range of discursive knowledge either. This is what we hint at in "understanding men" and "knowing their hearts." This knowing is not something easily said. It is the knowing that is like a recognition, when things begin to fall into place because something has been shown you by the person in what he does and says. For then his language also falls into place. It is understood not only for what is said by it, but also by its role and by what it is "of," not just "about." And that can't be said.

Again to say that one knows the "heart" of a man is a metaphorical and non-discursive way of summarizing this kind of knowing. Certainly there are people, probably those we call "wise" and graced with human understanding, who can piece behavior and people together with uncommon accuracy, who are fooled less often. These are the people whose judgments issue from a "better knowledge of mankind." Wittgenstein is probably right that we can learn this kind of thing but not by taking courses. It is only through experience and, one can add, thoughtful preoccupation. It might be like learning taste in aesthetic matters, where a correct judgment made by a master is the way one is taught, for there is no technique and no methodology. The correct judgment will, of course, be only a dogma to the thoughtless and the hapless student. But to the careful and concerned man, that very judgment will force the student to realize for himself those powers in which the judgment will come to life.

Learning the judgment is not the same as becoming tasteful. But it is all that can really be taught. So it is with most things of the heart, including morals and religion; but also the sort of things one reads about in Shakespeare's *Macbeth*, *King Lear*, *As You Like It*, when the characters and what they say and do is all there is. The rest, the requisites for the reader, cannot be stated for him, but must be done by him.

This is why Kierkegaard thought "indirect communication" as a concept had so much merit. For in important matters of aesthetic, moral, and religious significance, where the heart was painfully involved, all that one man could say to another was to speak categorically and in the "of" mood, while simultaneously, never allowing the learner only to repeat what was said—in the same mood. Instead a range of hints would have to goad the student into activating his subjectivity, his heart, so that the issues could actually come to exist for him.[17] Where capacities were necessary, even the language would have to be understood to reflect that capacity. The road to this understanding would be via the realizing of those capacities, and disinterested description and logical universals would here no longer be of much avail.

Putting this into a compact form requires metaphors. "Heart calleth unto heart," says the poet. Wittgenstein pushed another metaphor into prominence when he spoke about "forms of life." Certainly his expression covers, less graphically perhaps, much of the same territory. For is it not like this, that no longer to have a heart to discern what is cruel, disloyal, and morally outrageous, as Lear correctly sees his daughter, Regan, to be, is also to have lost a kind of form of life? Even what Regan says is nonsense to others.[18] But the metaphors "heart" and "form of life" are acknowledgments that subtle requisites (and they are a variety) are needed to perceive, to identify, and even to articulate human deeds and emotions. Of course, the "form of life" is also like a repository, as is the "heart," but it is also like a name for how the person becomes conventionalized after a while. One's deeds also count up—they bear fruit, they harden your heart and predispose you.

Many things that might count as reasons guiding one's action might be said to reflect one's heart or form of life too. After a while, these begin to hang together. One understands prospects and the future in ways that become standardized. Of course, it is also the case that even one's language becomes embedded in the form of life. And there are times when one cannot understand what another man is saying until one also understands his heart. There is a point to Wittgenstein's remark that is analogous: "What has to be accepted, the given, is—so one could say—*forms of life*."[19] No wonder the literary tradition, then, has been saying in effect for so long: "What has to be accepted, is—so one could say—the *human heart*."

17. Kierkegaard's *Concluding Unscientific Postscript* is a lengthy postscript to the *Fragments*, to this effect.

18. There is a kind of *connaître* as well as *savoir*. Language like Regan's does not belong to anything that Lear knows as a man of moral dignity but also tarnished by past ignobility; neither does he have *savoir* about it.

19. Wittgenstein, *Philosophical Investigations*, part II, p. 226.

IV

There is a point to saying that there are no hidden facts, that when revealed, will give us the terminological firmness and the nomological net that will amount to a science of human nature, for in one sense there is nothing much hidden. And the novelist, poets, and the dramatists, to whom we are all debtors, do not have another and sixth sense that the rest lack. It is a mistake to assume a greater sensitivity or a methodological scheme by which an epistemological advantage is secured.

But we cannot deny to Tolstoy and Shakespeare and other writers what seems obvious, namely, a plentitude of emotions, feelings, and other powers. These may, indeed, be the capacities that Kierkegaard, with sublime disregard for the difficulties, called poetic. By this he meant the power to project the possibilities of action, sentiments, and language, so that they were far more definite and idealized than they are in everyday life. These, in turn, become for a reader of the poetry a kind of mirror in which the reader sees what the quality of heart entails. Kierkegaard talked freely about the heart, but more particularly (and more akin to Wittgenstein) also about stages on life's way. So, too, he envisaged his own pseudonymous literature as a kind of educating of the human heart. It is as if the stages are paradigm instances of the way a man's heart and life may be formed.

But several issues can still be joined about the use of the concept "heart." There is a strong temptation to give the expression some kind of literal sense, a kind of trans-empirical grounding after all. One of these efforts is forced upon us by the long-standing and well-nigh universal hold that the expression "heart" has. The trans-cultural and trans-temporal use of the term is very likely to occasion our thinking that there is something unchangeable and fixed also about the human heart.

However, such a doctrine ought to be eschewed. It is almost as if we wish to explain the widespread use of such a metaphor by looking for another and more universal heart in men that is the foundation and referent of the term. And positing a fundamental likeness in human beings, which is metaphorically named as the heart, is exceedingly tempting. This is the kind of thing that has happened with the metaphor again and again. The business is deceptively attractive, both because we have a hard time explaining how, with all the differences that separate one age from another, we can still be appealed to by the classics, and secondly, it does look as if there are fundamental and necessary emotions that are grounded, almost ontologically. The "heart" seems a very good place to put them. Once more we have a transcendental metaphysics, this one suggested by a useful and common metaphor.

But the logic of the metaphor need not lead us in this direction at all. Neither do we have to posit fundamental emotions. For at bottom, even in their hearts, men are not the same. We all suffer a multitude of ideas and a cacophony of conviction; but it is inviting to think that where these are different, at least, our hearts are the same. Once, again, there is a temptation to make the heart the point of departure for a new metaphysics, perhaps like some existentialists and various literary philosophers. Then one is moved to think that there is, after all, a nature of man, testified to by his heart. And that, in turn is supposedly a symbolic way of speaking (if the argot is followed closely) about a man who has anxiety ontologically or who suffers insecurity just because of what he is. If this is the way a man is, then his nature is indeed a matter of description.

Obviously enough, if you remove everything different, what is left will be the same. Whether this kind of abstracting from this age or that, this circumstance or that, leaves one with anything at all is a moot point. I think not. Certainly we would have no feelings, no emotions, no wishes, not even words, if there were nothing to elicit them. For how can we talk at all about a man ontologically, independent of circumstances? That supposes knowing what a man is without any context at all. In such a barren environment, stripped of everything that had a name, a man could have no heart at all.

The logic of that metaphor "heart" is, on the contrary, all tied up to circumstances, people, and vicissitudes of all kinds. All emotions require targets and objects; and because there is an expectation built into our appraisals of things, we know in an appropriate way when fear, joy, and contentment are apt and when they are not. More than this, what we know about men, in general, is only something quite formal, namely, that they have a heart. But that means that they can acquire all kinds of abilities, all kinds of powers, to feel, to love, to hope, not just wildly but also as is suitable. Then it is that the temptation of John Falstaff can be understood so that you, too, will know a heart that can be beguiled by those merry but scheming wives of Windsor.

There is a way in which a well-developed sympathy and an insinuating intelligence will also enable a man to know how convictions and motive connect up for the scoundrels and rogues as well as the moral heroes and religious saints. To be practiced in this way is to have a heart for the multitudinous relations between thought and emotion, between wish and deed, between jealousy and murder, between lust and love, which relations again mark off one man's life from another. Here is where the logic of the heart is understood. Is it not like this? To recognize a desire is to see that a person or thing stands in a relation to a person. Knowing about persons and objects is to know the desire, for without these there is no desire *per se*. So, too, with fear, love, jealousy, anxiety, and the rest. After a while, great artistry, like personal understanding, gives voice to the great examples of the works of the human heart. Then we all easily participate in them, not as if we invent them, rather as if they simply are there in their own right.

It is far better, then, to fathom these changes in the heart, by whatever evidence is available; for in this manner, with novelist and poets, dramatists, and one's own experienced eye, one begins to assimilate grounds and consequence, such as they are. Surely they are different here than in other domains, but this is all that we have. A variegated kind of observation can, indeed, inform us about how men are, whether they are really this or that, or only feigning. Great examples also begin to loom up after a while.

But the evidence is not the kind that leads to generalizations and law-like accounts. Instead it leads to competence in reading the human heart. What is the evidence like? Wittgenstein made a point on behalf of "imponderable evidence." He said it

> includes subtleties of glance, of gesture, of tone. . . . I may recognize a genuine loving look, distinguish it from a pretended one. . . . But I may be quite incapable of describing the difference. And this not because the languages I know have no words for it. . . . Ask yourself: how does a man learn to get a "nose" for something? And how can this nose be used.[20]

20. Ibid., part II, p. 228.

To understand men in this way supposes a concept like "heart" in order to put things together. For both understanding human behavior and indulging it in any recognizable way requires a form to one's life, a minimal coherence between thought and action, conviction and feeling, hope and realization. To identify ourselves and another supposes that we recognize why he acts and thinks as he does. To know a man's heart is to understand the actions that flow around him and from him and is, by the very act of recognition, also, to know why he did them.

Not everything crucial is said—some things are shown. If one gets a little practical and becomes a spy in the artifices of human life, one also begins to know a bit how things will fall out. We learn after a while that some human hearts are such that desire will overcome discretion whenever that person stands in a certain relation to the world or another person. The great paradigms of the works of the heart have an almost metaphysical cast about them, not because the heart is immutable but rather because our hearts are mutable and can so easily participate in them. This is why there is a subtle work of intelligence that does not consist in inventing a new hypothesis and torturing nature of her secrets. Instead it is as if the familiar components of daily life need a form, and this incumbent need presses us towards a firmer grip upon ourselves and upon certain elements in our common consciousness. Unlike those philosophers and other learned people who, like journalists seeking a scoop, always want something new, here the proposal is more modest.

Is it not that the intellectual life also must be like a force of nature? The familiar materials of human life, to which we all have first-hand access, get out of focus and almost strange to us. The metaphor of the heart proposes a range of capacities to do two things: one, to effect a growth in power and competence that will provide a new living synthesis, a new heart, but, also, an intellectual means of ingathering and exploitation, by which a synthesis of otherwise strange things in behavior can be explained and understood.

There is a point to saying that we can use concepts to describe the behavior of animals. But animals can only illustrate those concepts and never understand them. But for men themselves, their action can also be governed by concepts that describe it. The metaphorical concept, heart, has consequently a double-edge—it explains and it governs. I am supposing that to see this much is to see how noble it is.

CHAPTER 16

About Happiness and the Concept, "Happiness"

I AM PROPOSING TO do several things in this essay. First, to proffer a series of reminders about the extent of our familiarity with the concept "happiness." These remarks will etch in depth our life-long concern with and pursuit of happiness as well as give us a few clues to the extent and the power of the concept in our daily life. Second, I propose sharpening up the concept "happiness," thereby being able to say in what "happiness" consists. Last, I want to link theology and happiness in a variety of ways.

I

All of us give thought to happiness. It is not only Aristotle, Plato, Mill, Aquinas, Pascal, Augustine, church fathers early and late, whose splendid ruminations stimulate reflection upon it, but daily life itself calls forth thought about it. "Happiness," as a word and concept, is a fundamental and readily available notion for the most elemental criticisms we make of human lives. The term is something we all think with, and it is a term that is not contrived and invented. Instead, it seems pressed upon us by the commerce and traffic of daily life. This is why we can say that it is fundamental—it is not launched by learned men and then taken up by the unlearned. Instead it has its vitality in common activities, in ordinary pursuits. It is a kind of "umpire" notion, used by almost everyone, to judge the quality of daily life. Philosophers, theologians, moral teachers, and psychologists are humble debtors to the race for the expression. They are teachers respecting it only in so far as they make minor clarifications and propose strategic considerations.

The competencies that enable a man to become adept at using the word "happiness" in responsible ways are not technical, but they are not unwitting either. One has to put his mind to the matter. Using the word "happiness" and its cognates is not like coughing, though one can also learn to do that slyly, politely, and with style. It is not a noise, naturally derived, hence unreflectively achieved. Nor does it simply gather up our exclamations of pleasure—our sighs, grunts, our "ahs" and "ohs."

The concept "happiness" is an achievement. We come to it in virtue of competencies that have to do with self-assessment, with efforts to be responsible, with learning that one can have reasons for his actions, with the business of criticizing our lives. Thus, the concept "happiness" comes to the fore in circumstances that are widely available and quite plain. When we want to tell someone, old or young, that a contemplated mode of conduct is inadvisable and even wrong, we can say: "It won't make you happy." And the expression "happy" here has its natural setting. For serious people do learn after a while something of the fundamental criteria that govern human lives, and to be told that something is likely to make another unhappy is to be reminded, not simply informed, of what does in fact govern many of our own wants.

Now, happiness (not just the concept "happiness") is not discovered the way gold is in the hills. We speak of "finding" happiness, but "finding" here is not identical with "discovering" and "uncovering" in their most familiar senses. Happiness often is inexplicable, as when we admit to days that are "happy beyond all words" and we cannot quite say why. God's grace is richly credited by Augustine with being the only explanation at all for happiness. But momentary periods of contentment and happiness are not enough for a way of life. We wish happiness to be life-long and not episodic. To have a happy life requires that one become happy, and one must "become" happy in ways that require all sorts of things besides, "finding," "uncovering," and "discovering."

The world has been full of happiness merchants since time began. Political nostrums and religious panaceas frequently get their hold upon us in virtue of their promise of happiness. An almost untold number of books are written on the arts, crafts, techniques of human happiness, all of them testifying, if to nothing else, to the extraordinary need and the readiness of the audience to seek it out. Even the promise of wisdom seems trivial to most of us if it does not also make us happy. But this happiness-literature seems to fail us unless the author has a way of making us more strenuous in pursuit and ardent in our concern for it. For the costs of human happiness—as Socrates reminded the Sophists, as Aristotle repeatedly noted, as Mill said to his critics—are high, but, I think, not incredibly so.

For human happiness is not a "thing," not a "secret" waiting to be disclosed. It is indeed a state of mind, but it does not float idly there either. It is not induced, it is not euphoria made by a drug, it is not unconscious bliss, it is not the pleasantry of oblivion as in sleep, it is not a false belief ("There is no evil," "Everything always comes out all right in the end," "Keep playing your deck, everybody's hand has happiness in it," and so forth). Instead, it is all bound up with one's way of life. Happiness accrues and emanates, it is an emergent in one's life history and is seldom, if ever, directly mounted.

But this is why the range of things that matter is so involved. We have to do with almost as much here as when we talk about a way of life or a view of life. This is why the concept is so notoriously difficult to be tidy about, why it seems diffuse and muddled, even when masters of analysis like Augustine, Mill, Aristotle, and Aquinas get to work on it. The concept, like happiness itself, is embedded in such enterprises as "making one's life meaningful" and "finding the sense" of things. Everything in these phrases, however poignant in a specific use, smack of cheapness on the one side, and opaqueness to clear thought on the other.

But this is all the more reason why the notion that all men are endowed with a desire for happiness needs no defense and little or no explanation. "We wish to be happy, do we not?" Augustine asks of his hearers. "No sooner had I said this, than they agreed, with one voice."[1] For the sentence is like an explication of the way it really is with us,

1. Augustine, *The Happy Life*, 2.10.

as if something confusing but elemental is being admitted. And there is surely widespread consensus upon the thought that a human life without happiness is not even a life—almost as if in not being happy one is not living. For "happiness" and "life" impinge upon one another and even overlap in large part. The more profound the happiness, the more significant and abundant that life is.

Happiness is, indeed, life's vital fluid, the breath of the nostrils, a basic human right, the stuff of human concern. So deeply rooted is the need for happiness that the desire for it is universal, instinctive, ineradicable, and absolutely imperative. It sets a limit to our thinking, a boundary to intellectual playfulness, for it is "unthinkable," in a very strong sense, to judge and to evaluate things human without invoking it. Men are made for happiness, but so much is this a depth-remark that it is almost silly to state it like that. For it seems to invite a recitation of cases to see whether we can find one negative instance— enough to deny the generalization. But to say what I have said is to put into indicative form what is something like a sense of propriety, a sense for where things belong, a nose for the way things are among men. One can see that men "choose" their policies, allegiances, wives, friends. They "choose" to exercise power, to have knowledge, to read a book. Some of them do these things after much thought. But it is obviously absurd to have someone say: "After due reading and much thought, much consultation and discussion, I think I will now choose a happy life."

Men do not "choose" happiness as they choose other things; they do not "desire" happiness as they desire books, sex, or fame; nor do they "want" it as one more thing among other things generally "wanted." And it is not quite so easy as some would have it, that "happiness" is a general "end" or "aim" and that other things are only "means" and specific objects of interest, desiring, wanting, and the rest. No, the remark about man being "made for happiness" sets the limit to the human community—it has to do with telling us what a fundamental criterion for being human is like. That is what being human means. To be essentially unhappy is to have missed one's goal and to fail to realize one's humanity. It is to fail in the difficult business of being a man.

To talk about happiness and to talk with the concept "happiness" are certainly to share something of the very grammar of human life itself. But here the notion of "grammar" gets a little too deep for most of us; and "depth" here has little to do with either philosophical-speculative propensities or purely technical-intellectual skills. Physics might be said to be "deep" because it supposes so much, namely, mathematical knowledge; and Heidegger is deep for most of us because you have to speculate about *Sein* and *Dasein*, and for many of us these words stay odd and obscure. But "depth" on the happiness issue is not like either of these kinds. I have said that remarks about happiness seem to me to be about the morphology and shape of human life itself. To be good at it supposes not quite being a scholar, not quite being learned about Aristotle and others who have written about pleasure, joy, and happiness. So it is almost as Wittgenstein suggested, that whatever propositions you want to learn, they are of equal value at least respecting the sense of life and its happiness. Know whatever you will, whatever field you choose, have few truths or many, but "happiness" does not loom up as something to be thereby encompassed.

It is more as if something else is prerequisite rather than discursive learning. And whatever is therein involved makes the matter "deep" in another way. One must be long concerned and not just concerned; one must be preoccupied and not just occupied by fits and starts with the quality of one's life; one must have learned to care and care a great deal about who and what one is, not just in passing. These characteristic behavior traits also begin to qualify people. They make them serious and are the necessary requisites for giving a certain gravity of life. I submit that such a kind of life-history is what gives depth to remarks, say in *The Brothers Karamazov* and in Wittgenstein's *Tractatus* as over against Walter Pitkin's eloquent and highly plausible and easily assimilable remarks about happiness in *Life Begins at Forty*. The notion of putting on the concepts of "happiness," of many emotions like "grief," "hope," and "love," in virtue of a clever book or a slick argument then becomes laughable. To be competent in these requires a peculiar depth indeed.

For these reasons, then, the grammar of such expressions supposes a kind of competence that is not easily learned or easily taught. On the other hand, the difficulties are not the ordinary variety either.

It is not quite a low intelligence quotient that is decisive or a lack of general culture. This is not to deny what was said earlier, namely, that all kinds of people happen upon the use of the word "happiness." In fact the expression is almost vulgar. But truly telling deployments of the expression, such that it gets hooked up responsibly with antecedents and alternatives, such that it gets a defined role rather than an incidental and fortuitous play, these are rare indeed. I suggest that one way to explicate that, albeit not very tellingly, is to say that one has not really become at all clear about the morphology and shape of one's life. This is still different from doing what Aristotle and others have done, namely, to describe the connections and intimate linkages, behavioral and linguistic, in which the concept functions.

Again the competencies that make us both able to talk like that and to respond to talk like that, to agree, disagree, to mend our ways, to consider our manner of life, these extend even further. There are ways of being pleasantly absorbed in the present, oblivious to both the prospects and the retrospects, void of both hope and regret, which, upon a little thought, we know is not a true happiness. There are other considerations that are borne in upon us quickly enough, so that even if we do not mouth the words, the thoughts find congruence in us. Momentary satisfactions, immediacies, feelings of pleasure—these are not all that make up happiness. We know that there is a frivolous happiness that belongs only to the thoughtless, to the young, to the teenager. I saw a young girl who had won a dollar on her father's gasoline purchase ticket leaping for joy, tears running down her cheeks, saying: "I'm so happy, I'm so happy." I thought it a credit to the father that he said, lamely, "Well, I'm happy too." But really he was glad for her, not in the deep moral sense "happy."

There is a logic to happiness, a kind of grading too, to which we fall heirs. We know, after a while, if we know something about human life, that there is a possibility of error. There are hollow satisfactions, meretricious joys, empty pleasures, pseudo-happiness. One can believe himself to be happy, even seem to be happy to others, yet be a deeply miserable man. One can be self-deceived, cheated almost by life itself, into ways of life that are productive of a false happiness. A life can be a failure even when full of pleasures. And pain by itself, like deprivation of this or that, is not enough to say that a life was a failure. But to miss true contentment, true happiness—this is to fail in living one's life.

By the same token, one can stand in possession of the greatest treasure, and yet, in thoughtlessness and light-mindedness, insist that he is absolutely destitute. So the person who does not feel pleasure every moment might be tempted to think that, therefore, he is not happy every moment. But this mistake is a trivial one. Suppose a Christian context, as an example. And then one's quest for happiness is indeed full of danger. Indeed one might be bold to say that there are false and trivial joys and pleasures that beguile men's hearts and cause them to miss the mark of a real human calling. High callings and somewhat lower, that of the New Testament as well as those described by Plato in *The Republic*, Aristotle in his *Nicomachean Ethics*, Augustine among the "Academics,"[2] are threatened by false happiness as much as they are by false beliefs, by pseudo-satisfaction as much as by delusions.

But all of this points up the fact that familiarity with the need for happiness is widespread. And the function of a certain range of discourse about it is not to supply information as much as it is to force one to self-consciousness about himself—to make him really human by making him concerned with happiness. This is not so much a matter about which men quarrel—it is a matter where men fail to be men. That is the kind of concept "happiness" is. It has its locus and arena in such a context. This is why, I believe, "happiness" has never been an obvious academic subject. It is too important! Preoccupation with it supposes personal seriousness, a kind of crying human need, and it suffers the same fate as does "wisdom" with which it is historically always linked. "Nobody, however," Augustine says, citing the wisdom tradition of Greece and Rome, "is wise if he is not happy."

II

But not everything is immediately clear about the concept. Therefore, I want to see if "happiness" can be made a little more transparent, by taking a couple of examples of major reflective works about happiness, both of which seem to me to be instructive and yet wrong.

2. Note Augustine's remarks in *The City of God*, bk. 19, where the academics are discussed on happiness.

Aristotle tells us that the aim of all men is happiness, which is the subject, he says, of all exhortation and discussion. In his *Rhetoric*, which is a book designed for public speakers, he tells us that happiness must be known if one is going to prepare men to deliberate on matters that are important and yet relatively free of rules. So he tells us that happiness may be defined as "Prosperity combined with virtue," "independence of life," "secure enjoyment of . . . pleasure," "a good condition of property and body." And, he adds, "That happiness is one or more of these things, pretty well everybody agrees."[3] But then he goes on to say that the conditions necessary for it are: good birth, many and good friends, wealth, health, beauty, fame, honor, and virtue—these among others. In short, happiness is highly conditional. Though it is "the" good, it is not widely available. It is no accident that he summarizes things by saying that one must have fortune and good luck on his side. Even in the remarks about happiness in his ethical writings, where he says that happiness is "an activity of the soul in accordance with virtue," he indicates that it is a rare happening, open only to those who are especially favored by fortune. It is no wonder that he asks: "Must no one at all, then, be called happy while he lives?"[4]

There is, of course, a certain obvious sense in this view. Being rooted in fortunate circumstances and special privilege does seem to most of us, who are not schooled by any kind of lofty disinterestedness, to be the sesame to what is desirable, inviting, and natural. There is no obvious rule that says you cannot mean by happiness just what Aristotle describes.

Some things seem remarkably the same, yesterday and today, for note what Walter B. Pitkin, a happiness merchant if there ever was one, held out as the promise of life in modern times: moderate wealth for all creative work, beautiful things, sports, a little daydreaming, a good fight in a decent cause, a community where beauty abounds, where a man may dress as he pleases, work that suits him, arts and letters, leisure, and a fine church with a great nave, from which the organ and the sounds of vespers ripple across the fields. Maybe we want a little more exotic sex thrown in since the appropriate skills

3. Aristotle, *Rhetoric*, 1.5.
4. Aristotle, *Nicomachean Ethics*, 1.10.

have been so well developed and well documented lately. But, be this as it may, Aristotle, Pitkin, Hefner, and most of us much of the time, are inclined to think that happiness is a matter of fortuitous and external conditions—that without these the minimal conditions are not even present.

It is hard to say what is wrong with this account. Surely what is wrong is not that it is an old view or expresses a Greek and aristocratic culture. Many of us would feel the difficulty in the following circumstance. If Aristotle found a man who was wealthy, healthy, intelligent, and fully independent who also said, "I do not feel happy, I feel miserable," then he would be inclined to say: "But if you are so fortunate, you are in fact happy—and that's the end of it." For if the constituents of happiness are these conditions, then happiness is a kind of "state" word. When you are in that state, you are happy whether you feel so or not.

Aristotle said "health" and "happy" were alike in this respect, that health was the highest assessment of a body's condition whereas happiness was the same of a man's total condition. We know that this analogy cannot be carried very far. One can say that another man is healthy even if he insists that he feels terrible, but it is a little odd to say that a man is happy in the face of his vehement denial thereof. For, surely, the business of being a man carries with it the noble task of being at rest with oneself, with being satisfied, with also being pleased with one's self-judgments. Indeed it is absurd to make a man's assessments the sole ground. But his assessment is a part of his total condition, and it is more important depending almost upon what kind of man he is.

I want to say then that men cannot be just "made and manufactured" happy. Happiness is not only a matter of being well placed. Just what connections there are between what fortune, politics, time and tide to men and their happiness is by no means obvious or clear. John Stuart Mill, ardent champion of the power of legislation to change the "social arrangements" and to effect greater happiness, is also the man who most clearly thought happiness was a psychological matter, if you will, a state of mind. He struck a note that seemed almost too blatantly obvious to qualify for being profound, saying that "each man desires his own happiness" as if this were an obvious psychological fact, and that "by happiness is intended a balance of pleasure over pain." So his argument is that we "feel" pleasure, and, of course, each of us "feels" his own pleasures and pains. Thus, being happy is fairly clearly a matter of having these states of mind, these feelings of pleasure over against the feelings of pain—physical, psychological, and what have you.

For better or worse, Mill had a very "average" view of what happiness is. It is almost as if he chooses to give voice to the statistical majority—he's terribly democratic about these matters. Where fortune has dealt unfairly and even unjustly with men—some are stupid, poor, friendless, ill—Mill thinks we can do a great deal to help them. For like Aristotle, Mill knew that there were immense differences in natural endowment and given circumstances. But Mill was also a man with great discernment and a powerful passion. He thought, too, that the "social arrangements" were, in his language, "wretched." It is almost as if where fortune had failed, legislation—the acts of men in concert—will succeed. Men can be liberated by education and legislation to find that pleasure, instead of the deprivation thereof, that will make them happy. Walter Rauschenbusch, who is often credited with being a new kind of theologian, was surely an old kind of utilitarian, very much like Mill. He said, identifying happiness, divine purpose, and human industries: "What is all the machinery of our industrial organization worth if it does not make human life healthful and happy?"[5]

But it was a happiness one "feels." Watching someone who is thirsty slake his thirst, we say, "Feel better?" This is the kind of "happiness" we all have talent for: "Happiness is a warm blanket," "Happiness is Snoopy's warm nose on a dark night," "Happiness is the teacher knowing your name on the first day." It is easy to conclude that happiness is a felt satisfaction of desire, a relieved drive, a resolved want, or an end to one's need. This means that for Mill one fundamental constituent of happiness is very clear—against Aristotle, one must *feel* happy in order to be happy. So "happiness" belongs roughly to what we can call then "a state of mind"—not only to circumstantial conditions. And surely he is right about that.

5. Rauschenbusch, *Christianity and the Social Crisis*, 370.

But there are hard cases. Augustine tells of one Sergius Orata, a relative of Catiline (referred to by Cicero) who was "a man of great riches, luxuries, and delights, not lacking anything in regard to pleasure, influence, dignity, and having a healthy constitution. . . . He had in abundance whatever his heart desired. . . . Perhaps one of you may say that this man desired to have more than he actually had. But this is unknown to us." Then Augustine tells us: "Through the greater sharpness of his mind he gained a deeper realization of the contingency of his possessions. Therefore he was bent down by fear . . . was miserable because of fear, not because of want."[6]

So there are occasions in human life when men are not happy even with wants satisfied. Euripides says: "If wealth flows in upon one, one may be perhaps luckier than one's neighbor, but still not happy."[7] In fact, happiness is not conceptually tied, nor actually tied, to any one set of facts in a human situation. One can be fortunately placed and not be happy—have blankets, acknowledging teachers, warm puppy-dog noses on one's hand, and still not be happy. Happiness is not engineered quite the way Mill thought it would be by general education and benign legislation. But this is not to say that happiness is simply an accident, completely unrooted, chancy, and fortuitous. Some are prone to say—well, if you can't tell me what the objective conditions are, then it must be only subjective! Happiness is not any one feeling, no one kind of satisfaction. It is not simple; but neither is it simply fortuitous and odd, rankly subjective.

A happy man cannot be simply accounted for. This has to do, surely, with the fact that he probably has a responsible way of life that he has practiced for a long time, and matters like that are not disclosed in five minutes or while you stand on one leg. But more than this, "happiness" has no particular target, no particular desire, no particular object, no particular emotion to which it is tied. Emotions, typically, have targets or objects. I'm afraid "of" something; I'm anxious about tomorrow; I'm sorry about "that." We can be joyful over lots of things, pleased (and we say "happy") about an election, but being "happy" as a man is not just being "pleased at" this or that. Nor is happiness simply a string of emotional states.

6. Augustine, *The Happy Life*, 4.26–27.
7. Euripides, *Medea*, lines 1229–30.

When Augustine says that Sergius was miserable, his misery was because of his fear of the contingency of his life and his possessions; but his unhappiness did not have the target the way his fear did. The man is unhappy and miserable, but he is not "unhappy at" or "miserable at" something or other.

But we can say more here that shows us how the concept works. For we do not like to use the word, except in extended and almost bracketed ways, about drunks, about the unconscious, about the dead. For though we find difficulty in calling people "happy" merely because luck is on their side, we also have difficulty calling them "happy" just because they are so virtuosic that they have lots of pleasures. Feelings are usually "feelings of" something; pleasure, for example! Feelings have targets and objects. But I have argued that one must "feel" happy in order to be happy, but now I want to add that there is no special object or pleasure-feeling that is thereby called for. No, what the word "feel" does here is simply to make it obvious that only to conscious creatures can "happiness" be ascribed, and, furthermore, only for periods of time, but not typically episodes. We have spasms of hunger, thirst, pleasure, and pain, but happiness must frame longer periods. And the criticism of men's lives, when we say that they are wretched and unhappy, is usually the sort of thing we say to fit a long period, not a short. People in pain, after surgery, are miserable but not in the strong sense "unhappy." We could still say "There is a happy man, but he surely is suffering." And it would be appropriate for him, were he asked, to say: "It hurts like hell, but I'm not an unhappy man. In a way, this doesn't matter." So, too, could he say about a sorrow, about a failure, about a worry over his future, etc.

Therefore, thinking over this range of instances, it seems to me, indeed, that happiness also becomes not just pleasure, not just the work of fortune, but another kind of state of mind. The sort I am talking about is borne in upon us when we have to choose in certain hard cases between deep incompatibles. Wanting incompatibles is the old story, and then one has to choose, and be free to choose, what one really wants. And we can even choose what we do not want. But there is no certain way of knowing, when we have got what we want, whether we will like it or not. But "liking it," namely, what one has got, is the necessary condition for a truly human happiness.

Therefore, I think it a mistake, really a mistake in a way of life, to assume that happiness will ensue when one fulfills the next desire or when one satisfies the next want. There is no telling about this. To make happiness dependent upon hitting a particular "target," in a range within a large target, seems to me to do violence both to the way we are as people and also to the very possibility of happiness.

Just as, to revert to Aristotle for a moment, a man can be healthy and one-legged, so one can be happy and have a lot of things be wrong. But one must be able to admit to being happy—one must feel happy—whereas with health, one can be it without feeling so. One can be crippled but healthy, one cannot be tubercular and healthy, jaundiced and healthy. One can be crippled and happy, in pain and happy, unsuccessful and happy, rich and happy, poor and happy, a victim and happy, adjudged unscrupulous and happy. There is not even, despite what Aristotle says, any necessary connection between being virtuous and happy. Happiness is, in the respects noted above, non-specific, but still nothing essential must be wrong.

But what is essential—that is the rub. Much of what a man thinks is essential and finds to be essential reflects his fundamental way of life. That is why the essentials are not quite what Aristotle said they were—fortune smiling, health, wealth, intellect, and friends. But nothing essential must be wrong in order to be happy. If it is wrong, then one is unhappy. But there is no neat formula. How many wishes do you need? One will never do. Wealth, celebrity, love—all are hazardous and temporary too. Pleasure and virtue have usually been thought to be minimum needs, almost guarantees of happiness.

It is not even that all that one prefers or wants has to be satisfied. One can give up everything for one's children's education and be happy in that self-deprivation; one can fulfill obligations that are onerous and be happy; one can die for the faith or for one's country or his friends and be happy; one can sacrifice his future for the sake of his wife's health and be happy. One can be happy—even find happiness, in things that are not pleasant to do. We can do things even gladly that are not pleasurable. But all of this seems to me to argue that happiness is not, therefore, again simply fortuitous and odd, idiosyncratic and strange. One must, in order to be happy, also learn to like and to enjoy what one is, what one has, what is prospective for oneself.

This is why being happy requires that one learn a kind of welcoming and accepting attitude. One can be alone and be happy; but he cannot be lonely and happy. One can be in the middle of peril and be happy; but he cannot be anxious and happy. One can be unsuccessful and happy; but he cannot be frustrated and happy. One can be guilty and happy; but he cannot be remorseful and happy. It is not a situation or one's place in life *per se* that guarantees happiness. Being lonely, poor, or suffering in themselves do not produce happiness or unhappiness. It is also how we take them—our feelings, emotions, responses, that determine whether we are happy or not.

Aristotle remarked long ago upon the fact that there were at least two kinds of pleasure. There were, he noted, obvious pleasure states, those associated with sex, hunger, comfort, which were rather obviously bodily. But there were others, too, the sort of pleasure one takes in something—in your child's accomplishment, in a good game, in a piece of music. John Stuart Mill tended to identify pleasures with "feeling" pleasures, therefore, mostly with the first group. But here I wish to note that taking pleasure in something is really accepting it heartily, doing and/or watching something with relish, even excitement. That seems to me to be a matter coming very close, indeed, to being happy. Except that happiness is surely like taking pleasure in something, in being more like an attitude and less like a feeling, but in order to be happiness it must extend over finally a large portion of human life. The truly happy man is the one who takes pleasure in living; he welcomes the prospect of more life and looks forward to his days. This is why, then, happiness, in the deepest moral sense, is not a felt pleasure or a succession of such pleasures. It is an attitude, which like all attitudes bespeaks a way of taking anything and everything that occurs. It is felt, but it is felt the way we feel an attitude.

Of course, all of this can be said in a Pollyannaish way—so that we simply tinker with attitudes or tinker with human conditions. But in a very deep sense, happiness requires a fundamental and very deep change in a man, something like a frame of life, a view of life that involves both his apprehension of the world and all that he is. Danger may produce anxiety in all of us, but danger is not enough to make one unhappy. It is in being prepared for any of the consequences, even allowing anxieties to excite one a bit, that allows happiness to flow forth.

If one is "bored," then one does not like what one is doing, one has no interest in what one is doing, and one becomes unhappy. If one is full of resentment, then one is terribly vulnerable, anything wounds one, even slights, and then, of course, one is a miserable man. Feeling happy is not the same as being happy, clearly enough, but feelings here are also dependent upon the view of life we have adopted.

A man can say, "I'm happy," and be wrong. He is not happy, he only thinks he is. "I'm so happy when I'm with her," the lover says. But he is either self-deceived or a liar. For we see him anxious, timid, perhaps in tears. He may be dishonest, lazy, forgetful, careless about himself. He may not understand himself, or he even may misunderstand the word "happy." So happiness is not a private state, to which only an individual has access. Even the feeling-component is subject to social and interpersonal criteria.

But to say one is happy indicates a state of mind. But something has to be right. Both his voluntary and involuntary behavior have to bear him out. Relationships are complex. If he sits hunched up, bites his nails, weeps, groans, and never smiles, there are the symptoms of unhappiness. No matter what he says, we judge him to be unhappy.

III

But now we turn to theological matters. Everyone needs reasons, at one time or another, for his actions. One needs a defensible general arrangement of human life that gives one reasons for this or that. I want to argue that theology is not only an account of beliefs, others' or your own, but that it is also something additional. For human life is not completely mad. There are connections of all sorts. A big reason for being a Christian is simply "because I'm happier that way." With Augustine, it is moot to declare that the Christian way is a wise way to go. And the task of theology is to make clear this pragmatic upshot of the faith. This is not a matter of feeling good while the tremolo stop is being played; it is not a matter of worship contrivance; neither is it an immediate "pop" pleasure, albeit under religious auspices.

Theology has proposals to make about the general arrangements of human life. Beliefs are that. They tell you that the earth is the Lord's; they tell you about the beginning and the end of things, within which arrangement a man can find his way and his happiness. This is a form of Christian rationality—within which one can arrange needs, desires, pleasures, hopes, pains, fears, and anxieties. There are dangers everywhere, but it is God's world. There are grounds for all the emotions you please, but the Christian kind of believing is the kind that should allow for rejoicing, not in just some things (anybody can do that), but in all things. We can welcome the world, its problems and lacks, not by denying them but by being strenuously motivated by them.

This is why Christian theology must also suggest and be responsible for a strategy. The concern for happiness is an absolutely minimal one. If we meet a man who lives only for the moment, who does not care whether he lives, or even whether he cares, who does not seek to be either content or discontent, happy or unhappy, then he has no motives for engaging in one set of activities or desires rather than any other. If either happiness or the concern for happiness is altogether absent, then he cannot be reasoned with at all. Such a man requires another kind of communication—perhaps something like psychotherapy. But theology always must be responsible to happiness and the need for it. Here its reasoning begins. Here is where God and man meet, and theology helps to prepare the liaison. This is why we must always, in a Christian interest, and even in a theological interest (if that is more intellectual and less a matter of soul care) be sure that the notion of happiness is still made clear and held up for everyone's wish!

And Christian happiness has its special character too. If a man is happy-oriented, but is not concerned with other people's happiness, then there is a Christian objection. To love God and to love man requires that one care about others' happiness; for God is a man's happiness and others' lives are indeed a matter of seeking happiness, and, also not finding it. But to show the shape of that kind of happiness, a kind that admits the ways of men but does not produce boredom or despair, but allows one to go on, even to welcome the struggle—this is also the task of theology.

To prosecute one's life, then, with an eye to this attitude and state of mind is also to seek happiness. Most people have no strategy at all, and those who have a strategy, even a Christian way of ordering their interests and beliefs and desires, often fail to apply it to certain regions of their life. That is why it is untheological, and irrational, not to plan one's life in a way to secure that happiness. There is then a rational way to live, in which a criterion for rationality is whether you are happy or not. Christian theology is rational in this respect. It proposes a kind of happiness one can have in God and a strategy by which to secure it.

It is a commonplace in our lives that a deep personal concern is what often makes a man biased if not downright prejudiced. And, of course, the issue is easily joined. But theology, as a form of reflection, engages a man on an issue that makes him think about his life—not just things in it. The concern for happiness indeed makes the world go round; not only that, it is also what makes men capable of certain powerful kinds of reflection—about the meaning of life and about Cicero's great question, "Where in the world are we going?"

Theology celebrates that range of issues that are often thought to be very deep. But when you get on the happiness issue, it turns out that the problems of life and the problems of theology start to get the same shape and form. And these problems are solved only when they disappear—and answers are arrived at only when there are no longer questions—when, as it were, our lives are the accounts that have settled them. That is why so many theological problems do not long stay on paper—they call for a religious life, a working strategy, a new way of seeing things and taking them one by one.

Theology impinges upon and helps us also to plot a strategy and way of life in which, so to speak, one starts to get the hang of himself and where he mounts his own problem. Then, like Augustine, he has less and less to say about what he has learned, because his whole life becomes the learning; and if one's life is successful and happy, there is no longer a problem that one's words really match.

Theology, when it has finally passed into a strategy, is content not only to sketch the world of a happy man but also requires that one be started on the move from being an unhappy man to a happy man. Theology does this by making us indeed look at what we say, and it helps us, then, to bring our own way of life to consciousness. But it is not only diagnosis—it is also part of the cure, for it promises the happiness that will give us coherence, inward and outward, in which life can go on. It sublimates the wish for happiness in its texture. It is no mean thing, in our day, to bring these intimate and heartfelt things once more into the reach of intellectual and personal assessment.

I suppose this is a lengthy way to say what we know already: that the more perfectly a man resembles God, the greater happiness he enjoys. And conversely, the less God-like, the more he wanders from his own happiness. But the best part of the Christian story, especially to those who want happiness and cannot manage it either by wishing or more strenuous kinds of discipline, is that the happy life is what can be properly called a gift of God.

CHAPTER 17

Something about What Makes It Funny

I

A THEORY OF HUMOR does not have to be funny. And it is not the worse for that. Does a theory about logical fallacies also have to be fallacious? Does a description of health have to be healthy and an hypothesis about humility itself humble? Of course not, we hasten to say. But it still seems odd to be serious, even to the extent of proposing a theory, about humor.

If being scholarly about humor were laughable, that at least would show us something about laughter. For often a laugh works like a judgment, putting things straight for a while. It sometimes gets us a little closer to the way things are. Maybe that is rather seldom. More common is our recognition that much of the laughter of the world is dreadfully stupid, and we can scarcely glean any sense from it at all. How pitiable it is to find someone who laughs at everything or laughs always; for then we are not only at the very nadir of human culture and taste, but worse, in the presence of one who makes little or no sense.

Even with a little thought, though, we can say with moderate confidence that most laughter is not completely random or altogether unpredictable. But we must distinguish a bit. Not every instance of hilarity is worthy of notice any more than every wordy noise, every bit of speech, is a part of a pattern of meaningfulness. Some people talk to keep themselves an ill company. Others talk because they can.

Others, indeed, because they cannot, and they take a paltry solace in the hum they create. But if one concluded therefore that talking was only random and chaotic, that it had neither cause nor motive, logic nor meaning, one would be quite wrong. Because talk that does something has its rules, we also know when talk is fortuitous and discontinuous. Laughter does not belong to people only because some of them have funny bones any more than speech does because they have larynxes.

But neither is talking necessitated by a general law. It does not follow from the supposed high-level principle that man is *homo loquens* that, therefore, every person must talk. And pompous Polonius is quite clear about those circumstances under which his son must not talk. He tells Laertes, who is about to embark on an untimely venture:

> Give thy thoughts no tongue,
> Nor any unproportioned thought his act.
> ... Give every man thy ear, but few thy voice;
> Take each man's censure, but reserve thy judgment.[1]

Indeed, we talk variously—for reasons, on impulse, with motive, on occasion, to this end or that, irrationally, rationally, with thinking and without. Men, being what they are, never quite talk as dogs bark. When talk sounds like a bark, we think it not quite talking; and then it probably would be subject to a psychological and lawlike explanation. More often, men talk for a wide variety of purposes, and one must discover from a wide knowledge of men the range of ad hoc possibilities that there are. This is what knowing men and human nature finally amounts to.

It would be very odd to say that people talk only in order to assert themselves. If this were stated as a general law, it would be both patently absurd and formally empty, not least when juxtaposed against the innumerable instances of talking. We cannot explain talking in a general way at all. So, too, is it with laughter. For how silly it is to say with Freud that all laughter and wit are but a vast sublimation and a way that the unconscious has of meeting pleasantly the exigencies that the authorities and necessities of social life impose upon us. On the other hand, how easy it is to crave for yet another general theory

1. Shakespeare, *Hamlet*, act 1, scene 3.

that will gather up the multifarious modes of the comic and give it a single and manageable interpretation.

We have some capacities at birth, we get more by a resolute use of our talents, some more by our profession and station in life. It would be odd to get our guilt by talent; and it is unbecoming to have repentance only by one's profession. But how is it with laughter? Are its boundaries fixed by nature? By culture? By accident? Does existence itself never require the laugh? When Santayana notes the contingency of daily life he does so in the interest of showing that that is what makes all of our experience inherently comic. It is funny in the same way that an accident is funny, except that when seen right there is a kind of perpetual accident of existence. But we have gone too far afield. Already we are suggesting that a view of life gives the setting and engenders the capacities for seeing the comical.

We might better start, perhaps, with simpler things. I read: "It is not generally known that the newt, although one of the smallest of our North American animals, has an extremely happy home life. It is just one of those facts which never gets bruited about." Robert Benchley wrote that with due solemnity in his *Of All Things*.[2] How different that is from the sardonic question asked Mary Todd Lincoln: "Aside from that, Mrs. Lincoln, did you enjoy the play?"

It is tempting, indeed, to believe that the concept "humor" must somehow capture the essence of these as well as other instances of jokes, situations, persons, at which we are likely to laugh. So Henri Bergson thought that the imposition of the mechanical and the physical categories upon the personal and moral made for the funny. "They had a volcano and they let it go out." If one says all humor is but an instance of contradiction, then one has another theory; and a theory here tells you what makes anything funny, though it might not tell you what makes people laugh. For there are fools who do not see the contradiction like there are those who laugh because others laugh but do not see the point of the joke. Already, though, we can see that the concept "humor" covers so many things it seems almost hopeless to insist upon an identifying universal, common to all the cases.

What is one supposed to say, too, when one hears W.C. Fields being asked for his opinion about the usefulness of clubs for women

2. Benchley, *Of All Things*, 3.

and being told that they were all right if all other forms of persuasion failed? Juxtaposing that remark against Kierkegaard's free rendering of a line from Shakespeare's *Twelfth Night*, "Better well hung than ill wed," is like trying to measure incommensurables. The guffaw that is right for one is quite unlike the wry smile for the other. But more than kinds of expressions are involved. The second remark, appearing as it does as a motto for an extraordinary book, is all the more wry for that. To be able to smile understandingly here supposes a very complicated mode of life and all kinds of subtle judgments. Without these, the words would be quite pointless. Without further ado, then, we will turn to another range of issues altogether. We will give up the theory of the comic and look around the motley that is humor and see if any other kind of accounting can be given.

II

Surely laughing by itself is not enough. Think of an analogy. If a child is counting one through ten, and correctly, but over and over, we might worry a bit. To get the sequence right is an achievement, but it does not qualify for "knowing how to count" except in the most restricted and primitive sense. One must learn when to count; but that is not a part of the sequence of numbers, and it has to be evinced by something besides another digit. One must learn that one counts, not the numbers, but with the numbers, and one counts almost anything else you please. If "counting" stops with repeating the numbers in sequence, something is wrong.

The child also smiles and chuckles—then it laughs. Maybe it is all because of gas bubbles or fresh clothes. But laughter cannot stay that way for very long. For the smile is not a very significant smile if it is only linked with a moving bubble. As the weave of a child's life gets a little more comprehensive that infantile smile is not thought to be a smile anymore. For smiles and chuckles must also get knotted into the fabric of life. Soon it becomes important to know what a child is smiling at, just as what goes before and what follows from a recitation of numbers will tell us whether the recitation signifies anything.

It is not amiss to say that laughter that goes on and on is an exceedingly queer phenomenon. If a man laughs too much, his laughter

290 PART FOUR: EMOTIONS, PASSIONS, AND VIRTUES

makes no sense. If a person cries about everything, then his crying makes no sense. It is important to ask "What are you crying about?" and "What are you laughing about?" Laughter, by itself, is an activity. But like all processes and activities of men it must be incorporated into other contexts before it becomes meaningful and human. Perhaps this can be sketched first schematically, then subsequently in a variety of other more specific ways.

We cannot infer much of anything from laughter that is never directed nor targeted. A grin is silly and pointless if it is constant and never proportioned to the world. So, too, the person who laughs at anything and everything himself becomes absurd and a subject of laughter, rather than his laughter being a clue to something else. Likewise that individual who weeps for anything or for nothing himself becomes sad, rather than his sadness being a part of a judgment we might share about how things are. But observe how strange that is, for the logic of weeping, the paradigm, one might say, is that it be over or about something. When it becomes clear that the person weeps irrelevantly, then the grief is understood to be something else, almost a symptom of oddity or illness or a deep personal pathology.

So the primitive and plain point is that laughter (and smiling, tittering, giggling, as well as suppressing laughter, smirking, and a host of other bits of behavior) also is brought into the stream of human vitality when connected both to a person's history and life and also to the world around us. One can laugh at things one remembers about oneself, but one can also assimilate the world around one with a laugh. In both cases we can say that a person laughs significantly when he laughs "at" or "about" something. That is what also counts for being conscious. If one laughs and laughs and no one knows why, we are likely to say that he or she is unconscious or, even worse, "ill" or "hysterical" or mentally ill. But if he laughs at what is not funny, we think him probably mistaken, or a fool, or uneducated. In the latter case, there is at least some sense; but that is because the laugh was about something, even though not about the right thing.

III

But this is not the only thing to be said about laughter. Laughter is subjective as are all activities, for subjects do them. This is not to say that laughter is without rules or that laughter depends only upon radically individuated facts of a personal sort. On the contrary, the comical and funny also have to be there. There must be something objective as the correlate. It is not enough to merely laugh "at" something; the something also has to be appropriate. Here, again, a theory becomes very tempting. We are prone to look for a standard case, a kind of invariant criterion in the state of affairs, that makes for the funny and the comical. Then the standard case justifies not just some laughter, but all. The point is not to deny the objectivity, but to deny that it is singular. Instead we have cases and not the case.

For is it that everything is simply neutral and that only thinking makes it good or bad? Does laughter make the world funny? We are likely to conclude that laughter depends upon the individual more particularly than does the judgment of an object's color. It seems obvious to us that the redness is very much "of" the object, whereas the humor of the situation is not quite what we call an objective matter. We acknowledge rather generally a sense of humor. It ranks with a sense of contrition, a sense of guilt, something like aesthetic taste, but very different from "sensing" an odor, seeing the streak of light, hearing the old refrain, or even grasping the point.

There is an odd way in which we have to say that looking, too, is a kind of activity. One can keep his eyes open and so, too, his ears. He can look and listen all the day long but never see or hear very much. The point of the ancient remark—they have eyes and see not, ears and hear not—has not been blunted by the passage of time. For it is also possible to enlarge capability, so that looking issues in seeing and listening in hearing. There seems scarcely any way to enumerate all that can be seen and heard, for there is no way to exhaust the capacities. But what is there, we continue to think, is there to be seen and to be heard. But the capacity creates the occasion for knowing what is there. Without capacities we have no way of saying in what our world consists. Seeing and hearing are still discoveries, not inventions.

Laughter and grieving are similar to these sensibilities in some respects; but they are also different. Certainly laughter begins like

crying, without any obvious direction and teleology. But in the normal course of affairs, human life becomes such that both laughter and
crying have their place. They cannot long remain totally unrelated.
They acquire significance, not quite like words, but not unlike words
in every respect, either. At least, laughing and crying must occur
in recognizable circumstances. Laughter belongs with the comic,
not with grief; crying belongs with grief, not with what is funny. Of
course there is the matter of laughing so hard that you cry, but we all
understand that kind of crying well enough. Likewise one can grieve
so long and deeply that one laughs irrationally. But the logic is already
established; otherwise we could not recognize such crying and laughter to be as odd as they are.

"Seeing" is tied to the visible in a different way, however, than
"laughing" is to the laughable. Laughing becomes more subtle. One
has had the language of hearing, as a sensibility, made more firm with
the syncopation of Brahms' intermezzi, which are audible, than one's
laugh is with the joke. We seem freer not to laugh, we are less obligated by the joke, than we are not to see the fury of the clouds or not to
hear the feigned madness in Hamlet's talk. This is to remark upon the
fact, then, a grammatical feature, that laughter is rather more bound
up with how one takes the whole of life, with the way one has formed
himself over a long period of time. Let us imagine instead the requirement of hearing the cricket's chirp in the cacophony of a city. Our
teacher trains us to hear what ordinary listening does not provide. So,
too, we can be taught to see what Aristotle saw with his naked eye,
whereas our untutored 20/20 vision alone does not permit us to do it.

There is, indeed, a matter of training, of fixing one's attention,
of discriminating, of recognizing, of giving names; and usually the
capacity comes along. We also can be trained to like, to feel dismay,
pleasure, or disdain, for those things that are likeable, dismaying,
pleasurable, or hateful. The linkage between having eyes and ears
and the visible and the audible is, however, fixed by a host of more
common activities in which we engage. They are rather plain activities, done in circumstances that are often to scale. We acquire capacities to see and to hear in a variety of ways that are well established
within our cultural contexts. One might almost say that our everyday
natural language also helps to elicit these capacities and to secure a

large number of the links between my psychological processes and the world around us. As we mature, formal learning provides a comprehensive conceptual system within which the link between seeing and what is visible is even more refined and declared, though never completely circumscribed.

Part of what is meant by being reasonable is to get the objective and the subjective very firmly tied together. After a while a well-trained person does get crying linked with the sorrowful and laughter with what is funny. We are not free to change those macroscopic connections, and we would only make ourselves utterly absurd and nonsensical if we tried. Nonetheless, within that general pattern, there are differences that mark off hearing and seeing as capacities from grieving and the delineation of what is comical. New factors enter in, and they are very subtle. They involve the fact that laughter is often connected, not exclusively with the descriptive language, the "about" language, that all of us assimilate and use continually, but also with those kinds of talk that are "of" a way of taking things, those stretches of languages that are evaluative and are the very means of making character, not describing it, of being a person, not tracing it, of qualitatively delineating our world, not enumerating its features. Therefore, laughter also becomes "of" and not only "about."

IV

In doleful remembrance of the dire predictions of the Democrats before the election of 1964, a newspaper columnist said (some twenty months thereafter): "Think where we'd be if Goldwater got in—we might be bombing Vietnam, have our fleet out there, maybe landing troops. . . ." One could not laugh unless one understood a number of things here. Someone fed up with the moral pomposity of the liberal tradition might have sardonically enjoyed seeing a Democratic president and Congress, liberal all the way, stumbling into the very behavior that once was held up as the threat of conservatism. But laughing here is not quite like hearing the cricket. The laugh is not required unless the anomaly is pointed out. There are a number of conditions laid down, depending upon how one has formed his confidences and convictions that are involved. There is a stronger dependence upon how one has taken up the everyday affairs of politics that will affect one's perception. These factors are not stateable in totality, which is why we have to say with Dostoevsky that what you laugh at will often be more important than a life-attitude. The laugh "shows" what language cannot "say." So, though the objective state of affairs has to be there, it is also the case that the quality of the person, the manner of his subjectivity, also counts a great deal.

The man who takes the above newspaperman's wry comment as one more sign that politics is a joke, that nothing is finally worthwhile, that all is absurd, also laughs because something has been omitted. There is that kind of laughter that is not utterly fatuous but which is posited on the notion that life never makes any sense at all. But this, again, is not a judgment that is often articulated; it is rather evinced in cynicism and shows itself in the refusal to take seriously anything between now and the end of all things. And this is, of course, a clue as to how a view of life really functions, not in being something stateable in and of itself so much as it affects the how of everything else, including one's humor. Laughing derisively is not a sign of cynicism—it is cynicism. Here, then, human foibles and mistaken prognostications are fitted by a laugh so that they make one's judgment on life. This is what having a view of life amounts to. One might as well play billiards or trade in wine. Trivialities are as much in order as anything else. But this, too, shows the logic of such laughter.

Therefore one is not quite so sure why people laugh. One man laughs impartially and generously—everything is funny and nothing matters; another because of the contradiction that is so blatant. There is no one factor guaranteeing the laugh. But this is not to say that laughing is without all principle, either, or that it is only invidiously subjective, for we don't laugh with him who laughs at everything. It might be that one man who laughs at everything laughs because of immaturity, for he has never hooked up his psychological propensities with anything at all. He may be then a fool, or a lovable simpleton whose laughter does not count. But the other man who laughs at everything might be the kind who has foreshortened human life and sees everything from the point of view of the very long run. In that perspective, of course, nothing at all matters. Then everything ethical gets omitted and the energies of life are like sound and fury, signifying nothing. Men are funny for behaving as if their lives really mattered. Omitting the ethical is to overleap the privilege and the arduous business of making everything you do count in a qualitative game of life. But if life is not a game with rules, if it has no quality and is never dependent upon oneself and others, then it will likewise be an immense comedy. Then Goldwater and Democrats get wafted together into the ludicrous along with the rest. Men are absurd because they tried at all.

This kind of laughter obliterates the differences between success and failure, trying and not trying, the less good and the greater, some and more. To omit the ethical is not only to be without a scale by which to weigh human circumstances—for few moral men are capable of such explicitness anyway—but rather it is to be without the capacity to make even laughter discriminating. The laughter, too, becomes indeterminate and overgeneralized, almost like a mood or an undisciplined emotion.

After Khrushchev's five-hour rambling press conference, James Thurber reported: "Great oafs from little ikons grow," a remark he knew full well would not have been permitted just anywhere. Humor often takes a beating from the intellectual left as well as from the political right. This brings us to still another permutation. Ideologies of almost any kind find laughter quite dangerous. Philip Sidney, that courtly gendarme of literary manners, thought that laughter might lead a man to enjoy sin. In any case, laughter put to a use is often thought to be dangerous, and it really is; our day is not the first to witness a kind of boundary-fixing here. Most ideologies are born of some kind of quasi-moral passion in which the reworking of mankind is projected. But people are notoriously stubborn and very slow to choose their own good, as Voltaire so cunningly said. So terror and tension are quickly created. Then, too, given the enormity of the task and the seriousness of the aim, there is no time for comedy.

An ideological political system is one very obvious way to put the ethical and human life together. So, too, with religion when it is conceived exclusively in moral and political terms. Everything gets serious. God's will has to be done, time is short, injustices cry out for correction, and the stakes are high indeed. Ideologies, whether political, religio-moral, dictatorially inspired, or what-have-you, seldom permit a man that little bit of indifference in which he can laugh. For if one is always cranking up his emotions for an onslaught upon evil it is very difficult to smile. What if you had obligated yourself to keeping Switzerland the way it was—clear, orderly, everything working well, money flowing, and, above all, that peaceful way of life. Then you read Daudet's novel about Tartarin who is so amazed by the Alps. In his credulous appreciation he is convinced by an erstwhile acquaintance that the whole of Switzerland is run from below, from an area like the basement of an opera house, where an ingenious company has devised and maintained the machinery by which the waterfalls, the glaciers, crevasses, goats and shepherds, even the towns, are all kept working together.

One does need at least a moment or two, an indifferent moment, not crowded by pathos and principled pain, in order to laugh, for nothing blots out laughter more quickly than another strong emotion. Anxiety heads off almost every smile, while despair so blackens judgment that the comical is usually not seen at all. Most of all, though, the unremitting effort to synthesize the good with the everyday world will squeeze out almost anything funny.

When Robert F. Kennedy projected the possibility that Martin Luther King, Jr. might someday be President, his brother John said: "But do you think the country is ready for a Baptist?" Part of what is meant by a sense of humor is the capacity, for that is what it is, to practice a little detachment, to live a moment of *ataraxia*, amid a life of ardent endeavor, and thus to be able always to put things in a different light. An ethicality that is intelligent and civilized, where expectations are limited and men somewhat understood, is, besides being non-ideological, also the kind that creates room for the indifferent glance and the disinterested apprehension. Humor is often the means. Without the indifferent occasion, nothing warns us of the vast range of possibilities as well as a streak of intelligent humor. It is only a civilized ethicality, however, passionate but also rational, that permits a laugh like that.

If a person so perceived the world that caring at all was a waste of time, then the Kennedys and King would seem absurd for their effort. If, on the contrary, their efforts were so consuming that everything had to be sacrificed for it, then humor would be a distraction.

If the infinite and the good can really be programmed right now into everyday life, then a joke is always out of place. Then one is offended by disinterested thought along with laughter.

There is, too, that sickly humor that men enjoy because their own lives are mistaken and seldom serious. The man who postures, who slobbers and drools, who indulges in depravity, ignorance, drunkenness, irresponsibility, and finds that there are always those who will laugh, this man probably uses humor to keep the rendezvous with his own meaningless life. This is to laugh but almost without knowing why and being unable to afford the insight to find out. Men do use humor also as a kind of shield, protecting themselves from anything that might reveal the ugly puddle inside.

But we can laugh at Santayana's fanatic who redoubles his efforts after he has lost his aim, because we know that effort matters and so does the aim. That must be in the background; otherwise getting them confused would not seem so silly. The king who says he rules by divine right utters unwittingly a disclaimer when he says, "My kingdom for a fig." Is that better than morally earnest Americans buying cigarettes because "I'd walk a mile for a Camel"? If nothing were worth an effort, there would be nothing to smile at in either remark.

V

We have noted, then, several things. Laughter as an activity must become transitive and be directed at something. Then it is not empty pathos but becomes somewhat proportioned and ordered to the way things are. But how are things? There is a kind of humor that is dependent upon a form of life that is too comprehensive to be stated as a belief, a kind of cynicism that makes all of life a massive comedy and every man an unwitting comic figure. But this is to omit the ethical, whereby respective actions and deeds, thoughts and purposes, get a measure and criterion.

Once more, then, a deep way of life begins to intervene, casting up the affairs of self and others in a new light. Then putting moral needs and obligations together in the actual world becomes the fundamental teleology and the unwritten agenda. Then another kind of laugh is pressed out of one. For it is just a little funny that we are all such amateurs in living. We lack sophistication even in our customs, so that at least a sizeable number of us never learn our way around. The woman who seeks permission to establish herself as a public prostitute is one of those strange mishaps. If you miss the customs of language, as many of us do so often, then you miss a fundamental ordering agency, too. "Have you ever smoked after sex?" the young woman was asked by the solemn family-life researcher. "I don't know," she said, "I never looked."

Customs in speech and daily practice are a kind of minimal rule-governing that few of us can afford to neglect, save at inordinate cost. Students who marry in school—they put the heart before the course. Most of the time knowing the words is not the whole of it; we must also know their uses. How confusing it all can be, but only if you are committed to something—to the rule for the use. To confuse the uses on purpose supposes a committed mind, but also what we call wit. Dorothy Parker said about Katharine Hepburn that she "ran the gamut of emotion from A to B." The fact that you cannot have a "gamut" so limited, plus Hepburn who had it, requires again a disinterested intelligence, not completely ruled by the rule for "gamut" or by the charm of Hepburn.

Surely it is very important to accommodate to custom and rule. To miss either is to make our lives adiaphora and our speech meaningless. But it also is the case that being completely ruled is also absurd, for men have, after all, made the rules. Martin Luther saw that the scholarship of his day caused men to misread the indicatives and the imperatives of the Bible, so he stayed rather busy pointing out which was which. But think of that elderly Norwegian couple about whom the Swedes of Minnesota speak, who took twelve hours to traverse the new superhighway from Fargo to Minneapolis when it should have taken at most only five. Their explanation was simple: they had seen the sign "Clean Restroom," that there were thirty-seven of them, and cleaning that many had taken a lot of time.

Even though some humor is a little cruel, it is nice to know that "The pain in Twain stops mainly in the bwain." And custom carried to extremes also must be resisted. "I don't like working between meals" is a little different from not eating between them. Think also about education. It is, of course, the most serious business of all, for here is where the moral heritage, the established custom, the learning of men, the rules of language and life are all juxtaposed and given gentle instantiation in every young stripling. No wonder, then, the enthusiasm and the extraordinary concern and careful modulation given to every thought and expression. So, we read Artemus Ward, not too impressed with the teacher who says slowly and with great pathos, "The highest part of the mountain"—and there is a pause—"is the top." Pedantry is pedagogy gone mad; according to Elizabethan lore, the pretense of being able to outdo nature. Too many distinctions, useless words, pointless enunciation, rules gone mad!

How the world has laughed! But again only because there is something grave in it after all. So I read in a solemn and very detailed scholarly account of an ancient thinker about all those innumerable things that are now supposed to count: "When Plato died, the comedies of Aristophanes were found in his bed." It is a little bit like Cervantes who sketched the extraordinary good sense of Don Quixote on the most crazy expeditions imaginable. That absent-minded professor, renowned for his attention to every last detail, is the man who, Booth Tarkington tells us, scratched his pancake and poured the syrup down his back. From professor to pedant—an unwitting transition.

Then we have something new, he who is idiotic in his precision, who practices an excessive purism in grammar and in diction, and who is serious about the wrong things. Erasmus Montanus, who is full of zeal for the new learning, comes back to the village after his university career. Two of the villagers tell him:

> [We] are . . . honest, God-fearing people, who would rather wring our daughter's neck than marry her to anyone who says that the earth is round, and brings false doctrine into the village. . . . To tell the truth, we have always had pure faith here on the hill.[3]

It is all so derisive because Erasmus himself is too self-conscious in his caring and too zealous about the latest truths. How much genuine fun Molière and Holberg could have with both the newly educated and the professionals! Molière would have it that the world used to be interested in health, justice, and truth, but now the main endeavor seems to be to have more doctors, lawyers, and professors instead.

3. Holberg, *Erasmus Montanus*, act 4, scene 2.

Here the laughter is rooted not in deprecating one's society but rather in commitment to it. One has to be in the game of life; then the laughter is not stupid. It is the stupidity within the game at which one can smile. Thus if the reader were not committed to the truth there would not be much point to Kierkegaard's story of the poor fellow who, confined to a lunatic asylum, sought his escape. One day he leaped through the window to freedom but then thought that he surely would be recognized in the town and brought back. So he decided to prepare himself fully to convince everyone, by the objective truth of what he said, that all was in order with his sanity. Thinking about this as he walked along, he picked up a ball and placed it carefully in the tail pocket of his coat. Every time it struck, "politely speaking, on his hinder parts," he said: "Bang, the earth is round." Full of confidence he went to the city to convince his friends that he was sane, saying continually, "Bang, the earth is round." It was clear to all but the patient that he was not yet cured; but to the patient it added yet a new difficulty. As Kierkegaard wryly comments, "Does the asylum still crave yet another sacrifice for this opinion, as in the time when all men believed [the world] to be as flat as a pancake?"[4]

To return to our theme again. There is a kind of ridiculousness that depends for its recognition upon a commitment to what we have called moral factors as well as other rule-governed enterprises. One cannot pun in a language where anything goes. One cannot see insanity if all are insane; one cannot see the laughable unless the serious has its firm place; and there would be no dispassionate enjoyment unless there were passionate preoccupation, too. When every case in law is right, we are told in *King Lear*, we cannot but come to confusion. This is why, again, a moral way of life, involving decision, responsibility, a ruled life and speech, occasions the emergence of civilized humor. This is why a laugh so often puts things right and why a man who can laugh is never quite swallowed up like a victim. The comical also helps put him aright. It becomes a declaration, an instance of health, a clue to both a man and the world.

---

4. Kierkegaard, *Postscript*, 174.

VI

Just a concluding word, though, about religious matters and the laugh. We have all known the genre of Jewish humor and its great complexities; but Christian humor is not far behind. There is a kind that simply is about Christian things and is not, therefore, a prerogative nor a particular feature of being a Christian. So it is deliciously sad, knowing the custom of a Christian land like Denmark, to read about the poor gentleman who went down to the city hall to get a license to open up a brothel but was refused because he could not produce his baptismal certificate. There the whole confounded business of putting the Christian idea of God together with the world, so that it comes out like that, is a massive *reductio ad absurdum*. But then so is the priest, in the robes of the finest quality, reading the Scripture from a gold-encrusted lectern, in a cathedral of indescribable magnificence. The text is: "And God has chosen the base things of no repute," and nobody laughs.

I have always thought Mozart's Bassoon Concerto a little much; for with that throaty reediness squandered on exquisite developments it always has seemed to me a little like the battle between mind and matter, with matter winning again. But putting the Christian notion of God up against daily life is even a greater task, and any try is almost bound to provoke a laugh. For how could it ever be done? Surely it is serious, but that, too, is the condition for a significant laugh. For once you learn to laugh in this context you are absolutely done with laughter that is simply indeterminate, that is a feverish cackle of sensuous irritability and gratification, or that is plainly the smirk of recklessness and abandon. The idea of God puts an end to the indefinite excitement that unmitigated laughter produces. Indeed there is seriousness here, for without this God one can do nothing! A new understanding of where to laugh, and where not to, will then manifest itself.

If all have sinned and if none is good save God, then the human arrangement by which to accommodate to that, either socially or individually, is rather difficult, to say the least. Then the whole of existence is not only a kind of illness, it is also a comedy in a very special sense. It is a divine comedy, an extraordinary spectacle, but with a happy ending of God's own choosing. Like Graham Greene's novel, *The Comedians*, so are we all. All that effort, that planning, that seriousness—it is enough to drive one to cynicism. But the religious man as over against the sneering and sarcastically bemused man is not permitted not to care, not to work, not to be engaged. He need not, however, be full of pretense or promise, bombast or ideology, for the goal is *Paradiso*, eternal happiness, and his access to that is via the God-idea. An eternal unhappiness becomes increasingly unthinkable because no one who understands the words could make it a goal.

To see it from without is to see and perhaps be amused. But there is also permitted the laugh from within the effort and within the consciousness that without God one can do nothing. Then laughter gets a new ring to it—it becomes part of the joy that has no limit, that has no surcease and no terminus at all. One can afford to laugh, for human efforts are not that important; though they are required of each man, it is not as if God needs moral Atlases who will bear everything up for Him.

If one has appreciated life like this, humoristically, with the help of the God-idea, then one is close to faith itself. That was part of what Kierkegaard said. But we can note something else, namely, that this is the kind of humor also permitted a Christian, in addition to the others we have noted. "God has them in derision and laughs." We are in derision ourselves, and almost by effort sometimes; for there is also the harm that good men do and the good that bad men do— as Bertrand Russell so eloquently noted. Instead of slackening one's effort in cynical appraisal, however, one does all things through the power and command of Jesus Christ. One does them, but, it must be noted with an ease and a jest, that do not require a favorable accounting or a metaphysical certainty about the future or uniformity of effort on the part of all.

Someone wrote, "I was in that new alcove of the Museum of Modern Art studying the latest acquisition for thirty-five minutes before I realized it was the ventilator." How long does one have to live this life before one finds it to be something quite different than it initially appears? "One damn thing after another" says one seeker for wisdom about our common life. "A vale of tears," "a bridge of sighs to eternity," say others. Is it only privilege that can afford the laugh? Do poverty and sorrow and dismaying disappointments mitigate one's capacities for the humorous?

This, again, is the ideologist's and cynic's charge. This is why the laugh is so often like a theatrical trick, conjured up by privilege, opportunity, and talent. Of course there have been those who were so benefited that they could also buy their laughs along with comforts and ease. But the paid fool had a short life, for he did not please very long. Humor that is salvaged from the human scene by others is meretricious and desperate. Humor, like hope, like confidence, like courage, cannot always be vicarious. It has to get roots in one's way of life. And when it does, then a sense of humor shows itself continually, in a variety of ways.

For it might be that humor sometimes is a disguise for the hiddenness of one's faith, just when one is not prepared to go the next step and suffer openly for Jesus' sake. One sees how it is, Christianly speaking, but one does not effect the transition to discipleship—and then humor is an incognito for deeper things that one is not yet obedient enough to make plain. Under such circumstances a sense of humor is not an accidental feature but is really a part of the judgment about how things are. Amid the suffering contradictions there is a way, God's way through it and out of it; and that makes a life truly worthwhile. One learns by this means to take pleasure in living, as Aristotle noted long ago, even if one did not succeed to pleasures of the body in the ordinary sense. There are some laughs that give us a pleasure kick—"I've been as sick as a spy. I've had a code in my nose"—might be like that. And it's nice to know in these serious days, when we all have to be unusually earnest about women every minute, that there is a female life-force, named "Elaine Vitale," to match Bergson's male life-force, "Élan Vital."

But it is far better and more satisfying in the long run that humor produces not just a moment of pleasure but the thought that will motivate us to a gratification in being human. It is not that a laugh alone will dissolve terror and anxiety—a laugh is not quite enough. We also need that God-idea, which forces upon us the logic of God's comedy. The absurd has no logic and its laughter is hollow. But without overleaping the ethical and a life of striving—instead incorporating it *in toto*—the God-idea promises that taking pleasure in the spectacle is the beginning of eternal happiness. Taking it all with a smile, even a laugh, is part, then, of a way of life, Christian at that.

CHAPTER 18

The Case for the Virtues

I

M Y PROPOSAL HERE IS simply to vindicate the neglected concept of virtue both for the teaching of morals and for any account of morals. I am confident that I can retrace enough of the history of that neglect so that my regret about that neglect will not be mitigated thereby. The historical account does not suggest that theorizing has gotten that much better. In a small way, I hope herewith to restore the complex of concepts, those for vices and for virtues. My target is no one theorist; but it is a frame of mind, maybe even an attitude, within which the following is deemed plausible:

> The ethical theorist tries to understand the concepts we use in our everyday ethical decisions and judgments. Some of these concepts are perfectly fundamental: such are value, obligation and responsibility. It is the explicit or implicit presence of one of these concepts in a judgment which enables us to identify the judgment as ethical.[1]

I submit that these so-called fundamental concepts, plus some others like "the good," "the right," "ends," "aims," "imperatives," "rules," and even "universal" (and its derivatives), have blurred the moral life, on the one side, and also created a set of terms within which ethical theorizing has gone on to the detriment of agreement, certainty, and even sense itself.

1. Zink, *Concepts of Ethics*, ix.

My concerns will prove to be intertwined in much that follows. I am admitting that intertwining, but for a reason. Let me assume, for the sake of discussion here, a distinction between morals (and first-order moral talk) and ethical theory (second-order and in an "about" mood). I will be contending that the moral life is falsely described when "right," "good," "value," "imperatives," "obligation," etc., are assumed to be fundamental. But modern moral philosophers and a kind of popular morality surging through our common life has invariably pitched moral issues so that its terms have to construe wars, general social conditions, and widespread and generic issues. Obviously, then, the concept of virtue is dwarfed by such magnitude. I think this is a mistake; and it is a serious mistake both in moral teaching, where it is an omission, and in creating confusion and uncertainty about all moral issues. For if the primary moral issues are the rightness of the way, the responsibility of doctors in hard cases, private versus socialized medicine, distributive justice in this domain and that, then morals is also conjectural, shot full of ambiguity, and probably worse than it looks. I find the consequent skepticism about morals actually misplaced. On this scale of issue, we, indeed, do have a kind of uncertainty; but it is a mistake to assume that this range of concern is primary morality. More properly, it ought to be politics; and the range of possibilities are then admissible without misusing moral concepts or insisting even that these matters are fundamental.

But the second area of my concern is the meta-theory that is developed out of all of this. Here, again, where the uncertainties in the first-order discourse are so large, the second-order accounts can be nothing less than conjectural and indistinct. My proposal, then, in brief, is that by restoring the virtues to a first-order concern, moral teaching becomes feasible, attractive and even far more certain. My suspicion is that second-order moral theorizing begins also, therewith, to lose its attractiveness, if it does not disappear altogether. I will be arguing that there is a context in which it begins to look like nonsense; but more of that later. And I am not persuaded that the more recent ethical theory talk in philosophical circles and lately in the new sociological and anthropological contexts is any freer of skepticism. In fact, I find that ethical theory is now full of the intellectual dishevelment, of the making of parties and positions that once was found principally in metaphysics and clearly speculative domains.

And "vices" and "virtues" are not pushed into an historical niche, revived only to show the curious how far we have gotten since Aristotle, Aquinas, and maybe moralists like Dr. Johnson. Or one has had the concept of virtue associated with vulgar teaching, with Seneca, Cicero, mothers, Benjamin Franklin, Boy Scouts, and slogan-eering. Against all of that, we have sought another idiom altogether, in which idiom a generality might obtain and the very expression of which would have a logical sheen and even hardness that would seem worthy.

This is the situation demanding a re-evaluation. Perhaps more than that is in order—a rehabilitation of the vice-virtue conceptual language. For despite the apparent power of concepts like "value," "universality," and "imperatives," ethical theorizing seems to me to be artificial and almost completely unilluminating. For instead of bringing things to light, one finds that there is no one ethical theory; instead, there are ethical theories and no criteria by which to adjudicate their claims and to address their differences. This is how a new darkness of mind develops; and it is all the more surprising when the high-level terms that seemed so promising are being used. All of that logical-like talk, that rational discourse, that law-like generalization, that scientific prowess—yet the outcome is almost the opposite of what one was led to expect.

This line of argument also addresses, somewhat obliquely to be sure, the worry about moral epistemology. For there has been a notion made popular by the rise of epistemology that there is something called a general epistemology, which would be a theory of knowing. This theory might obtain in some independence of whatever, in this case or that, might be known. But I shall argue that there is very little to the idea of general epistemology, and certainly not enough to suggest remedies to moral uncertainty. On the contrary, in moral matters, as perhaps in some religious matters too, the knowing concerns are not mapped in either general logic or epistemology. Instead, the difficulties met in becoming virtuous are also the issues encountered in becoming certain and precise. So, one might say, in anticipation again of the argument, that becoming an ethical knower is all tied up with becoming virtuous.

It is tempting in all of this to conclude again that there is no point to the thinking about ethics, that it is all nonsense on cognitive grounds anyway. But this approach seems to me almost jejune and shallow. The issues are not quite caught up in that grandiloquent sweep. It is, in brief, that to conduct a discussion of moral issues is surely possible, but that beginning with terms like "value," "responsibility," "imperative," "obligation," etc., is to start altogether too high. For a variety of reasons, these lofty concepts do not require genuine competencies of us. We, in fact, are in the position of having to make these words mean something for us only by loose description and various kinds of stipulative and defining uses. At best, the work is done by the description, not by a genuine moral endeavor. Because this is so, the ethical theory talk is full of definitions and descriptions that beg definitions; and the disagreements keep getting multiplied the more clever the theorists and the more variegated the material described. So, too, with the large-scale talk about wars, about medical issues, and a host of policy issues.

By contrast I wish to suggest that there is another arena altogether where all of us do have to make sense. By being courageous, we achieve some semblance of meaningfulness in situations that are otherwise frightening and utterly bewildering; by being temperate, we modulate ourselves in situations that would tear us between extremes; by being honest, we stay legible where half-truths and duplicity otherwise completely confound us. The temptation is to think that larger terms, like "value" and "obligation," "good" and "right," will bring the understanding that moral confusion demands. In fact, these big concepts promise illumination and light. But in truth, they compound the difficulties and multiply the options even more. Furthermore, they are not fundamental, whereas the virtue concepts are.

But this set of concepts has been born out of an intimate acquaintance with the frightful business of making sense of every day and of an individual life. Here there are a host of concepts, too, some of them for virtues, some for vices (like envy, sloth, pride), some for emotions, some for passions, some for motives, activities, and capacities. I am choosing to talk principally with the "virtue" concept and concepts, but the close interconnection of the above kinds of concepts will entail another kind of blurring, a kind not altogether unwelcome, here and there.

II

Some of us remember, perchance, a few authors who became something like our moral teachers. There is that kind of novelist who provides more than recreation and becomes almost a didactic essayist, despite his literary delights. For example, Arnold Bennett was one of those for me. Both in his novels and in appended essays, Bennett separated morals, for a rebellious young reader, from religion and dulling conventional talk. In ways that seemed acute and also profitable, he brought the art of living to an exquisite pitch. It looked as though he knew, better than anyone else, how to arrange a life in order to extract the maximum satisfactions and abiding pleasure from all his actions. He declared a heretofore unthinkable possibility.

But the difficulty was that Bennett could not only describe such lives, but he also had to advocate a rational hedonism. He slipped into theory, as if theory were an improvement. This creed (with its thorny concepts) was not only praised in his pages, but the creedal theory ostensibly inspired, as an overt teaching, his successful characters. That hedonism supposedly inspired conduct. Whatever advantage his pages seemed to have for a young man, wanting a primer of instruction, was soon dissipated by the requisites of Bennett's instruction. For the moment one is asked to believe in rational hedonism, then, if you have a brain in your head, there are countless difficulties. Why this theory rather than that? And the greater Bennett's insistence upon his kind of hedonism as the only *fundamentum* for a worthy life, the less plausible a worthy life seemed to become.

Surely the logic is wrong here. Whatever the criticism one might want to level at the moral thrust made by Bennett's pages, there is still another issue. It is that he thinks, along with many writers on moral matters, that he can inspire with goodness in the abstract. There is a fatal flaw in all of this, an idea that intellectual standardization is necessary and that, thereby, a common kind of life is being proposed towards which all rational men and women will ultimately progress. The confusions are several. Because we recognize that there are indeed rules of a moral sort, too, we tend to think that human lives must be ruled and that individuality—motives, feelings, wishes—must also be conformed to a general scheme. But generality also is the curse.

There is another way altogether to conceive of all of this. For the issue is whether moral clarity can really be had at all in the abstract. The reason for much of the confusion in moral theory finally rests on the fact that there is nothing much to have a theory about. The subject matter, in one sense, is not there. And this is the case not because moral language and moral concepts are too gross for the subject matter—as if moral behavior were too refined or ethereal for words, but rather because the moral substance is not there to be scanned and circumscribed. The temptation, then, is to invent a general term, and by making the scope much larger hopefully to capture the essence. But it still is not there.

However, to speak thus sounds like one more denial of the objectivity of morals, and that is not the intent. Neither is it being suggested that moral language is, therefore, only subjective or emotive. The question is whether moral language is connected to anything moral, objective or subjective—whether and how it makes sense.

The issues are, at once, more complex and yet also more simple. We have to ask ourselves, "Of what are we ignorant?" When we ask for knowledge of the good, of the right, of pure obligation, or moral laws, what are we seeking? Are there such things to be found and to be known? The odd thing is that any answer to such questions seems to be a dogma. Most of the resplendent answers, in the schemes of Kant, Hegel, Hartmann, and even Richard Hare, have to share an ignoble fate. They join the ranks of the pretenders. Once more skepticism becomes rampant and, despite the lofty theory-like language, morality itself looks as though it were out of reach of responsible assessment.

But consider the logic again. Try as we will in recasting moral confusion in theoretical and general terms, we do not seem to be quite able to find an unequivocal moral law, the good *qua* good, or even the foundational value within which moral discourse gets its justification. Is it as Wittgenstein said, that all propositions are of equal value?[2] Then it would also be the case that trying to formulate ethical theories in such a way that there could be genuinely ethical propositions would be a vanity. For ethical propositions, propositions of value, would be clearly unequal and of tremendous importance. And if we say that ethical propositions are unequal and that ethics is tran-

2. Wittgenstein, *Tractatus,* 6.4.

scendental, then surely we are embarrassed having to defend propositions of a theory-sort about anything transcendental. So, it may be that the confusion and multiplicity of ethical themes, the disturbing and dogmatical character of even the meta-theories that claim to be neutral and very descriptive, is finally due to the attempt to say what cannot be said and to pretend to know what is, in principle, unknowable. But this, too, is a desperate way out, and we cannot conclude in such daring fashion until we have considered the issues again.

III

If we remember something about our lives and our everyday needs, we have a clue. For is it not true that most of us do not actually need big moral views, whereas we do need hope, courage, and rectitude? Most religious people are not in such exigent state that inclusive theologies will do more for them than charity, faith, and plain holiness. And certainly world-views and metaphysical schemes are a redundant kind of wisdom when we do not know what to do next. So we are back to the issues earlier noted. Most of us are quite without any kind of moral substance, and we lack, consequently, character and identity. We have no personality and no selfhood, and this we have to bring to birth.

However, this sounds esoteric and rare when stated so generally and abstractly. In more specific terms we live muddled lives, because we do not know what we want, what we ought to be, or how to conduct ourselves. The root difficulty is a personality vagueness. This does not mean that we are vague about a theory of personality. Consider for a moment the familiar situation of not knowing what we want. There is one way to think about wanting so that it will seem esoteric and inward, as if it takes a great skill to ascertain exactly what one's want, in fact, is. The thought seems to be that "wanting" is already going on inside of us, but that it goes on obscurely and in aphasic modes. The reason for our unclarity is then due to the character of "wanting," as though it were a drive, something moving us and directing us, about which we do not know until we set out to know.

But this is a long-standing and almost academic-like prejudice. "Wanting," as a concept, is thought to be vague because wanting, now considered as an internal process, is supposedly so various, so devious, and, above all, so haphazard. We tend to think that wanting must be unruly, chaotic, and surely individualistic. Obviously, if wanting is like that, then the not-knowing what you want is a matter of not being able to get clarity where none is to be had. The conceptual unclarity about "wanting" is then attributable to the chaos within, to the indefinite and vagrant mode of wants themselves. But we must also remember that what is said about wants is also said about most of human subjectivity and inwardness. Love, mercy, kindness, along with emotions, desires, passions, deep feelings, are thought about, as Kingsley suggested, as though they were squishy and squashy as a caterpillar.

But this is wrong. For "not knowing what you want" is not typically a matter of (1) having a want, and (2) not knowing it. Typically, again, we do not have, first, the want, and secondly, the knowing about the want. To have a want is to know it, and to know it is to have it. Our difficulty is not in being unaware and not clear, but in not having a want. And the personality clarification that is involved consists principally in learning to want steadily and long.

And what we say about wants can be said about love and hope, most deep feelings, and surely even encompassing passions. It is not the case that we already have these things and that they only lack expression and identification. The epistemological issue is not there. Rather, it is that in not having any deep feeling, any pathos, any want, we are doomed to not knowing because there is so little to know. The energy of life is missing, in consequence of which we could acquire these things.

But with a certain kind of wanting, hoping, loving—briefly what we are calling an energy of life—we begin to acquire a self and begin the process in virtue of which we are characterizable at all. There is, therefore, a very deep tragedy in hearing someone say: "My trouble is I've never known what I wanted." Again, it is not as though one's mind was clouded and that one did not pay attention to the want that was there, but rather that one never achieved that singularity and definition that comes from wanting. It was wanting itself that was missing—or if there was "wanting," it was probably episodic and random so that it never amounted to anything.

This is to remark then upon the logic of a lot of those psychological verbs. "Wishing," "proposing," "intending," "caring," "loving" are all, with some differences, like that too. All of them are not so much names of internal activities as much as they mark subtle achievements and capacities. What we often think about very generally as a kind of ignorance of ourselves can build into a very esoteric and false picture of the human being. Our ignorance of ourselves is attributed to the unavailability, the unassailable privacy if not completely opaque character of wants, purposes, drives, wishes, at least as understood from within. For if these are unconscious and dark, controlling us the way the pull of the moon does the action of the waves, then, of course, we are, very likely, similar to waves, objects, and events, in not being rational in themselves but only made rational to the extent that their behavior can be described, if at all, under general laws.

Then all knowledge of wants, drives, and wishes, would have, at best, to be inferred, and probably by an outsider at that. And if wants, desires, and wishes do inhabit us, almost like alien and enemy forces, so that it would take extraordinary courage to acknowledge them, then, again, the knowledge of them could only be teased out by the most subtle of methods. But I am proposing that this kind of talk is not that of another science at all. Neither is my resistance a stubborn anti-intellectualism nor a defense mechanism. Instead I want to make a claim that is of a logical sort. This esotericism about minds and men, personality and character, can only thrive where something elemental has been overlooked or plainly forgotten.

The vagueness we own to about ourselves—the lack of conceptual clarity about persons too—is due to a lack of personality qualification. Most of us are mysterious to ourselves in a way that is analogous to the mystery we see in most popular irrationalities. When little or no sense is being made, the logical criteria have no play at all. When persons talk sensibly and to the point, their arguments get a cumulative effect and the words begin to fall into place. But human lives also have to make sense. But that sense cannot be done on paper. Many of the obscurities we have intellectually about moral concerns (and even some religious matters) are traceable to the vagueness that our lives evince. For personality vagueness, not knowing oneself, is not initially a cognitive problem. It is not that personality is too spiritual a substance for the vulgarities of words; nor is language too symbolic and too public for the private self.

Personality vagueness is in consequence, usually, of there not being very much to know. For human life does not consist in having all these dark forces within and, then, learning about them. Rather it consists in learning also to will, to hope, to wish, to want, to feel deeply, etc. And such definitions and clarity as we are allowed of ourselves is mostly a function of how strenuously and continuously we have willed, wanted, hoped, and wished. It is not as if the human content is there, and it only remains to learn it; instead, the human content is not there, and the grand task, the moral task, is to establish it. That being done, there is usually little trick in knowing oneself.

But what about, then, the virtues? Of course, I am arguing that moral philosophy, in the enthusiasm for a kind of safe meta-ethics and theory talk, has not only failed to achieve that vaunted scientific neutrality and objectivity it aims at, but it leaves out something central to moral life. Inclining apparently to avoid moral trespassing and seeking above all to be scholarly, not admonitory and didactic, the ethicists, philosophical and religious, have left out what is crucial—the primary ethical stuff. For the depiction and pursuit of actual virtues, the terribly homely business of learning how to be polite in difficult circumstances; always prompt; courageous when threatened; temperate when zig-zagging looks right; "just" when advantages lie in injustices; these and more are the achievements, the habitual achievements, that make up the virtues. Without these, there simply is no primitive working context for the moral life. Surely, there is, then, no clarity about moral concepts either.

The oddest thing happens when wanting, wishing, and seeking get concentrated in our life histories. For by these and their virtues our lives make sense. Rather than the virtues being an alien imposition, it is the case that a life characterized by steady wanting, persistent desires, long-term loves, tempered likes and dislikes, etc., is also a rational life.

But a caveat must be entered here. I began by noting that much of the meta-theory talk today is distressingly uncertain. But its uncertainty reflects also the uncertainty of that kind of moral talk we have generated about right and wrong policies, the value of education, the issues in distributive justice schemes and the like. Here the persistent terms are "value," "obligation," and other second-level concepts. And the judgments in which they are exercised are invariably conjectural and hypothetical. Besides, there is no way to make them otherwise. The better part of wisdom here is to get used to the surmising character of policies and proposals and never to assume that the uncertainty here is the ground for moral skepticism. But meta-ethical accounts of medical ethics, of issues of war and peace, of distributive justice, can do little else but reflect the variety of options and likelihoods. Again, there is no way to greater moral certainty here; for this is not the arena in which fundamental moral concepts are born and in which they flourish. They are always extrapolated from a more primitive and simpler context.

Our general point is, thus, that there is a kind of moral language, that in which virtues are enjoined and practiced, which is hand-to-glove with primary moral life. Here the issue of moral knowing is simpler. To clarify the personality by the acquisition of deep feelings, powerful emotions, and standing virtues is also the means of clarifying the moral concepts and language. And the logic of these concepts and the relations between those concepts and the behavior, the virtues, is not quite another theory. But that logical delineation gives us the morphology of the moral life in something like a glance! Furthermore, such a grasp obviates the need of ethical theory in the more usual senses. The issues served by ethical theory, in effect, evaporate, once our life begins to serve as the epistemic occasion. Now, however, we can afford to turn again to the conventional stated difficulties we noted earlier with ethical theories.

IV

The character of moral theory talk is moot once more at this point. Wittgenstein, trying to explain the deep uncertainties about theory here, said plainly about ethics that it was transcendental.[3] And because it was transcendental, it is also an attempt to say what cannot be said. In all kinds of subtle and strange ways a large number of ethical thinkers seem to have been moved by some such notion

3. Ibid., 6.421.

as Wittgenstein articulated. For we have ethical propositions being made into all kinds of lesser things once the news got around. Any attempt to say something transcendental falls under a proscription— "hence also there can be no ethical propositions." So they were not propositions, but only emotive expressions; or those sentences were really nonsense and ought never to have been uttered at all; or, a simpler language of morals could be discerned within them and some meta-rules about that language could then be the subject matter for the ethicist's craft.

In all that something seems to be overlooked. We have talked and written ourselves into the notion that the high-level moral talk, discussion about policies and interpersonal matters, is actually the fundamental and foundational stuff of morals. We have, thus, become so enamored with "good," "right," "rules," and "imperatives" that we seem to think that these, plus the large position words (utilitarian, hedonic, and dozens of others) are decisive. This makes virtues and feelings, pathos and decisions, almost deductive derivatives. The big and general concepts look for us like the master achievements and powerfully descriptive, while the individually gained accomplishments are somehow thought to be consequences. But this is a reversal of the way things are.

Instead, ethical theorizing issued in skepticism and uncertainty and surely not in motivating behavior. For Wittgenstein and many other philosophical theorists, metaphysics and ethics, though undeniably about the most important of all matters, still become a scandal. Ethical theses, like metaphysical views, seem always a pretense. While promising knowledge of the good-in-itself and reality-in-itself, which knowledge most of us surely lack, these domains gave us nothing but a passel of competing themes and really no way to judge between them.

No wonder, then, the ignominious retreat of the moderns! All sorts of schemes are adduced to explain, to mollify, to reorient the science of ethics and the reader. Ethicists assert a kind of sociology of knowledge thesis in order to explicate the apparent skepticism; others maintain a kind of historicism and culture-bound notion of language and morals and faith; others insist that appraisal and evaluation are primitive and that morals are radically subjective.

All of this is done to make some sense out of the meta-ethics and, of course, also the first-order moral talk. The continually flailing about looks dangerously like an attempt to avert the outright charge of nonsense. And, from an outsider's standpoint, all of that energy being spent and the countless modifications, can make modern ethical theorizing look either very exciting—as if it is indeed where the action is—or else an hysterical effort to keep despair at bay.

I think it the latter, though I must admit that the twisting and turning has an aesthetic appeal, if nothing else. It surely is the case that the making of ethical theories is also scandalous, the more one wallows in that inconclusiveness. But it is too easy to say that ethical theorizing is simply a logical mistake—an attempt to say the unsayable. It is not quite "nonsense," by standards that are general, either logical or linguistic. Seeing how the theory talk arises here demands that one consider what the moral life and its achievements really are. Therefore, I propose, finally, to address the dissipation of sense in ethical theory, by thinking again about the virtues.

V

The difficulty with ethical theory, in brief, is not that it proposes being neutral or scientific or objective. One cannot fault the literature for being in that mood. The issue is deeper.

For ethical theories are indecisive in respect to two different areas. The vagueness we have about "right," "good," "obligation," "value," et al., is most probably due to the fact that these terms have their role in the context of judgment-making that has to do with policies, programs, decisions that are by the nature of the case tentative and logically uncertain. The point already made is that this range of issues, typically war and peace concerns, distributive justice matters, and others involving social action, is the range in which most people find themselves so easily preoccupied. And it is altogether simple to conjugate all such policy questions in a general conceptual rubric that give a moral-like color to the decision-making. Here it is that modern ethicists, religious talkers, and college moralizers get their audience and manage also to turn up the enthusiasm more than a little.

Any meta-talk here that tries to isolate the working concepts will soon enough discover that the uncertainties that dog the first also dog the second. Or at least we can say that the indecisiveness of the erstwhile moral agent is not materially resolved by ethical analysis and a restatement in a higher and disinterested conceptual medium. The motivation for ethical theory in this context would seem to me to disappear almost completely when one realizes that the meta-theory is not the means of achieving clarification and dispelling the ambiguities. One can say with some assurance that there is very likely no single way to get that anyway, granted the range of issues involved. But then the ethical theory need not be proposed as if transcendentals were involved or as if a genuine ethical proposition was being assayed. So much, then, for the effort in this context.

The other area, the second we noted, makes for a difficulty too. But it is finally that the vagueness of theory here, despite its meta-character, is due to the fact that the subject matter is not really at hand. Or rather, that what is at hand, namely, a frightful amount of moral meandering and indecisiveness, simply does not allow a clear and precise theory at all. For the difficulties are two-fold; there is, indeed, an imprecision of concept and definition—this exemplified in the plethora of theories and the inability of most of us to get understanding via the theory; the other, a non-linguistic matter, is simply that men and women do actually live by fits and starts and that their lives lack order, character, and anything that might match a definition.

But the subject matter, moral lives, is what we seem to overlook. In overlooking moral lives, we also seek to do by an ethical theory what only ethical effort can actually supply. Then the kind of nonsense we perpetrate is of an extremely complicated sort. For we speak vaguely about moral matters because we have no overpowering moral feeling. Our imprecision, our thoughtlessness, even the absence of moral concepts, is also due to the injustice of the rest of our behavior. It seems an inveterate tendency among us, augmented by long-standing academic prejudices, to push emotions and feelings to the periphery. It is as if pathos and caring are only an accompaniment, as if emotions are the adiaphora, and reasoning and moral discourse the mainstream of moral insight. But this is wrong. For one does not know his thoughts, he has them; and the man who says he does not know his own thoughts is only saying very clumsily that he does not have them. To become clear in thought is an achievement, not marked actually by becoming clear as much as it is, instead, by having a thought. So, too, with feelings. One is not ignorant of them. It is not right to say that one has them and is ignorant of them; instead, to be ignorant of them is, in everything except the most unusual of cases, not to have them.

Therefore, it is right to say, surely, that morals do involve emotions and feelings. But then to infer that ethical judgments are emotive, and also, thereby, trivial and unrevealing, is absurd. Emotions, feelings, and attitudes are not subjective and beyond an intellectual assessment. On the contrary, they are most properly either achievements or misachievements. We either win or lose, make or break, our life and character with them. And the achievements that the virtues name for us, such as being faithful, are not consequences of a formal obligation laid upon us, as much as they are composites of deep love for somebody and deep shame at being promiscuous. That is, the affection and shame, as deep feelings, are also achievements, and they have to be perpetrated and accomplished; and within their power in our lives, we are molded into faithful and persistent persons.

Besides, this is the story of most of the virtues. Ignorance of ourselves and of our own moral life is the refusal to act and to know. However, that refusal to know is a complex matter involving a reluctance to acknowledge plain needs and to respond positively by meeting them. We all want understanding without pain; but in morals, as in religion, understanding is, therefore, hedged. We cannot have it without inner change. As matters stand, moral issues are not resolvable by finding a new conceptual scheme, by refining the vocabulary and improving the powers of observation. All of these, obviously, can occur in moral matters; but they remain parenthetical unless we rid ourselves of self-deception. The self-deception, though, is never exclusively cognitive.

Once we take all the little steps and acquire the fear of being shallow, the dread of being a deceiver; once we conquer the anxiety of being deceived, the desire to be approved, the need to be popular; we are, also, in the position to be courageous when opposed, just when unrewarded, and maybe wise and temperate about a lot of little things.

No virtues are rewards; none are imposed; all are achievements. The large-scale questions about the good, obligation, value, and what is right do indeed float rather loosely over the human scene. With notions like that forming our questions, we seem to be seeking the hang of the world and ourselves. And the general ethical proposals look as if they are answers—systematic, cultural, historical—to those gnawing issues.

The difficulty is that they seem to ask for a knowledge we do not have. It looks often like the better part of wisdom to risk all that we can, even if we try to latch on to the transcendentals themselves! However, questions like that are finally not answerable in the same mode in which we raise them. To what use can we put that high-level ethical talk? With its inconclusiveness, the many answers, the equivocation, we might be tempted to say that the history of ethical theory shows us how nonsensical the whole inquiry is. There is another aspect. Let us admit that there is something odd about such questions and surely the answers. For in the human welter, it sometimes becomes manifest that the pursuit of low-scale achievements, feelings, emotions, and simple virtues also shows us that the high-scale quest was not quite genuine.

For when our lives are formed by hopes, by fears, by wants, by desires, and when these are trained and transmuted into the virtues, then our lives become a kind of answer in themselves. It is not as if the questions are answered *per se*, but rather as if the questions are no longer pertinent. It is as if the pursuit of virtues, not a purely abstract consideration, surely not a purely epistemological concern, straightens out the logical issue. Our lives are the accounts that settle the questions, not by answering them, but by being in their depth of pathos, depth of feeling, genuineness of preoccupation, that which makes the question of no account.

This is why virtuous people, who have in one sense "learned" the hang of themselves and their world, have that learning, not as something about which they can talk, but as an achievement. Then they have relatively little to say, not because they have omitted self-examination or forgotten something, but rather because nothing they would say would be the answer. The very problem has itself changed if it has not actually disappeared altogether.

We began by saying that the concept of virtue needs to be introduced into moral discourse again. Now I think we can begin to surmise why. For the virtue concepts, and the matrix of motive, pathos, feeling, want, emotion, desire, etc., within which they are embedded, have the power to phrase those elemental necessities that much of the rest of ethical talk often masks. These necessities most of us in inchoate and imprecise ways also know. But it is very human to deny them. And ethical theories, by always pitching everything in such lofty terms, become, unfortunately, one more way in which we omit consideration of them.

But to consider them makes us see that ethical propositions are not nonsensical because they are tries at saying something transcendental. Neither are they nonsensical because they are about value rather than facts, or imperatives disguised as indicatives. Instead, they are nonsensical because they make us look for a "good" or an "imperative," as if these were there to be seen, granted the right instrumentalities. We are not spectators to moral worth but its agents; and if anything can be known morally it is only by a moral achievement that makes the form of the proposition an irrelevancy. The pursuit of the virtues is the kind of activity that will, of itself, not answer the ethical problem; but it will show us, after a while, that there is no question left. Just this, as Wittgenstein says, is the answer. Yet more, they are nonsensical because they suggest that morals finally are sayable. But they cannot be said. They are shown by a life, in which virtues win over vices. To have sought them by an essay of words then looks like an all-too-human bit of foolishness.

CHAPTER 19

About Thankfulness

I

IN AN ANCIENT LITERARY source, we read something strange about human behavior. The author in an admonitory mood says rather boldly that there ought to be no filthiness and no silliness because these are not fitting; instead let there be, says the man of wisdom, thankfulness (Eph 5:4). From such a remark one can see readily enough that there is a kind of logic of the emotions, and of thankfulness in particular, that is being invoked. Unlike today's scene where we have knowledge about almost any topic that pleases us, and this without any great effort, that Apostle who said this could not turn to a library replete with books nor could he dial a lecture on any of a host of topics. He lived in a world that was poverty-stricken, at least if the quantity of knowledge marks a contemporary advantage. Yet that person, 1,900 years ago, could speak wisely and so uncommonly on a matter of behavior.

His wisdom obviously was a function of something besides an extensive objective knowledge. The Apostle Paul was party to a compelling "logic" of emotions and pathos, and this was apparently a great part of what made for his understanding and his wisdom. For hear him again. He says: "Let there be thanksgiving."

On the other hand, most of us have come to know ingrates whose behavior is the diametric opposite to what is appropriate. We can often see that clearly enough. But Paul suggests that ingratitude is not the only opposite to thankfulness; and that tells us something we do not expect to hear about the hidden structures of behavior. Ribaldry and silliness, coarseness and vulgarity, it would seem from Paul's remarks, get their sway in us when we lose our gratitude. Thankfulness has several opposites, not just one. There is more, for the same author insists that "always and for everything give thanks." Once more it looks as though the very notion of gratitude and thanks is being enlarged, probably by including too much and being thought of as a constant, whereas in everyday use that concept is highly selective and its occasions almost episodic.

In most settings, gratitude and the feeling of thankfulness are linked to those times when our wants and events begin to coincide. Wishes have to be fulfilled before we can be glad enough to manage a little praise; and desires need gratification in order that gratitude takes root. This is why the capacity for gratitude is customarily a bit fortuitous, and, equally, why we all come to think that grumbling has its justified large place in daily life. The ordinary and working conception of "thanks" is that the genuine and deserved causes for it are rather rare, as infrequent as those times when things appear to be working together for good. Mostly the machinations of the world look chaotic and the realization of a good is almost an accident. Furthermore, until our powers to change the world accord with our aspirations, plans, and thought of what the good is, it seems that gratitude will have to remain partial and its occasions very few.

All of this is a kind of ordering of thought that the everyday world effects in almost all of us. This is also what passes as worldly wisdom and a rather typical understanding. We need nothing esoteric to become a practitioner of such a lore. So too, in everyday life we have to postpone our happiness again and again. As long as the world remains as it is, not quite good enough to deserve praise, we must grumble and gripe our way from day to day. It is hard, indeed, to be both a grumbler and joyous except in moments of contrived forgetfulness of the world. Perhaps that, too, is how ribaldry and silliness get such a hold on us, almost as if they are the trivial formations of our spirit that permit us a few artificial satisfactions that the world does not otherwise provide. Refashioning the world is, obviously enough, a very strenuous activity; and the effort becomes ringed with pathos as soon as we think that our joy and our gratitude can only prosper when the world has been made good enough. Therein, amusements and distractions give us temporary relief and afford us interludes of happy endings and sequences without suffering.

Long ago, however, that eminent moralist and wise pagan, Plutarch, commented very gracefully and soberly about the price we pay for having tranquillity of mind only in moments of forgetfulness and induced amusement. He warned about the "insensible and thankless forgetfulness [that] steals upon the multitude and takes possession of them. . . . it does not allow life to become unified."[1] One does not have to live long to know how right that remark is. Most of us live by fits and starts. And that is part of the human predicament. Our lives lack order and symmetry. Envy takes root in us and we lose our sense of thankfulness once more. It is not enough to be learned, we also have to be wealthy; our good local repute shrinks with the thought of being more widely famous; the happily married revel in the thought of being single and free; and the healthy are dismayed that the future is not guaranteed; the gainfully employed become distressed with obligations that work brings.

We all recognize the pleasures of thankfulness and perhaps cherish special moments when the lineaments of the world and of our spirits seem to coalesce. The Psalmist says it very nicely: "Yea, a joyful and pleasant thing it is to be thankful" (Ps 147:1). In periods of gratefulness all seems well with our troubled lives, but usually we give credit to the turn of events. Appropriately enough, the thrust of Holy Scripture, while very much upon thankfulness, is scarcely at all upon the course of the events or even the nature of the world. It probably behooves us, therefore, to consider thankfulness once more, if for no other reason than to take measure of ourselves as genuine spiritual beings whose fate and happiness are not totally dependent upon the externalities amid which we live. For the Scripture clearly describes thankfulness as a kind of personality formation and we have to be sure that our lives evince it.

---

1. Plutarch, "On Tranquillity of Mind," *Moralia*, 6:217.

II

It has to be remarked that thankfulness is plainly commanded in the Scripture. Even the countless admonitions to "bless the Lord" suggest that much. More pointedly we are told to "be thankful," to give thanks always and for everything, and simply to live in Jesus Christ, "abounding in thanksgiving" (Col 2:7, cf. 3:15–17). Granted our everyday experiences, it seems rather bizarre to be commanded to be thankful, for any feeling, including gratitude, mostly comes of itself and not by command. We cannot tell anyone, "Be joyful!" and expect a ready response in kind. Emotions are typically transitive and they take a direct object. That portends that being full of thanks depends upon the objective circumstances being right, and circumstances are not usually subject to demands. Gratitude, we think, usually comes to us as an accompaniment to the train of events, not as a thing-in-itself. Scripture, however, does not bear out our common thought.

Furthermore, this is clearly to forget our dignity as spiritual persons, endowed so richly with powers and potentialities. We are in a world that often seems alien and contrary to our deepest passions. Our popular morality suggests that we always ought to remake the world and bring it into conformity with the moving consensus of mankind. But Scripture has another suggestion, one that is both flattering and yet demanding. It portrays us as potentially spiritual but not as yet in possession of our inheritance as children of God. Perhaps an analogue can be exploited. If we were marooned in a barren place, utterly cut off from home, friends, and familiarities, we would very likely quickly develop an intensity of pathos to go with our situation. If a few fragments of print were discovered from our country, think how it would be scrutinized and devoured. Every reference would be explored, every meaning would be essayed, and countless connections would soon be discovered. All kinds of capacities, heretofore only hinted at, would be developed in us. Memory, hope, and a current enthusiasm would blossom and keep that negligible piece of print a sesame to a familiar world. Even the dismal sequence of lonely hours would become livable once more.

This is precisely what it means to be a human spirit. We live not only by events and happenings, and we are not born to be tossed hither and yon by the tides of fortune. One of the most important features of a genuine Christian spirituality is thankfulness. With that attribute we can also begin to bear all kinds of things with gladness. However, we cannot simply concoct such attributes and put them on like new clothes. Nor do we acquire such qualities merely by admiration and by wishing. Other conditions have to be met.

There are times when we simply have no emotions left. We become like Querry in Graham Greene's *A Burnt-Out Case*. A host of difficulties and he was soon a man on the run. But everywhere his condition of spirit went with him. Settling in the leper colony was almost the most serious test of his deadened life. There he saw lepers without toes and fingers, but Querry was now unable to feel much of anything. Even pity escaped him. His pathos was gone and nothing much, even profound disasters, mattered thereafter.

Certainly we know ourselves to have that negative potential. Perhaps we have come dangerously close to the nadir point of defiant despair where nothing much touches us and little matters any longer. There is, however, a positive potential, too. It lurks there always soliciting our growth and threatening us with the violence and trauma of a new birth. It is to that possibility the Scripture calls us.

When we have nothing to be grateful for we are also sinking into a lethargy of spirit. We are prone always to blame the world as if circumstances justify our lack of feeling. But always we must return to the Scriptural context. Indeed our lives do depend in part upon the ecological scene. We are dependent but not radically so. Even in the best days, our surroundings do not always satisfy our wants and assuage every demand. Instead, the Scripture proposes some completely new conceptual surroundings. "Thou openest thy hand, thou satisfiest the desire of every living thing" (Ps 145:16). The world is also a tissue of illusion and make-believe and against all of that there is another scheme of things, the true reality.

As our lives unfold we all get at home in the everyday world. Soon a scheme of opinions, points of view, and even batches of knowledge begin to accompany that world and to guide our existence. Most of us come into a kind of competence and assurance within that complex. But this very complex of feeling, belief, expectation, and attitude soon is credited among us as the fruit of experience and the very distillate of working wisdom. We have referred already to this tissue of thought when we noted that after a while almost all of us are quite certain that we can only be legitimately thankful when the events in the world will permit it. The more we listen to the sirens of everyday experience and daily life, the more convinced we will be that our happiness is also very tentative, that our opportunities are hedged, and that like Guildenstern (in *Hamlet*) we are all beggars and must remain "poor even in thanks."

But, that is the very condition to which the commands of the New Testament faith are directed. A new reality is therein invoked. God is the *fundamentum*, the very source and foundation of all things. A new wine of remembrance is available for all to drink. Instead of being foolish and neglecting the state of the world as it is, we are asked to remember that the world and ourselves exist by this grace and mercy. Even if those benefits for which we long are not now at hand, there is another beneficence that is made vividly existent for all of us. This is what the Christian story provides. An entirely new conceptual surrounding is supplied by creed, Gospel, and Epistles. Once one gets the hang of the world thus conceived, the only appropriate response is thankfulness.

Indeed thankfulness is commanded, but it does not dangle there as an unsupported attitude. It is not a vagrant move of the personality, an immediate gift that some have by sheer force of their wish or disposition. Rather it is both appropriate to what we are as persons and also correct in respect to the reality of things. Christian teachings tear the veil of illusion away and they confute the erstwhile wisdom of experience. What may look like a scandal and an offense to the statistically normal apprehension is no longer a scandal at all—it makes sense. The token of that sense is the new capacity for thankfulness that makes every day worth living and every moment of opposition an occasion for spiritual strengthening.

III

Indeed it seems odd to command gratitude. But not if the rest of the conceptual surrounding, those teachings, also redescribe the world and oneself. In that newly conceived creation, it is as if all kinds of emotions become possible again. Instead of being stripped of feelings and pathos, as we so often are in the tragic everyday world, we are being offered also new joys, a peace that the world does not provide, and a thankfulness that can survive anything that happens.

We have said already that thankfulness is an attitude. Surely that is so, for the logic of an attitude is that it be not quite like an emotion that usually only targets a certain thing or event. We are afraid of this or that, hopeful about something, sorrowful over this loss, etc. Attitudes are more comprehensive and that is why typical attitudes are orientations in respect to everything. Patriotism is an attitude; so are pessimism, being trustful, suspicious, and careful. It is as if we pose the whole person towards the whole world. Furthermore, we hold each other responsible for attitudes, condemning and praising, as the case might be. Once more, we can say, then, that thankfulness is an attitude and that it is, indeed, to be manifested towards all things. The New Testament suggests repeatedly that we are responsible for staying thankful; otherwise Paul's commandment would make no sense at all.

But emotions are also involved. Most of the time we find the world to be, in Wordsworth's words, "too much with us; . . . Getting and spending, we lay waste our powers."[2] We need comfort and we want always to replace the loss of one thing with another. But this does not always work. Rather we have to be made congruent often with the thing or person we lost and surely with reality itself. Our wretched emotions like resentment, jealousy, envy, and greed always seem to strike root in us without any major provocation. They keep us in an anxious state and build up a thankless and complaining attitude that also becomes comprehensive and infinitely resilient. Nothing will satisfy after a while and gratitude is postponed indefinitely.

The spirit of thankfulness suggests another possibility, namely, that the person can be made compatible with the thing lost. One's self-surrender is a good part of being thankful, for then living does not require all the impediments of demand and dissatisfaction. A new set of emotions now become possible. Thankfulness casts out envy, greed, and strife. One's life coheres rather than divides. Furthermore, a thankful life is one that is easily motivated. A life can never be long enough if you are thankful; besides, one can relish every moment.

2. Wordsworth, "The World Is Too Much with Us," lines 1–2.

Another extraordinary feature is that an attitude like gratitude will also begin to make the events of everyday life look very good. Just as a foul mood can spoil almost anything that transpires, so a happy attitude can enable the individual to see the goodness in all things. In a dim way, we all know that there is goodness lurking everywhere, but we are seldom able to discern it. A thankful spirit is enabling in this very respect. One's perception of the realities begins to improve.

Of course, there is always the temptation to indulge only in psychological tinkering, to practice moods, and to simulate pathos. And such a psychologizing of Christian teachings turns them into a travesty. The fact is that Christians are also supposed to be educated not only into the faith but by it. Becoming a faithful believer also requires that we become eventually a knower of God. This is why thankfulness is not just a trick to be mastered, whereby we can be a practitioner of attitudes by the hour. On the contrary, by learning to be thankful we also become linked up with all things in a new way, but also with God. He who gives all things and knows that all that He made and gives is good is the creator and sustainer of all.

By being thankful we begin to see that all things are good, and our perceptive capacities are also His gift. More than this, by being thankful, we are objectively in the right. For the entire world is His and He made it. All of us are in His debt and we are in a state of owing. "The Lord gave, and the Lord has taken away" (Job 1:21). The radical contingency of all things must be acknowledged, for nothing has to be the way it is. We can regret it and spend our time scheming how to beat reality, or we can acknowledge the Lord and Giver of all. With the first, we thwart ourselves and see so little; with the second, we share a perspective that lets us see goodness in suffering and providence in pain. Gratitude is not an escape from reality; it is an access to it.

The Christian life is thus a life-long improvisation in the attitude of thankfulness. An attitude of this scope is, however, not a single-track phenomenon. If one is thankful eventually for all things, as the Apostle urges us to be, then a kind of unification of our life begins to take place. Instead of living spasmodically and tacking to catch every breeze, one can practice the luxury of taking existence in its own terms. This is never easy, for we will seldom outgrow the protest against sufferings that seem pointless and deaths that are so shattering. Once more, Christianity must never be identified with a bland puttying over of all the hardships and profound griefs. Faith does not deny these tragic features in the least and it does little to encourage a thoughtless sentimentality. But thankfulness need not be either systematic disregard or a trivializing by bland declamation of the brutish occurrences of daily life. The point is, rather, that thankfulness as an attitude changes the person and in a variety of ways. One begins to see differently and to evaluate differently. Then the goodness of God's providence begins to shine through even the most desperate events.

IV

There is something more. The stupendous proposal that Christianity makes to all of us is that we are not totally and completely dust and clay. We are also destined to be such as God Himself is. Indeed, life is frequently dogged by uncertainty and hurt by sorrows. However, we are not victims. Part of the godly life that is imparted to us is a radically different disposition towards all of the world. Some of that is shadowed for us by the theological teachings. There we learn that the world is created, that God is the Maker and Sustainer, and that we, too, are creatures, born to love and to acknowledge ourselves, God and the world, in a manner that is proper to "the mercies of God." It is as if "freely ye have received," therefore, freely we give (Matt 10:8). A new picture of a reasonable life begins to develop, almost as if our bodies could be presented as a living sacrifice, a lifelong service, "holy, acceptable unto God" (Rom 12:1). Then it becomes plausible to think that such a God has a will and disposition for us in Christ Jesus whereby we can "in every thing give thanks" (1 Thess 5:18). Gratitude, service, and a happy outlook begin to hang together.

There are kinds of hurt and varieties of difficulties. An attitude like thankfulness has a strange dispositional character. More than that, we might even describe it as dispositional in itself. It is not only an abstract teaching. A disposition describes a potential to behave in a certain way. A dog is prone to bark under certain circumstances and we think its barking a natural bit of behavior. The sugar will dissolve when placed in water and that again is its natural property. With a normal train of difficulties with which we are confronted, human beings are very likely to complain and to remonstrate. Then a host of negative emotions, highly unpleasurable, ensue. All of us know the agonies of spirit that are so likely.

But Christianity is also a mode of training in the new disposition, quite different than those that seem so natural and so obvious. Aristotle thought that all virtues were acquired and were secondary powers in contrast to the "things that exist by nature."[3] Christian literature simply assumes that what we are by nature must be converted and a second nature be acquired. The new life in Jesus Christ has strong things to say about how we can now be disposed as reborn creatures. What the theological teachings suggest in the abstract, our daily practice must also acquire. Our dispositions do not only change; rather it is the fact that God's grace will supply a new disposition, that of thankfulness. Thus, there are two factors, the teaching and the dispositions, both are a measure of grace.

Gratitude is a disposition in a variety of ways. For one thing, thankfulness is not innate or quite a possession the way our capacity to see is. We have the senses before we use them, but thankfulness we acquire only by exercising it. We are introduced to it by commands, those of the Old Testament and the New. The doctrines and teachings of the church are like a riverbed of thought, within which the practice of this new disposition can be realized. Sometimes, though, the straightforward teachings may be absent and the command may be all that we can cling to. But the doctrines and the commands do work together, and either of them creates in us the capacity for the other. What we say here about this disposition being acquired by exercise could also be said about most virtues. We are dependent upon a kind of training, and in this instance, a training in gratitude is a good part of the life of prayer, devotion, worship, and church-life.

There is another sense in which thankfulness is dispositional. When one is thus disposed, one is prone to choose life, to relish it, and even to sustain it. Some dispositions, like fidelity, would issue in a state of character in which a preference becomes habitual and predictable. One's choices become thereby fixed. But thankfulness has more to do with disposing one to appreciation, to a kind of gladful embracing of a lifetime of service. Instead of a life being a chore and

3. Aristotle, *Nicomachean Ethics*, 2.1.

a duty only to be borne with grim resolution, it is as if daily existence can be actually liked, even its oppositions and conflicts. Then one begins to acquire a sense for the meaning of life. More properly it might be said that for the individual who has learned to be thankful, the question of the meaning of life begins to lose its grip. After a while the issue fades away, not because it is answered, but rather because whatever chaos occasioned the doubt is now dissipated.

More must and can be said about thankfulness as a disposition. If Christians are thankful, is this to say that a state of the soul is also being described? Two points can be noted. There is such a thing surely as a state of being thankful, and that state would suggest a demeanor of peace, tranquillity of mind, and a quality of present life. A reduction of anxiety, a kind of contentment, and a willingness to be what one is—these are part of that state. But there is also the dispositional side, the potentiality and tendency to believe in certain ways that must be considered. For Christians have never admitted one fruit of the Spirit without seeing a host of others. They involve each other, not quite like a system of thoughts, but more like knots in a fishnet. To pull up one is to pull up some others. Certainly, thankfulness disposes us to love one another. The silliness and vulgarity noted in Paul's comments that we earlier alluded to are only conceivable where gratitude is absent. Grumbling, envy, malice, and rivalry can only prosper where other people are no longer thought about with any gladness of heart. But if one is genuinely thankful for a wife or a husband, for a friend or a neighbor, granted their idiosyncrasies and difference, then we can also rejoice in them. Pettiness disappears; and affection gets a little room in one's life.

This is to assert, then, something very small of the logic of the Christian virtues. For thankfulness is part of the new habituation and training of the Christian. We can be certain that God Himself is pleased with every person who thanks Him. "Bless the Lord, O my soul . . . bless His holy name" (Ps 103:1). The oddest thing about being thankful is that very soon that gratitude itself becomes an occasion for praise. The world and people for whom one is thankful are also a world and people one begins to enjoy more and more. This is why the command to be thankful might seem at first a little onerous and against the grain. It may seem as Aristotle said about virtues, not quite natural. But after a bit, the thankful person crosses a threshold into a kind of enjoyment that is truly contagious. This is why we are urged in the Psalms to praise just about everything. Thankfulness completes our joy and our joy sustains our thanks. But the person who thinks happiness and joy are only indices of natural pleasures over against pains has it wrong. We are spiritual beings, not just pawns of a material world. Because we are also spiritual, we bring capacities and dispositions to bear upon everything that is. That means dependency upon events is broken, and we can now have health of the spirit even while creation groans for the day of deliverance.

Thankfulness is, indeed, commanded. That makes it look almost like a bit of personality manipulation, but it is not. Being thankful for all things also is one of the deepest ways to approach God. To thank Him is to appreciate what He is. This, in turn, is to be fully alert and alive to the way the real world is. Not to be thankful is to have lost touch with reality itself. Besides it means missing one of the most refined and lovely human experiences that we can have. God not only demands thankfulness, but finally He communicates His presence to grateful hearts. This is why a virtue like that is both rewarding for what it is, but more, that in that thankfulness God is able to give Himself to tranquil spirits.

Afterword

Paul L. Holmer

Self-Effacing, Swaggering, Nonpareil

A N INKLING. AN INKLING, surely, but perhaps more as I attended Paul Holmer's Tuesday evening lectures on Kierkegaard at Yale Divinity School, spring semester, 1966. Perhaps I knew how very special this opportunity was, how fortunate I was. On Tuesday evening, April 12, Holmer said he was going to address again the "certainty / uncertainty" issues in Kierkegaard "because last week was such a travesty on my part." I had never heard a professor say anything like that. But I had never heard a professor like Paul Holmer. On May 17, he concluded the course by saying, "I hope the lectures haven't failed the quality of the man." I was sure the lectures had not.

Professor Holmer also remarked during that semester that "theology can only be communicated directly with a loss." With manifold indirections, he pitted himself against such loss. At Richard Bell's splendid symposium at The College of Wooster, March 1987, in honor of Paul Holmer, "The Grammar of the Heart: Thinking with Kierkegaard and Wittgenstein,"[1] many tributes were paid Paul Holmer. Mine was a reading of this passage from Johannes Climacus' *Philosophical Fragments*:

> . . . the fact that I have been instructed by Socrates or by Prodicus or by a servant-girl, can concern me only historically; or in so far as I am a Plato in sentimental enthusiasm,

1. See Richard H. Bell, ed., *The Grammar of the Heart: New Essays in Moral Philosophy and Theology* (San Francisco: Harper & Row, 1988).

it may concern me poetically. But this enthusiasm, beautiful as it is, and such that I could wish both for myself and all others a share of this εὐκαταφορία εἰς πάθος, which only a Stoic could frown upon; and though I may be lacking in the Socratic magnanimity and the Socratic self-denial to think its nothingness—this enthusiasm, so Socrates would say, is only an illusion, a want of clarity in a mind where earthly inequalities seethe almost voluptuously.[2]

Professor Holmer was appreciative of the selected passage and probably also of the irony that the celebration of a celebrated teacher be marked by a wariness of such celebration.

Yet there was swaggering, a polemical swagger; and that, of course, added to the interest. Professor Holmer concludes his "Preface" to *The Grammar of Faith*:

It would be most surprising if my debt to colleagues and teachers, students and authors, was not apparent. But a remark of Scipio's, the statesman and conqueror of Hannibal at Zama (202 B.C.), is appropriate. He said that he was never less idle than when he had nothing to do, and never less lonely than when he was by himself. The reflections in these pages have mostly come about when attempts were being made to make sense for and by myself.[3]

In an "interview" with Paul Holmer at St. Olaf College, June 1988, I asked Professor Holmer to retell a story he had mentioned in an earlier public address:

Well, she [Lillian Marvin Swenson] came with this letter [from Norman Malcolm]. She didn't know who Norman Malcolm was. He was a young graduate student, actually, at Cambridge University. And he had written to her because he had found out about the translation of Kierkegaard's *Works of Love*. She wanted to know who he was, and she wanted to know who Wittgenstein was, who was referred to in the letter. . . . I knew about Wittgenstein, but I didn't know Norman Malcolm. So I assured her that Wittgenstein was worthy of getting a copy of the book. And so Mrs. Swenson sent the volume, a new translation from Princeton Press, of Kierkegaard's *Works of Love*. And then some time later, almost within a

2. Kierkegaard, *Philosophical Fragments*, 14–15.
3. Holmer, *Grammar of Faith*, xii.

month, I think, Malcolm wrote back and said about this
... that ... [Wittgenstein] had received the book and read the
book and so on. Mrs. Swenson referred him [Malcolm] to me.
... He then corresponded further with me. I asked Malcolm
outright what Wittgenstein thought of Kierkegaard's *Works of
Love*. He told me that Wittgenstein had already read it in the
German translation, didn't like the German, had tried it in
Danish and, because of his knowledge of Norwegian, he was
able to read it; but it wasn't clear to him. So he wanted to try it
in English translation. But Malcolm told me that Wittgenstein
said it was much too high for him. And so I wrote to Malcolm
and said, "What does he mean by *that*?" And then he wrote
back and said, "It was as if he [Wittgenstein] couldn't manage those intense passions and feelings that were involved in
Kierkegaard's volume." And then Malcolm pointed out to me
that the lovely thing about Wittgenstein was that he didn't
blame Kierkegaard for that. He thought it was his own weakness. And I thought that was a right and true remark.[4]

Swagger (by indirect implication) seems eclipsed by self-effacement.
Paul Holmer lived and *was* a dialectic of earnestness and irony. Irony
perhaps had the edge—perhaps because of earnestness. His mouth
was a runaway, somewhere between a scowl and a smirk—or not between but *both*.

At the end of our time at Yale Divinity School, my wife Marlyne
and I invited Paul Holmer over to the Canner Street apartments for
a lunch to say thank you. This was May 31, 1967. I know because he
dated the guestbook and wrote: "Only the truth which edifies is truth
for you."

David Cain
Distinguished Professor of Religion
University of Mary Washington

4. Cain, "Appendix" to "Appreciation of Roger Poole," 480–81.

Appendix

Paul L. Holmer: A Select Bibliography

Books by Paul L. Holmer

Philosophy and the Common Life. Tully Cleon Knoles Lectures in Philosophy, 1960; College of the Pacific. Philosophy Institute Publications, vol. 10. Stockton, CA: Fitzgerald, 1960.

Theology and the Scientific Study of Religion. The Lutheran Studies Series. Minneapolis: Denison, 1961.

Youth Considers Doubt and Frustration. Youth Forum Series. Camden, NJ: Nelson, 1967.

C. S. Lewis: The Shape of His Faith and Thought. New York: Harper & Row, 1976.

The Grammar of Faith. San Francisco: Harper & Row, 1978.

Making Christian Sense. Spirituality and the Christian Life series. Edited by Richard H. Bell. 1984. Reprinted as *Making Sense of Our Lives.* Minneapolis: MacLaurin Institute, n.d.

Other Resources

Bell, Richard H., editor. *The Grammar of the Heart: New Essays in Moral Philosophy and Theology.* San Francisco: Harper & Row, 1988. Based on the March 1987 symposium, "The Grammar of the Heart: Thinking with Kierkegaard and Wittgenstein," to honor Paul L. Holmer, held at The College of Wooster, Wooster, Ohio.

————, and Ronald E. Hustwit, editors. *Essays on Kierkegaard and Wittgenstein: On Understanding the Self.* Wooster, OH: The College of Wooster, 1978. Based on the October 1976 symposium, "Søren Kierkegaard and Ludwig Wittgenstein: Philosophy as Activity and Understanding Forms of Life," held at The College of Wooster, Wooster, Ohio.

Cain, David. "Appendix" to "An Appreciation of Roger Poole." In *Kierkegaard Studies Yearbook 2005*, edited by Niels Jørgen Cappelørn and Hermann Deuser, with K. Brian Söderquist on behalf of the Søren Kierkegaard Research Centre, 480–81. Berlin: Walter de Gruyter, 2005.

Carlson, Bruce. "Tribute to Paul Holmer." *Pietisten* 19 (Fall 2004). n. p. Online: http://www. pietisten.org/fall04/paulholmer.html.

Cathey, Robert Andrew. *God in Postliberal Perspective: Between Realism and Non-Realism*, 49–82. Farnham, England, and Burlington, VT: Ashgate, 2009.

Lindbeck, George A. *The Nature of Doctrine: Religion and Theology in a Postliberal Age.* 25th Anniversary Edition. With a New Introduction by Bruce D. Marshall and a New Afterword by the Author. Louisville, KY: Westminster/Knox, 2009.

Sherry, Patrick. "Learning How to be Religious: The Work of Paul Holmer." *Theology* 77.644 (1974) 81–90.

Dissertations on Paul L. Holmer

Rollefson, Richard. "Thinking with Kierkegaard and Wittgenstein: The Philosophical Theology of Paul L. Holmer." PhD diss., Graduate Theological Union, 1994.

Stewart, T. Wesley. "Paul L. Holmer and the Logic of Faith: A Utilization of Kierkegaard and Wittgenstein for Contemporary Christian Theology." PhD diss., Southern Baptist Theological Seminary, 1991.

On Holmer as a Teacher

Hauerwas, Stanley. *Hannah's Child: A Theologian's Memoir.* Grand Rapids, MI: William B. Eerdmans, 2010, pages 53, 58, 59–60.

————. "How to Go On When You Know You Are Going to Be Misunderstood, or How Paul Holmer Ruined My Life, or Making Sense of Paul Holmer." In *Wilderness Wanderings: Probing Twentieth-Century Theology and Philosophy*, 143–52. Radical Traditions: Theology in a Postcritical Key. Boulder, CO: Westview, 1997.

Holmer, Phyllis. "Holmer and Students." *Christian Century* 122.9 (May 3, 2005) 45.

Horst, Mark. "Paul Holmer: A Profile." *Christian Century* 105.29 (October 12, 1988) 891–95.

Roberts, Robert C. "A Little Protector." In *God and the Philosophers: The Reconciliation of Faith and Reason*, edited by Thomas V. Morris, 113–27. Oxford: Oxford University Press, 1994.

Willimon, William H. "Hard Truths." *Christian Century* 122.4 (February 22, 2005) 25–28.

Online Resources

The "Guide to the Paul L. Holmer Papers" (Record Group No. 195) may be accessed electronically from Special Collections, Yale University Library, Divinity School Library. Online: http://www.library.yale.edu/div/colgpers.html.

The Holmer Lectures

The Holmer Lectures. Since 1996, The MacLaurin Institute, Minneapolis, MN, has sponsored annual Holmer Lectures, inaugurated in 1996 by Professor Holmer. Other Holmer lecturers have been George Marsden, Nicholas Wolterstorff, Glenn Tinder, Bruce Reichenbach, Jean Bethke Elshtain, Alvin Plantinga, Gilbert C. Meilaender, Dallas Willard, Richard John Neuhaus, Richard Swinburne, Stanley Hauerwas, David Gushee, J. Budziszewski, James K. A. Smith, and C. Stephen Evans. Online: http://www.maclaurin.org/home.

Bibliography

Anselm. "Why God Became Man" [*Cur Deus Homo*]. In *A Scholastic Miscellany: Anselm to Ockham*. Edited and translated by Eugene R. Fairweather. The Library of Christian Classics, 10:100–83. New York: Macmillan, 1970.

Aristotle. *Nicomachean Ethics*. In *The Basic Works of Aristotle*. Edited with an Introduction by Richard McKeon, 935–1112. New York: Random House, 1941.

———. *Rhetoric*. In *The Basic Works of Aristotle*. Edited with an Introduction by Richard McKeon, 1317–1451. New York: Random House, 1941.

Augustine. *The City of God*, bk. 19. Translated by Gerald G. Walsh and Daniel J. Honan. In *Writings of Saint Augustine*, 8:183–248. Fathers of the Church 24. New York: CIMA, 1954.

———. *Confessions*. Translated with an Introduction by R. S. Pine-Coffin. Harmondsworth, England: Penguin, 1961.

———. *The Happy Life*. Translated by Ludwig Schopp. In *Writings of Saint Augustine*, 1:29–84. Fathers of the Church 34. New York: CIMA, 1948.

Bedford, Errol. "Emotions." In *Essays in Philosophical Psychology*, edited by Donald F. Gustafson, 77–98. Garden City, NY: Anchor, 1964.

Benchley, Robert C. *Of All Things*. New York: Holt, 1921.

Bouwsma, O. K. "Anselm's Argument." In *The Nature of Philosophical Inquiry*, edited by Joseph Bobik, 252–93. Notre Dame: University of Notre Dame Press, 1970.

Collingwood, R. G. *An Autobiography*. London: Oxford University Press, 1939.

Cowley, Abraham, and Richard Crashaw. "On Hope, by way of Question and Answer between *A. Cowley* and *R. Crashaw*." In *The Metaphysical Poets*, edited by Helen Gardner, 169–73. London: Oxford University Press, 1967.

Durrell, Lawrence. "The Death of General Uncebuncke." In *A Private Country: Poems*, 33–48. London: Faber & Faber, 1943.

Ebeling, Gerhard. *The Nature of Faith*. Translated by Ronald Gregor Smith. Philadelphia: Fortress, 1961.

Eliot, T. S. "Hamlet and His Problems." In *The Sacred Wood: Essays on Poetry and Criticism*, 95–103. New York: Routledge, 1960.

———. "Shakespeare and the Stoicism of Seneca." In *Selected Essays*, 107–26. New edition. New York: Harcourt, Brace, 1950.

Engelmann, Paul. *Letters from Ludwig Wittgenstein, With a Memoir*. Translated by L. Furtmüller, edited by B. F. McGuinness. Oxford: Blackwell, 1967.

Euripides. *Medea*. In *The Complete Greek Tragedies*. Euripides, vol. 3, edited by David Grene and Richmond Lattimore. Chicago: University of Chicago Press, 1956.

Frege, Gottlob. *Logical Investigations*. Edited by Peter T. Geach. Translated by Peter T. Geach and R. H. Stoothoff. New Haven: Yale University Press, 1977.

Gardner, Helen. *The Metaphysical Poets*. 2nd ed. London: Oxford University Press, 1967.

Geach, Peter. *God and the Soul*. New York: Schocken, 1969.

Heidegger, Martin. *Aus der Erfahrung des Denkens*. Pfullingen: Neske, 1954.

——. *Holzwege*. 3rd ed. Frankfurt: Klostermann, 1957.

——. "Language." In *Poetry, Language, and Thought*, 187–210.

——. "The Origin of the Work of Art." In *Poetry, Language, and Thought*, 15–87.

——. *Poetry, Language, and Thought*. Translations and Introduction by Albert Hofstadter. New York: Harper & Row, 1971.

——. "The Thinker as Poet." In *Poetry, Language and Thought*, 1–14.

——. *Unterwegs zur Sprache*. Pfullingen: Neske, 1959.

——. "What Are Poets For?" In *Poetry, Language, and Thought*, 89–142.

——. "Wozo Dichter?" In *Holzwege*, 248–95.

Holberg, Ludvig. *Erasmus Montanus*. In *Comedies of Holberg*. Translated by Oscar James Campbell Jr., and Frederic Schenck. With an Introduction by Oscar James Campbell Jr., 119–78. New York: The American-Scandinavian Foundation, 1935.

Holmer, Paul L. "About Our Capacity to Talk." *The Philosophy Forum* 7.4 (1969) 29–42.

——. "Theology and Happiness," *Reflection* 67.4 (1970) 1–4.

James, William. *The Principles of Psychology*. 2 vols. New York: Holt, 1890.

Kant, Immanuel. "Introduction to The Metaphysic of Morals." In *The Doctrine of Virtue*, 7–28. Translated with Introduction and Notes by Mary J. Gregan. Foreword by H. J. Paton. Philadelphia: University of Pennsylvania Press, 1964.

——. *Philosophical Correspondence: 1759–99*. Translated and edited by Arnulf Zweig. Chicago: University of Chicago Press, 1967.

Kierkegaard, Søren. *The Concept of Dread*. Translated by Walter Lowrie. Princeton: Princeton University Press, 1944.

——. *Concluding Unscientific Postscript*. Translated by David F. Swenson. Princeton: Princeton University Press, 1941.

——. *Edifying Discourses: A Selection*. Edited with an introduction by Paul L. Holmer. Translated by David F. and Lillian Marvin Swenson. New York: Harper & Row, 1958.

——. *Either/Or*. 2 vols. Translated by David F. and Lillian Marvin Swenson and Walter Lowrie. Princeton: Princeton University Press, 1971.

——. *Fear and Trembling* and *The Sickness Unto Death*. Translated, with an introduction and notes by Walter Lowrie. Princeton: Princeton University Press, 1941.

——. *Johannes Climacus*. In *Philosophical Fragments, Johannes Climacus*. Edited and translated by Howard V. Hong and Edna H. Hong, 113–72. Princeton: Princeton University Press, 1985.

——. *On Authority and Revelation*. Introduction by Frederick Sontag. Translated and Edited by Walter Lowrie. New York: Harper & Row, 1966.

——. *Philosophical Fragments*. Originally translated and introduced by David F. Swenson. New Introduction and Commentary by Niels Thulstrup. Translation revised and Commentary translated by Howard V. Hong. 2nd ed. Princeton: Princeton University Press, 1962.

———. *The Point of View for My Work as an Author: A Report to History, and Related Writings*. Translated with Introduction and Notes by Walter Lowrie. Newly edited with a Preface by Benjamin Nelson. New York: Harper & Row, 1962.

———. *Samlede Vaerker*. 20 vols. Edited by A. B. Drachmann, J. L. Heiberg, and H. O. Lange. 3rd ed. Copenhagen: Gyldendal, 1962–1964.

———. *The Sickness Unto Death*. Translated by Walter Lowrie. Princeton: Princeton University Press, 1941.

———. *Søren Kierkegaard's Journals and Notebooks*. 5 volumes to date. Edited by Niels Jørgen Cappelørn, Alastair Hannay, David Kangas, Bruce H. Kirmmse, George Pattison, Vanessa Rumble, and K. Brian Söderquist. Published in Cooperation with the Søren Kierkegaard Research Centre, Copenhagen. Princeton and Oxford: Princeton University Press, 2007–.

———. *Søren Kierkegaard's Journals and Papers*. 7 vols. Edited and translated by Howard V. Hong and Edna H. Hong. Assisted by Gregor Malantschuk. Bloomington and London: Indiana University Press, 1967–1978.

———. *Søren Kierkegaard's Papirer*. 16 vols. Edited by P. A. Heiberg, V. Kuhr, and E. Torsting. 2nd ed., augmented, by Niels Thulstrup. Copenhagen: Gyldendal, 1968–1978.

———. *Training in Christianity, and the Edifying Discourse which "Accompanied" It*. Translated with an Introduction and Notes by Walter Lowrie. London, New York: Oxford University Press, 1941.

———. *Works of Love: Some Christian Reflections in the Form of Discourses*. Translated by Howard and Edna Hong. Preface by R. Gregor Smith. New York: Harper & Row, 1962.

Kuhr, Victor. *Modsigelsens Grundsaetning*. Kierkegaard Studier. Edited by P.A. Heiberg and Victor Kuhr. Copenhagen: Gyldendal, 1915.

Leibniz, Gottfried Wilhelm. *Logical Papers: A Selection*. Translated and edited with an introduction by G. H. R. Parkinson. Oxford: Clarendon, 1966.

Lewis, C. S. "On Criticism." In *Of Other Worlds*, edited by Walter Hooper, 43–58. London: Bles, 1966.

Moore, G. E. "Wittgenstein's Lectures in 1930–33." In *Philosophical Papers*, 252–324. London: Allen & Unwin, 1959.

Ott, Heinrich. "What Is Systematic Theology?" In *The Later Heidegger and Theology*, edited by James M. Robinson and John B. Cobb Jr., 77–111. New Frontiers in Theology 1. New York: Harper & Row, 1963.

Plutarch. "On Tranquillity of Mind." In *Moralia*. 16 vols. Translated by W. C. Helmbold, 6.163–241. Loeb Classical Library. Cambridge, MA: Harvard University Press, 1970.

Popper, Karl. *The Open Society and Its Enemies*. 2 vols. London: G. Routledge & Sons, 1945.

Quine, Willard Van Orman. *From a Logical Point of View*. Cambridge: Harvard University Press, 1961.

Rahner, Karl. "The Experiment with Man: Theological Observations on Man's Self-Manipulation." In *Theological Investigations*, 9:205–24. Translated by Graham Harrison. New York: Herder & Herder, 1972.

————. "Philosophy and Philosophising in Theology." In *Theological Investigations*, 9:46–63. Translated by Graham Harrison. New York: Herder & Herder, 1972.

————. "The Theology of the Symbol." In *Theological Investigations*, 4:221–52. Translated with an Introduction by Kevin Smyth. Baltimore: Helicon, 1966.

Rauschenbusch, Walter. *Christianity and the Social Crisis*. Edited by Robert D. Cross. New York: Harper & Row, 1964.

Revised Standard Version of the Bible.

Robinson, James M. "The German Discussion of the Later Heidegger." In *The Later Heidegger and Theology*, edited by James M. Robinson and John B. Cobb Jr., 3–76. New Frontiers in Theology 1. New York: Harper & Row, 1963.

————, and John B. Cobb Jr., editors. *The Later Heidegger and Theology*. New Frontiers in Theology 1. New York: Harper & Row, 1963.

Ryle, Gilbert. *The Concept of Mind*. New York: Barnes & Noble, 1949.

Schrag, Calvin O. "The Phenomenon of Embodied Speech." *The Philosophy Forum* 7.4 (1969) 1–27.

Swenson, David F. *Something about Kierkegaard*. Minneapolis: Augsburg, 1941.

Whitehead, Alfred North, and Bertrand Russell. *Principia Mathematica*. 3 vols. 2nd ed. Cambridge: Cambridge University Press, 1925–1927.

Wittgenstein, Ludwig. *The Blue and Brown Books: Preliminary Studies for the* Philosophical Investigations. 2nd ed. Oxford: Blackwell, 1960.

————. *Briefe an Ludwig von Ficker*. Edited by G. H. von Wright. Salzburg: Otto Müller Verlag, 1969.

————. *Culture and Value*. Edited by G. H. von Wright in collaboration with Heikki Nyman. Translated by Peter Winch. Oxford: Blackwell, 1980.

————. *Letters to Russell, Keynes, and Moore*. Edited with an Introduction by G. H. von Wright, assisted by B. F. McGuinness. Oxford: Blackwell, 1974.

————. *Notebooks 1914–1916*. Edited by G. H. von Wright and G. E. M. Anscombe. Translated by G. E. M. Anscombe. Oxford: Blackwell, 1961.

————. *On Certainty*. Edited by G. E. M. Anscombe and G. H. von Wright. Translated by Denis Paul and G. E. M. Anscombe. Oxford: Blackwell, 1969.

————. *Philosophical Grammar*. Edited by Rush Rhees. Translated by Anthony Kenny. Oxford: Blackwell, 1974.

————. *Philosophical Investigations*. Translated by G. E. M. Anscombe. 3rd ed. New York: Macmillan, 1958.

————. *Philosophical Remarks*. Edited by Rush Rhees. Translated by Raymond Hargreaves and Roger White. New York: Barnes & Noble, 1975.

————. *Philosophische Bemerkungen*. Edited by Rush Rhees. Oxford: Blackwell, 1964.

————. *Prototractatus: An Early Version of* Tractatus Logico-Philosophicus. Edited by B. F. McGuinness, T. Nyberg, and G. H. von Wright, with a translation by D. F. Pears and B. F. McGuinness. An historical introduction by G. H. von Wright and a facsimile of the author's manuscript. Ithaca, NY: Cornell University Press, 1971.

————. *Remarks on Colour*. Edited by G. E. M. Anscombe. Translated by Linda L. McAlister and Margaret Schättle. Berkeley: University of California Press, 1977.

————. *Remarks on the Foundations of Mathematics*. Edited by G. H. von Wright, Rush Rhees, and G. E. M. Anscombe. Translated by G. E. M. Anscombe. Oxford: Blackwell, 1956.

————. *Remarks on the Philosophy of Psychology*. 2 vols. Edited by G. E. M. Anscombe and G. H. von Wright. Translated by G. E. M. Anscombe. Chicago: University of Chicago Press, 1980.

————. *Tractatus Logico-Philosophicus*. Translated by D. F. Pears and B. F. McGuinness, with Introduction by Bertrand Russell. London: Routledge & Kegan Paul, 1922.

————. *Zettel*. Edited by G. E. M. Anscombe and G. H. von Wright. Translated by G. E. M. Anscombe. Oxford: Blackwell, 1967.

Wordsworth, William. "The World Is Too Much with Us." In *The New Oxford Book of English Verse, 1250–1950*, edited by Helen Gardner, 507–8. Oxford: Oxford University Press, 1972.

Yeats, William Butler. *The Collected Poems of W. B. Yeats*. New York: Macmillan, 1957.

Zink, Sidney. *The Concepts of Ethics*. New York: St. Martin's, 1962.

Index of Names

Index of Subjects